*Advances in*

# COMPUTERS

## VOLUME 68

# Advances in COMPUTERS

## Computational Biology and Bioinformatics

*GUEST EDITOR*

CHAU-WEN TSENG

Department of Computer Science
University of Maryland
College Park, Maryland

*SERIES EDITOR*

MARVIN V. ZELKOWITZ

Department of Computer Science
and Institute for Advanced Computer Studies
University of Maryland
College Park, Maryland

**VOLUME 68**



ELSEVIER

AMSTERDAM • BOSTON • HEIDELBERG • LONDON • NEW YORK • OXFORD
PARIS • SAN DIEGO • SAN FRANCISCO • SINGAPORE • SYDNEY • TOKYO
Academic Press is an imprint of Elsevier

ACADEMIC PRESS

Academic Press is an imprint of Elsevier
84 Theobald's Road, London WC1X 8RR, UK
Radarweg 29, PO Box 211, 1000 AE Amsterdam, The Netherlands
30 Corporate Drive, Suite 400, Burlington, MA 01803, USA
525 B Street, Suite 1900, San Diego, CA 92101-4495, USA

First edition 2006



ISBN-13: 978-0-12-012168-7
ISBN-10: 0-12-012168-9

ISSN: 0065-2458

For information on all Academic Press publications
visit our website at books.elsevier.com

Printed and bound in USA

06 07 08 09 10 11 10 9 8 7 6 5 4 3 2 1

# Contents

## Translocation Distance: Algorithms and Complexity

**Lusheng Wang**



## Computational Grand Challenges in Assembling the Tree of Life: Problems and Solutions

**David A. Bader, Usman Roshan, and Alexandros Stamatakis**



## Local Structure Comparison of Proteins

**Jun Huan, Jan Prins, and Wei Wang**



## Peptide Identification via Tandem Mass Spectrometry

**Xue Wu, Nathan Edwards, and Chau-Wen Tseng**

# Contributors

**Professor David A. Bader** is an Associate Professor in Computational Science and Engineering, a division within the College of Computing, Georgia Institute of Technology. He received his Ph.D. in 1996 from the University of Maryland, was awarded a National Science Foundation (NSF) Postdoctoral Research Associateship in Experimental Computer Science. He is an NSF CAREER Award recipient, an investigator on several NSF awards, a distinguished speaker in the IEEE Computer Society Distinguished Visitors Program, and is a member of the IBM PERCS team for the DARPA High Productivity Computing Systems program. Dr. Bader serves on the Steering Committees of the IPDPS and HiPC conferences, and was the General co-Chair for IPDPS (2004–2005), and Vice General Chair for HiPC (2002–2004). David has chaired several major conference program committees: Program Chair for HiPC 2005, Program Vice-Chair for IPDPS 2006 and Program Vice-Chair for ICPP 2006. He has served on numerous conference program committees related to parallel processing and computational science & engineering, is an associate editor for several high impact publications including the IEEE Transactions on Parallel and Distributed Systems (TPDS), the ACM Journal of Experimental Algorithmics (JEA), IEEE DSOnline, and Parallel Computing, is a Senior Member of the IEEE Computer Society and a Member of the ACM. Dr. Bader has been a pioneer the field of high-performance computing for problems in bioinformatics and computational genomics. He has co-chaired a series of meetings, the IEEE International Workshop on High-Performance Computational Biology (HiCOMB), written several book chapters, and co-edited special issues of the Journal of Parallel and Distributed Computing (JPDC) and IEEE TPDS on high-performance computational biology. He has co-authored over 75 articles in peer-reviewed journals and conferences, and his main areas of research are in parallel algorithms, combinatorial optimization, and computational biology and genomics.

**Prof. Guillaume Bourque** is an Adjunct Assistant Professor at the Department of Mathematics, National University of Singapore. He received his B.Sc. in Computer Science and Mathematics from Université de Montréal, Montreal, Quebec in 1998, his M.A. and Ph.D. in Applied Mathematics from the University of Southern

California, Los Angeles, CA in 2000 and 2002, respectively. He was a Bioinformatics Consultant at MazLab, Inc., in 2002 and was a Postdoctoral Researcher at the Centre de Recherches Mathématiques, Université de Montréal, Quebec from 2002–2004. He became a Group Leader at the Genome Institute of Singapore in 2004 and joined the Mathematics Department as an adjunct faculty in 2005. The main focus of Dr. Bourque's research is to explore questions in bioinformatics that can benefit from a comparative perspective. These analyses can be at the coarse whole-genome level but they can also be at the raw sequence level. The topics covered include: comparative genomics, genome rearrangements in evolution, genome rearrangements in cancer and evolution of regulatory sequences.

**Dr. Nathan Edwards** is an Assistant Research Scientist in the Center for Bioinformatics and Computational Biology (CBCB) at the University of Maryland, College Park. He received his B.S. degree in Mathematics and Computer Science in 1992 from the University of Western Australia. He received his M.S. and Ph.D. degrees in Operations Research in 1998 and 2001 from Cornell University. He joined Celera Genomics as a Computer Scientist in 2000, where he developed novel models and algorithms for high-throughput identification of peptides via tandem mass spectrometry for a wide variety of mass spectrometry platforms, technologies, and experimental protocols. From July 2002 he was Senior Staff Scientist at Applied Biosystems, Rockville, MD, where he developed software and algorithms for protein profiling workflows, compression of alternative splicing protein sequence databases, haplotype phasing, and PCR primer design. Now, at Maryland, Dr. Edwards works on software and algorithms for the rapid detection of microoganisms by their proteins, proteomic characterization of alternative splicing and coding SNPs, and genomic assay design.

**Jun Huan** is a Ph.D. candidate in the Department of Computer Science and a member of the Bioinformatics and Computational Biology Training Program at the University of North Carolina. He received his B.S. in Biochemistry from Peking University, China in 1997 and an M.S. in Computer Science from Oklahoma State University in 2000. He worked at Argonne National Laboratory and Nortel before he joined UNC and has current collaborations with GlaxoSmithKline. His research interests include data mining, bioinformatics, and high performance computing. He was a recipient of the UNC Scholar of Tomorrow Fellowship in 2001 and the Alumni Fellowship in 2005.

**Ying Chih Lin** received his BS degree in applied mathematics from National Chung Hsing University, Taichung, in 2002. He is currently a Ph.D. candidate in computer science at National Tsing Hua University, Hsinchu. His research interests include combinatorial optimization, computational complexity, and design and analysis of algorithms.

**Professor Jan Prins** is Professor and Chair of the Department of Computer Science at the University of North Carolina at Chapel Hill. He obtained a B.S. in 1978 in Mathematics from Syracuse University, and a Ph.D. in 1987 in Computer Science from Cornell University. His research interests center on high-performance computing, including algorithm design and applications in computational biology and bioinformatics. He is a member of the curriculum in molecular and cellular biology and the training program in bioinformatics and computational biology. Dr. Prins was a cofounder of Digital Effects, one of the first computer animation companies. He was a researcher in programming languages at Oxford University and at Univ. of Madison in Wisconsin and was a visiting professor at the Institute for Theoretical Computer Science at ETH Zurich in 1996–97. He is on the editorial board of Journal for Scientific Programming. His research sponsors include AFOSR, ARO, DARPA, DOE, EPA, NIH, NIEHS, NSF, ONR, and various companies.

**Professor Usman Roshan** is an Assistant Professor in the Computer Science Department at the New Jersey Institute of Technology. He received his Ph.D. in May 2004 from The University of Texas at Austin for his work on booster methods for large scale phylogeny reconstruction. His area of research is phylogenetic tree reconstruction, sequence alignment, and phylogenomics.

**Dr. Alexandros Stamatakis** received his Diploma in Computer Science in March 2001 from the Technische Universität München. His studies included internships at the Ecole Normale Supérieure de Lyon, France, at the Eurocontrol Experimental Center near Paris, France, and at the Instituto de Salud Carlos III/Universidad Politecnica de Madrid, Spain. In October 2004 he received his Ph.D. for research on Distributed and Parallel Algorithms and Systems for Inference of Huge Phylogenetic Trees based on the Maximum Likelihood Method from the Technische Universität München. From January 2005 to June 2006 he worked as postdoctoral researcher at the Institute of Computer Science of the Foundation for Research and Technology Hellas in Heraklion, Greece. Upon invitation he joined Bernard Morets group at the Swiss Federal Institute of Technology at Lausanne as a PostDoc in July 2006. His main research interest is on high performance computing and algorithmic solutions for inference of huge phylogenetic trees.

**Professor Chuan Yi Tang** (唐傳義) received the B.S. degree from the Department of Electrical Engineering and the M.S. degree from the Department of Computer

Science, National Tsing Hua University (NTHU), Taiwan, in 1980 and 1982, respectively. He received the Ph.D. degree from the Department of Computer Science and Information Engineering, National Chiao Tung University, Taiwan, in 1985. In the same year, he joined the Department of Computer Science, NTHU, Taiwan, where he became a Professor in 1992. From 1999 to 2003, he was the chairman of the department. Currently, he is the Deputy Dean of the Academic Affairs, NTHU, Taiwan. His research interests include the analysis and design of algorithms, computational molecular biology, parallel processing and computer aided engineering. He has published more than fifty of papers in prestigious journals of computer science. In past years, he developed tools for multiple sequence alignments and evolutionary trees by using the concept of compact set and the technologies of approximation. More recently, he developed tools to help the enzyme biologist search active sites, where the function of these new tools is to cover the sequence alignment and the consensus finding with structure information. In addition, for comparative genomics, he designed several different algorithms to predict exons and alternative splicing. He also has plentiful experiences to lead the cooperation of computer scientists and biologists.

**Professor Chau-Wen Tseng** is an Associate Professor in the Department of Computer Science at the University of Maryland, College Park. He received the A.B. degree in Computer Science from Harvard University in 1986 and the M.S. and Ph.D. degrees in Computer Science from Rice University in 1992 and 1993, respectively. He served as a Research Associate at the Computer Systems Laboratory at Stanford University from 1993–95 and was a consultant at Silicon Graphics before joining the faculty at the University of Maryland, College Park in 1995. He was awarded a NSF CISE Postdoctoral Fellowship in 1993 and a NSF CAREER Award in 1996. His Ph.D. thesis received the 1993 Budd Award for Best Thesis in the School of Engineering at Rice University. Dr. Tseng's research interests are in the field of bioinformatics, high performance computing, and optimizing compilers for high-performance architectures. His research investigates methods to exploit high performance computing to improve the speed and/or quality of bioinformatic algorithms in fields such as DNA sequence alignment and peptide identification via mass spectrometry.

**Professor Lusheng Wang** is an Associate Professor in the Department of Computer Science at the City University of Hong Kong. He received his B.S. degree from Shandong University, M.S. from the University of Regina, and Ph.D. from McMaster University. Prof. Wang is on the editorial boards of the Journal of Bioinformatics and Computational Biology and Journal of Global Optimization.

**Professor Wei Wang** is an Associate Professor in the Department of Computer Science and a member of the Carolina Center for Genomic Sciences at the University of North Carolina at Chapel Hill. She received a M.S. degree from the State University of New York at Binghamton in 1995 and a Ph.D. degree in Computer Science from the University of California at Los Angeles in 1999. She was a research staff member at the IBM T.J. Watson Research Center between 1999 and 2002. Dr. Wang's research interests include data mining, bioinformatics, and databases. She has filed seven patents, and has published one monograph and more than 90 research papers in international journals and major peer-reviewed conference proceedings. Dr. Wang received the IBM Invention Achievement Awards in 2000 and 2001. She was the recipient of a UNC Junior Faculty Development Award in 2003 and an NSF Faculty Early Career Development (CAREER) Award in 2005. She was named a Microsoft Research New Faculty Fellow in 2005. Dr. Wang is an associate editor of the IEEE Transactions on Knowledge and Data Engineering and ACM Transactions on Knowledge Discovery in Data, and an editorial board member of the International Journal of Data Mining and Bioinformatics. She serves on the program committees of prestigious international conferences such as ACM SIGMOD, ACM SIGKDD, VLDB, ICDE, EDBT, ACM CIKM, IEEE ICDM, and SSDBM.

**Xue Wu** received her B.E. degree in Computer Science from Tsinghua University in 1995. She is currently a Ph.D. candidate in the Department of Computer Science at the University of Maryland, College Park. Her research is in the field of bioinformatics, including DNA to genome alignment, peptide identification via mass spectrometry, and high performance BLASTs.

**Professor LouXin Zhang** is an Associate Professor in the Department of Mathematics, National University of Singapore. He received his B.S. and M.S. degrees in Mathematics from Lanzhou University, and his Ph.D. degree in Computer Science from Waterloo University. His research interests are mainly in the fields of Bioinformatics and Computational Biology, but also include theoretical aspects of parallel and distributed networks, algorithms, applied combinatorial mathematics, mathematical logic, and group theory. Prof. Zhang has served on the program committees of many international conferences and workshops, including APBC'07, COCOON'06, WABI'06, 3rd RECOMB Comparative Genomics Satellite Workshop 2005, WABI'04, and WABI'03. He is currently on the editorial board of the International Journal of Bioinformatics Research and Applications in Genomics, Proteomics and Bioinformatics.

# Preface

This volume is number 68 in the series **Advances in Computers** that began back in 1960. This is the longest continuously published series of books that chronicles the evolution of the computer industry. Each year three volumes are produced presenting approximately 20 chapters that describe the latest technology in the use of computers today. Volume 68, subtitled "Computational Biology and Bioinformatics," presents six chapters that examine exciting problems in the new field of computational biology.

The past decade has been an exciting period for the biological sciences. It seems every other week researchers discover a new gene responsible for some important physical trait, or establish some new evolutionary relationship between organisms. What is less clear to the public is that computer scientists have also contributed to many of these discoveries by developing bioinformatic algorithms implemented in software tools used by biologists.

The field of *bioinformatics* and *computational biology* arose due to the need to apply techniques from computer science, statistics, informatics, and applied mathematics to solve biological problems. Since James Watson and Francis Crick discovered the DNA double helix in 1953, scientists have been trying to study biology at a molecular level using techniques derived from biochemistry, biophysics, and genetics. Progress has greatly accelerated with the discovery of fast and inexpensive automated DNA sequencing techniques, enabling the completion of massive endeavors such as the Human Genome Project, which sequenced all the DNA (genome) found in human beings. Today, advances in molecular biology experimental techniques are producing huge amounts of biological data, making computational tools indispensable for biologists.

The field of computational biology includes many research areas, including sequence alignment, genome assembly, gene finding, gene expression, gene regulation, comparative genomics, evolutionary biology, protein structure prediction, protein structure alignment, determining gene and protein interaction networks, and experimental proteomics. This book focuses on the areas of phylogenetics, comparative genomics, and proteomics.

As the genomes of more and more organisms are sequenced and assembled, scientists are discovering many useful facts by tracing the evolution of organisms by measuring changes in their DNA, rather than through physical characteristics alone. This has led to rapid growth in the related fields of *phylogenetics*, the study of evolutionary relatedness among various groups of organisms, and *comparative genomics*, the study of the correspondence between genes and other genomic features in different organisms. Comparing the genomes of organisms has allowed researchers to better understand the features and functions of DNA in individual organisms, as well as provide insights into how organisms evolve over time. Useful concrete applications of phylogenetics and comparative genomics include identifying the basis for genetic diseases and tracking the development and spread of different forms of Avian flu.

The first four chapters of this book focus on different aspects of the fields of phylogenetics and comparative genomics. Chapter 1, "Exposing Phylogenetic Relationships by Genome Rearrangement" by Ying Chih Lin and Chuan Yi Tang provide a basic review of concepts and terms used in molecular biology, then explore techniques for comparing the closeness of evolutionary relationships between related organisms by modeling the manner in which genomes have been rearranged over long periods of time. The authors demonstrate how their techniques may be used when comparing the genomes of multiple species of bacteria.

In Chapter 2, "Models and Methods in Comparative Genomics" by Guillaume Bourque and LouXin Zhang, the authors discuss several topics biologists face when comparing the genomes of different organisms, focusing on mathematical models and algorithmic aspects of each topic. This chapter provides a glimpse of the different types of information that can be discovered when comparing DNA from different organisms, as well as the variety of difficulties and challenges that must be overcome.

Chapter 3, "Translocation Distance: Algorithms and Complexity" by Lusheng Wang, focuses on issues and techniques for using translocation distance as the principal metric for comparing the evolutionary distance between organisms. This chapter demonstrates how complicated algorithms and analyses may be needed even when considering just a single approach to solving phylogenetic problems.

Chapter 4, "Computational Grand Challenges in Assembling the Tree of Life: Problems & Solutions" by David A. Bader, Usman Roshan, and Alexandros Stamatakis addresses the issues encountered when attempting to extend phylogenetic techniques to handle a large number of organisms at once. Their goal is to be able to successfully analyze the genomes of all organisms together to assemble a full Tree of Life. This chapter exposes the difficulties of overcoming computational challenges in bioinformatics, even when exploiting the availability of fast computers and the power of parallel computing.

The last two chapters of this book focus on topics in the field of *proteomics*, the study of all proteins in an organism. While DNA may be thought of as the biological method used to store information required by an organism, *proteins* are the actual molecular machinery constructed using information stored in the DNA. Proteins are essential to the structure and function of all organisms, and are needed to perform a wide variety of useful and necessary biological processes. In many situations the presence and identity of proteins can be indirectly inferred from information available in DNA. However, more precise information and understanding may be obtained by studying proteins directly, giving rise to the field of proteomics.

Chapter 5, "Local Structure Comparison of Proteins" by Jun Huan, Jan Prins, and Wei Wang discuss methods for comparing the 3-dimensional structure of proteins. Protein structure is important because it can directly affect its biological function. Structure comparison techniques can thus help predict protein function by finding similarities to proteins with known functionality. The authors introduce the problem of protein structure comparison and discuss recently developed techniques that show promise.

Chapter 6, "Peptide Identification via Tandem Mass Spectroscopy" by Xue Wu, Nathan Edwards, and Chau-Wen Tseng discusses how tandem mass spectrometry, a technique from analytical chemistry, can be used to directly identify proteins in a high throughput setting. This chapter presents a review of how protein fragments (peptides) are produced and identified. Results from an experimental comparison of existing tools are used to point out limitations and potential improvements in current algorithms used for protein identification.

The past decade has seen many advances in the field of molecular biology. Techniques and tools developed by researchers in computational biology and bioinformatics have contributed immensely to these successes. I hope the chapters in this book can help you understand how computer scientists have enabled advances in molecular biology. Newer and even more efficient DNA sequencing technologies such as sequencing by hybridization, pyrosequencing, and nanopore sequencing are being developed that threaten to unleash even larger mountains of biological data on scientists. It appears researchers in computational biology and bioinformatics will have many future opportunities to continue contributing to advances in the biological sciences.

Chau-Wen Tseng
College Park, Maryland

# Exposing Phylogenetic Relationships by Genome Rearrangement

YING CHIH LIN AND CHUAN YI TANG

*Department of Computer Science*
*National Tsing Hua University*
*Hsinchu 300*
*Taiwan, ROC*
*d904399@oz.nthu.edu.tw*
*cytang@cs.nthu.edu.tw*

**Abstract**

Evolutionary studies based on large-scale rearrangement operations, as opposed to the traditional approaches on point mutations, have been considered as a promising alternative for inferring the evolutionary history of species. Genome rearrangement problems lead to combinatorial puzzles of finding parsimonious scenarios towards measuring what difference species have and explaining how a species evolves from another. Throughout this chapter, we will focus on the introduction of computing the genomic distance, arising from the effects of a set of rearrangement events, between a pair of genomes. In the end, two experiments on Campanulaceae and Proteobacteria are used to simply show how to exploit the genome rearrangement approach for exposing phylogenetic relationships.



ADVANCES IN COMPUTERS, VOL. 68


ISSN: 0065-2458/DOI: 10.1016/S0065-2458(06)68001-7

# 1. Introduction

Today molecular biology has become an information science in many respects with close ties to computer science. Large databases and sophisticated algorithms are developed as essential tools for seeking to understand complex biological systems, determine the functions of nucleotide and protein sequences, or reconstruct the evolution of species. Before understanding biological tools, the models of biological problems and biologically related algorithms, one should primarily learn about the background in both biology and algorithm theory. In this section, we first introduce some basics in biology, then in algorithm and complexity, and finally in a relatively young field, computational biology, which also contains the topics studied in this chapter.

## 1.1 Molecular Biology Primer

A complete way to describe each living organism is represented by its *genome*. From the view of computer science, this can be regarded as a "program" in some particular language, which describes a set of instructions to be followed by an organism for growth and living. In other words, the genome is a temple or a blueprint on which constructing a building relies. Therefore in order to understand and interpret the hidden information of genome, we first define the "life language" by the representation of *DNA codes*.

A genome is composed of the *deoxyribonucleic acid* (DNA) discovered in 1869 while studying the chemistry of white blood cells. The DNA appears in the cell of organisms and comprises two sequences, called *strands*, of tightly coiled threads of *nucleotides*. Each nucleotide is a molecule composed of a phosphoric group, a pentose sugar and a nitrogen-containing chemical, called a *base*. Four different bases

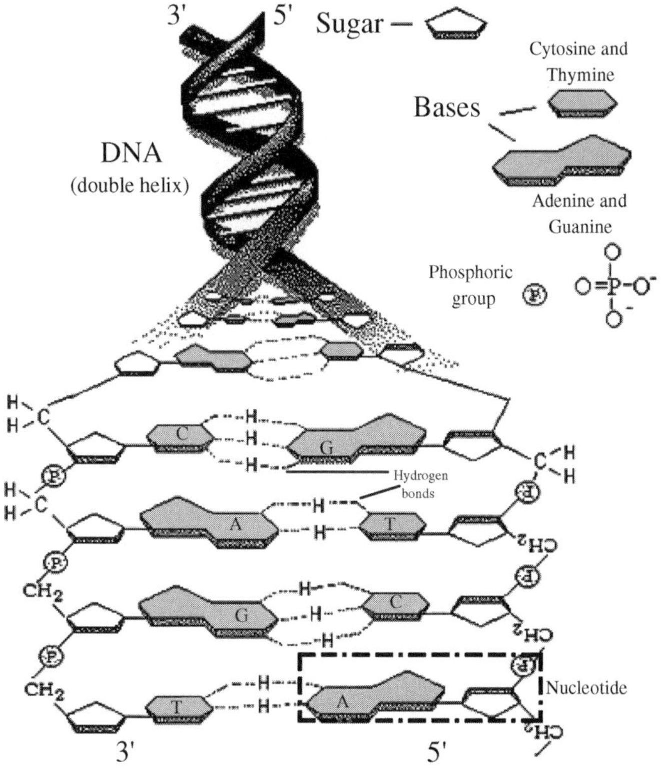


FIG. 1. The DNA is a double-stranded molecule twisted into a helix (like a spiral staircase). Each spiral strand, comprised of a sugar-phosphate backbone and attached bases, is connected to a complementary strand by non-covalent hydrogen bonding between paired bases. Two ends of a backbone are conventionally called the 5′ end and the 3′ end [2].

are adenine (A), thymine (T), cytosine (C) and guanine (G), as illustrated in Fig. 1. A particular order of the bases is called the *DNA sequence* which varies greatly from organism to organism. It is the content of this sequence specifying the precise genetic instructions to produce unique features of an organism.

Among the four bases, base A is always paired with base T, and C is always paired with G. Thus bases A and T (C and G) are said to be the *complement* of each other, or a pair of *complementary bases*. Two DNA sequences are *complementary* if one is the other read backwards with the complementary bases interchanged, e.g., ATCCGA and TCGGAT are complementary because ATCCGA with A $\leftrightarrow$ T and C $\leftrightarrow$ G becomes TAGGCT, which is TCGGAT read backwards. There are strong interac-

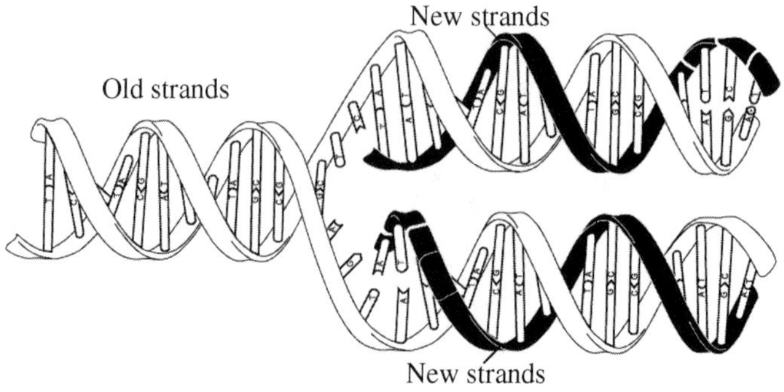


FIG. 2. Schematic DNA replication [2].

tions formed by hydrogen bonds between two complementary bases, called *base pairing*. Hence, two complementary DNA sequences are intertwisted in a double helix structure described by Watson and Crick in 1953 [173]. Despite the complex 3-dimensional structure of this molecule, the genetic material only depends on the sequence of nucleotides and can thus be described without loss information as a string over the alphabet {A,T,G,C}.

Because of this complementarity, the DNA has the capability to replicate itself. The full genome of a cell is duplicated when it divides into two new cells. At this moment, the DNA molecule unwinds and breaks the bonds between the base pairs one by one (Fig. 2). Each strand acts as a template for the synthesis of a new DNA molecule by the sequential addition of complementary base pairs, thereby generating a new DNA strand that is the complementary sequence to the parental DNA. By this way, each new molecule should be identical with the old one. However, although the replication process is very reliable, it is not completely error-free and it is possible that some bases are lost, duplicated or simply changed. The situation of variations to the original DNA sequence is known as *mutations*, and can make the diversity of organisms or their offspring. In most cases, mutations are harmful, but sometimes they can be innocent or advantageous for the evolution of species to adapt to new environments.

In spite of the huge variety among the existing forms of life, the basic mechanism for the representation of being is the same for all organisms. As a matter of fact, all the information describing an organism is encoded in the DNA sequence of its genome by means of a universal code, known as the *genetic code*. This code is used to describe how to construct the *proteins*, which are responsible for performing most of the work of cells, e.g., the aid of constructing structures and essentially biochemical reactions. It is interesting that not all of the DNA sequences contain the coding information. In fact it appears on small regions only, e.g., in human, the total size

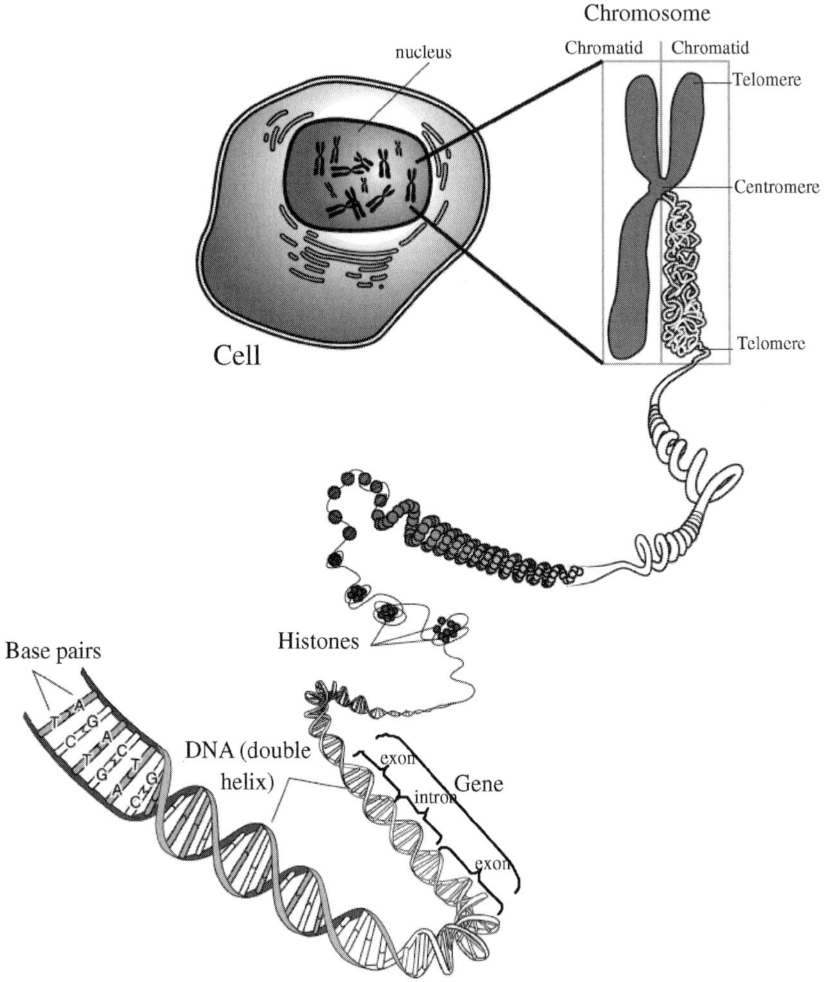


FIG. 3. A schema of chromosomes in eukaryotic [2].

of such regions covers about 10% of the whole DNA sequence. The coding DNA regions are the so-called *genes*, where each gene is mapped to a different protein. Gene sequence contains *exons* and *introns* (Fig. 3) of which the former are translated into proteins and the latter are the intervening sequences whose functions are obscure (in general, they are regarded as irrelevancies to the functions of organisms).

Genes are linearly located on *chromosomes* and are also the primary material of chromosome, as shown in Fig. 3. In the *eukaryotic cell* of higher organisms, there are several chromosomes in their nucleus, which are all linear sequences in general, e.g., human has 46 chromosomes (23 pairs). Their chromosome usually consists of one or two *chromatids*, *telomeres* and a *centromere*. In most case, the centromere roughly locates in the middle of a chromosome, but sometimes, it approaches the end. When a chromosome composes of two chromatids, we sometimes term it a *doubled chromosome*. Besides, in the *prokaryotic cell* of lower organisms, they usually contain chromosomes of circular molecules, e.g., bacteria have one circular chromosome while vibrio species have two. More background on molecular biology can be referenced in the textbooks of Clark and Russell [45], and Weaver [175].

## 1.2 Algorithm and Complexity

In a general sense, an *algorithm* is a well-defined and finite sequence of steps used to solve a *well-formulated problem* which is unambiguous and can be specified by *inputs* and *outputs*. An algorithm solves a problem which means that the algorithm gives the solution satisfying the requirement according to the instance of problem. A famous example in computer science is the Traveling Salesman Problem, or TSP for short. In this problem, a salesman has a map specifying a collection of cities and the cost of travel between each pair of them. He wants to visit all cities and eventually return to the city form which he started. The inputs of a TSP are the map and a starting city, while the output is the cheapest route for visiting all cities.

Most problems in computer science can be abstracted and then redescribed as graphs of vertices and edges connecting two vertices. For instance in TSP, the cities correspond to vertices and the cost of a pair of cities corresponds to the edge associated with a weight. The output is finding the shortest length of starting from one vertex, visiting all vertices and finally reaching the starting vertex, where the length is computed by sum of the edge weights in this tour. See Fig. 4 for a simple example of TSP.

In spite of the success in the example of Fig. 4, the TSP is indeed harder than most combinatorial optimization problems considered. The conjecture by Edmonds [65] in 1965 of why no efficient algorithm for TSP means that there is no algorithm which solves the problem on all instances in a reasonable time. However, he did not point out the precise meaning to what is the "reasonable time," but a common definition since then is that a reasonable running time is one where the number of steps is polynomial in the size of the input, i.e., if $n$ is the input size, then $f(n)$ is the number of steps where $f()$ is a polynomial function. Furthermore, the class of optimization problems having such algorithms is denoted as P introduced by Cobham [46]

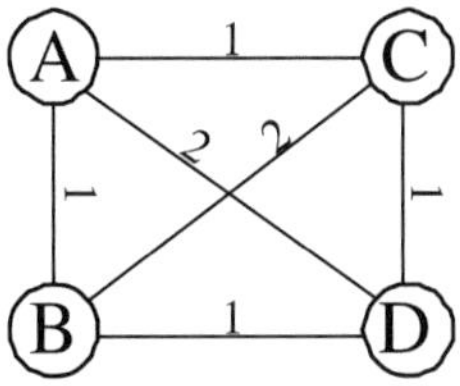


FIG. 4. An example has four vertices and the cost of each pair of vertices is labeled on the edge. A shortest tour starting from vertex A is A $\rightarrow$ B $\rightarrow$ D $\rightarrow$ C $\rightarrow$ A with cost 4.

and independently, Edmonds [65], where the problems are also referred to *tractable* problems.

In the early 1970s, we made a better progress on the problems for which no efficient algorithms were known. These harder problems are classified as *decision* and *optimization* problems according to what they ask. A decision problem is a problem where the answer is "yes" or "no," e.g., "Is there a TSP tour of distance at most 5?" while the optimization problem is as "What is the shortest tour of visiting all cities?," Cook [51] proposed a milestone paper presenting the class NP (Non-deterministic Polynomial time) and first showed that the *circuit-satisfiability problem* is NP-complete. NP contains the decision problems which can be solved in polynomial time by a *non-deterministic* machine. This machine has the capability to "guess" a solution non-deterministically and then verifies it in polynomial time. In some sense, the non-deterministic guessing is equivalent to try all possible solutions in parallel. For the TSP, we can design a non-deterministic machine as follows: Given a starting vertex $S$, it enumerates all paths with length $i$ from $S$, and verifies that a path passes through all vertices and ends in $S$. This verification can be done in polynomial time, thus implying TSP $\in$ NP.

A special class of optimization problems is NP-hard in which a polynomial-time solution to any problem in this class implies that all problems in NP have polynomial solutions. A problem is in the class NP-completeness if it is both NP and NP-hard. Thus NP-complete problems can be regarded as the hardest problems in NP. Clearly, P $\subset$ NP and whether P is equal to NP or not is one of the most notable open problems in both theoretical computer science and mathematics (one of the seven *Prize Problems* [3]). It is widely believed that P $\neq$ NP on which many results are based. Therefore, a polynomial-time algorithm for solving a problem in NP-completeness seems to be highly unlikely since that would imply polynomial solutions to all problems in NP and hence P $=$ NP. For this reason, NP-complete problems are also said to be *intractable*. For more properties and classes of computational complexity, we refer the reader to the books of Garey and Johnson [79], Hopcroft, Motwani and Ullman [99], Papadimitriou [142] and Sipser [156].

Many problems of practical significance are NP-complete implying that obtaining an optimal solution is intractable, but they are too important to be discarded directly. If the input size is small, an exhaustive algorithm for searching in exponential running time may be adequate. Nevertheless, for an input of large size, it is time-consuming, perhaps several years, to wait for the solution output by a computer. One way to attack such problems is to use heuristics, which is typically implemented with sophisticated searches in partial solution space. Solutions of heuristic methods often have no guarantees with respect to optimal solutions, i.e., there are no bounds on the degree of how near/far-optimal solutions are.

Although we are most unlikely to find a polynomial-time algorithm for solving an NP-complete problem exactly, it may still be possible to find *near-optimal* solutions in polynomial time. An algorithm that returns a near-optimal solution with theoretical proof is called an *approximation algorithm*. Graham [81] made the first attempt to introduce the concept of approximation algorithm, which is used to solve the *parallel-machine-scheduling problem*. Subsequently, Garey, Graham and Ullman [78] and Johnson [103] formalized the concept of a polynomial-time approximation algorithm.

We say that an algorithm for an optimization problem has an *approximation ratio* $\beta$ ($\beta$-approximation algorithm) if, for any input of size $n$, the cost $C$ of solution produced by the algorithm is under a factor of $\beta$ with respect to the cost $C^*$ of an optimal solution, i.e., $\max(C/C^*, C^*/C) \leqslant \beta$ [52]. The definition of approximation ratio applies to both minimization (ratio $C/C^*$) and maximization (ratio $C^*/C$) problems. Taking the TSP for an example, if there are $n$ cities, a brute-force search of at most $(n-1)!$ possibilities can find out the shortest tour. However, for the TSP with *triangle inequality*, even if it is still NP-complete, we have a simple 2-approximation algorithm [52, p. 1028], which outputs a tour of A $\rightarrow$ B $\rightarrow$ C $\rightarrow$ D $\rightarrow$ A with cost 6 in the example of Fig. 4. Therefore, the approximation ratio of this solution is $6/4 = 1.5$ (cost 4 is optimal), which is under 2. There is a handy website for recording the history and progress of TSP [4]. In addition, for more classic approximation algorithms, the books of Ausiello et al. [8], Hochbaum [97] and Vazirani [164] extensively include the topics.

## 1.3 Computational Biology

*Computational* (*Molecular*) *Biology* started in the late 1970s as an area that tends to solve the problems arising in the biological lab. In this period, computers became cheaper and simpler to use so that some biologists adapted them for storing and managing genomic data. By powerful ability in computation of computers, their projects and researches can be soon completed while they would cost much time before. An early striking example of a biological discovery by using a computer was in 1983 when Doolittle et al. [61] used the nascent genetic sequence database to show that a cancer-causing gene was a close relative of a normal gene. From this, it became clear that the cancer might arise from a normal growth factor being acted at the wrong time.

At that time, molecular biology labs throughout the world began installing computers to do database search via networks or develop their own database. Recently, due to convenience and robustness of the Internet, biologists can share their data and make them available worldwide through several genomic data banks, such as GenBank [18], PDB [25], EMBL [47], etc. Moreover, there is a well-developed website NCBI [176] established in 1988 as an interface for accessing these databases. These databases and other resources are valuable services not only to the biological community, but also to the computer scientists in searching the domain information.

Up to now, it is generally obscure on what "Computational Biology" means. Some researches use the two names, *Bioinformatics* and *Computational Biology*, interchangeably, but there actually exists a little difference. We adopt the definitions provided by Lancia [112] in which the *Bioinformatics problems* are concerned with storage, organization and distribution of large amounts of genomic data, while the *Computational Biology* deals with the mathematical and computational problems of interpretation and theoretical analysis of genomic data.

In general, the work of constructing algorithms that address problems with biological relevance, i.e., the work of constructing algorithms in computational biology, consists of two interacting steps. The first step is to present a biologically interesting question, and to construct a model according to the biological phenomenon that makes it unambiguous to formulate the posed question as a *computational problem*. We need to be careful in this step because almost every area of theoretical computer science starts as an attempt to solve applied problems, and later becomes more theoretically-oriented. These theoretical aspects may even become more important and scientifically precious than the original applications that motivate the entire area. Then, the second step is to design an algorithm for solving the computational problem of careful formulation. The first step requires the knowledge of molecular biology, while the second one needs the background of algorithm theory.

To measure the quality of a constructed algorithm, we traditionally use a standard algorithmic methodology on the cost of the resources, most prominently running time and used space, it requires to solve the problem. However, since the problem solved by the algorithm originates from a question with biological relevance, the algorithmic quality could also be judged by the biological relevance of the answer it produces. For example in Fig. 5(a), the distance matrix lists all distances between each pair of the four species, VC, VP, VV and VF, indicating the evolutionary relationship of them, where a bigger distance represents a far relationship of two species.

(a)

| | VC | VP | VV | VF |
|---|---|---|---|---|
| VC | 0 | 23 | 21 | 32 |
| VP | 23 | 0 | 5 | 24 |
| VV | 21 | 5 | 0 | 23 |
| VF | 32 | 24 | 23 | 0 |

(b)

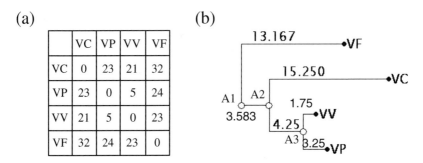

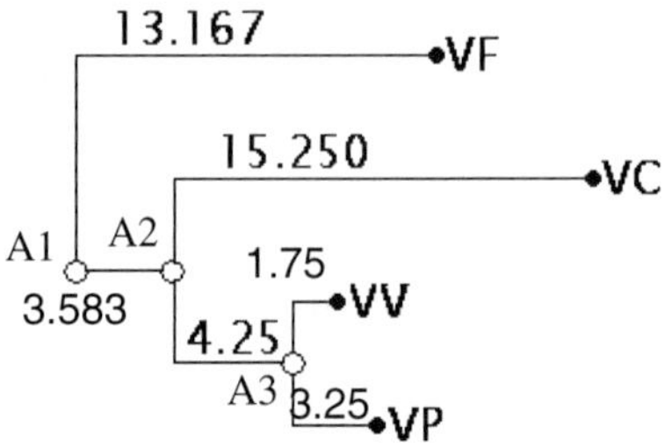


FIG. 5. A distance matrix (a) of four species, VC, VP, VV and VF, and a phylogenetic tree (b) represents the evolutionary relationship of them, where filled circles represent terminal nodes while open circles correspond to internal nodes, A1, A2 and A3. In particular, A1 is called *root*.

Now, we want to describe the distance matrix by using the *phylogenetic tree* made by arranging *nodes* and *branches* (Fig. 5(b)), where every node represents a distinct taxonomical unit. Nodes at the rights of branches (*terminal nodes* or *leaves*) correspond to genes or organisms for which data have actually been collected for analysis, while *internal nodes* usually represent an inferred common ancestor that give rise to two independent lineages at some point in the past. Furthermore, each branch of tree is labeled by a value to reflect the phylogenetic relationship at the distance matrix.

The problems of inferring evolutionary trees have been extensively studied for many years, and unfortunately, many of them are NP-hard or NP-complete. Here, we want to construct a tree such that the length of each path of two *leaves* on the tree is equal to the corresponding value at the distance matrix. Figure 5(b) is an example of a phylogenetic tree constructed by *neighbor-joining method* [147] whose input is the distance matrix in Fig. 5(a). In this tree, the path from VC to VF has length 32, while the distance of VC and VF is also 32 in Fig. 5(a). This tree construction method has polynomial running time from algorithmic view and thus we can expect to obtain the output in a reasonable time. However, it is obviously not an optimal solution due to unequal distances between VC and VV in the matrix (21) and the constructed tree (21.25). Besides, from biological point of view, evaluating the quality of this tree is made by the real relationships among four species. For example, VV is closer to VP than VC to VP in the tree, and if it is also true in real situation, we will believe that the tree is good, thereby implying the neighbor-joining method is superior. For more formulated problems and their corresponding algorithms, we refer reader to the textbooks of Gusfield [83], Jones and Pevzner [104], Pevzner [145], Setubal and Meidanis [154], and Waterman [171].

The details of a specific model and algorithm of course depend on the questions being asked. Most questions in computational biology are related to molecular or evolutionary biology, and focus on analyzing and comparing the composition of the key biomolecules, DNA, RNA and proteins, that together form the basic components of an organism. The success of ongoing efforts to develop and use techniques for getting data about the composition of these biomolecules, like the DNA sequencing technique for extracting the genetic material from species, e.g., the Human Genome Project [101,165], has resulted in a flood of available biological data to be compared and analyzed.

## 2. Genome Rearrangement Overview

The genome of an organism consists of a small number of segments called chromosomes, and genes are spread to the DNA sequence with a particular order in the chromosome that are responsible for encoding proteins. Each gene has an orientation, either forward or backward, depending on which direction it is assumed to be read. Therefore, a genome can be abstracted as a set of chromosomes and a chromosome is composed of an order set of oriented genes. The chromosomes of higher organisms like mammalian are generally linear (the DNA sequence has a beginning and an end), but of lower organisms like bacteria, are circular (their DNA sequences have no beginning or end).

Traditional comparison between two genomes pays attention to *local operations* (mutations), such as *substitution*, *insertion*, *deletion* and *duplication* (Fig. 6) which

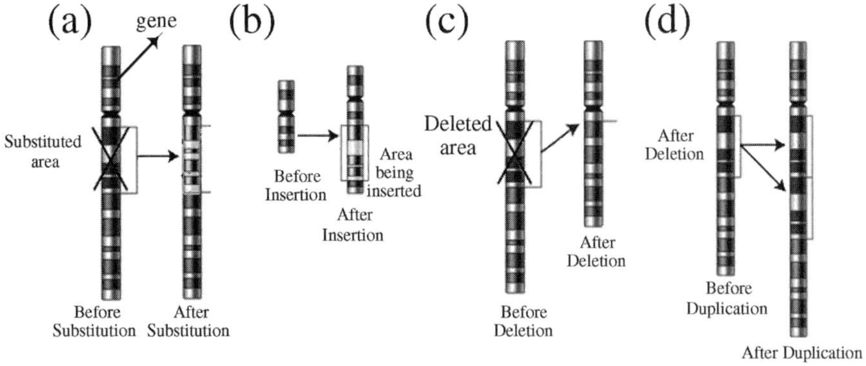


FIG. 6. The bar represents a chromosome and each black block indicates the position of its gene. The four types of local operations, substitution (a), insertion (b), deletion (c) and duplication (d) [2], which usually affect a very small number of genes in a chromosome.

affect only a small stretch on DNA sequence. These local operations have been widely observed by biologists due to their frequent occurrences in studying the difference between two genomes. Further, from theoretical point of view, the minimum difference caused by local operations between two genomes is regarded as the *edit distance* of them, and such value, in most cases, can be easily calculated by using *dynamic programming* method [52]. Most phylogenetic researches have been published based on these types of operations.

On the other hand, the study of *genome rearrangement* focuses on inferring the parsimonious explanation by using a set of *non-local operations* for the disruption in gene orders among two or more genomes. In general, such non-local operations are called *rearrangement events*. A rearrangement event occurs when a chromosome is broken at two or more positions which results in two or more segments reassembling with a different order. The rearranged DNA sequence is essentially identical to the original sequence, except exchanges in the order of reassembled segments. These non-local operations causing reassembly include *reversal* (or *inversion*), *transposition*, *block-interchange* and *translocation*.

A *reversal* event flips a segment in a chromosome and changes the directions of each element in the segment. Each *transposition* event exchanges two adjacent segments in a chromosome while the *block-interchange* swaps two non-intersecting segments. Due to the involving of segments in two chromosomes, the *translocation* event is more complicated and its effect will be introduced in Section 5. Moreover, most of non-local operations are derived from biological observations on the difference of DNA sequences among species. For example, in the late 1930s, Dobzhansky and Sturtevant [60] published a milestone paper presenting a rearrangement scenario with inversions for *Drosophila* fruit fly and it was taken as the pioneer of genome rearrangement in molecular biology. Moreover, in the late 1980s, Palmer and Herbon [140] compared the mitochondrial genome of *Brassica oleracea* (cabbage) and *Brassica campestris* (turnip) in which many genes are 99% identical but dramatically differ in gene order (Fig. 7). Palmer and his coworkers also found the similar phenomenon within the chloroplast genome of legume [141] and anemone [98]. These discoveries are convincing to prove that genome rearrangement plays a role in molecular evolution.

In contract to the edit distance, the *rearrangement distance* (or *genetic distance*) resulting from rearrangement events is commonly set to the minimum number of operations for the transformation between two genomes. For instance in Fig. 7, if only reversal is considered, the rearrangement distance between cabbage and turnip is 3 where the minimum can be verified by "pen-and-pencil" method. In case of genomes consisting of a small number of homologous genes (or conserved blocks), we can find the most parsimonious rearrangement scenarios by exhaustive search or observation. However, it is time-consuming for genomes consisting of more genes notwithstand-

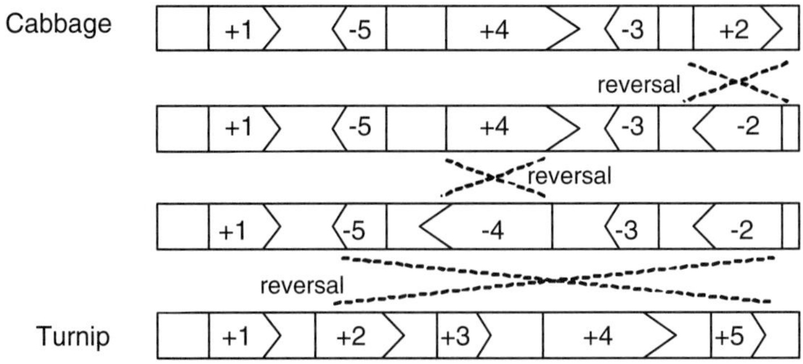


FIG. 7. The pentagons represent the positions, orientations and order of common genes shared by cabbage and turnip, and each pair of two dotted lines represents an inverted segment. As shown in this figure, three reversals can transform cabbage into turnip [145].

ing performing exhaustive search over all potential solutions by a computer. As a result, developing efficient algorithms is an urgent requirement to deal with genome rearrangement problems arising from the large-scale mapping of species.

The computational approach based on the comparison of gene orders was pioneered by Sankoff et al. [148,150,151]. According to which operations we consider, the genome rearrangement problems lead to different combinatorial puzzle. This model simply treats chromosomes as permutations and genes as the elements in the permutations associated with $+$ or $-$ sign indicating the direction of its transcription. Taking Fig. 7 as an example, cabbage ($\vec{\pi}$) is modeled as $+1\ -5\ +4\ -3\ +2$ and turnip ($\vec{\sigma}$) as $+1\ +2\ +3\ +4\ +5$, and thus, the problem becomes to find the minimum number of reversals for transforming $\vec{\pi}$ into $\vec{\sigma}$.

Let $\Sigma = \{1, 2, \ldots, n\}$, and $\vec{\pi} = \vec{\pi}_1\ \vec{\pi}_2 \ldots \vec{\pi}_n$ be a signed permutation on $\Sigma$, where each $\vec{\pi}_i$ is labeled by a sign of $+$ or $-$. For $1 \leqslant i \leqslant j < k \leqslant l \leqslant n$, we express three types of operations as the mathematical form:

- A reversal $r(i, j)$ affects $\vec{\pi}$, denoted as $r(i, j) \cdot \vec{\pi}$, by inverting the block $\vec{\pi}_i\ \vec{\pi}_{i+1} \ldots \vec{\pi}_j$ to $-\vec{\pi}_j\ -\vec{\pi}_{j-1} \ldots -\vec{\pi}_i$, i.e., $r(i, j) \cdot \vec{\pi} = \vec{\pi}_1 \ldots \vec{\pi}_{i-1}\ -\vec{\pi}_j\ -\vec{\pi}_{j-1} \ldots -\vec{\pi}_i\ \vec{\pi}_{j+1} \ldots \vec{\pi}_n$.
- A transposition $\mathrm{tr}(i, j, k)$ affects $\vec{\pi}$, denoted as $\mathrm{tr}(i, j, k) \cdot \vec{\pi}$, by swapping two consecutive segments $\vec{\pi}_i\ \vec{\pi}_{i+1} \ldots \vec{\pi}_j$ and $\vec{\pi}_{j+1}\ \vec{\pi}_{j+2} \ldots \vec{\pi}_k$, i.e., $\mathrm{tr}(i, j, k) \cdot \vec{\pi} = \vec{\pi}_1 \ldots \vec{\pi}_{i-1}\ \vec{\pi}_{j+1} \ldots \vec{\pi}_k\ \vec{\pi}_i \ldots \vec{\pi}_j\ \vec{\pi}_{k+1} \ldots \vec{\pi}_n$.
- A block-interchange $\mathrm{bi}(i, j, k, l)$ affects $\vec{\pi}$, denoted as $\mathrm{bi}(i, j, k, l) \cdot \vec{\pi}$, by swapping two non-intersecting segments $\vec{\pi}_i\ \vec{\pi}_{i+1} \ldots \vec{\pi}_j$ and $\vec{\pi}_k\ \vec{\pi}_{k+1} \ldots \vec{\pi}_l$, that is, $\mathrm{bi}(i, j, k, l) \cdot \vec{\pi} = \vec{\pi}_1 \ldots \vec{\pi}_{i-1}\ \vec{\pi}_k \ldots \vec{\pi}_l\ \vec{\pi}_{j+1} \ldots \vec{\pi}_{k-1} \vec{\pi}_i \ldots \vec{\pi}_j\ \vec{\pi}_{l+1} \ldots \vec{\pi}_n$.

Given two permutations $\vec{\pi}$ and $\vec{\sigma}$, *sorting by reversals* is the problem of finding a series of reversals $\rho_1, \rho_2, \ldots, \rho_t$ such that $\rho_t \cdot \rho_{t-1} \cdots, \rho_1 \cdot \vec{\pi} = \vec{\sigma}$, where $t$ is the minimum and considered as the *reversal distance* $d_r(\vec{\pi})$ between $\vec{\pi}$ and $\vec{\sigma}$. Usually, the target permutation $\vec{\sigma}$ is replaced by the *identity permutation* $\vec{I} = +1\ +2\ \ldots +n$ and this is why we call the transformation of $\vec{\pi}$ into $\vec{I}$ a *sorting problem*. Therefore, the *reversal distance* is the distance $d_r(\vec{\pi})$ of $\vec{\pi}$ and $\vec{I}$. In 1995, Hannenhalli and Pevzner [89] surprisingly provided a polynomial-time algorithm for exactly solving the sorting by reversals problem, which lead to great interest of later researchers. Other problems such as *sorting by transpositions*, *sorting by block-interchanges* and *sorting by translocations* can be similarly defined, except the difference in operations. For convenience, we use the term, genomic distance, to represent the distance of two permutations no matter what operations are used to sort.

## 2.1 Pancake Flipping Problem

Before introducing genome rearrangement problems defined later, we first present an interesting problem called *pancake flipping problem* originally inspired by Dweighter [64]. This problem comes out of a real-life situation that a waiter wants to rearrange a stack of pancakes with all different sizes by grabbing several from the top and flipping them over such that the smallest pancake winds up on top, and so on, down to the largest at the bottom. If there are $n$ pancakes, what is the minimum number of flips used to rearrange them? Moreover, the pancake flipping problem corresponds to the *sorting by prefix reversal* problem described as follows: Given an arbitrary permutation $\pi = \pi_1\pi_2 \ldots \pi_n$ (a stack of $n$ pancakes), each $\pi_i$ corresponds to a pancake according to its value, i.e., a bigger $\pi_i$ corresponds to a pancake with larger size. *Sorting by prefix reversal* problem is to find the minimum number of *prefix reversals*, denoted as $d_{\text{pref}}(\pi)$, of the form $r(1, i)$ to sort $\pi$. Since there is no difference between two sides of a pancake, the permutation $\pi$ is unsigned, i.e., each $\pi_i$ is always positive. A reversal thereby acts on $\pi$ by inverting the order of elements without changing the signs of them in a segment (Fig. 8). Specially, Bogomolny developed a website for simulating this problem [31].

The first result attempting to solve this problem was published by Gates and Papadimitriou [80]. They proved that the *prefix reversal diameter*, $D_{\text{pref}}(n) = \max_{\pi \in S_n} d_{\text{pref}}(\pi)$ where $S_n$ is the *symmetric group* containing all permutations of size $n$, has bounds of $D_{\text{pref}}(n) \leqslant (5n + 5)/3$ and that for infinitely many $n$, $17n/16 \leqslant D_{\text{pref}}(n)$. Subsequently, Heydari and Sudborough [94] improved the lower bound to $15n/14$. To our surprise, this seemingly effortless problem had no complexity result until Fischer and Ginzinger [75] recently gave a 2-approximation algorithm to find $d_{\text{pref}}(\pi)$.

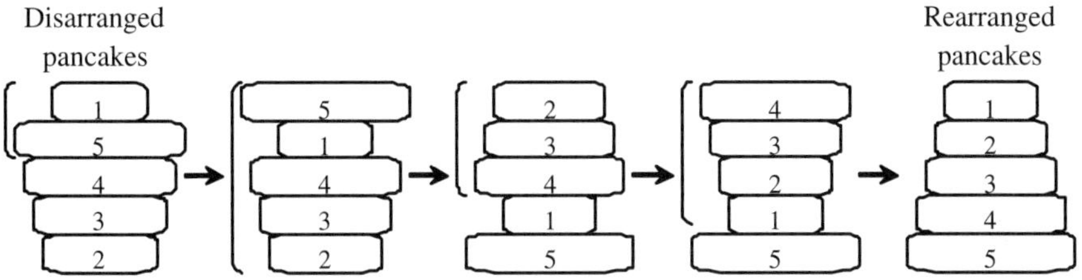


FIG. 8. Four prefix reversals can transform $\pi = 1\ 5\ 4\ 3\ 2$ into $I = 1\ 2\ 3\ 4\ 5$. The left-bracket segments show where reversals take place.

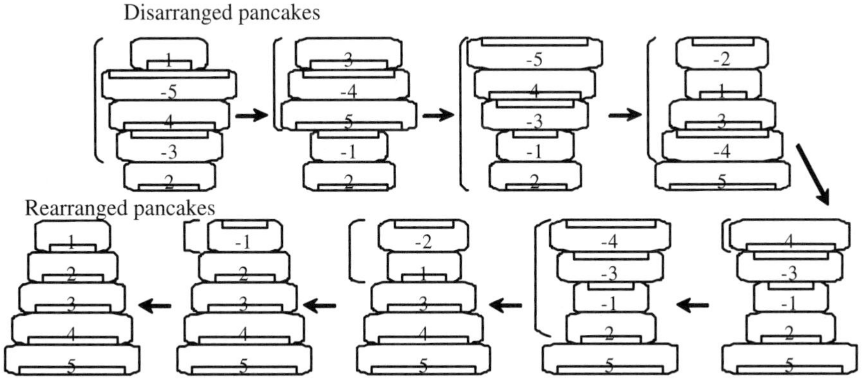


FIG. 9. $\vec{\pi}_i$ represents a pancake and moreover, a sign "−" is associated with $\vec{\pi}_i$ if its burnt side is up; otherwise, it has good side up, where the burnt side is indicated by the rectangle in a pancake. Eight prefix reversals can transform $\vec{\pi} = 1\ -5\ 4\ -3\ 2$ into $\vec{I} = 1\ 2\ 3\ 4\ 5$.

Gates and Papadimitriou [80] also considered a variation of pancake flipping problem in which a pancake has two sides and one side is burnt. These pancakes must be sorted to the size-ordered arrangement and every pancake has its burnt side down. Such a variation can also be transformed to an analogous sorting by prefix problem mentioned above. Moreover, due to the dissimilarity of two sides in a pancake, the permutation $\vec{\pi}$ becomes signed and each prefix reversal changes all signs of elements in an inverted segment (Fig. 9). Gates and Papadimitriou found that $3n/2 - 1 \leqslant d_{\text{pref}}(\vec{\pi}) \leqslant 2n + 3$ and this was further improved to $3n/2 \leqslant d_{\text{pref}}(\vec{\pi}) \leqslant 2n - 2$ by Cohen and Blum [50], where the upper bound holds for $10 \leqslant n$. However, there is little progress in either type, unsigned and signed, of pancake problem. Although Heydari [95] has proved the NP-completeness of a *modified version* of pancake problem (unsigned), it remains unknown whether or not the original problems are in P.

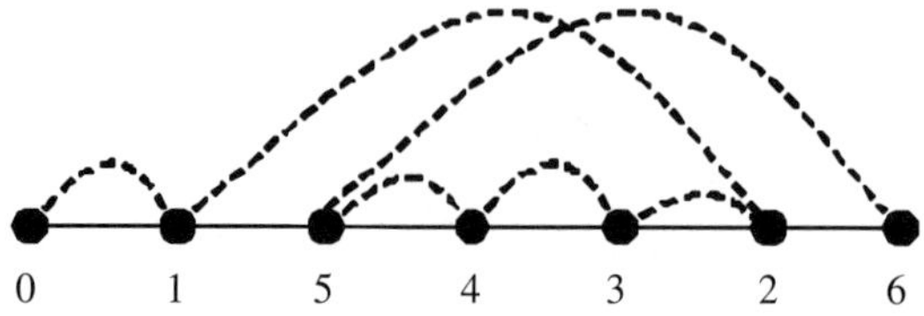


FIG. 10. The breakpoint graph $G(\pi)$ of $\pi = 1\ 5\ 4\ 3\ 2$, where black edges are represented as solid lines and gray edges as dotted lines.

## 2.2 The Breakpoint Graph

In the field of genome rearrangement, the most famous tool for analyzing is the *breakpoint graph* on which many results are based. Watterson et al. [174], and Nadeau and Taylor [135] introduced the notation of a *breakpoint*. They also noticed that there are some correlations between the number of breakpoints and the reversal distance. Below we define the breakpoint and show how to construct the breakpoint graph of an unsigned/signed permutation.

For an unsigned permutation $\pi = \pi_1\pi_2\ldots\pi_n$, we extend it by adding $\pi_0 = 0$ and $\pi_{n+1} = n+1$. A pair of elements $(\pi_i, \pi_{i+1})$, $0 \leqslant i \leqslant n$, is a *breakpoint* if $|\pi_i - \pi_{i+1}| > 1$. For instance, if $\pi = 1\ 5\ 4\ 3\ 2$, then there are two breakpoints $(1, 5)$ and $(2, 6)$. Since the identity permutation has no breakpoints, sorting $\pi$ corresponds to eliminating breakpoints. If we use only reversals, an observation that a reversal can eliminate at most two breakpoints immediately implies $b(\pi)/2 \leqslant d_r(\pi)$, where $b(\pi)$ is the number of breakpoints in $\pi$. Similar inferences can be applied to transposition and block-interchange so that we obtain the lower bounds of $b(\pi)/3 \leqslant d_{\mathrm{tr}}(\pi)$ and $b(\pi)/4 \leqslant d_{\mathrm{bi}}(\pi)$ for transposition and block-interchange distance, respectively.

There were several definitions for the breakpoint graph in previous researches and we choose one of the most common models introduced by Bafna and Pevzner [11] which we will use in the following sections. The *breakpoint graph* of an unsigned permutation $\pi$ is defined to be an edge-colored graph $G(\pi)$ with $n+2$ vertices $\{\pi_0, \pi_1, \ldots, \pi_{n+1}\}$ as the following. For $0 \leqslant i \leqslant n$, $\pi_i$ and $\pi_{i+1}$ are connected by a *black edge*, and $\pi_i$ is joined to $\pi_j$ by a *gray edge* if $|\pi_i - \pi_j| = 1$, as shown in Fig. 10. Sections below will introduce in detail how to use the breakpoint graph to assist in sorting a permutation.

# 3. Sorting by Reversals

The reversal event is our first discussed event: not only is it the first event observed in *Drosophila* species by Dobzhansky and Sturtevant [60], but also it commonly exists in virus [102], bacteria [66,100], Chloroplast of plants [54,111,141], animals and mammalian [74] thereby accepted by most biologists. Modeling the reversal distance for higher organisms is reasonable as biological lectures report that reversals are the primary mechanism of genome rearrangement for many genomes in eukaryote [125]. Furthermore, there are also practical results, both tools and theoretical analyses, in considering reversals only. Watterson et al. [174] made the first attempt to deal with reversal events, and gave definitions of the sorting by reversals problem associated with a heuristic for computing the reversal distance. Schöniger and Waterman [152] also presented a heuristic method when only non-overlapping inversions, whose inverted segments are non-overlapping, are allowed.

Biologists acquire gene orders either by sequencing entire genome or by constructing comparative physical mappings. Error-free sequencing can provide correct information about the directions of genes and thus allows one to representing a genome as a signed permutation. However, sequencing the whole genome is still expensive and may have some errors so that most available data on gene orders are based on comparative physical maps. Physical maps usually do not provide full information about the directions of genes, and hence, lead to representing a chromosome as an unsigned permutation. In general, unsigned permutations is a special case of signed ones with all positive elements implicitly implying that sorting an unsigned permutation is simpler than sorting a signed one, but on the contrary, the former is often harder than the latter in genome rearrangement. Even the sorting unsigned permutation by reversals problem is more "difficult" than the NP-complete problems. The coming part first focuses on sorting unsigned linear chromosomes, then considers the signed version and the last of this section demonstrates that the equivalence in sorting of linear chromosomes and circular ones.

## 3.1 Unsigned Permutations

When information about the directions of gene segments is not available, a chromosome can be modeled as an unsigned permutation $\pi = \pi_1\pi_2\dots\pi_n$. Thus given two unsigned linear permutations $\pi$ and $I$, the sorting by reversals problem is to find $\rho_t, \rho_{t-1}, \dots, \rho_1$ such that $\rho_1 \cdot \rho_2 \cdots \rho_t \cdot \pi = I$, where each $\rho_i$ is a reversal, and $t$ is the minimum. Caprara [33] first showed this problem to be NP-hard, and Berman and Karpinski [28] later proved it to be MAX-SNP hard implying that it is almost impossible to be approximated under $1 + \varepsilon$, for some $\varepsilon > 0$.

From two observations that a reversal eliminates at most 2 breakpoints and $n - 1$ reversals can create any permutation, we instantly obtain the bounds of $b(\pi)/2 \leqslant d_r(\pi) \leqslant n-1$, where $b(\pi)$ is the number of breakpoints in $\pi$. Taking $\pi = 6\,4\,1\,5\,2\,3$ as an instance for explaining the upper bound, the reversal $r(1, 3)$ can move $\pi_3 = 1$ to the right position when it acts on $\pi$, that is, a series of reversals, where the first

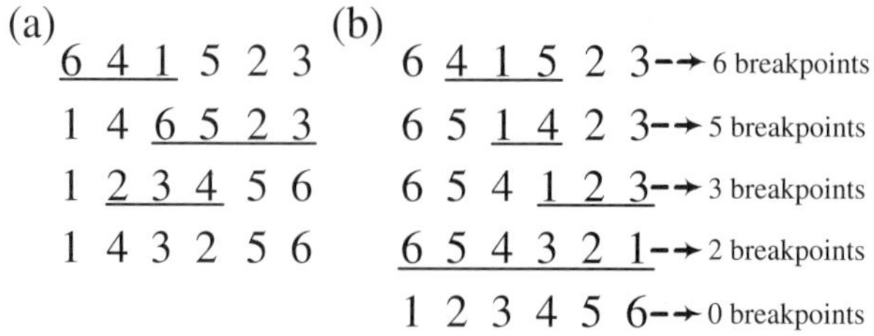


FIG. 11. (a) Three reversals optimally sort $\pi = 6\ 4\ 1\ 5\ 2\ 3$ and therefore, the reversal distance between $\pi$ and $I$ is 3; (b) The approximation algorithm developed by Kececioglu and Sankoff [109] can sort $\pi$ by using 4 reversals, where each reversal removes at least 1 breakpoint. Underlined segments indicate where reversals happen.

moves 1 to its right position, the second copes with 2, and so on, can sort $\pi$. One of the worst cases with this method is $\pi = n\ 1\ 2 \ldots n-1$, which can be sorted by $n-1$ reversals. In addition to the straightforward bounds, Kececioglu and Sankoff [109] also derived efficient bounds of $d_r(\pi)$ by simulation, allowing a computer to output $d_r(\pi)$ in a few minutes for $n \leqslant 30$.

On the other hand, Kececioglu and Sankoff obtained a 2-approximation algorithm for $d_r(\pi)$ based on the structure of *strip*, which is a maximal subsequence in $\pi$ without breakpoints. For example, if $\pi$ is the last mentioned permutation, $\langle 2, 3\rangle$ is a strip and moreover, the strip $\langle 2, 3\rangle$ is *increasing* whereas the strip $\langle 6\rangle$ is *decreasing*. By greedily choosing the reversals, deriving from the decreasing or increasing strip, to remove the most number of breakpoints, they proved that each one of such reversals removes at least 1 breakpoint, thereby obtaining a 2-approximation algorithm, as illustrated in Fig. 11.

They further conjectured that for every permutation, there exists an optimal sorting series composed of reversals with cutting no strips of size more than 2, and there also exists an optimal reversal series which never increases the number of breakpoints. Both conjectures are verified by Hannenhalli and Pevzner [88] by means of their duality theorem for signed permutation [89]. Nevertheless, they found an example for which this procedure fails with strips with size 2, and described an algorithm to fix this problem. In particular, the sorting by reversals problem for permutations without strips of size one, called *singletons*, can be solved in polynomial time by Hannenhalli and Pevzner, which thus implies that the singletons present the major obstacle on the way towards an efficient algorithm.

The approximation ratio of 2 derived from Kececloglu and Sankoff [109] was further improved to a factor of 1.75 by Bafna and Pevzner [11], then to a factor of 1.5 by Christie [43], and finally to 1.375 by Berman, Hannenhalli and Karpinski [27].

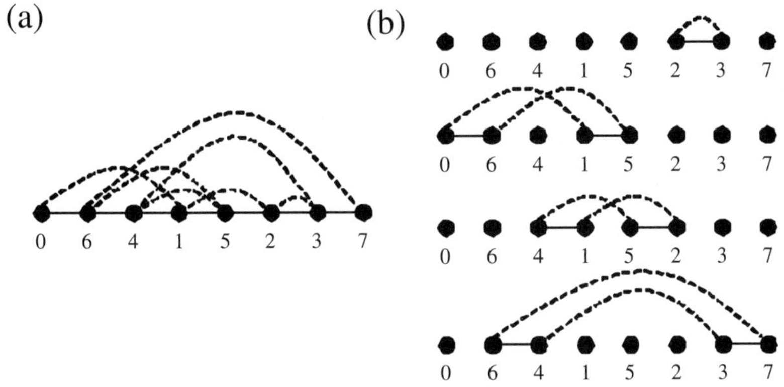


FIG. 12. The breakpoint graph $G(\pi)$ of $\pi = 6\ 4\ 1\ 5\ 2\ 3$ (a) and its maximum cycle decomposition is $c(\pi) = 4$ (b).

In Section 2, we have introduced the breakpoint graph $G(\pi)$ for a permutation $\pi$, where this graph can be recognized in linear time by Caprara [36]. Such a graph has tight relations to the sorting by reversals problem and can be used to explain why this problem is difficult. Gray and black edges in $G(\pi)$ constitute an *alternating cycle* if the colors of every two consecutive edges of this cycle are distinct. For instance in Fig. 12(a), the cycle of $1 \xrightarrow{b} 5 \xrightarrow{g} 6 \xrightarrow{b} 0 \xrightarrow{g} 1$ is alternating where $g$ and $b$ indicate gray and black edge, respectively. From the structure of $G(\pi)$, there are two gray edges and two black edges connected to every vertex, except $\pi_0$ and $\pi_n$ having a gray and a black edge. Since the number of gray edges incident to a vertex $v$ equals that of black edges incident to $v$, every vertex has even degree and thus, there exists a *cycle decomposition* of $G(\pi)$ into alternating cycles such that every edge in the graph belongs to exactly one cycle in the decomposition [13]. We are interested in the maximum number $c(\pi)$ of alternating cycles in $G(\pi)$. For example in Fig. 12, $c(\pi) = 4$.

A reversal can reduce the number of cycles in a maximum cycle decomposition by at most one, while the number of breakpoints by at most two. Bafna and Pevzner [11] presented a lower bound of $n + 1 - c(\pi)$ on the distance $d_r(\pi)$, which is much tighter than the bound of $b(\pi)/2$ derived from the concept of breakpoint. Besides, Caprara [36] described a transformation from the sorting by reversals problem to the maximum cycle decomposition problem. The latter was shown to be NP-hard thereby implying the same complexity as the former.

Extensively simulated studies [37,38,109] showed that $d_r(\pi) = n + 1 - c(\pi)$ in numerous cases, and Caprara [35] demonstrated that $d_r(\pi) = n + 1 - c(\pi)$ with probability $1 - \Theta(1/n^5)$ for a random permutation $\pi$ of size $n$. These results prompted us to derive algorithms of directly minimizing the parameter $c(\pi)$ to solve the sorting by reversals problem. The first approximation algorithm of computing $c(\pi)$ was obtained by Bafan and Pevzner [11] with the ratio of 1.75, and further improved to 1.5 by Christie [43]. Subsequently, Caprara and Rizzi [40] improved the ratio to a factor of $33/23 + \varepsilon \approx 1.4348 + \varepsilon$, for any positive $\varepsilon$, by reducing the problem to the *maximum independent set problem* and the *set packing problem* [79]. Lin and Jiang [114] recently extended the techniques of Caprara and Rizzi, and incorporated a balancing argument to further improve the approximation ratio to $(5073 - 15\sqrt{1201})/3208 + \varepsilon \approx 1.4193 + \varepsilon$, for any positive $\varepsilon$.

Due to the practicality of sorting by reversals problem, numerous researchers try to solve it optimally by implementing programs even if it may run in exponential time. Heath and Vergara [92] implemented an $O(n^3 n!)$ time algorithm by using the dynamic programming method for testing their conjectures. One of these interesting conjectures is that *there exists a sequence of reversals that optimally sort a permutation $\pi$ such that each reversal positions either the minimum or the maximum unpositioned element.* For example, the permutation $\pi = 3\ 4\ 2\ 5\ 1$ can be optimally sorted as the following sequence: $3\,4\,2\,5\,1 \Longrightarrow 3\,4\,2\,1\,5 \Longrightarrow 1\,2\,4\,3\,5 \Longrightarrow 1\,2\,3\,4\,5$. The three reversals sort $\pi$ on the positions 5, 1 and 3 (or 4) respectively, where the corresponding elements are either minimum or maximum unpositioned elements. This conjecture agrees with the intuition but however, their program found a counterexample when $\pi = 2\ 5\ 3\ 1\ 4$ sorted by the following process: $2\ 5\ 3\ 1\ 4 \Longrightarrow 2\ 1\ 3\ 5\ 4 \Longrightarrow 2\ 1\ 3\ 4\ 5 \Longrightarrow 1\ 2\ 3\ 4\ 5$. Note that the sorted element by first reversal is neither 1 nor 5 and attempting to do so requires more than 3 reversals to sort $\pi$. In particular, Tran [163] provided a special set of permutations, which can be optimally sorted by reversals in polynomial time by giving a graph-theoretical characterization of these permutations. Such permutations are when the number of breakpoints is twice as big as the reversal distance, and the last mentioned permutation is an example satisfying the requirement.

Caprara, Lancia and Ng [37–39] also attempted to find exact algorithms for the sorting by reversals problem. They first designed a *branch-and-bound* algorithm for this problem [37], and the lower bound is based on the result of Bafna and Pevzner [11] (a closely related work by Kececioglu and Sankoff [109]) where the reversal distance is related to $c(\pi)$. For estimating the parameter, they solved a *Linear Programming* problem containing a possible exponential number of variables by using *column generation* scheme, which has been shown to be efficient for many combinatorial optimization problems [15]. This algorithm optimally solved random instances of $n = 100$ within 2–3 minutes and was further improved to be more efficient by a new *Linear Programming* technique [38,39].

The following is the introduction of sorting by reversals problem on *signed permutations* which has been extensively studied in computer science and also receives many practical results.

## 3.2 Signed Permutations

From the above discussion on unsigned permutations, we know that in the general problem of finding genomic distance caused by disrupted gene order between two genomes it is very difficult to find algorithms coming up with better performance. However, it is the situation when we are short of the information about gene directions. In practice, every gene in a chromosome has a direction (it is the result of a fact that DNA is double stranded and single gene resides on one of the strand). Here we consider the sorting by reversals problem on the permutation where each element has either $+$ or $-$ sign indicting its direction. For example in Fig. 7, the gene content of cabbage is modeled as the signed permutation $\vec{\pi} = +1 -5 +4 -3 +2$. Furthermore, every reversal acting on a segment of signed case changes both the order and signs of elements in this segment. We are still interested in the minimum number of reversals $d_r(\vec{\pi})$ needed for transforming a signed permutation $\vec{\pi}$ into the identity permutation $\vec{I} = +1 +2 \ldots +n$.

Given a signed permutation $\vec{\pi}$ of $\{1, 2, \ldots, n\}$, Hannenhalli and Pevzner [89] first transfered it into an unsigned mapping $\pi = \pi_0 \equiv 0\ \pi_1 \ldots \pi_{2n}\pi_{2n+1} \equiv 2n + 1$ of $\{0, 1, \ldots, 2n + 1\}$, by replacing each positive element $x$ of $\vec{\pi}$ by $2x - 1$ and $2x$, and each negative element $-x$ by $2x$ and $2x - 1$. For example, if $\vec{\pi} = +1 -5 +4 -3 +2$, then we have $\pi = 0\ 1\ 2\ 10\ 9\ 7\ 8\ 6\ 5\ 3\ 4\ 11$. Clearly, $\vec{I}$ corresponds to $I$ and each reversal in $\vec{\pi}$ corresponds to a reversal in $\pi$. A reversal of the form $r(2i+1, 2j)$ is said to be *legal* for $\pi$ because it mimics the reversal $r(i+1, j)$ on $\vec{\pi}$. Then the problem of sorting $\pi$ by legal reversals is equivalent to the sorting $\vec{\pi}$ by reversals problem.

The analysis of Hannenhalli and Pevzner is based on the breakpoint graph. In Section 2, we present how to construct it, but it is for unsigned permutations. For the breakpoint graph of a signed permutation $\vec{\pi}$, we use the breakpoint graph of its unsigned mapping $\pi$ instead, which is also defined to be an edge-colored graph with $2n + 2$ vertices $\pi_0, \pi_1, \ldots, \pi_{2n+1}$ as follows: For $0 \leqslant i \leqslant n$, $\pi_{2i}$ and $\pi_{2i+1}$ are connected by a *black edge*, and $2i$ is joined to $2i + 1$ by a *gray edge*, as shown in Fig. 13.

In above section, finding the maximum cycle decomposition is a difficult problem and closely related to the sorting unsigned permutation by reversals problem. Fortunately, in the case of signed permutations, this problem is easy because each vertex in $G(\pi)$ has even degree. It is not hard to verify that the $G(\pi)$ in Fig. 13 is able to be uniquely decomposed into $c(\pi) = 3$ alternating cycles. Since the number of maximum cycle decomposition in $I$ is the maximum of all permutations with size

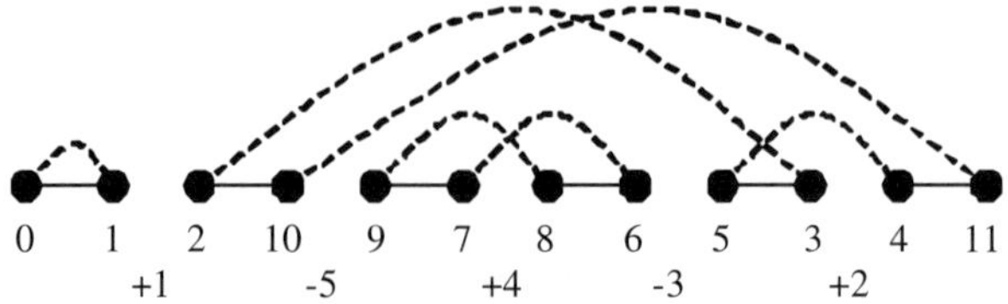


FIG. 13. The breakpoint graph $G(\pi)$ of $\pi = 0\ 1\ 2\ 10\ 9\ 7\ 8\ 6\ 5\ 3\ 4\ 11$, which is an unsigned mapping of $\vec{\pi} = +1\ {-5}\ {+4}\ {-3}\ {+2}$.

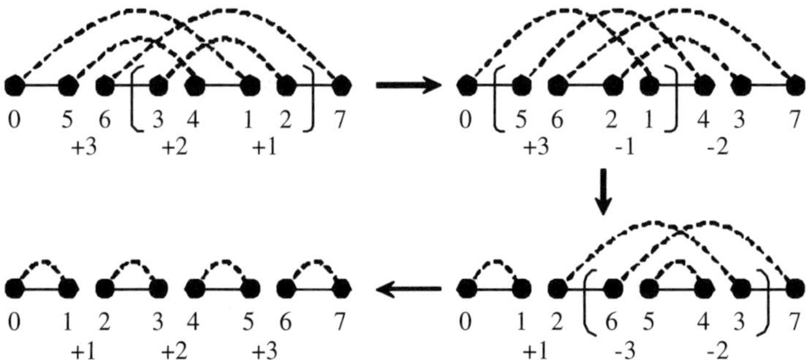


FIG. 14. The optimally sorting series for transforming $\vec{\pi} = +3\ {+2}\ {+1}$ into $\vec{I}$ contains at least a non-proper reversal.

$n$, finding the reversal distance $d_r(\vec{\pi})$ can be regarded as increasing the number of cycles in a most rapid manner. By demonstrating that $\Delta c_r = c(r \cdot \pi) - c(\pi) \leqslant 1$, Hannenhalli and Pevzner immediately obtained the lower bound of $n + 1 - c(\pi)$ on $d_r(\vec{\pi})$. Therefore, if the used reversals are all of $\Delta c_r = 1$, called *proper*, then we can optimally sort a permutation in $n+1-c(\pi)$ steps. As shown in the Fig. 13, the lower bound is $5 + 1 - 3 = 3$ suggesting that three proper reversals in Fig. 7 perform an optimal sorting.

Nevertheless, for the permutation $\vec{\pi} = +3\ +2\ +1$, there is no proper reversal in the first step and thus, it cannot be sorted in $n + 1 - c(\pi) = 2$ steps (an optimally sorting process is shown in Fig. 14), indicating that apart from the number of cycles, there exist hidden parameters for sorting a signed permutation. Hannenhalli and Pevzner defined the *hurdle* structure to describe such a hidden obstacle. An example of permutation shown in Fig. 14 needs one more reversal than the lower bound 2, as a result of a hurdle in it. For the detailed knowledge of hurdles, we refer reader to the paper by Hannenhalli and Pevzner [89].

Let the number of hurdles in a permutation $\pi$, an unsigned mapping of $\vec{\pi}$, be $h(\pi)$. Then they showed that $n + 1 - c(\pi) + h(\pi) \leqslant d_r(\pi) \leqslant n + 2 - c(\pi) + h(\pi)$ and however, there is still a little gap to obtain the optimal solution. With that, they found when $h(\pi)$ is odd in some cases, there is a singular structure called *fortress* which leads to the hardness of sorting. After identifying the fortress, they finally presented a duality theorem for optimally sorting a signed permutation by reversals as follows:

$$d_r(\vec{\pi}) = \begin{cases} n+1-c(\pi)+h(\pi)+1, & \text{if } \pi \text{ is a fortress,} \\ n+1-c(\pi)+h(\pi), & \text{otherwise.} \end{cases}$$

Furthermore, they also provided two algorithms for this problem, where the complicated one runs in $O(n^4)$ time and the running time of simpler one is $O(n^5)$.

Since the time-complexity of algorithm developed by Hannenhalli and Pevzner is a little high, Berman and Hannenhalli [26] first improved it to $O(n\alpha(n))$ time, where $\alpha()$ is the inverse Ackerman's function [5], by exploiting more combinatorial properties of breakpoint graph. Due to avoiding special data structures, Kaplan, Shamir and Tarjan [105] further improved the running time to $O(nd_r(\vec{\pi}) + n\alpha(n))$ based on a union-find structure for efficiently finding reversals. Since $\alpha(n)$ is a constant no longer than four for almost all practical purposes, their algorithm is efficient for implementation. Subsequently, Tannier and Sagot [160] proposed an algorithm running exactly in $O(n^{3/2}\sqrt{\log n})$ time, which has been the fastest practical algorithm to date, and also answers an open question of Ozery-Flato and Shamir [138] whether a subquadratic complexity could ever be achieved for solving the sorting by reversals problem. If only the reversal distance is needed, Bader, Moret and Yan [9] presented a simple and practical algorithm with linear running time for computing the *connected components*, which results in a linear-time algorithm for calculating the reversal distance.

Moreover, the following works try to reduce the computational complexity by using the concept of randomization. A randomized algorithm is an algorithm that makes arbitrary choices during its execution, which allows a savings in execution time of a program as it does not require time in finding optimal choices, and instead works with arbitrary ones. Although the major disadvantage of this method may be incorrect output, i.e., output of a non-optimal solution, a well-designed randomized algorithm will have a very high probability of returning a correct answer. For more detail about it, we refer reader to a textbook written by Motwani and Raghavan [133].

Bansal [14] classified all possible reversals and considered a probability of choosing reversals from the classes. Nevertheless, the reversals she chose have no guarantee of being helpful to the transformation of $\vec{\pi}$ into $\vec{I}$. Recently, Kaplan and Verbin [106,107] described a randomized algorithm to sort signed permutations by repeatedly drawing a random *oriented reversal*, which is a reversal making consecutive elements in the permutation adjacent with the same sign, e.g., either $i, i+1$ or $-(i+1), -i$ is adjacent. Their method relies on the observation that typically a very large percentage of oriented reversals is indeed part of a most parsimonious scenario [21]. Furthermore, Kaplan and Verbin designed some efficient data structures for supporting them to maintain a permutation after applying a reversal and drawing random oriented reversals from it, where each operation costs sub-linear time. Their randomized algorithm has running time of $O(n^{3/2}\sqrt{\log n})$ but fails with a very high probability on little permutations.

The first polynomial-time algorithm proposed by Hannenhalli and Pevzner [89] relied on several intermediate constructions that have been simplified since [9,26, 105,160], but grasping the whole details remains a challenge. Consequently, Bergeron focused on finding a simpler explanation relying directly on the *overlap graph* for Hannenhalli–Pevzner theory and also gave a *bit-vector* implementation for the reversal problem that runs in $O(n^2)$ *bit-vector* operations, or in $O(n^3/w)$ operations, where $w$ is the word-size of the processor [20,24]. Besides, instead of the annoying hurdles and fortress in the duality theorem derived from Hannenhalli and Pevzner, Bergeron, Mixtacki and Stoye [22] used the *PQ-tree* to deal with them, and yielded an efficient and simple algorithm to compute reversal distances. On the other hand, there may exist many sorting series for the optimal transformation of $\vec{\pi}$ and $\vec{I}$, but we have no idea about how to choose. Due to the absence of auxiliary information to determine a plausible scenario, Ajana et al. [7], and Siepel [155] found all minimum-length series of reversals to sort a signed permutation for the purpose of further tests.

Apart from the theoretical analyses, there are several practical tools. Mantin and Shamir [124] implemented their algorithm [105] with a Java applet. Furthermore, Tesler [162] developed an integrated website GRIMM for implementing the algorithms [9,88,89] to tackle the problems of sorting by signed/unsigned permutations with linear/circular type by reversals. Figure 15 is an example provided by GRIMM to show the possible rearrangement scenarios among *Herpes simplex virus* (HSV), *Epstein–Barr virus* (EBV) and *Cytomegalovirus* (CMV) [86], and their phylogenetic tree.

### 3.3 Circular Permutations

Watterson et al. [174] made the first attempt at the problem of computing reversal distance between the circular permutations $\pi^c$ and circular identity permutation $I^c$ of unsigned case. The circular unsigned permutation is the circular rearrangement of elements of a linear permutation in clockwise direction. Watterson et al. gave the rudimentary bounds that $b(\pi^c)/2 \leqslant d_r(\pi^c) \leqslant n-1$, where $d_r(\pi^c)$ is the reversal distance of $\pi^c$ and $I^c$, and also presented a stochastic algorithm for this problem. Subsequently, Solomon, Sutcliffe and Lister [158] assumed that there is no difference in rotations and reflections of an unsigned circular permutation, see Fig. 16 as an

(a)

**HSV** : 1 2 3 4 5 -6 -7 8 -9 -10 11 -12 -13 -14 15 16 17 -18 -19 -20 21 -22 23 24 25 26 27

**EBV** : 1 2 3 4 5 -6 -7 8 -9 -10 11 -12 -13 -14 15 16 17 -21 -18 -19 -20 -22 23 24 25 -27 -26

**CMV** : 1 2 3 4 5 -6 -7 8 -9 -10 11 14 13 12 -17 -16 -15 26 27 20 19 18 21 -22 23 24 25

(b)

| | HSV | EBV | CMV |
|---|---|---|---|
| HSV | 0 | 3 | 5 |
| EBV | 3 | 0 | 5 |
| CMV | 5 | 5 | 0 |

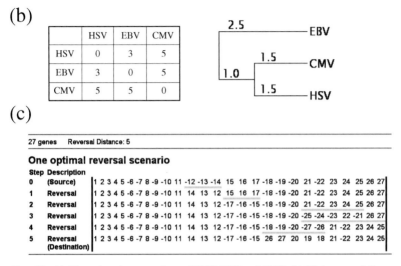

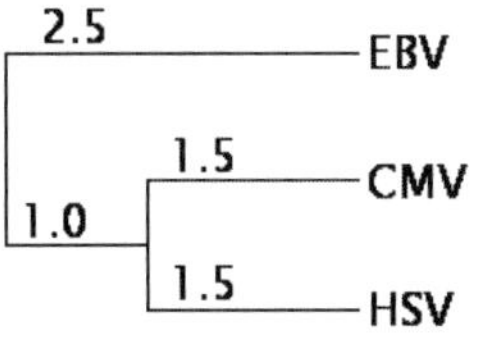


(c)

27 genes Reversal Distance: 5

**One optimal reversal scenario**

| Step | Description | |
|---|---|---|
| 0 | (Source) | 1 2 3 4 5 -6 -7 8 -9 -10 11 -12 -13 -14 15 16 17 -18 -19 -20 21 -22 23 24 25 26 27 |
| 1 | Reversal | 1 2 3 4 5 -6 -7 8 -9 -10 11 14 13 12 15 16 17 -18 -19 -20 21 -22 23 24 25 26 27 |
| 2 | Reversal | 1 2 3 4 5 -6 -7 8 -9 -10 11 14 13 12 -17 -16 -15 -18 -19 -20 21 -22 23 24 25 26 27 |
| 3 | Reversal | 1 2 3 4 5 -6 -7 8 -9 -10 11 14 13 12 -17 -16 -15 -18 -19 -20 -25 -24 -23 22 -21 26 27 |
| 4 | Reversal | 1 2 3 4 5 -6 -7 8 -9 -10 11 14 13 12 -17 -16 -15 -18 -19 -20 -27 -26 21 -22 23 24 25 |
| 5 | Reversal (Destination) | 1 2 3 4 5 -6 -7 8 -9 -10 11 14 13 12 -17 -16 -15 26 27 20 19 18 21 -22 23 24 25 |

FIG. 15. (a) Three signed permutations of HSV, EBV and CMV; (b) Their reversal distance matrix and the corresponding phylogenetic tree; (c) A possible rearrangement scenario consists of five reversals for transforming HSV into CMV outputted by GRIMM [162].

example, which are straightforward from three-dimensional view. Reversals applying to $\pi^c$ have similar results as that to linear permutation $\pi$, i.e., just reverse the order of elements in a segment (Fig. 16(c)). Therefore, the circular version of sorting by reversals problem is well defined. To our surprise, Solomon et al. showed that based on these assumptions, sorting circular permutations by reversals can be reduced to the same problem on linear case, thereby indicating that it is also NP-hard.

On the other hand, sorting signed circular permutations also has an analogous result. A signed circular permutation $\vec{\pi}^c = (\vec{\pi}_1^c \vec{\pi}_2^c \ldots \vec{\pi}_n^c)$ can be regarded as a circular arrangement of elements in a signed permutation $\vec{\pi}$, where the sign "+" indicates the clockwise direction and "−" represents the counterclockwise one. As shown in Fig. 17, rotations and reflections of $\vec{\pi}^c$ are similar to those of $\pi^c$, but a few differences exist in reflection. A reflection of $\vec{\pi}^c$ changes both the order and signs of elements in $\vec{\pi}^c$. Under these assumptions, Meidanis, Walter and Dias [128] demonstrated the equivalence of sorting by reversals on linear permutations and circular ones.

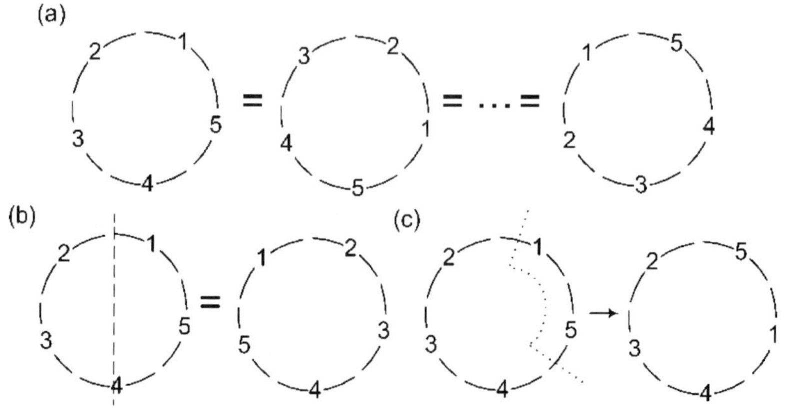


FIG. 16. (a) Rotations of a permutation, $\pi^c = (1\ 5\ 4\ 3\ 2) = (2\ 1\ 5\ 4\ 3) = \cdots = (5\ 4\ 3\ 2\ 1)$; (b) Reflection of a permutation, $\pi^c = (1\ 5\ 4\ 3\ 2) = (1\ 2\ 3\ 4\ 5)$; (c) The reversal acts on the segment containing 1 and 5 indicated by dotted line by inverting the order of them.

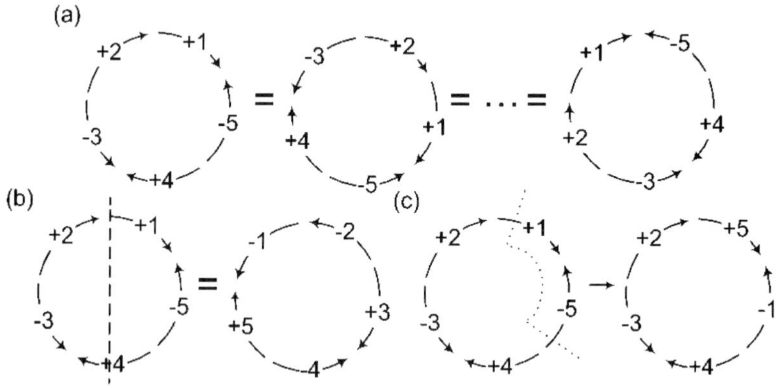


FIG. 17. (a) Rotations of $\vec{\pi}^c = (+1\ -5\ +4\ -3\ +2) = (+2\ +1\ -5\ +4\ -3) = \cdots = (-5\ +4\ -3\ +2\ +1)$; (b) Reflections of $\vec{\pi}^c = (+1\ -5\ +4\ -3\ +2) = (-1\ -2\ +3\ -4\ +5)$; (c) The reversal acts on the segment containing $+1$ and $-5$, which is indicated by dotted line, by changing both the order and signs of them.

In fact, there is a simple view of work in considering the relationship between linear and circular permutations. Figure 18 is an example with two equivalent reversals of a signed circular permutation $\vec{\pi}^c = (+1\ -5\ +4\ -3\ +2)$. Therefore, the reversal acting on $\vec{\pi}^c$ can always leave $\vec{\pi}_1^c$ unchanged, that is, if an inverted segment contains $\vec{\pi}_1^c$, then we use the equivalent reversal without involving $\vec{\pi}_1^c$ instead. With this re-

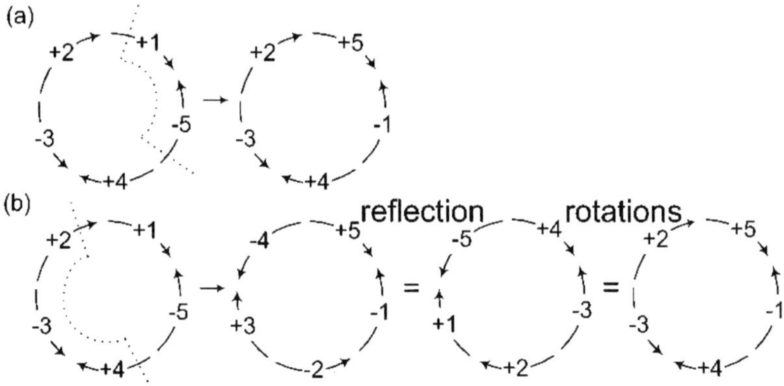


FIG. 18. (a) The reversal acts on the segment containing +1 and −5; (b) The reversal acts on the segment containing +2, −3 and +4, and its effect is the same as (a) since reflection and rotations are not included into account.

placement, the reversal series of sorting $\vec{\pi}^c$ is a feasible series to sort $\vec{\pi}$ implying that the problem of sorting signed linear permutation by reversals can reduce to that of sorting signed circular one. The other side from linear to circular can also be similarly proved. The sorting linear and circular permutations by reversals problems are consequently equivalent.

## 4. Sorting by Transpositions/Block-Interchanges

A *transposition* is an exchange of two adjacent segments on a chromosome, while a *block-interchange* swaps two non-intersecting segments without necessary adjacency, suggesting that the latter is a generalization of the former. Analogously, the effect of a transposition can be taken as the result caused by two steps of cutting a segment and placing it in another location on the chromosome. In this regard, some people call it *cut-and-paste* operation. In biology, transpositions are rare events in contrast with reversals, and usually accompany other events like reversals or *translocations* (introduced in next section). Liu and Sanderson [119] identified inversions and transpositions in the bacterium *Salmonella typhi*, while Seoighe et al. [153] estimated that gene adjacencies of yeast have been broken frequently by rearrangements as inversions, transpositions and translocations. Moreover, Coghlan and Wolfe [49] inferred that there are 517 chromosomal rearrangements including inversions, transpositions and translocations for the transformation between the nematodes, *Caenorhabditis elegans* and *Caenorhabditis briggsae*. Zhang and Peterson [180], in particular, demonstrated a new intramolecular transposition mechanism by which transpositions can greatly impact genome evolution.

Since block-interchange is a generalization of transpositions, it has come up much less than reversal, transposition and translocation. A justification may be that the large-scale exchanges of segments are much less observed by biologists. Fliess, Motro and Unger [76] presented that there are swaps of short fragments in protein evolution, and Slamovits et al. [157] also observed the similar phenomenon of swapping segments by the comparison of *Antonospora locustae* (formerly Nosema locustae) and human parasite *Encephalitozoon cuniculi*.

From the theoretical point of view, *sorting by transpositions* (resp. *sorting by block-interchanges*) is the problem of finding the minimum number of transpositions (resp. block-interchanges), denoted as $d_{\mathrm{tr}}(\pi)$ (resp. $d_{\mathrm{bi}}(\pi)$), for sorting an unsigned permutation $\pi$. In 1996, Christie [42] solved the sorting by block-interchanges problem in polynomial time, while it has been of unknown complexity for the problem of sorting by transpositions so far. However, it is interesting that the two problems both have equivalence between sorting linear permutations and circular ones, which can be shown by a simple observation. Below we will first introduce the history of several approximation algorithms for the transposition problem and some efficient implementations. Then, there are two approaches for optimally solving the block-interchange problem and simultaneously, two websites of ROBIN [121] and SPRING [117] can automatically find the rearrangement scenario among two or more homologous sequences as their input.

## 4.1 Sorting by Transpositions

In the late 1980s, Aigner and West [6] considered two rearrangement problems whose operations can be regarded as variations of the transposition. One is the restriction of operations by removing the leading element and reinserting it somewhere in the permutation. The other is an analogous restriction of above operation, except the leading element is always reinserted into the position equal to its value, e.g., $3\ 4\ 1\ 2 \Rightarrow 4\ 1\ 3\ 2$. As regards the sorting by transpositions problem, it was first studied by Bafna and Pevzner [12], who primarily derived a 1.75-approximation algorithm and further improved to a factor of 1.5 with running time $O(n^2)$.

Since no transposition can change the signs of elements when it acts on a permutation, all permutations discussed here are unsigned. Nevertheless, the breakpoint graph $G(\pi)$ of $\pi$ is established by imitation of a signed permutation $\vec{\pi}$, in place of the construction introduced in Section 2. In other words, we replace each element $x$ in $\pi$ by $2x - 1$ and $2x$, and add $\pi_0 = 0$ and $\pi_{2n+1} = 2n + 1$ to $\pi$. The remainder of the procedure on the connections of black and gray edges is the same as the breakpoint graph of $\vec{\pi}$. Besides, let the *size* of a cycle in $G(\pi)$ be the number of gray edges it contains. A cycle is *odd* if its size is odd and denote the number of odd cycles in a permutation $\pi$ as $c_{\mathrm{odd}}(\pi)$. Then, sorting $\pi$ by transpositions is equivalent to increasing the number of odd cycles to the maximum because all cycles in $G(I)$ are odd.

Bafna and Pevzner demonstrated that $d_{\mathrm{tr}}(\pi) \geqslant (n+1-c_{\mathrm{odd}}(\pi))/2$, where the lower bound was enhanced to $(n+1-c_{\mathrm{odd}}(\pi))/2+\lceil h(\pi)/2\rceil$ [44], and developed an algorithm to sort $\pi$ in at most $\frac{3}{4}(n+1-c_{\mathrm{odd}}(\pi))$ transpositions, thereby ensuring an approximation guarantee with ratio 1.5. Subsequent works mainly focused on simplifying the approximation algorithm mentioned above. Christie [44] gave a somewhat simpler algorithm with the same approximation ratio, but a bad running time of $O(n^4)$. Next, Hartman and Shamir [90] first undertook the transposition problem on circular permutations, and obtained a simple approximation algorithm despite the same running time and ratio as the result of Bafna and Pevzner. In order to tackle circular unsigned permutations, they also constructed the breakpoint graph of them, which is analogous to $G(\pi)$, as shown in Fig. 19. Specially, they also proposed the same result of ratio 1.5 and $O(n^2)$ time for the sorting by transpositions and transreversals problem, where a transreversal inverts one of two transposed segments [91].

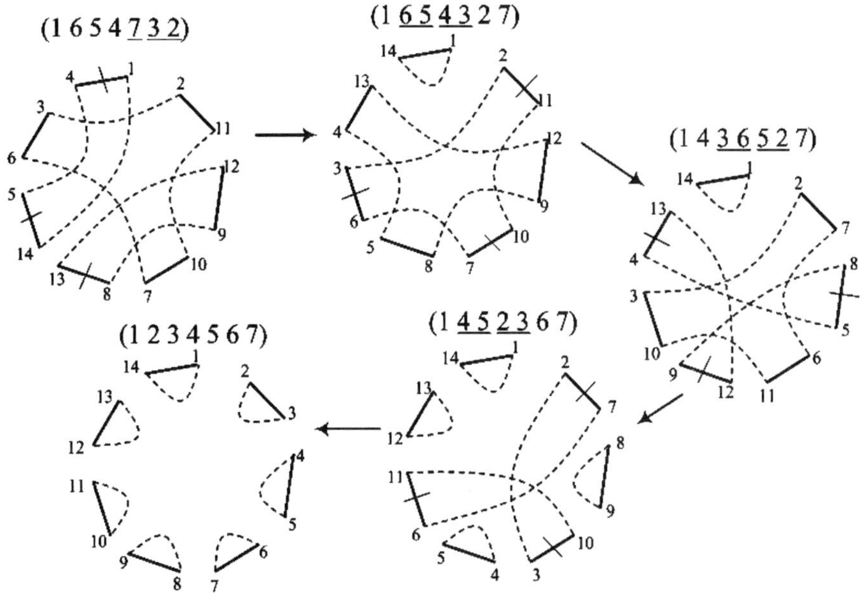


FIG. 19. An example of permutation $\pi^c$ = (1 6 5 4 7 3 2) can be sorted with 4 transpositions produced by the algorithm of Hartman and Shamir [90]. Each exchanged segment of a transposition is an intermediate region delimited by two short lines placed on two black edges in $G(\pi^c)$, and indicated by the underline in $\pi^c$ as well.

Furthermore, Walter et al. [167,169] developed implementations and slightly improved the results obtained by three algorithms mentioned late for transposition problem. Recently, an outstanding work presented by Elias and Hartman [67] is a 1.375-approximation algorithm using the aid of a computer to systematically generate the proofs. It improves a ten-year-old ratio 1.5 of finding $d_{\text{tr}}(\pi)$ obtained in 1995. On the other hand, Guyer, Heath and Vergara [84] provided several heuristic approaches and experiments of this problem.

The transposition diameter $D_{\text{tr}}(n)$ of the symmetric group $S_n$, which is the maximum number of $d_{\text{tr}}(\pi)$ among all permutations $\pi$ of size $n$, is still unknown. Bafna and Pevzner [12] presented that $\frac{3}{4}n$ is an upper bound for $D_{\text{tr}}(n)$, which was reduced to $\lfloor(2n-2)/3\rfloor$ for $n \geqslant 9$ by Eriksson et al. [71]. Christie [44], Eriksson et al. [71], and Meidanis, Walter and Dias [127] independently gave a lower bound of $\lfloor n/2\rfloor+1$ by showing that the transposition distance between a permutation and its reverse is $\lfloor n/2\rfloor + 1$. Furthermore, Elias and Hartman [67] provided the exact diameters for some kinds of permutations and an upper bound of $11\lfloor n/24\rfloor + \lfloor 3\frac{n/3 \bmod 8}{2}\rfloor + 1$ on the diameter of *3-permutation*, which is a special collection of permutations such that all cycles in $G(\pi)$ of a permutation $\pi$ have length 3. Also, this upper bound is the basis of obtaining ratio 1.375 for sorting by transpositions problem.

In addition, by restricting the operation to *prefix transposition* of the form $\text{tr}(1, i, j)$ for $1 < i < j \leqslant n$, Dias and Meidanis [59] obtained a 2-approximation algorithm for the problem of determining the minimum number of prefix transpositions to sort $\pi$. They conjectured that the diameter of prefix transposition distance is $n - \lfloor n/4\rfloor$ and also presented several tests to support it. Subsequently, Fortuna and Meidanis [77] gave a complete proof to show $d_{\text{pref}}(\pi) = n - \lfloor n/4\rfloor$ when $\pi = n\ n-1\ \ldots\ 1$, i.e., a reverse permutation of $I$.

## 4.2 Sorting by Block-Interchanges

As to block-interchange, Monammed and Subi [132] first mentioned it in 1987 to the best of our knowledge. Their problem is how can we effectively swap two non-overlapping blocks of continuous elements by using a minimum number of *constrained block-interchanges* of exchanging two elements at a time. For example, given the permutation $\pi = 1\ 8\ 9\ 5\ 6\ 7\ 2\ 3\ 4\ 10$, how to sort it by using the minimum number of constrained block-interchanges, such as swapping the elements 8 and 2. They exactly solved the problem and Fig. 20 is an example of their algorithm.

The sorting by block-interchanges problem was first studied by Christie [42], who gave an $O(n^2)$-time algorithm for optimally solving this problem based on the breakpoint graph. He also determined the diameter of block-interchange distance, which is $\lfloor n/2\rfloor$. Figure 21(b) is an example of his algorithm for sorting $\pi = 4\ 2\ 1\ 3\ 6\ 5\ 8\ 7$. Moreover, Lin et al. [116] studied the same problem on circular chromosomes based

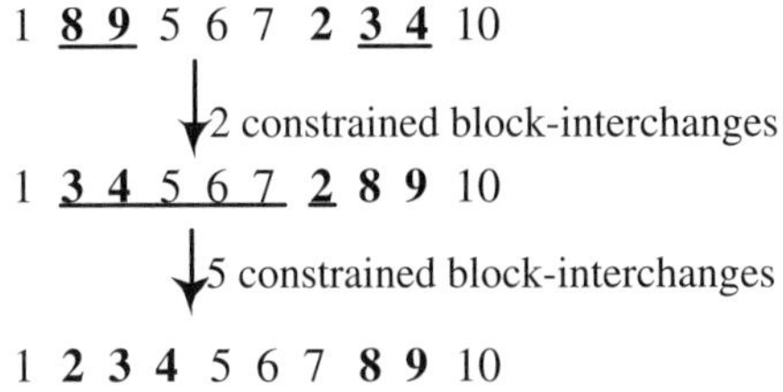


FIG. 20. The two swapping blocks are represented by the boldface integers. Let the number of elements in two swapping blocks be $S_1$ and $S_2$, respectively and the middle block between $S_1$ and $S_2$ be $M$, which may be zero. Then Monammed and Subi [132] showed that the minimum number of constrained block-interchanges, required to swap two blocks in this example, is $S_1+S_2+M-\gcd(S_1+M, S_2+M) = 2+3+3-\gcd(5,6) = 7$.

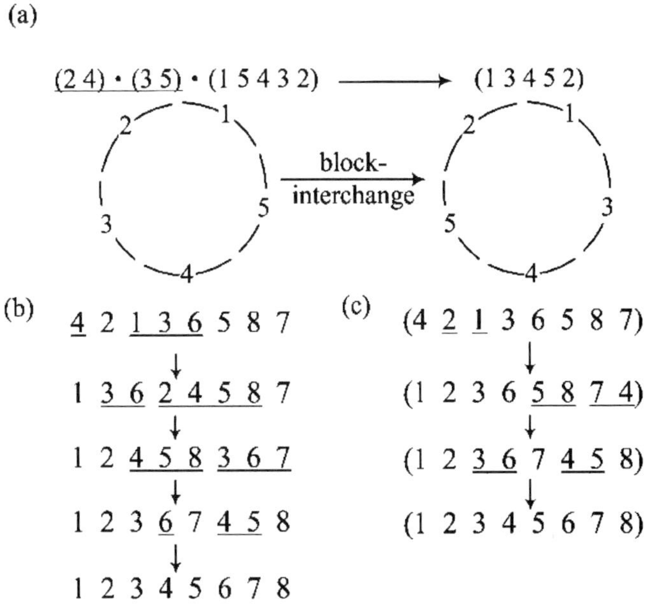


FIG. 21. (a) A circular chromosome is taken as a permutation with group form in algebra, and the effect of a block-interchange is modeled as the result of composition of two *2-cycles* indicated by the underline; (b) The permutation $\pi$ is optimally sorted by the algorithm of Christie [42] with $(n+1-c(\pi))/2 = 4$ block-interchanges, where $c(\pi)$ is the number of cycles in $G(\pi)$; (c) The permutation $\pi^c$ can be optimally sorted by $(n - f(I(\pi^c)^{-1}))/2 = (8-2)/2 = 3$ block-interchanges deriving form the algorithm of Lin et al. [116], where $f(I(\pi^c)^{-1})$ denotes the number of disjoint cycles in the *cycle decomposition* of $I(\pi^c)^{-1}$.

on the *permutation group* in algebra. Here we somewhat abuse the notation of permutation, since it appears in both *permutation group* in algebra and traditional model of genome rearrangement problems.

In their model, chromosomes correspond to permutations in group theory and block-interchange corresponds to two particular *2-cycles*. Besides, the effect of applying a block-interchange to a chromosome is modeled as *permutation composition* (*function composition*) of two 2-cycles to $\pi^c$, as illustrated in Fig. 21(a). Their strategy is to decompose $I(\pi^c)^{-1}$, where $(\pi^c)^{-1}$ is the inverse permutation of $\pi^c$, and $I(\pi^c)^{-1}$ is also a permutation in group. Even if starting from circular chromosomes, they also presented the equivalence between sorting linear permutations and circular ones. Figure 21(c) is an example of their algorithm for sorting $\pi^c = (4\,2\,1\,3\,6\,5\,8\,7)$. From their experimental results, Lin et al. concluded that the block-interchange events seem to play a significant role in the evolution of three vibrio species, *V. vulnificus*, *V. parahaemolyticus* and *V. cholerae*.

A website, called ROBIN, was developed by Lu et al. [121] for the sorting by block-interchanges problem. Instead of gene order, they use the order of landmarks to represent sequences and compute the block-interchange distance for each pair of them. ROBIN can automatically identify the Locally Collinear Blocks (LCBs) for representing the landmarks among input sequences by integrating the program of Darling et al. [58]. At the same time, Lu et al. repeated the experiment of Lin et al. and also obtained the coincident result.

## 5. Sorting by Translocations

We have introduced three kinds of events, reversal, transposition and block-interchange in previous sections, which all act on a single chromosome. In this section, we are interested in the translocation event acting on two segments of a multichromosomal genome, where the two segments belong to two different chromosomes. Before formulating this operation, some background must be introduced first to describe what the corresponding situation in biology is.

For a start, depending on the position of centromere along the length of a chromosome, chromosomes are classified into two types. One is the *acrocentric chromosome* in which the centromere occurs at one end of the chromosome, while the other is the *metacentric chromosome* whose centromere approaches the middle of chromosome (Fig. 22). Within a genome, every chromosome is either acrocentric or metacentric and furthermore, in acrocentric chromosome, there is a reading direction according to the location of centromere.

In the early 1930s, Creighton and McClintock [56] presented an elegantly simple experiment on Zea mays to show the interactions of two allelomorphic factors in the

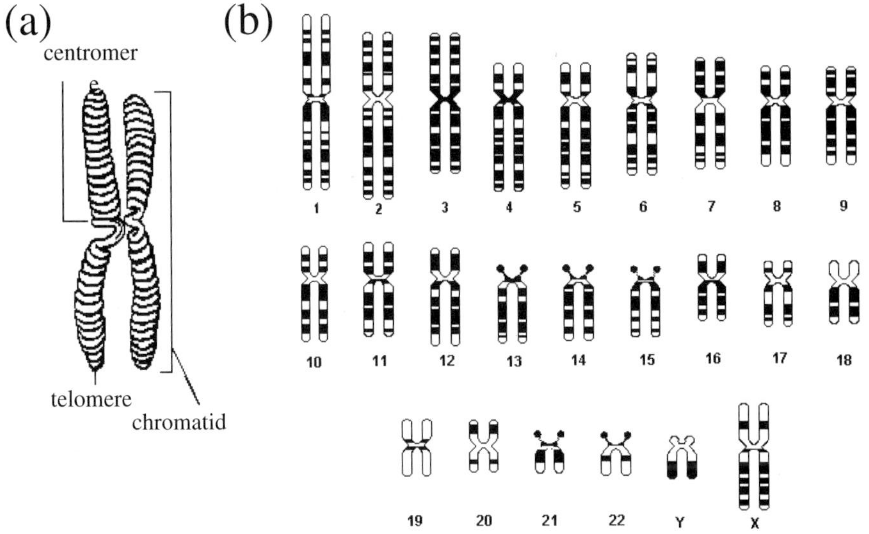


FIG. 22. (a) The structure of a chromosome [2]; (b) Representation of the 23 paired chromosomes (the chromosomes X and Y are paired) of the human male, where the chromosome 6 is a metacentric chromosome that constitutes about 6% [134] and the chromosome 13 is the largest acrocentric chromosome constituting about 4% of the human genome [62].

same linkage group accompanied by cytological and genetical crossing-over. Even if there was no clear mention about translocation events, from the description of their discovered phenomenon, it should be the first work related to translocations. Recently, Coe and Kass [48] reviewed the data surrounding the paper of Creighton and McClintock and provided a perspective on the significance of their findings. Translocation events occur as frequently as reversals and are commonly observed in virus [96], bacterium [100], yeast [63] and mammalian [172,110]. In particular, Courtay-Cahen, Morris and Edwards [55] demonstrated that the translocation event appears in breast cancer, and from clinical diagnosis on a patient, Heller et al. [93] reported that there is a complex translocation event between the two homologue chromosomes 5 in Philadelphia negative chronic myelogenous leukemia (CML).

On the theoretical progress, given two multichromosomal genomes $\Pi$ and $\Gamma$, which share the same set of genes, the *sorting by translocations problem* is finding the minimum number of translocations, denoted as $d_{tl}(\Pi)$, for transforming $\Pi$ into $\Gamma$. Here, $\Pi = \{\pi(1), \ldots, \pi(N)\}$ and $\Gamma = \{\gamma(1), \ldots, \gamma(M)\}$ are genomes consisting of $N$ and $M$ chromosomes respectively, and $\pi(i) = \pi(i)_1\ \pi(i)_2 \ldots \pi(i)_{n_i}$ composes of $n_i$ genes in the $i$th chromosome ($\gamma(i)$ is similar). Particularly, directions of each chromosome are irrelevant, i.e., $\pi(i) = -\pi(i)$.

Kececioglu and Ravi [108] first noticed this problem and provided two approximation algorithms with respect to two types of translocations in *directed* and *undirected* model. Given two chromosomes $X = \text{X1X2}$ and $Y = \text{Y1Y2}$, a *prefix-prefix translocation* exchanges X1 and Y1, and a *prefix-suffix translocation* exchanges X1 and Y2, as illustrated in Fig. 23(a). Note that one of the two swapped segments may be empty. For immediately grasping the definition, Fig. 23(b) is an example of a parsimonious scenario obtaining from the tool developed by Feng, Wang and Zhu [73] to transform $\Pi$ into $\Gamma$ by translocations.

The *directed model* concerns acrocentric chromosomes and allows only prefix-prefix translocations. In other words, there are no orientations in either genes or chromosomes. The other is *undirected model*, which deals with metacentric chromosomes and allows both prefix-prefix and prefix-suffix translocations. Signed data are considered only in the case of chromosomes with no absolute reading directions, i.e., the undirected model. In both the directed and undirected models, Kececioglu and Ravi had 2-approximation algorithms for sorting by translocations problem which runs in $O(k^2N^2)$ time, where $N$ is the number of chromosomes and $k$ is the maximum number of genes among all chromosomes. Cui, Wang and Zhu [57] recently improved the approximation ratio to a factor of 1.75. Furthermore, if the two swapped

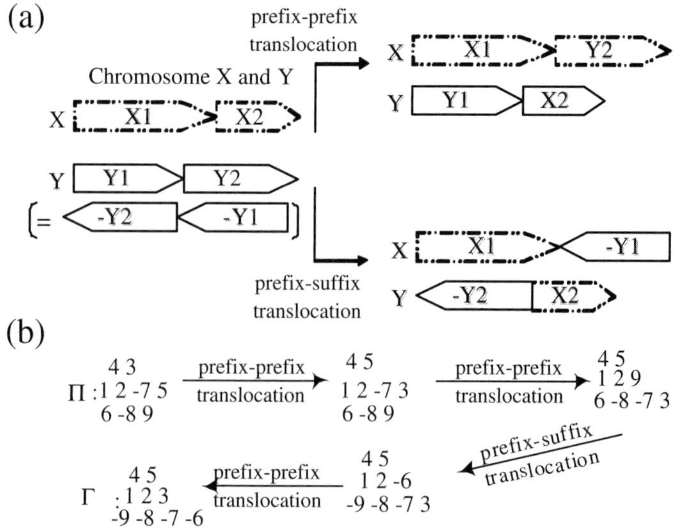


FIG. 23. (a) There are two types of translocations on signed chromosomes. Notice that directions of each chromosome are omitted for considering the unsigned chromosomes; (b) An example presents a parsimonious series of translocations for transforming $\Pi$ into $\Gamma$ acquired from the website CTRD [73].

segments of a translocation are restricted to be equal-length, Kececioglu and Ravi proposed an exact algorithm with $O(kN)$ time for both two models.

Later, Hannenhalli [85] studied the most common type of translocation, *reciprocal translocation*, in the direction model, where the four segments, X1, X2, Y1 and Y2, are assumed to be all non-empty. His analysis was also based on the breakpoint graph and omitted the existence of centromere for simplicity. Hannenhalli exactly solved this problem by providing an algorithm with $O(n^3)$ running time and a formula for $d_{tl}(\Pi)$, which can be further computed in linear time from a recent study proposed by Li et al. [113]. Afterward Wang et al. [170] gave an algorithm running in $O(n^2)$ time to show the optimal series composed of transformations, which improved the analogous result of algorithm with $O(n^2 \log n)$ time presented by Zhu and Ma [181]. However, the translocation distance calculated by Hannenhalli's algorithm may have an unexpected error leading to failure in finding the parsimonious scenarios of some cases. Recently, Bergeron, Mixtacki and Stoye [23] corrected the error and gave a new algorithm for sorting by translocations problem.

## 6. Sorting by Multiple Operations

In nature, considering different events during the evolution of species is more general in reflecting the real situation. For some group of species, rearrangement events appear to be strongly biased toward one type of event, but most of the time, all types of events can occur. Reversals are the most common events in the single chromosome, while translocations are the most general events in the multichromosomal genome. Even so, they usually accompany *fissions*, *fusions*, transpositions, block-interchanges, etc. Below we will introduce several combinations of operations in sorting the permutations and moreover, by assigning the weights to each operation, the evolutionary process can favor or disfavor some events, thereby exhibiting more diverse phylogenetic paths.

### 6.1 Reversal + Transposition/Block-Interchange

*Sorting by reversals and transpositions* is the problem of finding the cheapest series for transforming the permutation $\vec{\pi}$ (resp. $\pi$) into $\vec{I}$ (resp. $I$) by using reversals and transpositions. The minimum number of reversals and transpositions is conventionally taken as the distance between two permutations and denoted by $d_{r+tr}(\vec{\pi})$. A computational approach to analyze this problem was pioneered by Sankoff [148]. He designed a program DERANGE based on the techniques of *alignment reduction* and a branch-and-bound search. Figure 24 is an example of how the alignment reduction can help the sorting process.

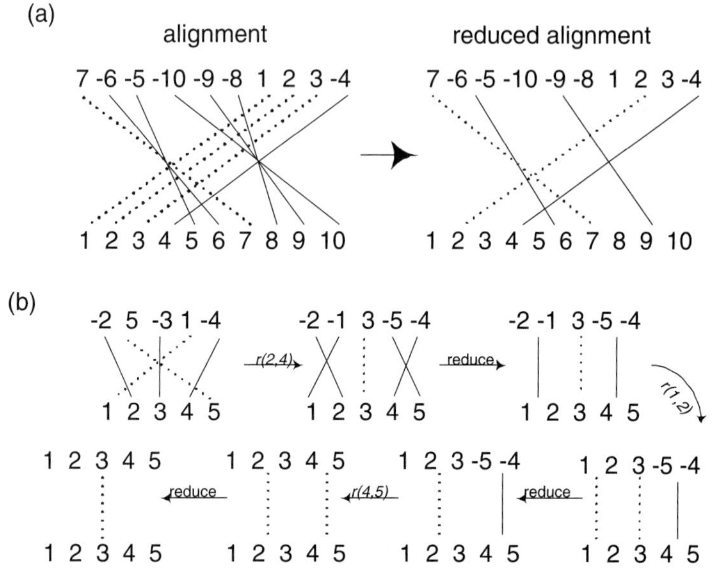


FIG. 24. (a) An example of alignment reduction. Dotted lines represent elements with same direction in both permutations, while solid lines indicate elements with opposite direction; (b) A sorting example of three reversals simply shows how to use the alignment reduction.

Furthermore, DERANGE can allow user-specified weights $w_r$ to reversals and $w_{\text{tr}}$ to transpositions, and look for the parsimonious series having the minimum sum of weights. Sankoff experimented on mitochondrial data of fungi with several possibilities of weights and concluded that assigning equal weights to reversals and transpositions is appropriate. Next, Blanchette, Kunisawa and Sankoff [30] improved the performance and provided a newer version DERANGE II [1]. They tested 37 homologous genes in human and Drosophila, and further concluded that $2w_r < w_{\text{tr}} < 2.5w_r$, obtaining by comparing Drosophila–human permutation with random permutation, is an appropriate weighting in their experiment.

On the other hand, Walter, Dias and Meidanis [168] gave 3-approximation algorithm for computing $d_{\text{r+tr}}(\pi)$ (unsigned case) and 2-approximation algorithm for calculating $d_{\text{r+tr}}(\vec{\pi})$ (signed case). Apart from the reversal and transposition event, Gu, Peng and Sudborough [82] added *inverted transposition* event as the transreversal (Fig. 25) into the consideration, and proposed a 2-approximation algorithm for this problem on signed permutations. Subsequently, Lin and Xue [115] also presented a 2-approximation algorithms for the two problems, sorting by reversals and transpositions problem and sorting by reversals, transpositions and inverted trans-

+1  -5 +4  -3  +2   $\xrightarrow{\text{transposition}}$   +1  -3  -5  +4  +2

$\xrightarrow[\text{transposition}]{\text{inverted}}$   +1  +3  -5  +4  +2

$\xrightarrow[\text{transposition}]{\text{inverted}}$   +1  -3  -4  +5  +2

$\xrightarrow[\text{transposition}]{\text{both inverted}}$   +1  -4  +5  -3  +2

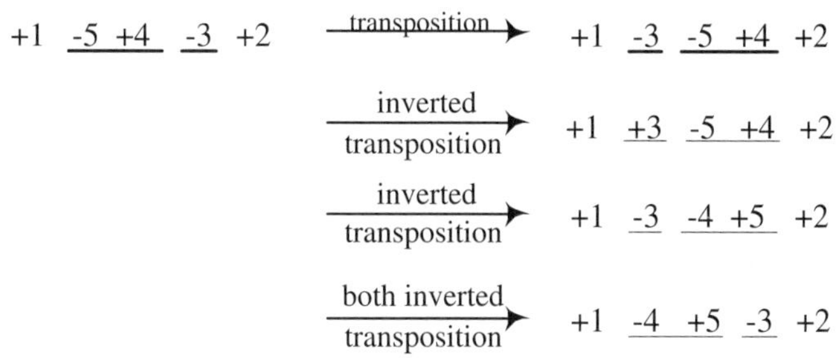

FIG. 25. Examples present the effects of transposition, inverted transposition and both inverted transposition where the two swapped segments are $-5$, $+4$ and $-3$ indicated by underlines.

positions problem. Furthermore, they allowed a special event called *both inverted transposition*, which inverts two adjacent segments at a time (Fig. 25), and presented a better 1.75-approximation algorithm for the problem of sorting by reversals and three types of transpositions shown in Fig. 25.

When $\vec{\pi} = -1 \ -2 \dots -n$, Meidanis, Walter and Dias [129] found that $d_{r+tr}(\vec{\pi}) = \lfloor n/2 \rfloor + 2$, for $n \geqslant 3$ and conjectured that this value is the diameter on the genomic distance. On the other hand, the combination of operations, reversal and (inverted) transpositions, was favored by several researchers when considering different weights to operations. Eriksen [70] designed a simulation to show that the suitable weight to reversal is 1 and to (inverted) transposition is 2, and also proposed a $(1 + \varepsilon)$-approximation algorithm for the sorting by reversals and (inverted) transpositions problem under such a weight assignment [69]. In particular, the approach proposed by Miklós [130] can estimate the weighted sum of reversals and (inverted) transpositions without specific weights to them beforehand by introducing the Markov Chain Monte Carlo (MCMC) method, based on a stochastic model of the three operations. Recently, Miklós, Ittzés and Hein [131] implemented a web server ParIS for a Bayesian analysis on the same three operations. Moreover, Erdem and Tillier [68] considered genome rearrangement as a planning problem, and allowed restrictions on the number/cost of events, the length of involved segments and additional constraints to guide the search. With this planning approach, they constructed the phylogenetic tree of chloroplast genomes of *Campanulaceae* (flowering plants) according to their reversal and transposition distance matrix. The groupings of chloroplast genomes on their tree coincided with the ones in the consensus tree proposed by Cosner et al. [53, Fig. 4].

Since there was less progress on the problem of sorting by reversals and transpositions, and transposition is a special case of block-interchange, a feasible approach is to consider the problem of sorting by reversals and block-interchanges. When the weight to reversals is 1 and to block-interchanges is 2, Lin, Lu and Tang [118] solved it by proposing a simple algorithm with $O(n^2)$ running time. Their algorithm first distinguished between *oriented* and *unoriented components*, and independently sorted them by reversals and block-interchanges, respectively. Furthermore, the number of block-interchanges in their sorting series is shown to be minimum under all optimal sorting sequences. Such a sorting series implicitly suggests that the scenario derived from it meets the biological observation that transpositions are rare in contrast to reversals [16].

## 6.2 Reversal + Translocation (Including Fusion and Fission)

Given two multichromosomal genomes $\Pi$ and $\Gamma$ as defined above, the problem considered in this section is to find a minimum number of operations composed of reversals and translocations for transforming $\Pi$ into $\Gamma$. In Section 5, using the reciprocal translocation with two non-empty swapped segments in two chromosomes can lead to a polynomial-time algorithm, hence being adopted here. Moreover, two special operations are additionally considered and described as follows: One is *fusion*, which concatenates two chromosomes $\vec{\pi}(i)$ and $\vec{\pi}(j)$ resulting in a new chromosome of $\vec{\pi}(i)_1\vec{\pi}(i)_2\ldots\vec{\pi}(i)_{n_i}\vec{\pi}(j)_1\vec{\pi}(j)_2\ldots\vec{\pi}(j)_{n_j}$ and an empty chromosome, and the other is *fission* in which one chromosome $\vec{\pi}(i)$ is broken into two chromosomes $\vec{\pi}(i)_1\vec{\pi}(i)_2\ldots\vec{\pi}(i)_{j-1}$ and $\vec{\pi}(i)_j\vec{\pi}(i)_{j+1}\ldots\vec{\pi}(i)_n$. Clearly, the fusion event reduces the number of chromosomes, whereas the fission event increases the number of (non-empty) chromosomes. The fusion and fission events bring about the difference in the number of chromosomes between two genomes, which is rather common in mammalian evolution. For example, the human genome has 46 chromosomes, while the mouse's contains 40 chromosomes.

Kececioglu and Ravi [108] first analyzed rearrangements of multichromosomal genomes, and proposed a 1.5-approximation algorithm based on the result of Bafna and Pevzner [11] for sorting by reversals alone. Nevertheless, they assumed that all chromosomes in a genome have the same number of genes, which conflicts with many organisms, e.g., human and mouse. Therefore, the subsequent model, including fissions and fusions, was first proposed by Hannenhalli and Pevzner [87], who gave the duality theorem for computing the genomic distance in terms of terrible 7 parameters associated with a polynomial-time algorithm. Their idea is to concatenate $N$ (resp. $M$) chromosomes of $\Pi$ (resp. $\Gamma$) into a new permutation $\vec{\pi}$ (resp. $\vec{\gamma}$) first, and then to mimic genomic sorting of $\Pi$ into $\Gamma$ through transforming $\vec{\pi}$ into $\vec{\gamma}$ by reversals (Fig. 26). However, the difficulty of this approach introduced $N!2^N$ different concatenates for $\Pi$ and $\Gamma$, and only some of them, called *optimal concatenates*, could mimic an optimal sorting of $\Pi$ into $\Gamma$. Hannenhalli and Pevzner used the techniques called *flipping* and *capping* to find an optimal concatenate from the numerous types of concatenates.

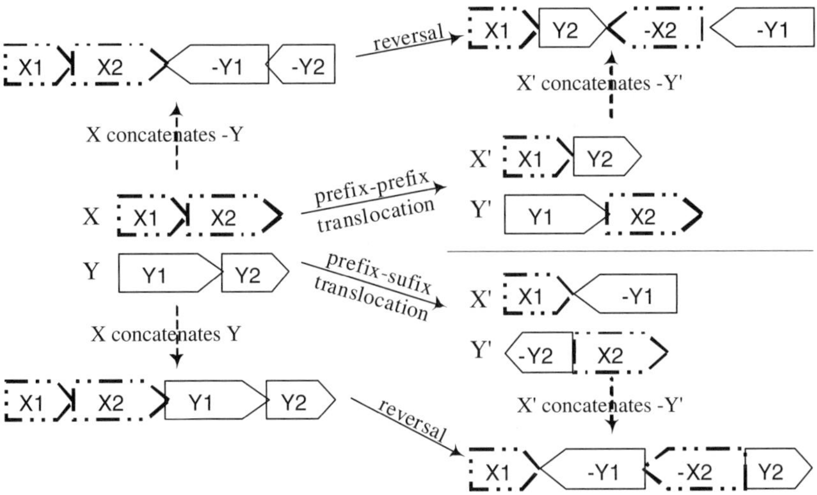


FIG. 26. Two types of translocations can be individually mimicked by a reversal in a concatenated permutation. Notice that $X = -X$ for a chromosome $X$.

Although the sorting by reversals and translocations problem was solved by Hannenhalli and Pevzner, there are some problems in constructing the rearrangement scenarios. First, they claimed that the rearrangement scenario can be exhibited from the sorting series of reversals obtained by solving the problem of sorting by reversals, but there is a gap in the construction. Next, the genomic distance $d_{\text{r+tl}}(\Pi, \Gamma)$ between $\Pi$ and $\Gamma$ is symmetric, i.e., $d_{\text{r+tl}}(\Pi, \Gamma) = d_{\text{r+tl}}(\Gamma, \Pi)$, but their algorithm requires that $\Pi$ has fewer number of chromosomes than $\Gamma$ when computing $d_{\text{r+tl}}(\Pi, \Gamma)$. Finally, their strategy is based on the algorithm for sorting only by reversals, and we are interested in whether a better algorithm for sorting by reversals problem leads to a better algorithm for this problem. With regard to the three problems, Tesler [161] closed the gap in construction, modified the unusual computation of $d_{\text{r+tl}}(\Pi, \Gamma)$, and improved the running time to compute genomic distance to $O(n)$ and rearrangement scenario to $O(n^2)$ by combining the algorithm of Bader et al. [9]. In addition, Ozery-Flato and Shamir [138] found that there is a case in which the two polynomial algorithms mentioned above will fail, and presented a revised duality theorem associated with an algorithm to deal with the problem.

## 6.3 Other Considerations

In this section, we will introduce two rearrangement problems with unequal weights to their sorting operations. One of the interesting considerations is the

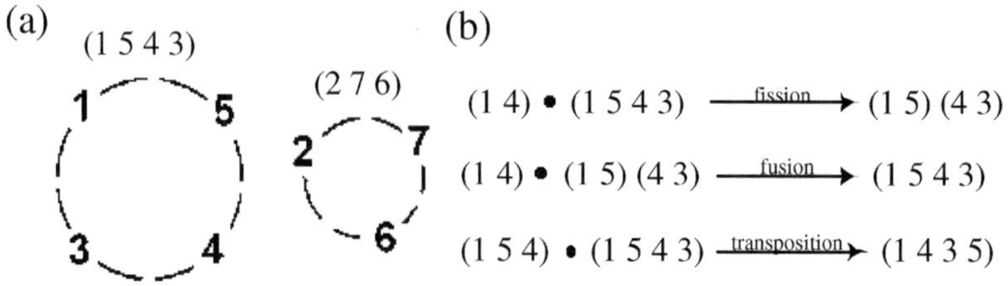


FIG. 27. (a) A genome with two chromosomes is modeled as a permutation with two cycles (1 5 4 3) and (2 7 6); (b) Fission, fusion and transposition can be mimicked by 2-cycles and a 3-cycle, respectively.

weighted composing of fusion, fission and transposition on circular unsigned multichromosomes, which was proposed by Meidanis and Dias [126]. They obtained a polynomial time algorithm for the minimum weighted series of three operations with transpositions weighted twice as much as fusions and fissions to transform one genome into another, which is based on the classical results of permutation group in algebra. In their model, a permutation may have several cycles to represent a multichromosomal genome (Fig. 27(a)) in which particularly all chromosomes are circular. The fusion or fission action on $\pi$ is mimicked by the composition of a special *2-cycle* to $\pi$, while the effect of a transposition corresponds to the composition of a *3-cycle* to $\pi$ (Fig. 27(b)). Therefore, sorting by fissions, fusions and transpositions problem is reduced to a special decomposition of $\pi$ to a series of 2- and 3-cycles, which has been well studied in algebra. Later, they made an attempt to assign an arbitrary weight $w_{\text{tr}}$ to transposition and concluded that this problem is at least as hard as the sorting by transpositions problem. Finally, they obtained an approximation algorithm with guaranteed ratio $2/w_{\text{tr}}$.

Recently, Yancopoulos, Attie and Friedberg [178] proposed an algorithm for solving the problem of sorting by reversals, translocations (including fusions and fissions) and block-interchanges on multi-linear chromosomal genomes. They used an universal *double-cut-and-join* operation that accounts for reversal, fission, fusion and translocation, but fails in describing the block-interchanges. In order to avoid complicated analysis, they assigned weight 1 to all operations except 2 to block-interchanges, which also is consistent with the biological observation that block-interchanges are relatively rare.

## 7. Experimental Results

A complete experimental procedure on genome rearrangement is starting with the sequence data as its input, next looking for genes, conserved segments or something for representing landmarks among the input sequences, and finally computing the distance matrix according to the considered operations. Sometimes, when the sequences are well annotated in the database, a set of homologous genes among them can be easily obtained from the biologists by identifying the gene functions, names or even similarity of gene segments. However, because of many reasons such as annotation errors, lack of annotations or insufficient knowledge in biology, it is hard to determine whether genes of two species are homologous or not. This problem has greatly perplexed not only biologists, but also anyone who wants to study related researches. Therefore, the approach of comparative mapping, which allows the observation of chromosomal segments conserved in both genomes since divergence from a common ancestor, arises by using the techniques in biology, statistics, computer sciences, etc. [32,41,179].

We consider the problem of sorting by weighted reversals and block-interchanges, where the weighted assignment is 1 to reversals and 2 to block-interchanges. In order to obtain the genomic distances automatically, the optimal algorithm of Lin et al. [118] is implemented by integrating the algorithm of Kaplan et al. [105]. Moreover, it seems that block-interchanges frequently appear in lower organisms from previous researches, and hence, we will have two experiments on 18 species of Campanulaceae and 29 $\gamma$-proteobacterial genomes for studying their evolutions in the rest of this section.

## 7.1 Chloroplast in Campanulaceae

In general, the Chloroplast DNA (cpDNA) of land plants is highly conserved in nucleotide sequence, gene content and order, and genome size. Chloroplast genomes of photosynthetic angiosperms average about 160 kilobase pairs (kb) in size and contain approximate 120 genes. The major disruption in gene order, such as caused by inversions, inverted repeat and gene losses, is usually rare. Its relatively slow rate of evolution makes it an excellent molecule for evolutionary studies [137].

We used gene maps released by Cosner et al. [54] to encode each of the 18 genera and the outgroup *Tobacco* as a circular ordering of signed gene segments. Her analysis suggested an unbelievable diversity of mutations, including inversions, insertions, deletions, duplications (inverted repeats) and putative transpositions. Transpositions in particular are only rare in the hypothesis of chloroplast evolution and therefore the inference for the Campanulaceae is surprising. The variety of rearrangements far exceeds the reports in any group of land plants, so that it is a challenge to determine the exact number and the evolutionary sequence of rearrangement events.

However, in order to apply our algorithm, we have to remove an incompletely mapped genus *Roella* from the dataset due to the lack of gene segment in some

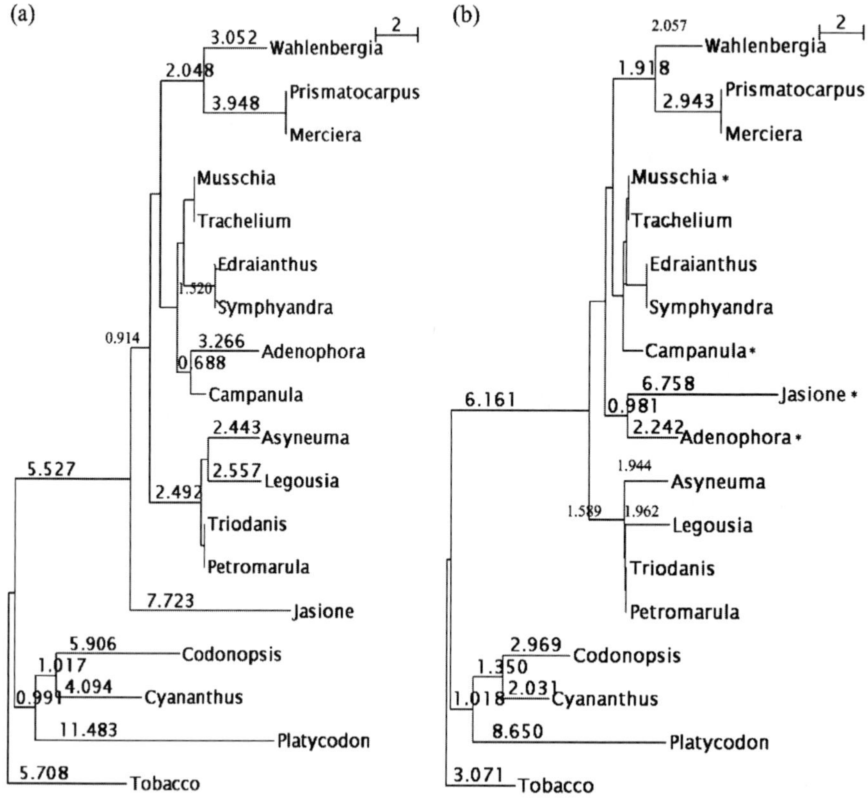


FIG. 28. Phylogenetic relationships among 18 genomes of Campanulaceae inferred from a breakpoint distance (a), and a reversal and block-interchange distance matrix (b). Values at clades reflect the distance among species. Too small distances are removed for readability of the whole tree. Asterisks in (b) represent the major differences with comparing the phylogenetic tree of Cosner et al. [54, Fig. 3]. The up bar indicates 2 breakpoints (a) or weight 2 of two reversals or a block-interchange (b) in the edge length of tree.

experimental segments. Moreover, the genes suffering repeated regions, gene duplications and losses are all eliminated, thereby reducing the original 105 genes to 91 genes ultimately. The quantity of gene numbers is enough for the analysis of reversal and block-interchange events, instead of reversals and putative transpositions in primary study. It deserves to be mentioned that previous researches have found that the differences in Campanulaceae are mainly in the mutations of duplications, insertions and the inverted repeats. Here, we bypass the effects of these mutations despite the consequence of making certain pair of genera indistinguishable.

We analyze the dataset of 18 circular genomes for their breakpoint distances, and reversal and block-interchange distances. By calculating the matrices for two distance measures, we further reconstruct the phylogenetic trees by means of the distance-base method *neighbor-joining* [147] contained in *PHYLIP package* [72]. Although this method has no guarantee on the constructed tree, it has been widely used up to now because it outputs a "better" tree topology than many tree construction methods. Moreover, a tree drawing program NJplot [144] is used to draw the phylogenetic tree according to the solution deriving from the neighbor-joining method.

Our breakpoint tree (Fig. 28(a)) is very similar to the *endpoint tree* of Cosner et al. [54, Fig. 2], even if we use different methods in constructing trees. However, in our reversal and block-interchange tree (Fig. 28(b)), there are four species indicated by asterisks, which does not agree with that in the tree constructed by Cosner et al. [54, Fig. 3]. The inconsistency may be caused by the disregard of other mutations or methods for tree construction. Except the four divergent species, the remaining genera of Campanulaceae are consistent with the result of Cosner et al.

## 7.2 $\gamma$-Proteobacteria

Within the Bacteria domain, the phylum Proteobacteria constitutes at present the largest and most diverse phylogenetic lineage. The Proteobacteria contain a lot of species, scattered over 5 major phylogenetic lines of descent known as the classes "$\alpha$-proteobacteria", "$\beta$-proteobacteria", "$\gamma$-proteobacteria", "$\delta$-proteobacteria" and "$\varepsilon$-proteobacteria" with length about 1–8 megabase pairs (mb), where $\gamma$-proteobacteria is the largest among these classes (at least 180 genera and 750 species). Genome rearrangements have been studied in several bacterial groups, and of course $\gamma$-proteobacteria is one of them, with inversions as one of the most frequent rearrangement types in interspecies comparisons.

Apart from the inversions and transpositions, there are other types of changes, e.g., deletion, duplication or *horizontal* (or *lateral*) *gene transfer*, may disrupt the gene order of $\gamma$-proteobacteria. The deletion and duplication events result in gaps and redundant genomic segments, respectively when the genomes of two species are compared. The horizontal gene transfer, sometimes named as *recombination*, predominates the evolution of prokaryotic genomes and may produce insertions throughout the genome. However, it is hard to include these changes beyond the ability of our algorithm. As usual, we ignore these effects for simplifying the experiment.

Recently, Belda, Moya and Silva [16] studied the breakpoint and inversion distance in 30 $\gamma$-proteobacterial complete genomes by comparing the order of 244 genes on the chromosome. They also presented the high correlation of two distance measurements by computing the correlation factor $r = 0.996$. Furthermore, the genes they used for analyzing the proteobacteria are recorded in the supplemen-

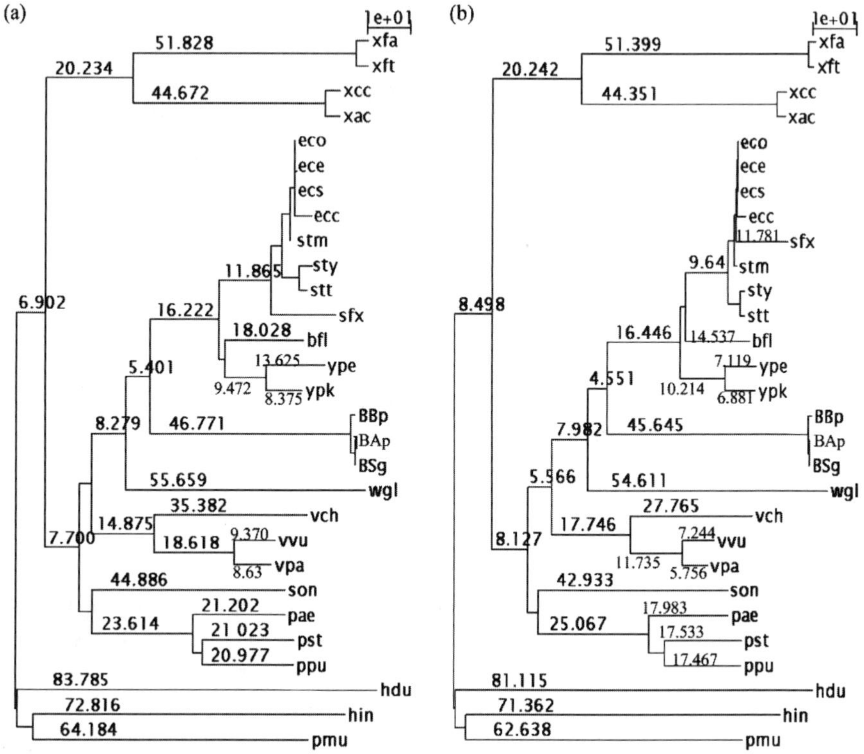


FIG. 29. Phylogenetic relationships among 29 $\gamma$-proteobacteria are inferred from a breakpoint distance (a), and a reversal and block-interchange distance matrix (b).

tary material of their paper, and thus can be conveniently available via the network. In this experiment, we extract the gene orders of 29 $\gamma$-proteobacteria released by Belda et al. as the input of our algorithm, and exclude *S. flexneri 301* (*sfl*) from our experiment as a result of its diversity in contrast with *S. flexneri 2457T* (*sfx*).

Figure 29 is our experimental results of two phylogenetic trees according to two distance measures. Due to the same consideration in both breakpoint distance and tree construction method (neighbor-joining) with that of Belda et al. [16, Fig. 5a], Fig. 29(a) is almost identical to their result. As to considering reversals and block-interchanges simultaneously, our tree in Fig. 29(b) seems to be superior than Belda et al. [16, Fig. 5b] in spite of the high similarity of two tree topologies. The *Shi. flexneri* (*sfx*) moves closer to *E. coli* (*ecc*, *eco*, etc.) in comparing two trees of Fig. 29, where the result of Belda et al. has the same variation, and however, the *She. oneidensis* (*son*) slightly changed its position in Belda et al. result, but not in ours. In other

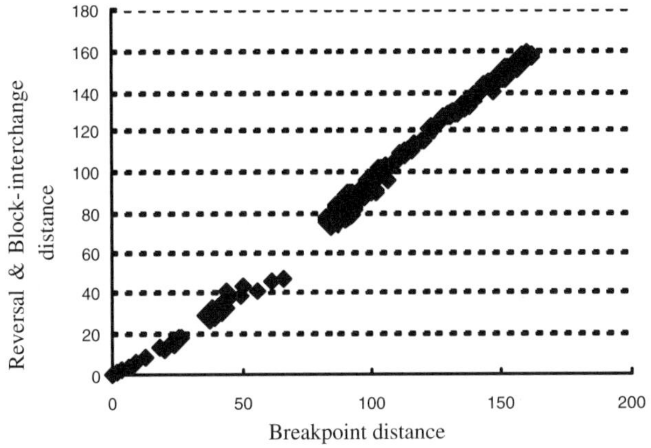


FIG. 30. Comparison of distance calculations on the dataset of 29 $\gamma$-proteobacteria with a correlation coefficient of $\gamma = 0.997$.

words, two tree topologies in Fig. 29 are more coincident in contrast to the comparison between breakpoint and reversal trees of Belda et al. This is why our correlation coefficient ($\gamma = 0.997$, see Fig. 30) is slightly higher than theirs ($\gamma = 0.996$ [16, Fig. 1]).

## 8. Conclusions

In this chapter we have taken a few primary introductions toward understanding the genome rearrangement problems. Almost all rearrangement events in this area came up in discussing the history and recent progress, which are further summarized in Table I. Not only theoretical analyses, but also biological evidences for rearrangement events are mentioned to connect the theory and application. However, there are still a lot of interesting topics related to the genome rearrangement but not included in our discussion. For example, we may have constraints on the length of inverted or transposed segments [17,122,123,136,159,166]. Furthermore, recent researches focus on inferring a special scenario called *perfect sorting*, which conserves all common intervals during the transforming process [19,146]. As to multiple genome rearrangement [149,177], the most mentioned problem is its special case, the so-called *median problem*, which is to find a median for a set of permutations under a specific genomic distance. Unfortunately, it has been shown to be NP-hard for both the breakpoint [143] and the reversal [34] distance. Very recently, Bernt et al. [29] proposed a heuristic algorithm for solving the median problem by considering only reversals without breaking the common gene intervals.

TABLE I

THE TABLE SUMMARIZES THE PROGRESS OF SOME GENOME REARRANGEMENT PROBLEMS COMING UP IN THIS CHAPTER

| (Unsigned) | Cycle decomposition | Prefix reversal | Reversal | Prefix transposition | Transposition | Transreversal | Block interchange | Translocation | Fusion & fission |
|---|---|---|---|---|---|---|---|---|---|
| $1.4193 + \varepsilon$-app. [114] | ✓ | | | | | | | | |
| 2-app. [75] | | ✓ | $\frac{15}{14}n \leqslant D_{\text{pref}}(\pi) \leqslant \frac{5n+5}{3}$ [80,94] | | | | | | |
| 1.375-app. [27] | | | ✓ | MAX-SNP hard [28], $D_r(\pi) = n - 1$ [11] | | | | | |
| 2-app. [59] | | | | ✓ | | | | | |
| 1.375-app. [67] | $\lfloor n/2 \rfloor \leqslant D_{\text{tr}}(\pi)$ [44,127] | | | | ✓ | $D_{\text{tr}}(\pi) \leqslant 11\lfloor n/24 \rfloor + \lfloor 3\frac{n/3 \bmod 8}{2} \rfloor + 1$ [67] | | | |
| | $O(n^2)$, $O(n)$ [42,116] | | | | | | ✓ | | |
| 1.75-app. [57] | MAX-SNP hard [182] | | | | | | | ✓ | |
| 3-app. [168] | | | 1 | | 1 | | | | |
| | $O(n^2)$, $O(n)$ [120] | | | | | | 1 | | 1 |
| | $O(n^2)$, $O(n)$ [126] | | | | 2 | | | | 1 |
| (Signed) | | ✓ | $\frac{3}{2}n \leqslant d_{\text{pref}}(\vec{\pi}) \leqslant 2n - 2$ [50] | | | | | | |
| 1.5-app. [91] | | | 1 | | 1 | 1 | | | |
| 1.5-app. [10] | | | 1 | | $1 < w_t < 2$ | $1 < w_t < 2$ | | | |
| | $O(n^{3/2}\sqrt{\log n})$ [139], $O(n)$ [113] | | | | | | | ✓ | |
| | | | ✓ | $O(n^{3/2}\sqrt{\log n})$ [160], $O(n)$ [9], $D_r(\vec{\pi}) = n + 1$ [89] | | | | | |
| 2-app. [82,115,168] | | | 1 | | 1 | $\lfloor \frac{1}{2}n \rfloor \leqslant D_{\text{r+tr}}(\vec{\pi})$ [129] | | | |
| 2-app. [82,115] | | | 1 | | 1 | 1 | | | |
| $(1 + \varepsilon)$-app. [69] | | | 1 | | 2 | | | | |
| | $O(n^2)$, $O(n)$ [118] | | 1 | $D_{\text{r+bi}}(\vec{\pi}) = n - 1$ [118] | | | 2 | | |
| | | | 1 | $O(n^2)$, $O(n)$ [138,161] | | | | 1 | 1 |
| | $O(n^2)$, $O(n)$ [178] | | 1 | | | | 2 | 1 | 1 |

If a column indicating an operation $\rho$ has the sign "✓," then the corresponding row is the result of sorting by $\rho$ problem. Otherwise, if a field contains an integer, 1 or 2, then it corresponds to the sorting by multiple operations problem and moreover, the integer represents its weight. Besides, we list two time complexities in a row if the corresponding problem is polynomial solvable, where the bigger one represents the running time of finding the sorting series and the smaller expresses that of computing the genomic distance.

## REFERENCES

[1] "Derange II", ftp://ftp.ebi.ac.uk/pub/software/unix/derange2.tar.Z.
[2] "Graphics gallery of the National Human Genome Research Institute (NHGRI)", www.accessexcellence.org/RC/VL/GG/.
[3] "The seven Prize Problems", www.claymath.org/millennium/.
[4] "Traveling Salesman Problem", www.tsp.gatech.edu/.
[5] Ackermann W., "Zum hilbertshen aufbau der reelen zahlen", *Math. Ann.* **99** (1928) 118–133.
[6] Aigner M., West D.B., "Sorting by insertion of leading elements", *J. Combin. Theory Ser. A* **45** (1987) 306–309.
[7] Ajana Y., Lefebvre J.-F., Tillier E.R.M., El-Mabrouk N., "Exploring the set of all minimal sequences of reversals—an application to test the replication-directed reversal hypothesis", in: *Proceedings of the 25th Workshop on Algorithms in Bioinformatics, WABI2002*, in: *Lecture Notes in Computer Science*, vol. 2452, Springer-Verlag, Berlin/New York, 2002, pp. 300–315.
[8] Ausiello G., Crescenzi P., Kann V., Marchetti-Spaccamela A., Gambosi G., Spaccamela A.M., *Complexity and Approximation: Combinatorial Optimization Problems and Their Approximability Properties*, Springer-Verlag, Berlin/New York, 1999.
[9] Bader D.A., Moret B.M.E., Yan M., "A linear-time algorithm for computing inversion distance between signed permutations with an experimental study", *J. Comput. Biol.* **8** (2001) 483–491.
[10] Bader M., Ohlebusch E., "Sorting by weighted reversals, transpositions, and inverted transpositions", in: Apostolico A., Guerra C., Istrail S., Pevzner P.A., Waterman M.S. (Eds.), *Proceedings of the 10th Annual International Conference on Research in Computational Molecular Biology, RECOMB2006*, in: *Lecture Notes in Computer Science*, vol. 3909, Springer-Verlag, Berlin/New York, 2006, pp. 563–577.
[11] Bafna V., Pevzner P.A., "Genome rearrangements and sorting by reversals", *SIAM J. Comput.* **25** (1996) 272–289.
[12] Bafna V., Pevzner P.A., "Sorting by transpositions", *SIAM J. Discrete Math.* **11** (1998) 221–240.
[13] Balakrishnan R., Ranganathan K., *A Textbook of Graph Theory*, Springer-Verlag, Berlin/New York, 2000.
[14] Bansal S.A., "Genome rearrangements and randomized sorting by reversals", unpublished, 2002.
[15] Barnhart C., Johnson E.L., Nemhauser G.L., Savelsbergh M.W.P., Vance P.H., "Branch-and-price: Column generation for solving huge integer programs", *Oper. Res.* **46** (1998) 316–329.
[16] Belda E., Moya A., Silva F.J., "Genome rearrangement distances and gene order phylogeny in $\gamma$-proteobacteria", *Mol. Biol. Evol.* **22** (2005) 1456–1467.
[17] Bender M.A., Ge D., He S., Hu H., Pinter R.Y., Skiena S., Swidan F., "Improved bounds on sorting with length-weighted reversals", in: *Proceedings of the 15th Annual ACM–SIAM Symposium on Discrete Algorithms, SODA2004*, ACM/SIAM, New York, 2004, pp. 919–928.

[18] Benson D.A., Karsch-Mizrachi I., Lipman D.J., Ostell J., Wheeler D.L., "GenBank", *Nucleic Acids Res.* **34** (2006) D16–D20.

[19] Bérard S., Bergeron A., Chauve C., Paul C., "Perfect sorting by reversals is not always difficult", in: Casadio R., Myers G. (Eds.), *Proceedings of the 10th Annual European Symposium on Algorithms, ESA2002*, in: *Lecture Notes in Computer Science*, vol. 3692, Springer-Verlag, Berlin/New York, 2005, pp. 228–238.

[20] Bergeron A., "A very elementary presentation of the Hannenhalli–Pevzner theory", *Discrete Appl. Math.* **146** (2005) 134–145.

[21] Bergeron A., Chauve C., Hartman T., St-Onge K., "On the properties of sequences of reversals that sort a signed permutation", in: *Proceedings of JOBIM, JOBIM2002*, 2002, pp. 99–108.

[22] Bergeron A., Mixtacki J., Stoye J., "Reversal distance without hurdles and fortresses", in: Sahinalp S.C., Muthukrishnan S., Dogrusöz U. (Eds.), *Proceedings of the 15th Annual Symposium on Combinatorial Pattern Matching, CPM2004*, in: *Lecture Notes in Computer Science*, vol. 3109, Springer-Verlag, Berlin/New York, 2004, pp. 388–399.

[23] Bergeron A., Mixtacki J., Stoye J., "On sorting by translocations", *J. Comput. Biol.* **13** (2006) 567–578.

[24] Bergeron A., Strasbourg F., "Experiments in computing sequences of reversals", in: Gascuel O., Moret B.M.E. (Eds.), *Proceedings of the 1st Workshop on Algorithms in Bioinformatics, WABI2001*, in: *Lecture Notes in Computer Science*, vol. 2149, Springer-Verlag, Berlin/New York, 2001, pp. 164–174.

[25] Berman H.M., Westbrook J., Feng Z., Gilliland G., Bhat T.N., Weissig H., Shindyalov I.N., Bourne P.E., "The protein data bank", *Nucleic Acids Res.* **28** (2000) 235–242.

[26] Berman P., Hannenhalli S., "Fast sorting by reversal", in: Hirschberg D.S., Myers E.W. (Eds.), *Proceedings of the 7th Annual Symposium on Combinatorial Pattern Matching, CPM1996*, in: *Lecture Notes in Computer Science*, vol. 1075, Springer-Verlag, Berlin/New York, 1996, pp. 168–185.

[27] Berman P., Hannenhalli S., Karpinski M., "1.375-approximation algorithm for sorting by reversals", in: Mohring R.H., Raman R. (Eds.), *Proceedings of the 10th Annual European Symposium on Algorithms, ESA2002*, in: *Lecture Notes in Computer Science*, vol. 2461, Springer-Verlag, Berlin/New York, 2002, pp. 200–210.

[28] Berman P., Karpinski M., "On some tighter inapproximability results", in: Wiedermann J., Boas P.E., Nielsen M. (Eds.), *Proceedings of the 26th International Colloquium on Automata, Languages and Programming, ICALP1999*, in: *Lecture Notes in Computer Science*, vol. 1644, Springer-Verlag, Berlin/New York, 1999, pp. 200–209.

[29] Bernt M., Merkle D., Middendorf M., "Genome rearrangement based on reversals that preserve conserved intervals", *IEEE/ACM Trans. Comput. Biol. Bioinform.* **3** (2006) 275–288.

[30] Blanchette M., Kunisawa T., Sankoff D., "Parametric genome rearrangement", *Gene* **172** (1996) 11–17.

[31] Bogomolny A., "Interactive mathematics miscellany and puzzles", www.cut-the-knot.org/SimpleGames/Flipper.shtml.

[32] Bourque G., Zdobnov E.M., Bork P., Pevzner P.A., Tesler G., "Comparative architectures of mammalian and chicken genomes reveal highly variable rates of genomic rearrangements across different lineages", *Genome Res.* **15** (2005) 98–110.

[33] Caprara A., "Sorting by reversal is difficult", in: *Proceedings of the 1st Annual International Conference on Research in Computational Molecular Biology, RECOMB1997*, ACM Press, New York, 1997, pp. 75–83.

[34] Caprara A., "Formulations and hardness of multiple sorting by reversals", in: Istrail S., Pevzner P.A., Waterman M. (Eds.), *Proceedings of the 3rd Annual International Conference on Research in Computational Molecular Biology, RECOMB1999*, ACM Press, New York, 1999, pp. 84–93.

[35] Caprara A., "On the tightness of the alternating cycle lower bound for sorting by reversals", *J. Combin. Opt.* **3** (1999) (1999) 149–182.

[36] Caprara A., "Sorting permutations by reversals and Eulerian cycle decompositions", *SIAM J. Discrete Math.* **12** (1999) (1999) 91–110.

[37] Caprara A., Lancia G., Ng S.K., "A column-generation based branch-and-bound algorithm for sorting by reversals", in: Farach-Colton M., Roberts F.S., Vingron M., Waterman M. (Eds.), in: *DIMACS Series in Discrete Mathematics and Theoretical Computer Science*, vol. 47, AMS Press, New York, 1999, pp. 213–226.

[38] Caprara A., Lancia G., Ng S.K., "Faster practical solution of sorting by reversals", in: *Proceedings of the 11th Annual ACM–SIAM Symposium on Discrete Algorithms, SODA2000*, ACM/SIAM, New York, 2000, pp. 12–21.

[39] Caprara A., Lancia G., Ng S.K., "Sorting permutations by reversals through branch-and-price", *INFORMS J. Comput.* **13** (2001) 224–244.

[40] Caprara A., Rizzi R., "Improved approximation for breakpoint graph decomposition and sorting by reversals", *J. Combin. Opt.* **6** (2002) 157–182.

[41] Chen C.Y., Wu K.M., Chang Y.C., Chang C.H., "Comparative genome analysis of vibrio vulnificus, a marine pathogen", *Genome Res.* **13** (2003) 2577–2587.

[42] Christie D.A., "Sorting by block-interchanges", *Inform. Process. Lett.* **60** (1996) 165–169.

[43] Christie D.A., "A 3/2-approximation algorithm for sorting by reversals", in: *Proceedings of the 9th Annual ACM–SIAM Symposium on Discrete Algorithms, SODA1998*, ACM/SIAM, New York, 1998, pp. 244–252.

[44] Christie D.A., "Genome rearrangement problem", PhD thesis, University of Glasgow, 1999.

[45] Clark D.P., Russell L.D., *Molecular Biology Made Simple and Fun*, second ed., Cache River Press, 2000.

[46] Cobham A., "The intrinsic computational difficulty of functions", in: *Proceedings of the 1964 Congress for Logic, Methodology and the Philosophy of Science*, 1964, pp. 24–30.

[47] Cochrane G., et al., "EMBL nucleotide sequence database: developments in 2005", *Nucleic Acids Res.* **34** (2006) D10–D15.

[48] Coe E., Kass L.B., "Proof of physical exchange of genes on the chromosomes", *Proc. Natl. Acad. Sci. USA* **102** (2005) 6641–6646.

[49] Coghlan A., Wolfe K.H., "Fourfold faster rate of genome rearrangement in nematodes than in *drosophila*", *Genome Res.* **16** (2002) 857–867.

[50] Cohen D.S., Blum M., "On the problem of sorting burnt pancakes", *Discrete Appl. Math.* **61** (1995) 105–120.

[51] Cook S.A., "The complexity of theorem-proving procedures", in: *Proceedings of the 3rd Annual ACM Symposium on Theory of Computing, STOC1971*, ACM Press, New York, 1971, pp. 151–158.

[52] Cormen T.H., Leiserson C.E., Rivest R.L., *Introduction to Algorithms*, second ed., MIT Press, Cambridge, MA, 2001.

[53] Cosner M.E., Jansen R.K., Moret B.M.E., Raubeson L.A., Wang L.-S., Warnow T., Wyman S., "An empirical comparison of phylogenetic methods on chloroplast gene order data in Campanulaceae", in: Sankoff D., Nadeau J.H. (Eds.), *Comparative Genomics: Empirical and Analytical Approaches to Gene Order Dynamics Map Alignment and the Evolution of Gene Families*, Kluwer Academic Press, Dordrecht/Norwell, MA, 2000, pp. 99–122.

[54] Cosner M.E., Raubeson L.A., Jansen R.K., "Chloroplast DNA rearrangements in Campanulaceae: phylogenetic utility of highly rearranged genomes", *BMC Evol. Biol.* **4** (2004) 1471–2148.

[55] Courtay-Cahen C., Morris J.S., Edwards P.A.W., "Chromosome translocations in breast cancer with breakpoints at 8p12", *Genomics* **66** (2000) 15–25.

[56] Creighton H.B., McClintock B., "A correlation of cytological and genetical crossing-over in Zea mays", *Proc. Natl. Acad. Sci. USA* **17** (1931) 492–497.

[57] Cui Y., Wang L., Zhu D., "A 1.75-approximation algorithm for unsigned translocation distance", in: Deng X., Du D. (Eds.), *Proceedings of the 16th Annual Symposium on Algorithms and Computation, ISAAC05*, in: *Lecture Notes in Computer Science*, Springer-Verlag, Berlin/New York, 2005.

[58] Darling A.C.E., Mau B., Blattner F.R., Perna N.T., "Mauve: multiple alignment of conserved genomic sequence with rearrangements", *Genome Res.* **14** (2004) 1394–1403.

[59] Dias Z., Meidanis J., "Sorting by prefix transpositions", in: Laender A.H.F., Oliveira A.L. (Eds.), *Proceedings of the 9th International Symposium on String Processing and Information Retrieval, SPIRE2002*, in: *Lecture Notes in Computer Science*, vol. 2476, Springer-Verlag, Berlin/New York, 2002, pp. 65–76.

[60] Dobzhansky T., Sturtevant A.H., "Inversions in the chromosomes of drosophila pseudoobscure", *Genetics* **23** (1938) 28–64.

[61] Doolittle R.F., Hunkapiller M.W., Hood L.E., Devare S.G., Robbins K.C., Aaronson S.A., Antoniades H.N., "Simian sarcoma *Onc* gene, *v-sis*, is derived from the gene (or genes) encoding platelet derived growth factor", *Science* **221** (1983) 275–277.

[62] Dunham A., et al., "The DNA sequence and analysis of human chromosome 13", *Nature* **428** (2004) 522–528.

[63] Dunham M.J., Badrane H., Ferea T., Adams J., Brown P.O., Rosenzweig F., Botstein D., "Characteristic genome rearrangements in experimental evolution of Saccharomyces cerevisiae", *Proc. Natl. Acad. Sci. USA* **99** (2002) 16144–16149.

[64] Dweighter H., "Elementary problems", *Amer. Math. Monthly* (1975) 1010.

[65] Edmonds J., "Paths, trees and flowers", *Canadian J. Math.* **17** (1965) 449–467.

[66] Eisen J.A., Heidelberg J.F., White O., Salzberg S.L., "Evidence for symmetric chromosomal inversions around the replication origin in bacteria", *Genome Biol.* **1** (2000).

[67] Elias I., Hartman T., "A 1.375-approximation algorithm for sorting by transpositions", in: Casadio R., Myers G. (Eds.), *Proceedings of the 5th Workshop on Algorithms in Bioinformatics, WABI2005*, in: *Lecture Notes in Computer Science*, vol. 3692, Springer-Verlag, Berlin/New York, 2005, pp. 204–215.
[68] Erdem E., Tillier E., "Genome rearrangement and planning", in: Veloso M.M., Kambhampati S. (Eds.), *Proceedings of the 20th National Conference on Artificial Intelligence and the Seventeenth Innovative Applications of Artificial Intelligence Conference, AAAI2005*, AAAI Press/The MIT Press, 2005, pp. 1139–1144.
[69] Eriksen N., "$(1+\varepsilon)$-approximation of sorting by reversals", *Theoret. Comput. Sci.* **289** (2002) 517–529.
[70] Eriksen N., "Combinatorial methods in comparative genomics", PhD thesis, Royal Institute of Technology, 2003.
[71] Eriksson H., Eriksson K., Karlander J., Svensson L., Wästlund J., "Sorting a bridge hand", *Discrete Math.* **241** (2001) 289–300.
[72] Felsenstein J., "PHYLIP", http://evolution.genetics.washington.edu/phylip.html.
[73] Feng W., Wang L., Zhu D., "CTRD: a fast applet for computing signed translocation distance between genomes", *Bioinformatics* **48** (2004) 3256–3257.
[74] Feuk L., MacDonald J.R., Tang T., Carson A.R., Li M., Rao G., Khaja R., Scherer S.W., "Discovery of human inversion polymorphisms by comparative analysis of human and chimpanzee DNA sequence assemblies", *PLOS Genetics* **1** (2005) 489–498.
[75] Fischer J., Ginzinger S.W., "A 2-approximation algorithm for sorting by prefix reversals", in: Brodal G.S., Leonardi S. (Eds.), *Proceedings of the 13th Annual European Symposium on Algorithms, ESA2005*, in: *Lecture Notes in Computer Science*, vol. 3669, Springer-Verlag, Berlin/New York, 2005, pp. 415–425.
[76] Fliess A., Motro B., Unger R., "Swaps in protein sequences", *Proteins* **48** (2002) 377–387.
[77] Fortuna V.J., Meidanis J., "Sorting the reverse permutation by prefix transpositions", Technical Report IC-04-04, Institute of Computing, 2004.
[78] Garey M.R., Graham R.L., Ullman J.D., "Worst-case analysis of memory allocation algorithms", in: *Proceedings of the 4th Annual ACM Symposium on Theory of Computing, STOC1972*, 1972, pp. 143–150.
[79] Garey M.R., Johnson D.S., *Computers and Intractability: A Guide to the Theory of NP-Completeness*, W.H. Freeman, New York, 1979.
[80] Gates W.H., Papadimitriou C.H., "Bound for sorting by prefix reversals", *Discrete Math.* **27** (1979) 47–57.
[81] Graham R.L., "Bounds for certain multiprocessor anomalies", *AT&T Tech. J.* **45** (1966) 1563–1581.
[82] Gu Q.P., Peng S., Sudborough H., "A 2-approximation algorithms for genome rearrangements by reversals and transpositions", *Theoret. Comput. Sci.* **210** (1999) 327–339.
[83] Gusfield D., *Algorithms on Strings, Trees, and Sequences: Computer Science and Computational Biology*, Cambridge Univ. Press, Cambridge, MA, 1997.
[84] Guyer S.A., Heath L.S., Vergara J.P.C., "Subsequence and run heuristics for sorting by transpositions", Technical Report TR-97-20, Virginia Polytechnic Institute and State University, 1997.

[85] Hannenhalli S., "Polynomial algorithm for computing translocation distance between genomes", *Discrete Appl. Math.* **71** (1996) 137–151.

[86] Hannenhalli S., Chappey C., Koonin E., Pevzner P.A., "Genome sequence comparison and scenarios for gene rearrangement: a test case", *Genomics* **30** (1995) 299–311.

[87] Hannenhalli S., Pevzner P.A., "Transforming men into mice (polynomial algorithm for genomic distance problem)", in: *Proceedings of the 36th IEEE Symposium on Foundations of Computer Science, FOCS1995*, IEEE Comput. Soc., Los Alamitos, CA, 1995, pp. 581–592.

[88] Hannenhalli S., Pevzner P.A., "To cut ... or not to cut (applications of comparative physical maps in molecular evolution)", in: *Proceedings of the 7th Annual ACM–SIAM Symposium on Discrete Algorithms, SODA1995*, ACM/SIAM, New York, 1995, pp. 304–313.

[89] Hannenhalli S., Pevzner P.A., "Transforming cabbage into turnip: Polynomial algorithm for sorting signed permutations by reversals", *J. ACM* **46** (1999) 1–27.
Preliminary version in: *Proceedings of the 27th Annual ACM Symposium on Theory of Computing, 1995, STOC1995*, pp. 178–189.

[90] Hartman T., Shamir R., "A simpler and faster 1.5-approximation algorithm for sorting by transpositions", *Inform. Comput.* **204** (2006) 275–290.

[91] Hartman T., Sharan R., "A 1.5-approximation algorithm for sorting by transpositions and transreversals", *J. Comput. Syst. Sci.* **70** (2005) 300–320.

[92] Heath L.S., Vergara J.P.C., "Some experiments on the sorting by reversals problem", Technical Report TR-95-16, Virginia Polytechnic Institute and State University, 1995.

[93] Heller A., et al., "A complex translocation event between the two homologues of chromosomes 5 leading to a del(5)(q21q33) as a sole aberration in a case clinically diagnosed as CML: characterization of the aberration by multicolor banding", *Internat. J. Oncol.* **20** (2002) 1179–1181.

[94] Heydari H., Sudborough H.I., "On the diameter of the pancake network", *J. Algorithms* **25** (1997) 67–94.

[95] Heydari M.H., "The Pancake Problem", PhD thesis, University of Wisconsin at Whitewater, 1993.

[96] Ho T.-C., Jeng K.-S., Hu C.-P., Chang C., "Effects of genomic length on translocation of Hepatitis B virus polymerase-linked oligomer", *J. Virol.* **74** (2000) 9010–9018.

[97] Hochbaum D.S., *Approximation Algorithms for NP-Hard Problems*, PWS Publishing Company, Warsaw, 1997.

[98] Hoot S.B., Palmer J.D., "Structural rearrangements, including parallel inversions, within the chloroplast genome of anemone and related genera", *J. Mol. Biol.* **38** (1994) 274–281.

[99] Hopcroft J.E., Motwani R., Ullman J.D., *Introduction to Automata Theory, Languages and Computation*, second ed., Addison–Wesley, Reading, MA, 2001.

[100] Hughes D., "Evaluating genome dynamics: the constraints on rearrangements within bacterial genomes", *Genome Biol.* **1** (2000).

[101] International Human Genome Sequencing Consortium, "Initial sequencing and analysis of the human genome", *Nature* **409** (2001) 860–912.

[102] Jancovich J.K., Mao J., Chinchar V.G., Wyatt C., Case S.T., Kumar S., Valente G., Subramanian S., Davidson E.W., Collins J.P., Jacobsa B.L., "Genomic sequence of a ranavirus (family iridoviridae) associated with salamander mortalities in North America", *Virology* **316** (2003) 90–103.

[103] Johnson D.S., "Approximation algorithms for combinatorial problems", *J. Comput. Syst. Sci.* **9** (1974) 256–278.

[104] Jones N.C., Pevzner P.A., *An Introduction to Bioinformatics Algorithms*, The MIT Press, Cambridge, MA, 2004.

[105] Kaplan H., Shamir R., Tarjan R.E., "A faster and simpler algorithm for sorting signed permutations by reversals", *SIAM J. Comput.* **29** (1999) 880–892.

[106] Kaplan H., Verbin E., "Efficient data structures and a new randomized approach for sorting signed permutations by reversals", in: Baeza-Yates R.A., Chávez E., Crochemore M. (Eds.), *Proceedings of the 14th Annual Symposium on Combinatorial Pattern Matching, CPM2003*, in: *Lecture Notes in Computer Science*, vol. 2676, Springer-Verlag, Berlin/New York, 2003, pp. 170–185.

[107] Kaplan H., Verbin E., "Sorting signed permutations by reversals, revisited", *J. Comput. Syst. Sci.* **70** (2005) 321–341.

[108] Kececioglu J.D., Ravi R., "Of mice and men: algorithms for evolutionary distances between genomes with translocation", in: *Proceedings of the 6th ACM–SIAM Symposium on Discrete Algorithms, SODA1995*, ACM/SIAM, New York, 1995, pp. 604–613.

[109] Kececioglu J.D., Sankoff D., "Exact and approximation algorithms for the inversion distance between two permutations", *Algorithmica* **13** (1995) 180–210.

[110] Kent W.J., Baertsch R., Hinrichs A., Miller W., Haussler D., "Evolution's cauldron: duplication, deletion, and rearrangement in the mouse and human genomes", *Proc. Natl. Acad. Sci. USA* **100** (2003) 11484–11489.

[111] Kim K.-J., Choi K.-S., Jansen R.K., "Two chloroplast DNA inversions originated simultaneously during the early evolution of the sunflower family (Asteraceae)", *Nucleic Acids Res.* **22** (2005) 1783–1792.

[112] Lancia G., "Applications to computational molecular biology", in: Appa G., Williams P. (Eds.), *Modeling for Discrete Optimization* in: *International Series in Operations Research and Management Science*, Kluwer Academic Publishers, Dordrecht/Norwell, MA, 2004, in press.

[113] Li G., Qi X., Wang X., Zhu B., "A linear-time algorithm for computing translocation distance between signed genomes", in: Sahinalp S.C., Muthukrishnan S., Dogrusöz U. (Eds.), *Proceedings of the 15th Annual Symposium on Combinatorial Pattern Matching, CPM2004*, in: *Lecture Notes in Computer Science*, vol. 3109, Springer-Verlag, Berlin/New York, 2004, pp. 323–332.

[114] Lin G., Jiang T., "A further improved approximation algorithm for breakpoint graph decomposition", *J. Comb. Opt.* **8** (2004) 183–194.

[115] Lin G.H., Xue G., "Signed genome rearrangement by reversals and transpositions: models and approximations", *Theoret. Comput. Sci.* **259** (2001) 513–531.

[116] Lin Y.C., Lu C.L., Chang H.Y., Tang C.Y., "An efficient algorithm for sorting by block-interchanges and its application to the evolution of vibrio species", *J. Comput. Biol.* **12** (2005) 102–112.

[117] Lin Y.C., Lu C.L., Liu Y.-C., Tang C.Y., "SPRING: a tool for the analysis of genome rearrangement using reversals and block-interchanges", *Nucleic Acids Res.* **34** (2006) W696–W699.

[118] Lin Y.C., Lu C.L., Tang C.Y., "Sorting permutation by reversals with fewest block-interchanges", manuscript, 2006.

[119] Liu S.-L., Sanderson K.E., "Rearrangements in the genome of the bacterium *Salmonella typhi*", *Proc. Natl. Acad. Sci. USA* **92** (1995) 1018–1022.

[120] Lu C.L., Huang Y.L., Wang T.C., Chiu H.-T., "Analysis of circular genome rearrangement by fusions, fissions and block-interchanges", *BMC Bioinform.* 7 (2006).

[121] Lu C.L., Wang T.C., Lin Y.C., Tang C.Y., "ROBIN: a tool for genome rearrangement of block-interchanges", *Bioinformatics* **21** (2005) 2780–2782.

[122] Mahajan M., Rama R., Vijayakumar S., "Towards constructing optimal strip move sequences", in: Chwa K.-Y., Munro J.I. (Eds.), *Proceedings of the 10th International Computing and Combinatorics Conference, COCOON2004*, in: *Lecture Notes in Computer Science*, vol. 1644, Springer-Verlag, Berlin/New York, 2004, pp. 33–42.

[123] Mahajan M., Rama R., Vijayakumar S., "On sorting by 3-bounded transpositions", *Discrete Math.* **306** (2006) 1569–1585.

[124] Mantin I., Shamir R., "An algorithm for sorting signed permutations by reversals", www.math.tau.ac.il/~rshamir/GR/, 1999.

[125] McLysaght A., Seoighe C., Wolfe K.H., "High frequency of inversions during eukaryote gene order evolution", in: Sankoff D., Nadeau J.H. (Eds.), *Comparative Genomics: Empirical and Analytical Approaches to Gene Order Dynamics, Map Alignment and the Evolution of Gene Families*, Kluwer Academic Press, Dordrecht/Norwell, MA, 2000, pp. 47–58.

[126] Meidanis J., Dias Z., "Genome rearrangements distance by fusion, fission, and transposition is easy", in: Navarro G. (Ed.), *Proceedings of the 8th International Symposium on String Processing and Information Retrieval, SPIRE2001*, in: *Lecture Notes in Computer Science*, IEEE Comput. Soc., Los Alamitos, CA, 2001, pp. 250–253.

[127] Meidanis J., Walter M.E.T., Dias Z., "Transposition distance between a permutation and its reverse", in: *Proceedings of the 4th South American Workshop on String Processing, WSP1997*, Carleton Univ. Press, 1997, pp. 70–79.

[128] Meidanis J., Walter M.E.T., Dias Z., "Reversal distance of signed circular chromosomes", Technical Report IC-00-23, Institute of Computing, 2000.

[129] Meidanis J., Walter M.E.T., Dias Z., "A lower bound on the reversal and transposition diameter", *J. Comput. Biol.* **9** (2002) 743–746.

[130] Miklós I., "MCMC genome rearrangement", *Bioinformatics* **19** (2003) 130–137.

[131] Miklós I., Ittzés P., Hein J., "ParIS genome rearrangement server", *Bioinformatics* **21** (2005) 817–820.

[132] Monammed J.L., Subi C.S., "An improved block-interchange algorithm", *J. Algorithms* **8** (1987) 113–121.

[133] Motwani R., Raghavan P., *Randomized Algorithms*, Cambridge Univ. Press, Cambridge, UK, 1995.

[134] Mungall A.J., et al., "The DNA sequence and analysis of human chromosome 6", *Nature* **425** (2003) 805–811.

[135] Nadeau J.H., Taylor B.A., "Lengths of chromosomal segments conserved since divergence of man and mouse", *Proc. Natl. Acad. Sci. USA* **81** (1984) 814–818.

[136] Nadeau J.H., Taylor B.A., "Sorting by restricted-length-weighted reversals", *Genomics Proteomics Bioinform.* **3** (2005) 120–127.

[137] Olmstead R.G., Palmer J.D., "Chloroplast DNA systematics: a review of methods and data analysis", *Amer. J. Bot.* **81** (1994) 1205–1224.

[138] Ozery-Flato M., Shamir R., "Two notes on genome rearrangement", *J. Bioinform. Comput. Biol.* **1** (2003) 71–94.

[139] Ozery-Flato M., Shamir R., "An $O(n^{3/2}\sqrt{\log(n)})$ algorithm for sorting by reciprocal translocations", in: Lewenstein M., Valiente G. (Eds.), *Proceedings of the 17th Annual Symposium on Combinatorial Pattern Matching, CPM2006*, in: *Lecture Notes in Computer Science*, vol. 4009, Springer-Verlag, Berlin/New York, 2006, pp. 258–269.

[140] Palmer J.D., Herbon L.A., "Plant mitochondrial DNA evolves rapidly in structure, but slowly in sequence", *J. Mol. Evol.* **28** (1988) 87–97.

[141] Palmer J.D., Osorio B., Thompson W.R., "Evolutionary significance of inversions in legume chorloplast DNAs", *Curr. Genetics* **14** (1988) 65–74.

[142] Papadimitriou C.H., *Computational Complexity*, Addison–Wesley, Reading, MA, 1994.

[143] Péer I., Shamir R., "The median problems for breakpoints are NP-complete", Technical Report TR98-071, Electronic Colloquium on Computational Complexity, 1998.

[144] Perrière G., Gouy M., "WWW-query: an on-line retrieval system for biological sequence banks", *Biochimie* **78** (1996) 364–369.

[145] Pevzner P.A., *Computational Molecular Biology: An Algorithmic Approach*, MIT Press, Cambridge, MA, 2000.

[146] Sagot M.-F., Tannier E., "Perfect sorting by reversals", in: Wang L. (Ed.), *Proceedings of the 11th International Computing and Combinatorics Conference, COCOON2005*, in: *Lecture Notes in Computer Science*, Springer-Verlag, Berlin/New York, 2005.

[147] Saitou N., Nei M., "The neighbor-joining method: a new method for reconstructing phylogenetic trees", *Mol. Biol. Evol.* **4** (1987) 406–425.

[148] Sankoff D., "Edit distance for genome comparison based on non-local operations", in: Apostolico A., Crochemore M., Galil Z., Manber U. (Eds.), *Proceedings of the 3rd Annual Symposium on Combinatorial Pattern Matching, CPM1992*, in: *Lecture Notes in Computer Science*, vol. 644, Springer-Verlag, Berlin/New York, 1992, pp. 121–135.

[149] Sankoff D., Blanchette M., "Multiple genome rearrangement and breakpoint phylogeny", *J. Comput. Biol.* **5** (1998) 555–570.

[150] Sankoff D., Cedergren R., Abel Y., "Genomic divergence through gene rearrangement", *Methods in Enzymology* **183** (1990) 428–438.

[151] Sankoff D., Leduc G., Antoine N., Paquin B., Lang B.F., Cedergren R., "Gene order comparisons for phylogenetic inference: Evolution of the mitochondrial genome", *Proc. Natl. Acad. Sci. USA* **89** (1992) 6575–6579.

[152] Schöniger M., Waterman M.S., "A local algorithm for DNA sequence alignment with inversions", *Bull. Math. Biol.* **54** (1992) 521–536.

[153] Seoighe C., et al., "Prevalence of small inversions in yeast gene order evolution", *Proc. Natl. Acad. Sci. USA* **97** (2002) 14433–14437.

[154] Setubal C., Meidanis J., *Introduction to Computational Molecular Biology*, PWS Publishing, Warsaw, 1997.

[155] Siepel A.C., "An algorithm to enumerate sorting reversals for signed permutations", *J. Comput. Biol.* **10** (2003) 575–597.

[156] Sipser M., *Introduction to the Theory of Computation*, PWS Publishing, Warsaw, 1997.

[157] Slamovits C.H., Fast N.M., Law J.S., Keeling P.J., "Genome compaction and stability in microsporidian intracellular parasites", *Curr. Biol.* **14** (2004) 891–896.

[158] Solomon A., Sutcliffe P., Lister R., "Sorting circular permutations by reversal", in: Dehne F.K.H.A., Sack J.-R., Smid M.H.M. (Eds.), *Algorithms and Data Structures, 8th International Workshop, WADS2003*, in: *Lecture Notes in Computer Science*, vol. 2748, Springer-Verlag, Berlin/New York, 2003, pp. 319–328.

[159] Swidan F., Bender M.A., Ge D., He S., Hu H., Pinter R.Y., "Sorting by length-weighted reversals: dealing with signs and circularity", in: Sahinalp S.C., Muthukrishnan S., Dogrusöz U. (Eds.), *Proceedings of the 15th Annual Symposium on Combinatorial Pattern Matching, CPM2004*, in: *Lecture Notes in Computer Science*, vol. 3109, Springer-Verlag, Berlin/New York, 2004, pp. 32–46.

[160] Tannier E., Sagot M.-F., "Sorting by reversals in subquadratic time", in: Sahinalp S.C., Muthukrishnan S., Dogrusöz U. (Eds.), *Proceedings of the 15th Annual Symposium on Combinatorial Pattern Matching, CPM2004*, in: *Lecture Notes in Computer Science*, vol. 3109, Springer-Verlag, Berlin/New York, 2004, pp. 1–13.

[161] Tesler G., "Efficient algorithms for multichromosomal genome rearrangements", *J. Comput. Syst. Sci.* **65** (2002) 587–609.

[162] Tesler G., "GRIMM: genome rearrangements web server", *Bioinformatics* **18** (2002) 492–493.

[163] Tran N., "An easy case of sorting by reversals", *J. Comput. Biol.* **5** (1998) 741–746.

[164] Vazirani V.V., *Approximation Algorithms*, Springer-Verlag, Berlin/New York, 2001.

[165] Venter J.C., et al., "The sequence of the human genome", *Science* **291** (2001) 1304–1351.

[166] Vergara J.P.C., "Sorting by bounded permutations", PhD thesis, Virginia Polytechnic Institute and State University, 1997.

[167] Walter M.E.T., Curado L.R.A.F., Oliveira A.G., "Working on the problem of sorting by transpositions on genome rearrangements", in: Baeza-Yates R.A., Chavez E., Crochemore M. (Eds.), *Proceedings of the 14th Annual Symposium on Combinatorial Pattern Matching, CPM2003*, in: *Lecture Notes in Computer Science*, vol. 2676, Springer-Verlag, Berlin/New York, 2003, pp. 372–383.

[168] Walter M.E.T., Dias Z., Meidanis J., "Reversal and transposition distance of linear chromosomes", in: *Proceedings of String Processing and Information Retrieval, SPIRE1998*, in: *Lecture Notes in Computer Science*, IEEE Comput. Soc., Los Alamitos, CA, 1998, pp. 96–102.

[169] Walter M.E.T., Sobrinho M.C., Oliveira E.T.G., Soares L.S., Oliveira A.G., Martins T.E.S., Fonseca T.M., "Improving the algorithm of Bafna and Pevzner for the problem of sorting by transpositions: a practical approach", *J. Discrete Algorithms* **3** (2005) 342–361.

[170] Wang L., Zhu D., Liu X., Ma S., "An $O(n^2)$ algorithm for signed translocation problem", in: Chen Y.-P.P., Wong L. (Eds.), *Proceedings of 3rd Asia-Pacific Bioinformatics Conference, APBC2005*, Imperial College Press, London, 2005, pp. 349–358.

[171] Waterman M.S., *Introduction to Computational Biology: Maps, Sequences and Genomes*, Chapman & Hall, London/New York, 1995.

[172] Waterston R.H., et al., "Initial sequencing and comparative analysis of the mouse genome", *Nature* **420** (2002) 520–562.

[173] Watson J.D., Crick F.H.C., "Molecular structure of nucleic acids: a structure for deoxyribose nucleic acid", *Nature* **171** (1953) 737–738.

[174] Watterson G.A., Ewens W.J., Hall T.E., Morgan A., "The chromosome inversion problem", *J. Theor. Biol.* **99** (1982) 1–7.

[175] Weaver R.F., *Molecular Biology*, second ed., McGraw–Hill, New York, 2001.

[176] Wheeler D.L., et al., "Database resources of the National Center for Biotechnology Information", *Nucleic Acids Res.* **33** (2006) D173–D180.

[177] Wu S., Gu X., "Algorithms for multiple genome rearrangement by signed reversals", in: *Pacific Symposium on Biocomputing, PSB2003*, 2003, pp. 363–374.

[178] Yancopoulos S., Attie O., Friedberg R., "Efficient sorting of genomic permutations by translocation, inversion & block interchange", *Bioinformatics* **21** (2005) 3340–3346.

[179] Yogeeswaran K., Frary A., York T.L., Amenta A., Lesser A.H., Nasrallah J.B., Tanksley S.D., Nasrallah M.E., "Comparative genome analyses of *Arabidopsis* spp.: Inferring chromosomal rearrangement events in the evolutionary history of *A. thaliana*", *Genome Res.* **15** (2005) 505–515.

[180] Zhang J., Peterson T., "Transposition of reversed Ac element ends generates chromosome rearrangements in maize", *Genetics* **167** (2004) 1929–1937.

[181] Zhu D.M., Ma S.H., "Improved polynomial-time algorithm for computing translocation distance between genomes", *Chinese J. Comput.* **25** (2002) 189–196 (in Chinese).

[182] Zhua D., Wang L., "On the complexity of unsigned translocation distance", *Theoret. Comput. Sci.* **352** (2006) 322–328.

# Models and Methods in Comparative Genomics

GUILLAUME BOURQUE

*Genome Institute of Singapore*
*60 Biopolis Street*
*#02-01 Genome*
*Singapore 138672*
*bourque@gis.a-star.edu.sg*

LOUXIN ZHANG

*Department of Mathematics*
*National University of Singapore*
*2 Science Drive 2*
*Singapore 117543*
*matzlx@nus.edu.sg*

**Abstract**

Comparative genomics is the analysis and comparison of genomes from different species. In recent years, in conjunction with the growing number of available sequenced genomes, this field has undergone a rapid expansion. In the current survey, we review models and methods associated with four important research topics in this area that have interesting computational and statistical components: genome rearrangements, gene duplication, phylogenetic networks and positional gene clustering. The survey aims at balancing between presenting classical results and promising new developments.



ADVANCES IN COMPUTERS, VOL. 68


ISSN: 0065-2458/DOI: 10.1016/S0065-2458(06)68002-9

## 1. Introduction

Advances in sequencing and comparative mapping have enable a new period in biology referred to as the *Genomics Era*. The tremendous efforts invested into this domain have provided the community with the complete sequence of whole genomes for a wide range of organisms ranging from atypical bacteria living in harsh conditions to large eukaryotic genomes such as Human [94] and Mouse [159].

Although the availability of these genomic sequences has facilitated great leaps in our understanding of many biological processes, they have also highlighted the complexity of fully deciphering genomes. Even questions as simple as determining the exact number of genes in the human genome have turned out to be quite difficult [146]. In this context, it is of no surprise that more elaborate problems, such as fully understanding how genes are being regulated (e.g. which genes are expressed, when are they expressed, etc.), have remain very challenging. This last question in particular is important because a lot of the animal diversity is thought to be harbored in gene regulation [99]. Other similarly exciting questions will hopefully incite the development of computational and statistical tools that will help further our comprehension of the forces that shape modern genomes.

Decoding the sequenced genomes is analogous to decoding a hard disk with no information about the file structure or even the type of information that is encoded. The difference is that we expect the challenge of decoding the genome to be greater given the complexity of the final product. In this setting, comparative genomics comes in as a powerful tool to contrast and recognize some of the features that play a crucial role in the different genomes. By the identification of similarities and differences, the hope is that we will gain a first handle on some of these important problems [124]; this is the field of Comparative Genomics.

The chapter focuses on mathematical and algorithmic aspects of four general research topics in comparative genomics. In Section 2, we first introduce models and methods used in the analysis of genome rearrangements. In this section we present some of the similarity measures use to study gene order conservation across genomes. This section also includes some of the details of the Hannenhalli–Pevzner algorithm for computing the inversion distance between two genomes, probably one of the strongest algorithmic result in computational molecular biology. We also present two recently introduced alternative model for genome evolution: the block-interchange and the double-cut-and-join operation. Finally, we summarize the recent progress in genome rearrangement with gene family and with partial order genomes. In Section 3, we summarize the mathematical models for dating both large scale genomic duplications and tandem duplications. In Section 4, we presents three different network models for studying horizontal gene transfer, recombination and other reticulations. We also summarize different methods for reconstructing these networks from gene trees and sequences. In Section 5, we point out two basic statistical models for analytically testing positional gene clusters.

## 2. Genome Rearrangements

The study of genome rearrangements is the analysis of mutations affecting the global architecture of genomes as oppose to local mutations affecting individual regions. This type of analysis dates back to the early 1920s with pioneering studies on the evolution of the *Drosophila* genome (e.g. [114]). To study genome rearrangements, it is in general sufficient to view genomes as permutations on a set of markers common to the group of genomes. Different types of marker can be used for this purpose but the key is that these markers must be unambiguously identifiable across genomes. In most of the current section (except Section 2.4), we restrict the comparison to a common set of markers such that each marker is found exactly once in each genome. See also Section 3 for other results where this restriction is alleviated to allow unequal marker content.

An obvious set of markers than can be use for this purpose is the set of genes observed in the group of genomes. Based on sequence similarity, a set of homologous genes can be identified across genomes and by labeling these genes from 1 to $n$, one can obtain permutations that encapsulate the relative order of these markers in the genomes. If available, the relative orientation can also be associated to the set of

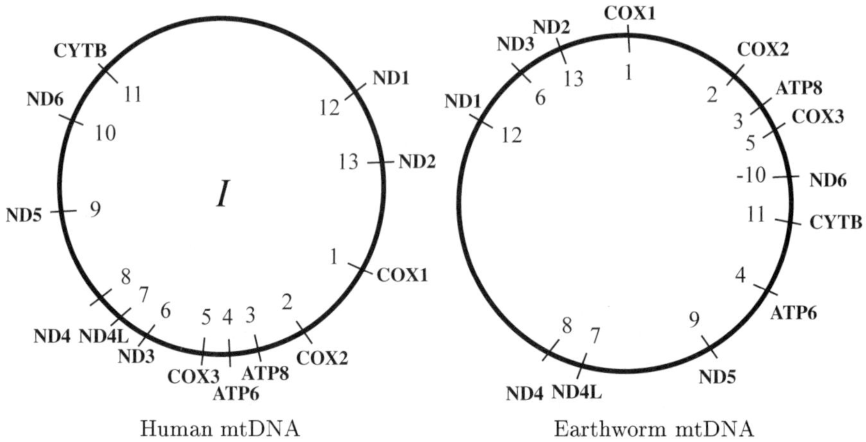


FIG. 1. Coding genes on the Human and on the Earthworm mitochondria circular genomes (mtDNA). The genes are the same but their order differs. We encapsulate these differences with permutations by labeling the genes from 1 to $n = 13$ using Human as a reference, starting with COX1 and going clockwise until ND2. This leads to the two permutations displayed inside the circular genomes ($I$ for Human and $\pi$ for Earthworm). The only gene transcribed on the reverse strand in these two genomes is ND6 in Human but because this genome is used as the reference permutation, the "-" is associated to ND6 only in Earthworm.

markers (e.g. for genes-based markers, the direction of transcription can be used) and leads to *signed permutations*. Otherwise *unsigned permutations* will be used. For an example with two small mitochondria DNA (mtDNA) genomes and their signed permutations see Fig. 1. By convention, since the labeling is arbitrary, we set one of the permutation to be the identity $I$. For instance, with two genomes, we get:

$$I = 1\,2\,3\,\ldots\,n, \qquad \pi = \pi_1\,\pi_2\,\pi_3\,\ldots\,\pi_n.$$

Although genes represent a natural choice of markers, we note that in many cases it is also interesting to use other types of markers (e.g. strictly based on sequence similarity), especially in large eukaryotic genomes where genes cover only a small fraction of the genomes (see [25,116]). In the remainder of this chapter we will use the terms gene and marker interchangeably.

We will first review different measures that can be used to characterize the extent of differences between two genomes. Next, we will show that alternative models of genome rearrangements lead to different challenges when computing edit distances. Finally, we will present some of the extensions of these pairwise approaches to multiple genomes.

## 2.1 Similarity Measures Between Two Genomes

### 2.1.1 Breakpoint Distance

The simplest unit for the comparison of gene orders is the adjacency, i.e. a pair of adjacent markers common to both genomes. To obtain a distance measure, we actually use breakpoints which are pairs of markers adjacent in one genome but not the other. This easily calculated measure was first explicitly presented in the context of genome rearrangements by Watterson et al. 1982 [162]. Formally, we get:

**Definition 1.** The *breakpoint distance*, $b(\pi)$, is the number of pairs $(\pi_i, \pi_{i+1})$, $0 \leqslant i \leqslant n$ such that $(\pi_{i+1} - \pi_i) \neq 1$ where $\pi_0 = 0$ and $\pi_{n+1} = n + 1$.

In the example shown in Fig. 1, there are 9 such pairs:

$$(3, 5), (5, -10), (-10, 11), (11, 4), (4, 9), (9, 7), (8, 12), (12, 6), (6, 13),$$

and so $b(\pi) = 9$. See also Fig. 2.

### 2.1.2 Common and Conserved Intervals

Recently, two new criteria were introduced as an extension of the breakpoint distance to measure the similarity between sets of genomes: common intervals [156, 77] and conserved intervals [10]. We introduce these definitions in the context of two general permutations of size $n$, $\pi$ and $\gamma$. When one of these permutation is the identity we have $\gamma = I$ as above.

**Definition 2.** A *common interval* is a set of two or more integers that is an interval in both $\pi$ and $\gamma$.

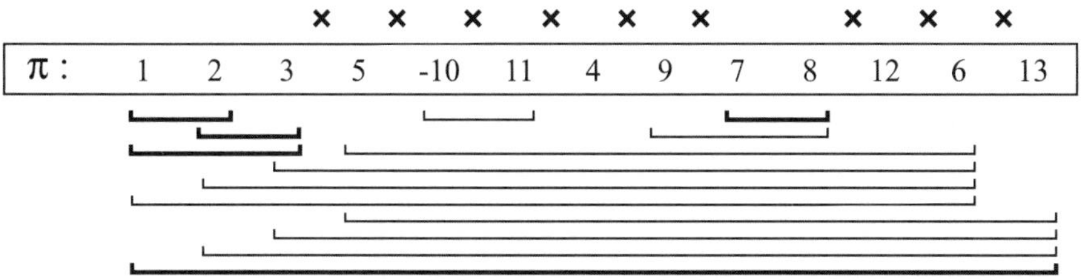


FIG. 2. Breakpoints, common and conserved intervals for $\pi$, the permutation associated with Earthworm (see Fig. 1). The 9 breakpoints are indicated using crosses above the permutation. The 14 common intervals are shown below the permutation. The 5 conserved intervals correspond to a subset of the common intervals and are shown in black.

Uno and Yagiura [156] presented three algorithms for finding all common intervals between two permutations $\pi$ and $\gamma$: two simple $O(n^2)$ time algorithms and one more complex $O(n+K)$ time algorithm where $K \leqslant \binom{n}{2}$ is the number of common intervals between $\pi$ and $\gamma$. Heber and Stoye [77] extended on this result by developing an algorithm to find the common intervals in a family of $m$ permutations in optimal $O(nm + K)$ time where $K$ is the number of common intervals in the $m$ permutations defined similarly to Definition 2.

To continue with the example of the two mtDNA shown in Fig. 1, we see that these two permutations harbor 14 common intervals displayed only in $\pi$ in Fig. 2. For two permutations of size $n$, the maximum number of common intervals is $\binom{n}{2}$ and so, in this case, the maximum would have been $\binom{13}{2} = 78$ common intervals.

We now define a conserved interval between two arbitrary permutations as introduced by Bergeron and Stoye [10].

**Definition 3.** A *conserved interval* $[a, b]$ is an interval such that $a$ precedes $b$, or $-b$ precedes $-a$ in both $\pi$ and $\gamma$, and the set of elements, without signs, between $a$ and $b$ is the same in both $\pi$ and $\gamma$.

Conserved intervals are common intervals with additional constraints on their endpoints. In Fig. 2 we see that 5 of the 14 common intervals of the two mtDNA also qualify as conserved intervals.

Although the definition of conserved intervals may seem unnatural at first, it is intimately connected to the concept of *subpermutations* [73] in the Hannenhalli–Pevzner theory (see Section 2.2). Moreover, it was shown that it can be used to efficiently sort permutations by reversals [11].

## 2.2 Edit Distance Between Two Genomes

In the early 90s, a series of paper revived the interest in the problem of computing the edit distance between a pair of genomes under different edit operations [137, 89,14]. This problem had been posed by Watterson et al. [162] and even earlier in the genetics literature (e.g. [150]). Examples of edit operations that are frequently considered are displayed in Table I. These operations can be considered separately or in different combinations and lead to different models of evolution of gene order. We now review some of the key results in this area and also present recent advances.

### 2.2.1 Reversal Distance

The reversal-only, or inversion-only, edit distance is probably the most studied edit distance in the context of gene order. Initially, we will focus on the problem of computing the reversal distance between two signed permutations.

TABLE I
EXAMPLES OF CHROMOSOMAL MUTATIONS, OR EDIT OPERATIONS, AFFECTING GENE ORDER

| Mutation type | Before | | After |
|---|---|---|---|
| Reversal | 1 2 3 4 5 6 7 8 9 10 | ⇒ | 1 2 3 4 −7 −6 −5 4 8 9 10 |
| Translocation | 1 2 3 4 5 6<br>7 8 9 10 | ⇒ | 7 8 5 6<br>1 2 3 4 9 10 |
| Fusion | 1 2 3 4 5 6<br>7 8 9 10 | ⇒ | 1 2 3 4 5 6 7 8 9 10 |
| Fission | 1 2 3 4 5 6 7 8 9 10 | ⇒ | 1 2 3 4 5 6<br>7 8 9 10 |
| Transposition | 1 2 3 4 5 _ 6 7 8 9 10 | ⇒ | 1 4 5 2 3 6 7 8 9 10 |
| Block interchange | 1 2 3 4 5 6 7 8 9 10 | ⇒ | 1 6 7 8 4 5 2 3 9 10 |

**Definition 4.** Given a permutation $\pi$, a *reversal* $\rho_{i,j}$, $1 \leqslant i, j \leqslant n$, applied to $\pi$ produces:

$$\rho_{i,j}(\pi) = \pi_1 \ \ldots \ \pi_{i-1} \ -\pi_j \ \ldots \ -\pi_i \ \pi_{j+1} \ \ldots \ \pi_n$$

In this context, the *reversal distance*, $d_{\text{rev}}(\pi)$, is defined as the minimum number of reversals required to convert $\pi$ into the identity permutation $I$. Since every reversal can reduce by at most two the number of breakpoints, a trivial first result is the following:

**Lemma 1.** [87]

$$d_{\text{rev}}(\pi) \geqslant \frac{b(\pi)}{2}.$$

To obtain an exact formula to compute the reversal distance, we now present a summary of the terminology frequently referred to as the *Hannenhalli–Pevzner theory* [14,74]. First, we convert $\pi$, a signed permutation, into $\pi'$, an unsigned permutation, by mimicking every directed element $i$ by two undirected elements $i^t$ and $i^h$ representing the tail and the head of $i$. Since $\pi$ is a permutation of size $n$, $\pi'$ will be a permutation of size $2n$. The permutation $\pi'$ is then extended by adding $\pi'_0 = 0$ and $\pi'_{2n+1} = n + 1$. Next, we construct the breakpoint graph associated with $\pi$.

**Definition 5.** The *breakpoint graph* of $\pi$, $G(\pi)$, is an edge-colored graph with $2n+2$ vertices. Black edges are added between vertices $\pi'_{2i}$ and $\pi'_{2i+1}$ for $0 \leqslant i \leqslant n$. Grey edges are added between $i^h$ and $(i + 1)^t$ for $0 < i < n$, between 0 and $1^t$, and between $n^h$ and $n + 1$.

In the breakpoint graph, black edges correspond to the actual state of the permutation while grey edges correspond to the sorted permutation we seek. See Fig. 3 for an example.

Bafna and Pevzner [14], and later Hannenhalli and Pevzner [74], showed that $G(\pi)$ contains all the necessary information for efficiently sorting the permutation $\pi$. The first step is to look at the maximal cycle decomposition of the breakpoint graph. Finding the maximal cycle decomposition of a graph in general can be a very difficult problem but, fortunately, because of the way the breakpoint graph was constructed for a signed permutation, each vertex has degree two and so the problem is trivial. Suppose $c(\pi)$ is the maximum number of edge-disjoint alternating cycles in $G(\pi)$. The cycles are *alternating* because, in the breakpoint graph of a signed permutation, each pair of consecutive edges always has different colors. We then get:

**Lemma 2.** [14,89]

$$d_{\text{rev}}(\pi) \geqslant n + 1 - c(\pi).$$

An edge in $G(\pi)$ is said to be *oriented* if it spans an odd number of vertices (when the vertices of $G(\pi)$ are arranged in the canonical order $\pi'_0, \ldots, \pi'_{2n+1}$). A cycle is said to be *oriented* if it contains at least one oriented gray edge. Cycles which are not oriented are said to be *unoriented* unless they are of size 2 in which case they are said to be *trivial*. The term oriented comes from the fact that if we traverse an oriented cycle we will traverse at least one black edge from left to right and one black edge from right to left. In the breakpoint graph shown in Fig. 3(I), there are only two non-trivial cycles: one where the gray edges are displayed using solid lines and one where the gray edges are displayed using dashed lines. The cycle with solid lines is unoriented since it does not contain an oriented edge but the cycle with dashed lines is oriented because it contains an oriented edge (e.g. $(10^h, 11^t)$).

For each grey edge in $G(\pi)$ we will now create a vertex $v_e$ in the *overlap graph*, $\mathrm{O}(G(\pi))$. Whenever two grey edges $e$ and $e'$ overlap or cross in the canonical representation of $G(\pi)$, we will connect the corresponding vertices $v_e$ and $v_{e'}$. A *component* will mean a connected component in $\mathrm{O}(G(\pi))$. A component will be *oriented* if it contains a vertex $v_e$ for which the corresponding grey edge $e$ is oriented. As for cycles, a component which consists of a single vertex (grey edge) will be said to be *trivial*. In Fig. 3(I), there are 5 trivial components and one larger oriented component since at least one of its grey edge is oriented. The challenge in sorting permutations comes from unoriented components.

Unoriented components can be classified into two categories: hurdles and protected nonhurdle. A *protected nonhurdle* is an unoriented component that separates other unoriented components in $G(\pi)$ when vertices in $G(\pi)$ are placed in canonical order. A *hurdle* is any unoriented component which is not a protected nonhurdle.

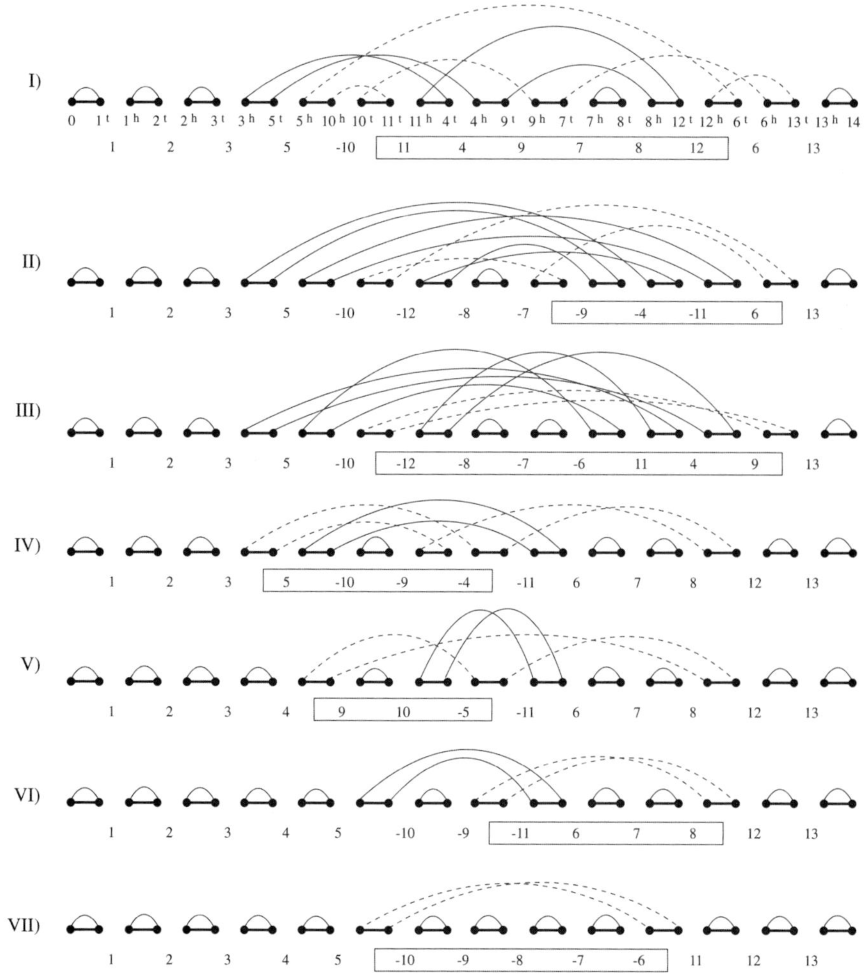


FIG. 3. (I) Breakpoint graph associated with the two permutations from Fig. 1. Black edges are shown using think lines. All other lines (both solid and dashed) correspond to grey edges. (I–VII) A sequence of sorting reversals. The fragment of the permutation to be inverted is shown using a box. Dashed lines are used to highlight the cycle that will be affected by the reversal. Black edges represent the "current" state of the permutation to be sorted while grey edges represent the "desired" state corresponding to a sorted permutation. Note that in the final stage (not shown) the black and grey edges are perfectly matched.

A hurdle is a *superhurdle* if deleting it would transform a protected nonhurdle into a hurdle, otherwise it is said to be a *simple hurdle*. Finally, $\pi$ is said to be a *fortress* if there exists an odd number of hurdles and all are superhurdles in $O(G(\pi))$ [143]. We then get the main result of the HP theory:

**Theorem 1.** [72]

$$d_{\text{rev}}(\pi) = n + 1 - c(\pi) + h(\pi) + f(\pi),$$

*where $h(\pi)$ is the number of hurdles in $\pi$ and $f(\pi)$ is 1 if $\pi$ is a fortress and 0 otherwise.*

For instance, using Fig. 3(I), we see that the reversal distance between Human mtDNA and Earthworm mtDNA is $d_{\text{rev}}(\pi) = 13 + 1 - 7 + 0 + 0 = 7$. In [72], Hannenhalli and Pevzner also showed how to recover an optimal sequence of sorting reversals using the breakpoint graph in $O(n^4)$ (see Fig. 3(II–VII) for an example).

Since these initial results, there has been a number of improvement on the performance of these algorithms. Berman and Hannenhalli [17] improved the bound for the sorting problem to $O(n^2\alpha(n))$ (where $\alpha$ is the inverse of Ackermann's function) and Kaplan et al. [85] reduced it further to $O(n^2)$. Later, Bader et al. [4] showed that without recovering an actual optimal sequence of steps, the reversal distance can be computed in linear time ($O(n)$). Finally, Bergeron and Stoye [10] have described an alternative sorting algorithm that takes $O(n^2)$ but bypass much of the complexity of the earlier algorithms.

So far, the discussion was centered around the problem of sorting two signed permutations. In this context, it is interesting to highlight the following result by Caprara [31].

**Theorem 2.** [31] *The problem of sorting an unsigned permutation by the minimum number of reversals is NP-hard.*

### 2.2.2 Transposition Distance

A transposition is an edit operation, in which a segment is cut out of the permutation, and pasted in a different location (for an example, see Table I).

**Definition 6.** Given a permutation $\pi$, a *transposition* is an operation $\theta_{i,j,k}$, $1 \leqslant i, j \leqslant n$, $k < i$ or $k > j$, that once applied to $\pi$ produces:

$$\theta_{i,j,k}(\pi) = \pi_1 \ \ldots \ \pi_{i-1} \ \pi_{j+1} \ \ldots \pi_{k-1} \ \pi_i \ \ldots \ \pi_j \ \pi_{k+1} \ \pi_n$$

The problem of sorting by transposition was first studied by Bafna and Pevzner [13] who presented a 1.5 approximation algorithm which runs in $O(n^2)$ time. Using an alternative data structure, Walter et al. [158] developed a 2.25 approximation algorithm for the same problem. More recently, Elias and Hartman [50] improved on these bounds by presenting a 1.375 approximation algorithm that required an elaborate computer assisted proof. The complexity of sorting by transpositions remains an open problem.

### 2.2.3 Block Interchange Distance

The notion of a block interchange operation in the context of genome rearrangements was introduced by Christie [38]. In a block-interchange, two non-intersecting substrings of any length are swapped in the permutation. This type of event can be viewed as a generalized transposition.

**Definition 7.** Given a permutation $\pi$, a *block-interchange* is an operation $\beta_{i,j,k,l}$, where $1 \leqslant i < j \leqslant k < l \leqslant n$, that once applied to $\pi$ produces:

$$\beta_{i,j,k,l}(\pi) = \pi_1 \ \ldots \ \pi_{i-1} \, \pi_k \ \ldots \ \pi_l \, \pi_{j+1} \ \ldots \pi_{k-1} \, \pi_i \ \ldots \ \pi_j \, \pi_{l+1} \, \pi_n$$

Note that the special case of $j = k$ leads to an alternative and equivalent definition of a transposition.

Christie [38] showed that by considering the block interchange operation, one can efficiently sort unsigned permutations in $O(n^2)$. This algorithm can also serve as a 2-approximation algorithm for the problem of sorting by transpositions.

**Theorem 3.** [38] *The block-interchange distance for an unsigned permutation, $d_{\mathrm{BI}}(\pi)$, is*

$$d_{\mathrm{BI}}(\pi) = \frac{1}{2}\big[(n+1) - c(\pi)\big],$$

*where $c(\pi)$ is the number of alternating cycles in the cycle graph of $\pi$ (note here that the cycle graph is defined slightly differently since the permutations are unsigned, see* [38]).

Recently, the analysis of block-interchanges was revisited by Lin et al. [101]. By focusing on circular chromosomes (such as the mtDNA in Fig. 1), that are also unsigned, and making use of permutations groups in algebra, they designed an algorithm for sorting by block-interchanges with time-complexity $O(\delta n)$, where $\delta$ is the minimum number of block-interchanges required for the transformation and can

TABLE II
SORTING USING BLOC-INTERCHANGES THE TWO PERMUTATIONS, VIEWED AS UNSIGNED, ASSOCIATED WITH THE MTDNA DISPLAYED IN FIG. 1

| | | | | | | | | | | | | | |
|---|---|---|---|---|---|---|---|---|---|---|---|---|---|
| Earthworm | 1 | 2 | 3 | 5 | 10 | 11 | 4 | 9 | 7 | 8 | 12 | 6 | 13 |
| $\beta_{4,6,8,10}$ | 1 | 2 | 3 | 5 | 10 | 11 | 4 | 9 | 7 | 8 | 12 | 6 | 13 |
| $\beta_{4,4,7,12}$ | 1 | 2 | 3 | 9 | 7 | 8 | 4 | 5 | 10 | 11 | 12 | 6 | 13 |
| $\beta_{6,8,9,12}$ | 1 | 2 | 3 | 4 | 5 | 10 | 11 | 12 | 6 | 7 | 8 | 9 | 13 |
| Human | 1 | 2 | 3 | 4 | 5 | 6 | 7 | 8 | 9 | 10 | 11 | 12 | 13 |

The scenario requires only 3 steps.

be calculated in $O(n)$ time in advance. The approach was also implemented in a tool called `ROBIN` [102].

Taking the permutations displayed in Fig. 1 and treating them as unsigned, we can compute an optimal scenario with 3 block-interchange operations, see Table II.

### 2.2.4 Reversal, Translocation, Fusion and Fission Distance

The results presented thus far have been centered around unichromosomal genomes, i.e. genomes that have a single chromosome. Table I shows examples of events that specifically affect genomes with multiple chromosomes, mainly: translocations, fusions and fissions.

Kececioglu and Ravi [88] began the investigation of translocation distances by giving a 2-approximation algorithm for multichromosomal genomes when the orientation of the genes are unknown ("unsigned permutation"). We also use the terminology permutation when dealing with multichromosomal genomes because, by using special markers to delimitate chromosome boundaries, it is still possible to represent such genomes using permutations. For signed permutation, Hannenhalli and Pevzner [73] derived an equation related to Theorem 1 to compute the rearrangement distance between two multichromosomal genomes when permissible operations are: reversals, translocations, fusions and fissions. We refer the reader to Pevzner [133] and Tesler [154] for the details of the calculation but we will briefly present how the formula can be obtained.

The main idea to compute the rearrangement distance between two multichromosomal genomes $\Pi$ and $\Gamma$ is to concatenate their chromosomes into two permutations $\pi$ and $\gamma$. The purpose of these concatenated genomes is that every rearrangement in a multichromosomal genome $\Pi$ can be mimicked by a reversal in a permutation $\pi$. In an *optimal* concatenate, sorting $\pi$ with respect to $\gamma$ actually corresponds to sorting $\Pi$ with respect to $\Gamma$. Tesler [154] also showed that when such an optimal concatenate does not exist, a *near-optimal* concatenate exists such that sorting this concatenate mimics sorting the multichromosomal genomes and uses a single extra reversal which corresponds to a reordering of the chromosomes. The algorithm was implemented into a program called GRIMM [155]. Ozery-Flato and Shamir [127] identified a case where the algorithm does not apply but also suggested a correction.

### 2.2.5 Double-Cut-and-Join Distance

Recently, in an attempt to reconcile the various edit distances, Yancopoulos et al. [165] presented a universal edit operation, the *double-cut-and-join* (DCJ), that could seamlessly model inversions, transpositions, translocations, fusions and fissions. The last two had already been identified as special cases of translocations [73]. This elementary operation is a local operation on four markers initially forming two adjacent pairs. It consists of cutting two adjacencies in the first genome and rejoining the resulting four unconnected markers to form two new pairs [165].

Under this model, any rejoining is *proper* as long as $b(\pi) - c(\pi)$ is reduced by 1. The major difference with the HP-theory presented above is that some of the proper ways of reconnecting these two pairs cannot be associated with a reversal (or a reversal mimicking a translocation). Actually, some of these operations lead to the creation of a circular intermediate (CI). Reabsorbing the CI actually correspond to doing a block-interchange (see [165]) but since it required two steps, it will be associated with a weight of two in the final edit scenario.

**Theorem 4.** [165] *The double-cut-and-join distance for a permutation $\pi$, $d_{\mathrm{DCJ}}(\pi)$, is*

$$d_{\mathrm{DCJ}}(\pi) = b(\pi) - c(\pi).$$

## 2.3 Genome Rearrangements with Multiple Genomes

Extending the two way measures and edit distance algorithms to multiple genomes has proven to be challenging. Formally, the problem is the following:

**Definition 8.** Given a set of $m$ genomes, the *Multiple Genome Rearrangement problem* is to find an unrooted tree $T$, where the $m$ genomes are leaf nodes, and assign internal ancestral nodes such that $D(T)$ is minimized where:

$$D(T) = \sum_{(\pi,\gamma)\in T} d(\pi, \gamma),$$

and $d(\pi, \gamma)$ can be any distance measure discussed in Sections 2.1, 2.2.

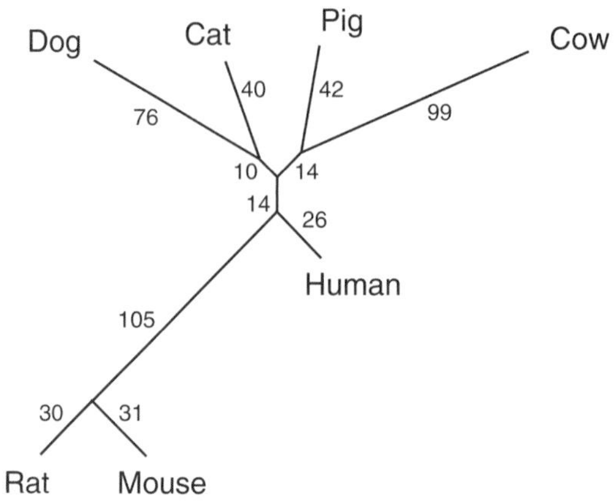


FIG. 4. Unrooted binary tree showing phylogenetic relationships between 7 mammalian genomes recovered by MGR. The number on each edge indicates the minimum number of rearrangements (reversals, translocations, fusions, fissions) required to convert between the two genomes connected by the edge. Extracted from Murphy et al. [116].

The problem is also known as the problem of reconstructing the most parsimonious phylogenetic tree under the metric $d$ [138] (see Fig. 4 for an example).

The simplest extension, the case with $m = 3$ signed permutations, also called the *Median problem*, was shown to be NP-hard [32] for both the breakpoint distance ($d = b$) and the reversal distance ($d = d_{\text{rev}}$). Nonetheless, we now present a few heuristic that have been developed for this problem under various distance metrics.

### 2.3.1 Breakpoint Phylogenies

Sankoff and Blanchette [139] studied the median problem for the breakpoint distance; they showed how the problem could be reduced to an instance of the Traveling Salesman Problem (TSP), a problem for which reasonably efficient algorithms are available. Using this result, Blanchette et al. [19] developed `BPAnalysis`, a method to recover the most parsimonious scenario for $m$ genomes under the breakpoint distance. The approach was to look for an optimal assignment of internal nodes for a given topology by solving a series of median problem (this is also known as the small parsimony problem). The next step in the approach was to scan the space of all possible tree topologies to the find the best tree (large parsimony problem). One of the downside of this approach is that the tree space quickly becomes prohibitive. This limitation was partially addressed by Moret et al. [112] who developed

GRAPPA which, by computing tight bounds, was able to efficiently prune the tree space.

### 2.3.2 Conservation Phylogenies

The first method that use the concept of conserved intervals as the criterion for the phylogenetic reconstruction problem was presented by Bergeron et al. [12]. Even though the problem was restricted to finding an optimal assignment of internal nodes on a fixed phylogeny (small parsimony problem), this is an auspicious area of research.

### 2.3.3 Rearrangement Phylogenies

Siepel and Moret [113] also studied the median problem but under a different metric: the reversal distance. They presented a branch-and-bound algorithm to prune the search space using simple geometric properties of the problem. Concurrently, Bourque and Pevzner [24] implemented a method called MGR for both the median and the full phylogeny by making use of properties of additive or nearly additive trees. This approach, combined with GRIMM [155] was shown to be applicable to both unichromosomal genomes for the reversal distance [24] and for multichromosomal genomes for a rearrangement distance that combines reversals, translocations, fusions and fissions [24,25]. In a recent analysis [116], this algorithm was applied to 7 mammalian genomes (Human, Mouse, Rat, Cat, Dog, Pig, Cow) and for which the recovered unrooted tree is shown in Fig. 4 (see [116] for full rearrangement scenario including recovered ancestral genomes).

## 2.4 Genome Rearrangement with Gene Families

As we have seen in the last several sections, each genome is viewed as a permutation in which each gene has exactly one copy in the traditional study of genome rearrangement. While this may be appropriate for small viruses and mitochondria genomes, it may not realistic when applied to eukaryotic genomes where paralogous genes often exist. Hence, a more generalized version of the genome rearrangement problem was proposed by Sankoff [140] where multiple copies of the same gene can now be found in the same genome. His idea is to delete all but one member of a gene family in each genome, so as to minimize the total breakpoint (or other) distance between the reduced genomes. In this approach, the retained copies are called exemplars. One of the applications of the exemplar problem is in orthologous gene assignment [33,151].

Even though it is almost trivial to calculate the breakpoint distance between two genomes with single-gene families, the exemplar problem for breakpoint distance is not only NP-hard [29], but also unlikely to have polynomial-time constant-ratio approximation algorithm unless NP = P [122,34]. Nevertheless, by observing the monotonicity of the exemplar problem, Sankoff proposed a branch-and-bound method to tackle this problem [140]. His idea is to work on each gene family separately, choosing the pair of exemplars that least increases the distance when inserted into the partial exemplar genomes already constructed.

Recently, Nguyen, Tay and Zhang [123] proposed a divide-and-conquer approach to calculating the exemplar breakpoint distance. Their idea is to partition the gene families into disjoint subsets such that two gene families in different subsets are 'independent', then to find the pair of exemplars of gene families in each independent subset at a time, and finally to merge all the exemplars together to obtain good exemplars of the given genomes. Tests with both simulated and real datasets show that the combination of the divide-and-conquer and branch-and-bound approaches is much more efficient than the branch-and-bound approach.

Finally, an alternative way to look at the exemplar problem is to identify the gene copies that maximize the conserved or common intervals (see Section 2.1). Using this approach, Bourque et al. [26] showed that, under certain conditions, it is possible to improve on a method that would only utilize breakpoints.

## 2.5 Genome Rearrangement with Partially Ordered Genomes

Another restriction in the traditional study of genome rearrangement is the total order of genes in a genome inherent in the representation of the genome as a permutation. In practice, the total order of genes can only be determined after the sequenced genomes are completely annotated. Many genomes are currently only sequenced at a level that prevents a whole and accurate assembly and this problem will probably not be fixed in the near future because of the prohibitive sequencing costs. When the complete sequence of a genome is not available, one can rely on gene mapping data as input for rearrangement studies but even for these datasets, due to the relatively low resolution, several genes are often mapped to the same chromosomal position.

To deal with these ambiguities but also to work in general context of partial gene orders, it is possible to represent a chromosome, or genome, as directed acyclic graph (DAG) [168,169]. The genome rearrangement problem with partially ordered genomes can be restated as the problem of inferring a sequence of mutational operations which transform a linearization of the DAG for one genome to a linearization of the DAG for the other genome that minimizes the number of operations required [168,169,141]. Obviously, such a general rearrangement problem is computationally challenging. Therefore, the development of efficient heuristic algorithms that could tackle some of the real datasets in the near future are highly desired.

# 3. Gene Duplication and Multigene Families

In the human and other higher organisms, there are numerous gene families. The number of genes in each gene family ranges from several to hundreds. Some families contain genes with similar functions; others contain genes with very diverse functions. The large copy number of members in some gene families such as histone families is due to need for large amounts of gene product.

Gene duplication has been proposed as a major mechanism for generating multigene families, because duplicated genes provide raw genetic materials for the emergence of new functions through point mutation, natural selection and random drift [125]. Such gene duplication processes include polyploidization, tandem duplication, and retrotransposition. During polyploidization, whole genomes are duplicated. Tandem duplication is responsible for positional clustered gene families. It is probably caused by unequal crossing over during meiosis and mitosis in a germ cell lineage [144]. Although repetitive sequences derived from reverse transcription are numerous in the human genome, there are not many retrogenes.

Since 1970s, phylogenetic analysis has been used for understanding relationships of gene family members, identifying gene duplication events and for orthologous gene assignment.

## 3.1 Gene Trees and Species Trees

Bifurcating trees (called *phylogenies* or *phylogenetic trees*) have been used as models to represent the evolution of species, in which evolutionary lineages splits and evolve independently for each other, since Charles Darwin first pointed out that the simplest pattern that might lie in the heart of evolutionary history can be represented by a tree [41]. Indeed, Darwin called the evolution of species the Tree of Life.

For a set $I$ of $N$ taxa, their evolutionary history is represented by a rooted full binary tree $T$ where there are $N$ leaves each uniquely labeled by a taxon in $I$ and $N - 1$ unlabeled internal nodes. Here the term "full" means that each internal node has exactly two children. Such a tree is called a *species tree*. In a species tree, we also consider an internal node as a subset (called a *cluster*) which includes as its members its subordinate species represented by the leaves below it. Thus, the evolutionary relation "$m$ is a descendant of $n$" is expressed using set-theoretic notation as "$m \subset n$."

The model for gene evolution is a rooted full binary tree with leaves labeled by gene copies. Usually, a gene tree is constructed from a collection of genes each having several copies appearing in the studied species. For example, the gene family of hemoglobin genes in vertebrates contains $\alpha$-hemoglobin and $\beta$-hemoglobin. A gene

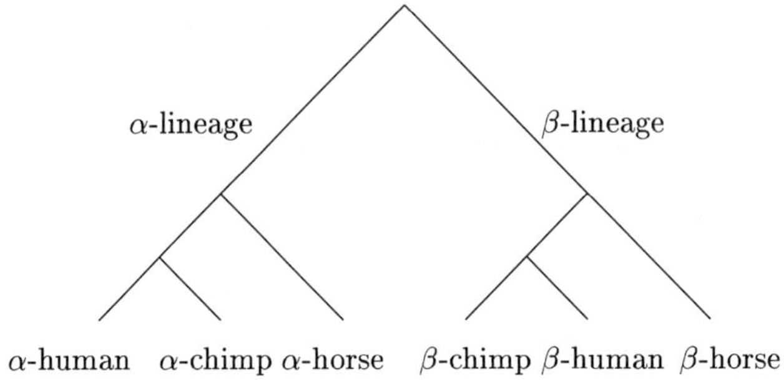


FIG. 5. A gene tree based on $\alpha$-hemoglobin and $\beta$-hemoglobin.

tree based on these two genes in human, chimpanzee and horse is shown in Fig. 5. We use the species to label the genes appearing in it. Thus, the labels in a gene tree may not be unique since there are usually multiple genes under consideration in each species. Therefore, each internal node $g$ in a gene tree corresponds to a multiset $\{x_1^{i_1}, x_2^{i_2}, \dots, x_m^{i_m}\}$, where $i_j$ is the number of its subordinate leaves labeled with $x_j$. The *cluster* of $g$ is simply the set

$$S_g = \{x_1, x_2, \dots, x_m\}.$$

Finally, we use $L(T)$ to denote the set of leaf labels in a species or gene tree $T$.

## 3.2 Gene Duplications and Losses

Detecting gene duplication and loss events is based on a node mapping from a gene tree to a species tree. Such a mapping was first considered by Goodman et al. [59] and later was popularized by Page in a series of papers [128–132]. Given a gene tree $G$ and a species tree $S$ such that $L(G) \subseteq L(S)$. For any node $g \in G$, we define $M(g)$ to be the least common ancestor (lca) of $g$ in $S$, i.e. the smallest node $s \in S$ such that $S_g \subseteq s$. Here we used term "smallest" to mean "farthest from the root." We call $M$ the *LCA mapping* from $G$ to $S$. Obviously, if $g' \subset g$, then $M(g') \subseteq M(g)$, and any leaf is mapped onto a leaf with the same label. For an internal node $g$, we use $c(g)$ (sometimes $a(g)$ and $b(g)$) to denote a child of $g$ and $G(g)$ the subtree rooted at $g$.

If $M(c(g)) = M(g)$ for some child $c(g)$ of $g$, then we say a *duplication* happens at $g$. The total number $t_{\text{dup}}(G, S)$ of duplications happening in $G$ under the LCA mapping $M$ is proposed as a measure for the similarity between $G$ and $S$ [59,128]. We call such a measure the *duplication cost*.

Let $a(g)$ and $b(g)$ denote the children of $g$. For $c(g) = a(g), b(g)$, if $M(c(g)) \neq M(g)$, we let $P$ be the path from $M(g)$ to $M(c(g))$. We say that the gene gets lost on each lineage between a species $X$ on the path $P$ to its child $c(X)$ that is not on $P$ [63]. Therefore, the *number of gene losses* $l_g$ associated to $g$ is

$$l_g = \begin{cases} 0 & \text{if } M(g) = M(a(g)) = M(b(g)); \\ d(a(g), g) + 1 & \text{if } M(a(g)) \subset M(g) \ \& \ M(g) = M(b(g)); \\ d(a(g), g) + d(b(g), g) & \text{if } M(a(g)) \subset M(g) \ \& \ M(b(g)) \subset M(g). \end{cases}$$

The *mutation cost* is defined as the sum of $t_{\text{dup}}$ and the total number of losses $t_{\text{loss}}(G, S) = \sum_{g \in G} l_g$. This measure turns out to have a nice biological interpretation [109,166,51].

Since the LCA mapping from a gene tree to a species tree can be computed in linear time [166,35,170], the gene duplication and loss events can be identified effectively.

## 3.3 Reconciled Tree

The *reconciled tree* concept gives another way to visualize and compare the relationship between gene and species trees [59]. Such a tree is constructed from a gene tree and a species tree and has two important properties. The first property is that the observed gene tree is a 'subtree' of the reconciled tree. The second property is that the clusters of the reconciled tree are all clusters of the species tree. Formally, the reconciled tree is defined as follows.

Let $T'$ and $T''$ be two rooted trees, we use $T' \vartriangle T''$ to denote the rooted tree $T$ obtained by adding a node $r$ as the root and connecting $r$ to $r(T')$ and $r(T'')$ so that $T'$ and $T''$ are two subtrees rooted at the children of $r$. Further, let $t$ be an internal node in $T'$, then, $T'|_{t \to T''}$ denotes the tree formed by replacing the subtree rooted at $t$ with $T''$. Similarly, $T'|_{t \to T_1,\, t' \to T_2}$ can be defined for disjoint nodes $t$ and $t'$.

For a gene tree $G$ rooted at $g$ and a species tree $S$ rooted at $s$ such that $L(G) \subseteq L(S)$, let $M$ be the LCA mapping from $G$ to $S$ and let $s' = M(a(g))$ and $s'' = M(b(g))$. The *reconciled tree* $R = R(G, S)$ of $G$ with respect to $S$ is defined as:

$$R = \begin{cases} R(G(a(g)), S) \vartriangle R(G(b(g)), S) & \text{if } s' = s'' = s, \\ S|_{s' \to R(G(a(g)),\, S(s'))} \vartriangle R(G(b(g)), S) & \text{if } s' \subseteq a(s),\ s'' = s, \\ S|_{s' \to R(G(a(g)),\, S(s')),\ s'' \to R(G(b(g)),\, S(s''))} & \text{if } s' \subseteq a(s),\ s'' \subseteq b(s), \\ S|_{a(s) \to R(G, S(a(s)))} & \text{if } M(g) \subseteq a(s). \end{cases} \quad (1)$$

Such a concept is illustrated in Fig. 6. An efficient algorithm was presented in [128] for computing a reconciled tree given a gene and species tree. It is easy to see that the reconciled tree $R(G, S)$ satisfies the following three properties, of which the first two are mentioned above:

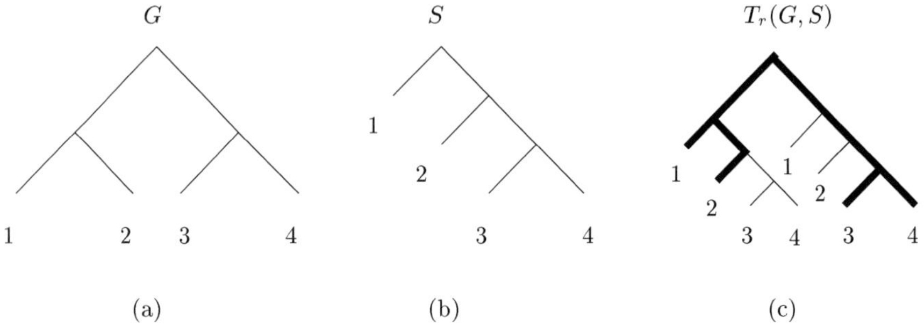


FIG. 6. (a) A gene tree $G$; (b) a species tree $S$; (c) the reconciled tree $T_r(G, S)$ of $G$ with respect to $S$.

(1) It contains $G$ as a subtree, i.e. there is a subset $L$ of leaves such that $R(G, S)|_L$ is isomorphic to $G$;
(2) All clusters are in $S$, where a cluster is defined as a subset of species below an internal node in $S$ (see Section 3.1);
(3) For any two children $a(g)$ and $b(g)$ of a node $g \in R(G, S)$, $a(g) \cap b(g) = \emptyset$ or $a(g) = b(g) = g$.

Actually, Page also defined the reconciled tree $R(G, S)$ as the smallest tree satisfying the above properties. However, these two definitions are not obviously equivalent. A rigorous proof of this equivalence is given in [21].

Obviously, duplication events are one-to-one correspondent to the internal nodes with two identical children in the reconciled tree. Moreover, in [61], Gorecki and Tiuryn proved an earlier conjecture that the number of gene losses is also equal to the number of the maximal subtrees that do not contains any nodes in the image of the gene tree in the reconciled tree.

## 3.4 From Gene Trees to Species Trees

Over the years, biomolecular sequence information has been applied effectively toward to reconstructing the species tree—the evolution history of species. Under the gene duplication model, the problem is formulated:

**Definition 9** (*Species Tree Problem*). Give a set of gene trees $G_i$ ($1 \leqslant i \leqslant n$), find a species tree $T$ that has the minimum duplication cost $\sum_{1 \leqslant i \leqslant n} t_{\text{dup}}(G_i, T)$ or mutation cost $\sum_{1 \leqslant i \leqslant n}(t_{\text{dup}}(G_i, T) + t_{\text{loss}}(G_i, T))$.

For either cost, this problem was proved to be NP-hard by Ma, Li and Zhang in [103] and the parametric complexity of this problem was studied by Fellows et al. in [149,52]. Moreover, various heuristic algorithms have been proposed By Page [130], Arvestad et al. [3] and Durand, Halldorsson and Vernot [46].

## 3.5 Tandem Gene Duplication

### 3.5.1 Tandem Duplication Tree Model

In the study of tandem duplication history of human hemoglobin, Fitch first observed that tandem duplication histories are much more constraint than speciation histories and proposed to model them assuming that unequal crossover is the biological mechanism from which they originate [54], and the corresponding trees are now called *tandem duplication trees*.

Assume $n$ sequences $\{1, 2, \ldots, n\}$ were formed from a locus through a series of tandem duplications, where each duplication replaced a stretch of DNA sequences containing several repeats with two identical and adjacent copies of itself. If the stretch contains $k$ repeats, the duplication is called a $k$-duplication.

A rooted *duplication tree* $\mathcal{M}$ for tandemly repeated segments $\{1, 2, \ldots, n\}$ is a rooted binary tree that contains blocks as shown in Fig. 7. A node in $\mathcal{M}$ represents a repeat. Obviously, the root represents the original copy at the locus and leaves the given segments.

A *block* in $\mathcal{M}$ represents a duplication event. Each non-leaf node appears in a unique block; no node is an ancestor of another in a block. If the block corresponds to a $k$-duplication, it contains $k$ nodes, say, $u_1, u_2, \ldots, u_k$ from left to right. Assume $lc(u_i)$ and $rc(u_i)$ are the left and right children of $u_i$, $1 \leqslant i \leqslant k$. Then, in the model $\mathcal{M}$,

$$lc(u_1),\ lc(u_2),\ \ldots,\ lc(u_k),\ rc(u_1),\ rc(u_2),\ \ldots,\ rc(u_k)$$

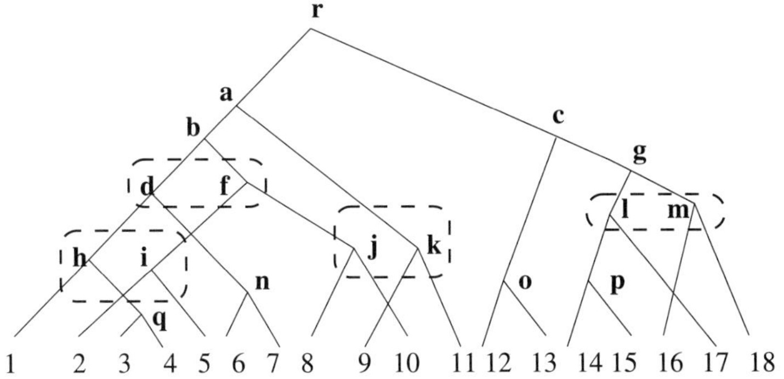


FIG. 7. A rooted duplication tree $\mathcal{M}$. Multi-duplication blocks are $[d, f]$, $[h, i]$, $[j, k]$ and $[l, m]$.

are placed from left to right. Hence, for any $i$ and $j$, $1 \leqslant i < j \leqslant k$, the directed edges $(u_i, rc(u_i))$ and $(u_j, lc(u_j))$ cross each other. But no other edges cross in the model. For simplicity, we will only draw blocks corresponding to multi-duplication events that contain more than one internal nodes.

The leaves representing given segments are placed from left to right in the same order as the segments appear on the chromosome. Here we assume such an order is the increasing order.

### 3.5.2 Combinatorics of Tandem Duplication Models

Duplication trees containing only 1-duplications are called *ordered phylogenies*. They form a proper subclass of the duplication models. Since an ordered phylogeny with $n$ leaves corresponds uniquely to a triangulation of a regular $(n+1)$-polygon, the number of ordered phylogenies with $n$ leaves is just $\binom{2(n-1)}{n-1}/n$, the $n$th Catalan number [167,48].

Like phylogenies, both rooted and unrooted duplication trees are studied. An unrooted phylogeny is a duplication tree if it can be rooted (on some edge) into a duplication tree.

**Theorem 5.** [58] *The number of rooted duplication trees for n segments is twice the number of unrooted duplication trees for n segments.*

A simple non-counting proof of this theorem is given by Yang and Zhang in [163]. Moreover, using a recurrence relation in [58], they also obtained the following recurrence relation for computing the number of rooted duplication trees.

**Theorem 6.** [163] *Let $r_n$ denote the number of rooted duplication trees for n segments. For any $n \geqslant 2$,*

$$r_n = \begin{cases} 1 & \text{if } n = 2, \\ \sum_{k=1}^{\lfloor (n+1)/3 \rfloor} (-1)^{k+1} \binom{n+1-2k}{k} r_{n-k} & \text{if } n \geqslant 3. \end{cases}$$

### 3.5.3 Reconstruction Algorithms

Tandem repeats are everywhere in the genome of higher organisms. A good method for reconstructing the parsimonious duplication tree is extremely useful for identifying orthologous genes in genome annotation. However, there has not been a good solution for it up to now.

Since the duplication model space is huge, the problem of constructing a parsimonious duplication tree given a set of duplicated sequences is believed to be NP-hard. Indeed, Jaitly et al. proved that finding the parsimonious ordered tree is NP-hard

[84]. Therefore, one approach to the problem is to search the phylogenetic trees that are duplication trees after the parsimony score is computed. Indeed, whether a phylogeny is a duplication tree or not can be determined efficiently. Tang, Waterman and Yooseph first gave a quadratic time algorithm for the problem [152]. Later, Zhang et al. and Elemento, Gascuel and Lefranc presented two different linear-time algorithms for the problem [167,49]. Other heuristic reconstructing methods can be found in [152,47].

Finally, different algorithms for reconstructing parsimonious ordered trees were developed in [9,84,152].

## 4. Phylogenetic Networks

### 4.1 Tree of Life or Net of Life?

As we mentioned in the last section, phylogenetic trees have a long history as models to represent the evolution of species. However, in the last decade, the large-scale availability of genomic sequences indicates that horizontal gene transfer (HGT), gene conversion, and recombination events have often occurred in genome evolution.

Horizontal gene transfer events occur when genetical material transfers across from a species to another distantly related species. They are common in the prokaryotes, especially bacterial genomes [95,44,119]. Additional evidence suggests that it might also occur in eukaryotes [79]. In many cases, horizontal gene transfers are very interesting in their own. Indeed, many reflect the most innovative adaptations in all of biology such as bacterial photosynthesis and nitrogen fixation. Horizontal transfers are not restricted to single genes. Genes, operons and a large segment of genomes are commonly exchanged among prokaryotes.

Recombination is another important mutational process that is common to most forms of life. A species is defined as a potentially interbreeding group of organisms that are capable of producing fertile offspring. Within a species, gene phylogenies are often inconsistent due to high rate gene flow and meiotic recombination. Meiotic recombination takes two equal length sequences and produces a third one of the same length by concatenating a prefix of one sequence and a suffix of another one. Other forms of recombination such as transformation, conjugation and transduction allow the sharing of genetic material between species as indicated by the recent completion of the sequences of different bacterial genomes. Efforts to identify patterns of recombination and the location of recombination are central to modern genetics.

In a nutshell, genomes have evolved not only vertically, but also horizontally. As a result, directed networks (i.e. trees with reticulation branches) are probably more appropriate mathematical model for the study of genome evolution. Here, we shall present the recent study of the algorithmic aspects of reconstructing phylogenetic networks. Readers are refereed to [115,134] for more information on phylogenetic networks.

## 4.2 Horizontal Gene Transfer Detection and Models

### 4.2.1 G+C Content-Based Detection

The G+C content of a genome is determined by mutation and selection pressures. Hence, the sequences from a genome share a common feature of compositional bases, codons and oligonucleotides [62,86]. This makes it possible to identify horizontally transfered genes as those whose G+C content is atypical for a particular genome [95,79,171]. For example, M. thermoautotrophicum contains several regions that have about 10% lower G+C content than that of the whole genome on average [145]. ORFs in these regions exhibit a codon usage pattern atypical of M. thermoautotrophicum, suggesting that they code some genes acquired by HGT. HGT genes are usually G+C poor. However, this method should be used with caution since sequences can quickly adjust to the new genome pattern and a gene with different G+C content does not necessarily originates in distant organisms [42].

### 4.2.2 Phylogeny-Based Detection Model

Comparison of a gene tree and a species tree provides a reliable method for identifying horizontally transfered genes [1,70,71,60,104,110]. It is based on the following simple idea: If A and B are siblings in the gene tree, then, either the parent gene AB must present in the last common ancestor of A and B in the species tree or a horizontal gene transfer has occurred from the lineage A to the lineage B or vice versa. Horizontal gene transfers are modeled as a species graph formed from a species tree by adding additional horizontal edges [70,60,93]. The horizontal edges represent the hypothetic horizontal gene transfers.

Let $S = (V, E)$ be a rooted tree in which each internal node has at most two children. A time stamp for $S$ is a function $t$ from $V$ to non-negative integers with the following property: for any $v \in V$, $t(p(v)) < t(v)$, where $p(v)$ is the parent of $v$ in $S$.

A relation $H \subset V \times V$ is *horizontal* for $S$ with respect to a time stamp $t$ if the following conditions are true:

(H1) $(v, v) \notin H$;
(H2) for each $(v, w) \in H$, both $v$ and $w$ have only one child;
(H3) for any different $(v, w), (v', w') \in H$, $\{v, w\} \cap \{v', w'\} = \emptyset$;

(H4) for any $(v, w) \in H, t(v) = t(w)$;
(H5) for any different $(v, w), (v', w') \in H, t(v) \neq t(v')$.

Each element of $H$ is a *horizontal transfer*. Intuitively, (H3) prevents more than one horizontal transfer events from occurring on the same lineage and (H4) indicates that the ends of a horizontal transfer should exist at the same time.

A *species graph* $\mathcal{G} = (S, t_S, H)$ consists of a rooted tree $S$, a time stamp $t_S$ and an horizontal relation $H$ on $S$ with respect to $t_S$. We use $S(H)$ to denote the directed graph obtained by adding elements in $H$ as arcs on $S$. Then, the following condition is true:

> For each directed path $v_1, v_2, \ldots, v_k$ in $S(H)$, $t_S(v_1), t_S(v_2), \ldots, t_S(v_k)$ is a non-decreasing integer sequences.

Obviously, the above property implies that $S(H)$ is a directed acyclic graph.

Let $G$ be a gene tree and $T$ a species tree. A rooted binary tree $S$ is an extension of $T$ if $T$ can be obtained from $S$ by contracting all the degree-2 nodes. Each species graph $(S, t_S, H)$ is a *model* of horizontal transfers of the gene occurring in the gene tree $G$ on the species tree $T$ if $S$ is an extension of $T$ and $G$ can be embedded into $S(H)$ as illustrated in Fig. 8. Notice that the time stamp and condition (H5) are used to prevent inconsistent transfer events as indicated in Fig. 9.

The problem of inferring horizontal gene transfers is formulated as follows:

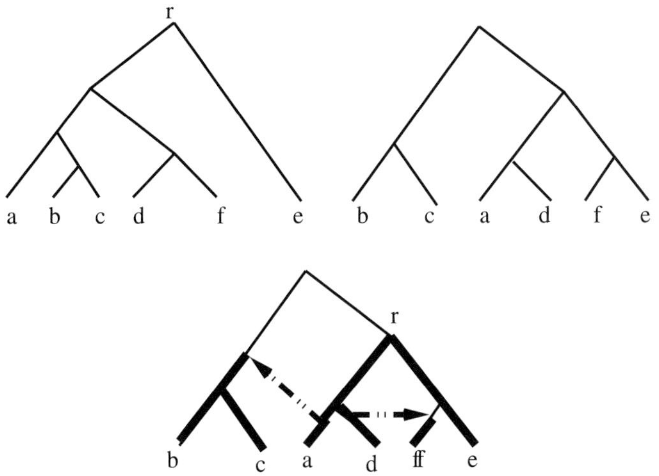


FIG. 8. A species graph. On the top, the left tree is a gene tree, the right one is a species tree. The species graph is shown at the bottom, in which the gene tree is embedded.

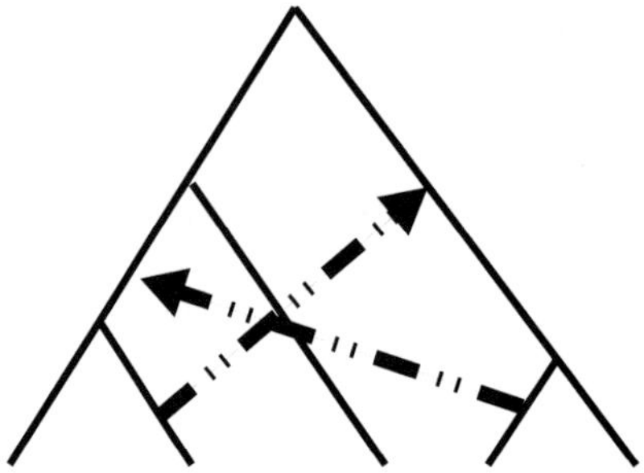

FIG. 9. Inconsistent transfer events that could not occur in genome evolution.

**Definition 10** (*HGT Inference Problem*). Given a species tree $T$ and a gene tree $G$, find a horizontal gene transfer model $(S, t_S, H)$ with the smallest gene transfer set $H$ over all the models.

Combining the horizontal gene transfer model and the concept of reconciliation tree described in the last section, one obtains a mathematical model for simultaneously detecting gene duplication, loss and horizontal transfer events [60,71]. Like duplication inference problems, the HGT inferring problem and its generalization to simultaneously detecting gene duplication, loss and horizontal transfers are obviously NP-hard [40]. Hence, an important and practical problem is to develop efficient algorithm for these two problems.

## 4.3 The Recombination Model

A recombination network $\mathcal{N}$ over a set $S$ of 0–1 sequences of length $L$ has four basic components:

(i) The topology structure of $\mathcal{N}$ is a directed acyclic graph $D$. It contains a unique node (called the *root*) with no incoming edges, a set of internal nodes that have both incoming and outgoing edges, and a set of nodes (called the *leaves*) with no outgoing edges. Each internal node has one or two incoming edges. A node with one incoming edge is called *tree node*; a node with two incoming edges is called *recombination* node. An edge is called a *tree edge* if it enters a tree node, and called *recombination edge* if it enters a recombination node.

(ii) There is a mapping $w$ from the integer set $[1, L]$ to the set of tree edges of $D$. It assigns a site $i$ in the sequences to a unique tree edge $e$. We write

$i = w^{-1}(e)$. It is possible that there are more than $L$ tree edges in $D$ and hence some tree edges might not receive a site assignment.

(iii) There are exactly two recombination edges entering each recombination node. These two edges are labeled with $p$ and $s$ respectively. In addition, a site is associated with a recombination node.

(iv) There is also a mapping that labels each node of $D$ with a 0–1 sequence. The labels satisfy the following conditions:

(a) For a tree-node $v$, let $e$ be the edge entering into $v$. Then, the label of $v$ is only different from its parent's label in site $w(e)$. This models a mutation in site $i$ occurring on edge $e$.

(b) For a recombination node $v$, let $e$ and $e'$ be the edges coming into $v$ from $v'$ and $v''$, labeling with $p$ and $s$ respectively, and let the integer assigned to $v$ in (iii) is $i$. The label of $v$ is identical to $v'$s label in the first $i - 1$ sites and to $v''$s label in the last $L - i + 1$ sites. This models a single-cross recombination occurring at site $i$.

(c) All the leaves are uniquely labeled with the given sequences in $S$.

One phylogenetic network is shown in Fig. 10. In this network, the ancestral sequence is 0000000, the leaves are labeled with sequences $a$, $b$, $c$, $d$, $e$, and there are three recombination nodes. The model presented here can be generalized in different ways. This simple version is the one that has been extensively studied currently. It is also the topology part of the stochastic process model called an ancestral recombination graph (ARG) in the population genetics study (see [120] for example).

In recombination model, the central problem is to infer a rooted or unrooted phylogenetic network with minimum number of recombination nodes on a set of given sequences. Although such a problem is NP-hard [161]. it is polynomial-time solvable for two classes of phylogenetic networks: perfect phylogeny and galled phylogenetic networks [64–66,68,161].

### 4.3.1 Perfect Phylogeny

A *perfect phylogeny* is a recombination network without recombination nodes. This is a simple combinatorial characterization for the 0–1 sequences that can be derived from a perfect phylogeny. Given a set $S$ of 0–1 sequences, two sites in the sequences are said to be *incompatible* in $S$ if and only if $S$ contains four rows where sites $i$ and $j$ contains all four possible ordered pairs: 00, 01, 10, 11. A site is *compatible* if it does not form any incompatible pair together with any other site. For a sequence $s$, two sites $i$ and $j$ in $S$ are said to *conflict* relative to $s$ if $i$ and $j$ are incompatible in $S \cup \{s\}$. A classical theorem when studying perfect phylogeny is the following theorem (see [64] for example).

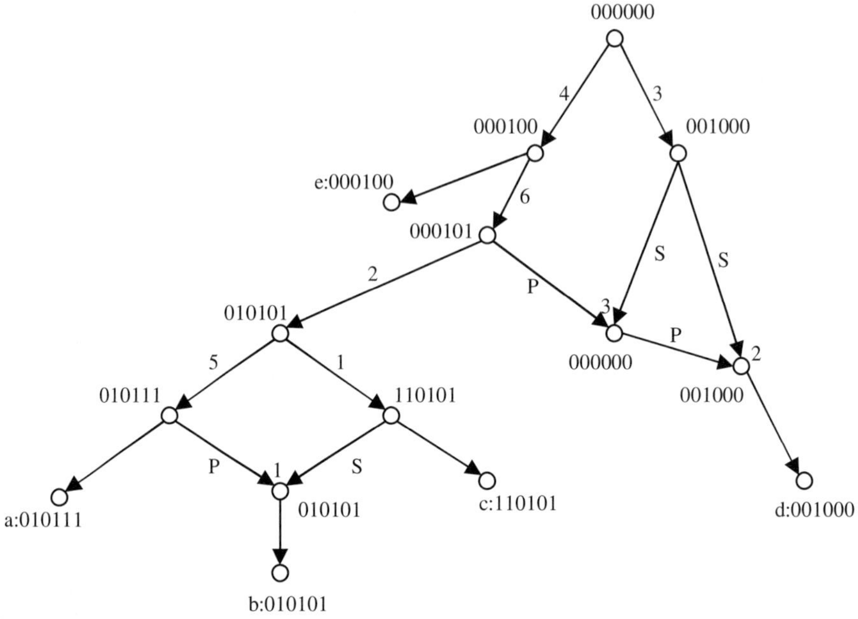


FIG. 10. A phylogenetic network for sequences {010111, 010101, 110101, 001000, 000100} in the recombination model.

**Theorem 7.** *Let S be a set of* 0–1 *sequences and s be a* 0–1 *sequence.*

(i) *There is an unrooted perfect phylogeny that derives the sequences in S if and only if all the sites are compatible in S*;

(ii) *there is a rooted prefect phylogeny, with ancestral sequence s, that derives sequences in S if and only if there is no pair of conflicting sites* (*relative to S*).

## 4.3.2 Galled Phylogenetic Networks

In a phylogenetic network with recombination nodes, for each recombination node $x$, there are two directed paths that come out of some tree node $y$ and meet at $x$. These two paths together define a *recombination cycle*. A recombination cycle is called a *gall* if it shares no nodes with other recombination cycles. For example, the left recombination cycle in the model shown in Fig. 10 is a gall. A phylogenetic network is called *galled network* if every recombination is gall. In [161], Wang, Zhang and Zhang first proposed to study the problem of determining if a set 0–1 sequences can be derived from a galled network or not.

Given a set $S$ of 0–1 sequences, we defined the *incompatibility graph* $G(S)$ for $S$ as a graph in which there is one node for each site in $S$ and there is an edge connecting two nodes if the corresponding sites are incompatible. Similarly, given a sequence $s$, we can define the "conflict graph" $G_s(S)$ for $S$ (relative to $s$).

A *connected component* of a graph is a maximal subgraph in which for any two nodes in it there is at least one path between them in the graph. If all the sites are compatible, then $G(S)$ has only trivial components that have only one node and no edges.

In a series of papers [68,67,66], Gusfield and his collaborators studied the structural properties of a connected component that corresponds to a gall in a phylogenetic network. By giving an efficient algorithm to determine how the sites in a connected component with the desired structural properties are arranged on a gall, they obtained the following theorem.

**Theorem 8.** *There is a polynomial-time algorithm that determines whether a set of* 0–1 *sequences can be derived from a galled phylogenetic network or not and constructs such a galled network.*

### 4.3.3 Full-Decomposition Optimality Conjecture

In a non-galled phylogenetic network, recombination cycles are not necessarily edge-disjoint. A maximal set of cycles $C_1, C_2, \ldots, C_k$ form a *blob* if they can be arranged in such a way $C_{i_1}, C_{i_2}, \ldots, C_{i_3}$ that the successive cycles share edges. In [65], Gusfield and Bansal proved the following theorem.

**Theorem 9.** *Let $S$ be a set of* 0–1 *sequences of equal length. Then*

(i) *there is an unrooted recombination network $\mathcal{N}$ deriving $S$ in which each blob contains exactly all sites in a single non-trivial connected component in $G(M)$, and every compatible site is assigned to a tree edge*;
(ii) *there is a recombination network $\mathcal{N}$ that derives $S$, with ancestral sequence $s$, in which each blob contains exactly all sites in a non-trivial connected component of $G_s(S)$ and any non-conflicting site is assigned to a tree edge.*

Obviously, there are other recombination networks that derive $S$, where a blob may contain sites from difference connected components in $G(S)$. Therefore, the following conjecture arises. It is considered as one of the most important open problems in the study of phylogenetic networks.

**Conjecture 1** (*Full-Decomposition Optimality Conjecture*). [65] For any 0–1 sequence set $S$, there is always a recombination network that satisfies the condition in the above theorem and has the minimum number of recombinations over all possible phylogenetic networks for $S$.

In [66], Gusfield showed that for the sequence set that can be derived from a galled network, there is an efficient algorithm for producing a galled network with the minimum number of recombinations, over all possible phylogenetic networks for the sequences. Recent progress toward this conjecture can be found in [69].

## 4.4 The Hybrid Model

In the hybrid model, a phylogenetic network for a set of taxa (species, DNA, protein sequences, or other objects) has all the properties of a recombination network except for edge site-labels. It is a directed acyclic graph in which there is a unique node (the *root*) without coming edges, a set of nodes (*leaves*) without outgoing leaves, and some other nodes with one outgoing edges and one or two incoming edges. The leaves are one-to-one labeled with given taxa. The nodes with one incoming edge are *tree nodes*; the nodes with two incoming edges are *reticulation nodes*. The edges entering tree nodes are tree edges; the edges entering reticulation nodes are network edges. As in the recombination model, we can define the reticulation cycle similarly. A reticulation network without overlapping reticulation cycles is galled.

Different variants of the hybrid model have been proposed. For example, a phylogenetic network is not necessarily binary. A phylogenetic network may have 'time-weighted' edges that satisfy time constraints so that two parents of a reticulation nodes should coexist in the same time [111].

### *4.4.1 Network Reconstruction from Gene Trees*

In genomic evolution, one usually obtains a set of gene trees that have evolved from a common ancestor in a series of reticulate events, and would like to reconstruct the underlying phylogenetic network from these gene trees. By removing exactly one of the two edges entering every reticulation node in a network, we obtain a phylogenetic tree. Such a tree is said to be induced by the network. Formally, the computing problem arise from above procedure is

**Definition 11** (*Parsimonious Reticulate Network from Gene Trees Problem*). Given a set $S$ of gene trees over a taxon set $X$, construct a phylogenetic network that induces all the trees in $S$ and has the minimal number of reticulation nodes, over all the phylogenetic networks.

In 1997, Maddison first proposed this problem and studied how to construct a phylogenetic network with one reticulation node for two gene trees [105]. Since this problem is NP-hard in general [161], different algorithms have been proposed recently [37,82,83,111,118,147]. In particular, the problem is also polynomial-time solvable for galled phylogenetic networks. More specifically, Nakhleh et al. proved the following theorem

**Theorem 10.** [118] *Given two binary trees $T_1$ and $T_2$, it is polynomial-time computable a galled phylogenetic network, if existence, that induces $T_1$ and $T_2$ and has the minimum number of reticulation nodes, over all the galled phylogenetic networks.*

The above theorem is recently generalized to multiple (not necessarily binary) trees by Huynh et al. Let $T$ and $t$ be two arbitrary trees. We say $T$ refines $t$ if $t$ can be obtained by a series of edge contractions. A phylogenetic network $\mathcal{N}$ refines $t$ if $\mathcal{N}$ induces a binary tree that refines $t$.

**Theorem 11.** [83] *Given a set of trees, it is polynomial-time computable a galled phylogenetic network, if existence, that refines the given trees and has the minimum number of reticulation nodes, over all the galled phylogenetic networks.*

When a set of phylogenetic trees cannot be combined into a galled phylogenetic network, one may be interested in knowing to what extend, these trees admit a solution. Hence, the following problem is interesting:

**Definition 12** (*Phylogenetic Network Compatibility Problem*). Given a class of phylogenetic network, and a set of trees over a taxon set $X$, find a largest subset $X'$ of $X$ such that the set of trees restricted on $X'$ have a refined network in the given class.

This problem is believed to be NP-hard. For the class of galled phylogenetic networks, the following result was obtained.

**Theorem 12.** [83] *Given a set of $k$ trees each with maximum degree $d$ over a taxon set $X$, it is $O(2^{3kd}n^{2k})$-time computable a largest subset $X'$ of $X$ such that the restriction of the given trees on $X'$ admit a refining galled phylogenetic network.*

### 4.4.2 Network Reconstruction from Sequences

All phylogeny reconstruction methods can and will probably generalize to phylogenetic network reconstruction in future. Here, we shall examine how the parsimony method is generalized in detail.

Let $S$ be a set of equal-length DNA or protein sequences. For two sequences $x, y \in S$, we use the Hamming distance $H(x, y)$ between them to measure their dissimilarity. It is defined as the number of mismatch positions between $x$ and $y$. Let $T$ be a rooted phylogeny over $S$. Then, each internal node is implicitly labeled with a sequence $s_v$ of the same length as those in $S$; each leave is labeled uniquely with a sequence in $S$. The *parsimony score* $s(T, S)$ of $T$ is defined as $\sum_{(u,v)\in E(T)} d(u, v)$, where $E(T)$ denotes the set of tree edges in $T$. The parsimony phylogeny for sequence set $S$ is a rooted phylogeny that has the minimum parsimony score overall the phylogenies.

The *parsimony problem* is, given a set $S$ of equal-length sequence set, to compute a parsimony phylogeny for $S$. It is known that this problem is NP-hard (see [57] for example). Therefore, one practical approach is through exhaustive search over the phylogeny space after the parsimony score of a phylogeny is computed, which is linear-time solvable (see [53] for example). In literature, computing the parsimony score of a phylogeny for a set of equal-length sequences is called the *small parsimony problem*.

Three parsimony problems arise from reconstructing a phylogenetic network from biomolecular sequences. Since each phylogenetic network $\mathcal{N}$ induces a set of phylogenies $P(\mathcal{N})$, we have the following problem:

**Definition 13** (*Small Parsimony Phylogenetic Network Problem*). Given a phylogenetic network $\mathcal{N}$ for a set $S$ of equal-length sequences, find a labeling of the internal nodes of $\mathcal{N}$ that has the minimum parsimony score $s(\mathcal{N}, S) = \min_{T\in P(\mathcal{N})} s(T, S)$.

To take non-point-mutation events such as recombination into account, we assume the given sequences are partitioned into different blocks $b_i$ $(1 \leqslant i \leqslant n)$ such that only point-mutation events occurred in each block and non-point-mutation events combined sequences from different blocks, where each block is specified by start and end positions. If we use $S|_{b_i}$ to denotes the resulting sequence set in the block $b_i$, then, the parsimony problem for phylogenetic networks is formulated as

**Definition 14** (*Parsimony Phylogenetic Network Problem*). Given a set $S$ of equal-length sequences that are partitioned into block $b_i$ $(1 \leqslant i \leqslant n)$, find a phylogenetic network $\mathcal{N}$ with the minimum score $s(\mathcal{N}, S, \{b_i\}) = \sum_{i=1}^{n} s(\mathcal{N}, S|_{b_i})$.

In the study of genomic evolution, we are only given a set of genomic sequence from different species. Without knowing the true evolutionary history of these sequences, we do not have the true partition blocks on the sequences. Hence, the following problem is also interesting and practical:

**Definition 15** (*Large Parsimony Phylogenetic Network Problem*). Given a set $S$ of equal-length sequences and an integer $k$, find a phylogenetic network $\mathcal{N}$ and a block partition $\{b_i \mid 1 \leqslant i \leqslant k\}$ of $S$ such that the parsimony score $s(\mathcal{N}, S, \{b_i\})$ is minimum.

The parsimony phylogenetic network problem was proposed by J. Hein in early 1990s [75,76]. With more and more genomic sequences available, researchers re-draw attention to the problem recently. Nakhleh et al. presented a heuristic algorithm for the parsimony phylogenetic network problem in [117]. It is easy to see the small parsimony phylogenetic network problem is polynomial-time solvable for the given network has a constant number of reticulation nodes. But, it is NP-hard in general [121]. In addition, it is not clear whether the first and third problems are polynomial time solvable for galled phylogenetic networks or not.

Other heuristic parsimony methods include statistical parsimony [153], median networks [6,7] and the netting method [55].

### 4.4.3 Distance-Based Reconstruction Methods

Different distance-based methods have also been proposed for reconstructing phylogenetic networks [5,28,43]. Split decomposition was proposed to decompose the distance matrix into weighted splits (a bipartition of the given taxon set) [5]. When these splits are compatible, they induce a phylogenetic tree, in which each split corresponds an edge. Otherwise, a network (called *split graph*) is used to realize them. Split decomposition is implemented in the package SplitsTree [81]. Strictly speaking, split graphs are not phylogenetic networks. They are just used to visualize the possible recombination events.

Neighbor-Net is a kind of combination of the NJ method and the split decomposition method [28]. It first constructs a collection of weighted splits using a generalization of the NJ method, then realizes these splits using a splits graph.

The Pyramid Clustering works agglomeratively like the UPGMA method for phylogeny reconstruction [43]. The UPGMA method generates a binary tree, whose internal nodes correspond the nested, non-overlapping clusters of taxa. In contrast to this, the Pyramid Clustering constructs overlapping clusters, forming a network.

### 4.4.4 Combinatorial Aspect of Phylogenetic Networks

Phylogenetic network reconstruction also raises some interesting combinatorial problems. One of such problems is, given a set of trees, to estimate the number of reticulation nodes in any phylogenetic network that contains the given trees as induced trees. Another problem is to study the combinatorial properties of special classes of phylogenetic networks such as unicyclic and galled networks. The readers are referred to [15,16,82,142] for recent results.

# 5. Gene Clusters

## 5.1 Positional Gene Clusters in Eukaryotic Genomes

Study of gene order within a genome is one of the key areas of genetics and genomics [126,80]. It is important in terms of understanding how genomes have evolved and how they function. For example, recent analysis indicates that genomic regions with the most actively expressed genes are those of highest gene density [157]. It also has important medical implications. An intact gene in a novel location could lead to a pathological phenotype [90].

It has long been known that genes are organized into operons in prokaryotic genomes such as bacteria genomes. However, gene order seems not random neither in eukaryotic genomes [80]. Recent analyses suggest that tissue (or function)-specific genes often cluster together in eukaryotic genomes (Table III). As a result, information about co-localised genes can be used for functional inferences of unknown genes through the 'guilt by association' principle [2].

## 5.2 Statistical Tests

In most of all the literatures, testing for non-random clustering of specific genes is done by simulation. The simulation process starts with formulating a test function. Then, generate a random genome and calculate the test function for many times. The

TABLE III
GENOME-WIDE ANALYSES ON GENE CLUSTERS

| Species | Clusters observed |
|---|---|
| P. falciparum | Clusters of co-expressed proteins [56] |
| S. cerevisiae | Clusters of cell-cycle-dependent genes [36]<br>Pairs of co-expressed neighboring genes, independent of orientation [39,92] |
| A. thaliana | Clusters of co-expressed genes [18,160] |
| D. melanogaster | Clusters of adjacent co-expressed or function-specific genes [148]<br>Clusters of tissue-specific genes [23] |
| C. elegans | Operons that contain about 15% genes [20]<br>Clusters of muscle-specific genes [136]<br>Clusters of co-expressed neighboring genes [96] |
| M. musculus | Clusters of tissue-specific genes [91,135,100] |
| H. sapiens | Clusters of tissue-specific genes [107,22,164]<br>Housekeeping genes [97,98] |

whole process generates the null distribution of the test function. The real value of the test function is then compared with the null distribution.

However, the results of different simulation studies are often difficult to compare. This motivates researchers to seek alternative analytic test methods.

### 5.2.1 Neighborhood Model

In study of testes-specific gene clustering in the mouse genome, Li, Lee and Zhang used the neighborhood model [100]. Under this model, two testis-specific genes are in a cluster if and only if there is a series of the testis-specific genes locating between them such that the distance between any two successive testis-specific genes in the series is less than a specified threshold ($D$). To incorporate the variance of gene density in different regions on a chromosome, each chromosome is divided into disjoint regions of a fixed length ($L$). Consider a length $L$-region containing $N$ genes in total. By Poisson approximation theory, the p-value of a cluster with $n$ tissue-specific genes in that region is about $(1 - e^{ND/L})^n$, the probability that a cluster has more than $n$ genes in that region.

The neighborhood model was also studied in earlier works [45,78]. A cluster in the neighborhood model is called a *max-gap* cluster in [78]. Hoberman, Durand and Sankoff showed that the exact probability that all the $m$ interesting genes form a max-gap cluster with distance threshold $D$ in a genome with $N$ genes is

$$P(N, m, D) = \frac{\max(0, N - w + 1) \cdot (D + 1)^{m-1} + d_0(m, D, \min(n, w - 1))}{\binom{n}{m}}$$

where $w = m + D(m - 1)$ and

$$d_0\big(m, D, \min(n, w - 1)\big) = \sum_{r=m}^{\min(n,w-1)} \sum_{i=0}^{\lfloor \frac{r-m}{D+1} \rfloor} (-1)^i \binom{m-1}{i} \binom{r - i(D+1) - 1}{m-1}.$$

They also presented a dynamic programming algorithm for computing the probability of observing a cluster of $h$ (out of $m$) interesting genes in a chromosome that contains $N$ genes.

### 5.2.2 Adjacent Gene Clustering

Order statistics can be a very powerful tool for removing the effect of non-uniform distribution of genes on statistical test although its power in clustering test has not been fully investigated. For instance, Li, Lee and Zhang considered the positional rank of a gene rather than its specific position by ordering all the genes according to their positions on a chromosome [100]. By treating the set of testis-specific genes and the set of other genes as two types of identical objects, a gene distribution on a chromosome is modeled as a binary string with 0 represents a tissue-specific gene. An *adjacent gene cluster* corresponds to a 0-subsequence in the resulting string.

Assume there are $M$ genes in a chromosome and $T$ of them are the testis-specific genes. Then, the probability that a random chromosome has a $r$-adjacent testis-specific gene cluster is

$$P_r = \binom{M-T+1}{r}\binom{T-1}{r-1}\Big/\binom{M}{T}.$$

Hence, the mean number of adjacent testis-specific clusters in a random chromosome is

$$\mu = \sum_{r=1}^{T} r P_r = (M-T+1)T/M$$

and the standard deviation is

$$\sigma = \sqrt{(M-T+1)(M-T)T(T-1)/\big(M^2(M-1)\big)}.$$

Using these values, one can estimate the significance of a real testis-specific gene distribution on a chromosome.

## 6. Conclusion

We have briefly introduced the current research status in genome rearrangements, gene duplication, phylogenetic network and positional gene clustering. Classical results were presented in these four areas but many open problems were also highlighted. For instance, promising new developments for the analysis of genome rearrangements include: new measures of similarity that generalize simple gene order adjacencies, alternative evolutionary edit operations that facilitate the modeling of transpositions, efficient approaches for genome rearrangement with gene families and rearrangement of partially ordered genomes. Similarly, interesting future directions for the analysis of gene duplications include how to identify true orthologous genes across species using the duplication models presented in Section 3 and how to identify large-scale duplications occurring along a lineage in the evolutionary history. In the study of phylogenetic networks, one important problem is to infer horizontal gene transfers among the bacterial genomes. Another major challenge is to develop a solid method for inferring phylogenetic network over a set of genomes given their genomic sequences. Finally, given that gene cluster analysis is a relatively new research topic, it is expected that more gene cluster testing methods based on order or other statistics will be developed. In its application end, the gene clustering analysis will probably become a routine task for every newly sequenced genome in the future.

This survey is far from being comprehensive as computational comparative genomics is a fast growing research topic. One topic which was not covered, for instance, involves studying the biological aspects around genomic structure. Other examples of important research areas missing from the current survey include: genomic sequence alignment problems and discovery of functional elements in genomic sequences. For genomic sequence alignment methods, we recommend a recent survey [8] of Batzoglou. For discovery of functional elements, we recommend the survey papers [30,106,27]. For further information on comparative genomics, the reader is also referred to another recent survey [108].

## ACKNOWLEDGEMENTS

GB is supported by funds from the Agency for Science, Technology and Research (A*STAR) of Singapore. LXZ is supported by a grant from Singapore BMRC and a grant from ARF, National University of Singapore.

## REFERENCES

[1] Addario-Berry L., Hallett M., Lagergren J., "Towards identifying lateral gene transfer events", in: *Proc. of Pacific Symp. Biocomput.*, 2003, pp. 279–290.

[2] Aravind L., "Guilt by association: contextual information in genome analysis", *Genome Res.* **10** (8) (2000) 1074–1077.

[3] Arvestad L., Berglund A.C., Lagergren J., Sennblad B., "Bayesian gene/species tree reconciliation and orthology analysis using MCMC", *Bioinformatics* **19** (Suppl. 1) (2003) i7–i15.

[4] Bader D.A., Moret B.M.E., Yan M., "A linear-time algorithm for computing inversion distance between signed permutations with an experimental study", in: *Proceedings of the 7th Internat. Workshop on Algorithms and Data Structures, WADS '01*, 2001, pp. 365–376.

[5] Bandelt H.J., Dress A., "A canonical decomposition theory for metrics on a finite set", *Adv. Math.* **92** (1992) 47–105.

[6] Bandelt H.J., Forster P., Sykes B.C., Richards M.B., "Mitochondrial portraits of human populations using median networks", *Genetics* **141** (2) (1995) 743–753.

[7] Bandelt H.J., Forster P., Rohl A., "Median-joining networks for inferring intraspecific phylogenies", *Mol. Biol. Evol.* **16** (1) (1999) 37–48.

[8] Batzoglou S., "The many faces of sequence alignment", *Brief Bioinform.* **6** (1) (2005) 6–22.
[9] Benson G., Dong L., "Reconstructing the duplication history of a tandem repeat", in: *Proc. Internat. Conf. Intell. Syst. Mol. Biol.* 1999, pp. 44–53.
[10] Bergeron A., Stoye J., "On the similarity of sets of permutations and its applications to genome comparison", in: *Proceeding COCOON*, 2003, pp. 68–79.
[11] Bergeron A., Mixtacki J., Stoye J., "Reversal distance without hurdles and fortresses", in: *Proceedings CPM*, 2004, pp. 388–399.
[12] Bergeron A., Blanchette M., Chateau A., Chauve C., "Reconstructing ancestral gene orders using conserved intervals", in: *Proceedings of WABI*, 2004, pp. 14–25.
[13] Bafna V., Pevzner P.A., "Sorting by transpositions", *SIAM J. Discrete Math.* **11** (2) (1998) 224–240.
[14] Bafna V., Pevzner P.A., "Genome rearrangements and sorting by reversal", *SIAM J. Comput.* **25** (1996) 272–289.
[15] Baroni M., Semple C., Steel M., "A framework for representing reticulate evolution", *Ann. Combin.* **8** (2004) 391–408.
[16] Baroni M., Grunewald S., Moulton V., Semple C., "Bounding the number of hybridisation events for a consistent evolutionary history", *J. Math. Biol.* **51** (2005) 171–182.
[17] Berman P., Hannenhalli S., "Fast sorting by reversal", in: *Proceedings Combinatorial Pattern Matching*, in: *Lecture Notes in Comput. Sci.*, vol. 1075, Springer-Verlag, Berlin, 1996, pp. 168–185.
[18] Birnbaum K., Shasha D.E., Wang J.Y., et al., "A gene expression map of the Arabidopsis root", *Science* **302** (2003) 1956–1960.
[19] Blanchette M., Bourque G., Sankoff D., "Breakpoint phylogenies", in: *Genome Informatics Workshop, GIW 1997*, 1997, pp. 25–34.
[20] Blumenthal T., Evans D., Link C.D., et al., "A global analysis of Caenorhabditis elegans operons", *Nature* **417** (2002) 851–854.
[21] Bonizzoni P., Della Vedova D., Dondi R., "Reconciling gene trees to a species tree", in: *Proc. Italian Conference on Algorithms and Complexity, CIAC2003, Rome, Italy*, in: *Lecture Notes in Comput. Sci.*, vol. 2653, Springer-Verlag, Berlin, 2003, pp. 120–131.
[22] Bortoluzzi S., Rampoldi L., Simionati B., et al., "A comprehensive, high-resolution genomic transcript map of human skeletal muscle", *Genome Res.* **8** (1998) 817–825.
[23] Boutanaev A.M., Kalmykova A.I., Shevelyov Y.Y., et al., "Large clusters of co-expressed genes in the Drosophila genome", *Nature* **420** (2002) 666–669.
[24] Bourque G., Pevzner P.A., "Genome-scale evolution: reconstructing gene orders in the ancestral species", *Genome Res.* **12** (2002) 26–36.
[25] Bourque G., Zdobnov E.M., Bork P., Pevzner P.A., Tesler G., "Comparative architectures of mammalian and chicken genomes reveal highly variable rates of genomic rearrangements across different lineages", *Genome Res.* **15** (1) (2005) 98–110.
[26] Bourque G., Yacef Y., El-Mabrouk N., "Maximizing synteny blocks to identify ancestral homologs", in: *Proceedings of RECOMB Satellite Meeting on Comparative Genomics*, in: *Lecture Notes in Bioinform.*, vol. 3678, Springer-Verlag, Berlin, 2005, pp. 21–34.
[27] Brent M.R., Guigó R., "Recent advances in gene structure prediction", *Curr. Opin. Struct. Biol.* **14** (3) (2004) 264–272.

[28] Bryant D., Moulton V., "NeighborNet: an agglomerative algorithm for the construction of phylogenetic networks", *Mol. Biol. Evol.* **21** (2) (2004) 255–265.

[29] Bryant D., "The complexity of calculating exemplar distance", in: D. Sankoff, J.H. Nadeau (Eds.), *Comparative Genomics*, Kluwer Academic Publishers, Dordrecht/Norwell, MA, 2000.

[30] Bulyk M.L., "Computational prediction of transcription-factor binding site locations", *Genome Biol.* **5** (1) (2003) 201.

[31] Caprara A., "Sorting by reversals is difficult", in: *RECOMB '97: Proceedings of the 1st Annual International Conference on Computational Molecular Biology*, 1997, pp. 75–83.

[32] Caprara A., "The reversal median problem", *INFORMS J. Computing* **15** (1) (2003) 93–113.

[33] Chen X., Zheng J., Fu Z., Nan P., Zhong Y., Lonardi S., Jiang T., "Assignment of orthologous genes via genome rearrangement", *IEEE/ACM Trans. Comput. Biol. Bioinform.* **2** (2005) 302–315.

[34] Chen Z.X., Fu B., Zhu B.H., "The approximability of the exemplar breakpoint distance problem", Manuscript, 2005.

[35] Chen K., Durand D., Farach-Colton M., "NOTUNG: a program for dating gene duplications and optimizing gene family trees", *J. Comput. Biol.* **7** (3–4) (2000) 429–447.

[36] Cho R.J., Campbell M.J., Winzeler E.A., et al., "A genome-wide transcriptional analysis of the mitotic cell cycle", *Mol. Cell.* **2** (1) (1998) 65–73.

[37] Choy C., Jansson J., Sadakane K., et al., "Computing the maximum agreement of phylogenetic networks", *Theoret. Comput. Sci.* **335** (1) (2005) 93–107.

[38] Christie D.A., "Sorting permutations by block-interchanges", *Inform. Process. Lett.* **60** (4) (1996) 165–169.

[39] Cohen B.A., Mitra R.D., Hughes J.D., Church G.M., "A computational analysis of whole-genome expression data reveals chromosomal domains of gene expression", *Nat. Genet.* **26** (2) (2000) 183–186.

[40] DasGupta B., Ferrarini S., Gopalakrishnan U., Paryani N.R., "Inapproximability results for the lateral gene transfer problem", in: *Proc. 9th Italian Conf. on Theoret. Comput. Sci., ICTCS'05*, in: *Lecture Notes in Comput. Sci.*, vol. 3701, Springer-Verlag, Berlin, 2005, pp. 182–195.

[41] Darwin C., *On the Origin of Species by Means of Natural Selection or the Preservation of Favored Races in the Struggle for Life*, John Murray, London, 1859.

[42] Daubin V., Lerat E., Perrière G., "The source of laterally transferred genes in bacterial genomes", *Genome Biol.* **4** (9) (2003) R57.

[43] Diday E., "Une représentation visuelle des classes empiétantes: les pyramides", *RAIRO Autoat.-Prod. Inform. Ind.* **20** (1984) 475–526.

[44] Doolittle W.F., "Phylogenetic classification and the universal tree", *Science* **284** (1999) 2124–2149.

[45] Durand D., Sankoff D., "Tests for gene clustering", *J. Comput. Biol.* **10** (2003) 453–482.

[46] Durand D., Halldorsson B.V., Vernot B., "A hybrid micro-macroevolutionary approach to gene tree reconstruction", in: *Proc. of RECOMB 2005*, 2005, 250–264.

[47] Elemento O., Gascuel O., "An efficient and accurate distance based algorithm to reconstruct tandem duplication trees", *Bioinformatics* **18** (Suppl. 2) (2002) S92–S99.
[48] Elemento O., Gascuel O., "An exact and polynomial distance-based algorithm to reconstruct single copy tandem duplication trees", in: *Proceedings of the 4th Annual Symp. on Combinatorial Pattern Matching, CPM R03, Mexico*, in: *Lecture Notes in Comput. Sci.*, vol. 2676, Springer-Verlag, Berlin, 2003, pp. 96–108.
[49] Elemento O., Gascuel O., Lefranc M.P., "Reconstructing the duplication history of tandemly repeated genes", *Mol. Biol. Evol.* **19** (3) (2002) 278–288.
[50] Elias I., Hartman T., "A 1.375-approximation algorithm for sorting by transpositions", in: *Proceedings WABI*, in: *Lecture Notes in Bioinform.*, vol. 3692, Springer-Verlag, Berlin, 2005, pp. 204–215.
[51] Eulenstein O., Mirkin B., Vingron M., "Duplication-based measures of difference between gene and species trees", *J. Comput. Biol.* **5** (1) (1998) 135–148.
[52] Fellows M., Hallett M., Stege U., "On the multiple gene duplication problem", in: *Proc. the 9th Internat. Symp. on Algorithms and Comput., ISAAC '98*, in: *Lecture Notes in Comput. Sci.*, vol. 1533, Springer-Verlag, Berlin, 1999, pp. 347–356.
[53] Fitch W., "Toward defining the course of evolution: minimum change for a specified tree topology", *Syst. Zool.* **20** (1971) 406–416.
[54] Fitch W., "Phylogenies constrained by cross-over process as illustrated by human hemoglobins in a thirteen cycle, eleven amino-acid repeat in human apolipoprotein A-I", *Genetics* **86** (1977) 623–644.
[55] Fitch W., "Networks and viral evolution", *J. Mol. Evol.* **44** (1997) S65–S75.
[56] Florens L., Washburn M.P., Raine J.D., et al., "A proteomic view of the Plasmodium falciparum life cycle", *Nature* **419** (2002) 520–526.
[57] Foulds L., Graham R., "The Steiner problem in phylogeny is NP-completed", *Adv. Appl. Math.* **3** (1982) 43–49.
[58] Gascuel O., Hendy M.D., Jean-Marie A., McLachlan R., "The combinatorics of tandem duplication trees", *Systematic Biol.* **52** (2003) 110–118.
[59] Goodman M., Czelusniak J., Moore G.W., et al., "Fitting the gene lineage into its species lineage, a parsimony strategy illustrated by cladograms constructed from globin sequences", *Syst. Zool.* **28** (1979) 132–163.
[60] Gorecki P., "Reconciliation problems for duplication, loss and horizontal gene transfer", in *Proc. of RECOMB*, 2004, pp. 316–325.
[61] Gorecki P., Tiuryn T., "On the structure of reconciliations", in: *Proc. RECOMB Comparative Genomics Workshop 2004*, in: *Lecture Notes in Comput. Sci.*, vol. 3388, Springer-Verlag, Berlin, 2005, pp. 42–51.
[62] Grantham R., Gautier C., Gouy M., Mercier R., Pave A., "Codon catalog usage and the genome hypothesis", *Nucleic Acids Res.* **8** (1) (1980) r49–r62.
[63] Guigó R., Muchnik I., Smith T., "Reconstruction of ancient molecular phylogeny", *Mol. Phys. Evol.* **6** (2) (1996) 189–213.
[64] Gusfield D., *Algorithms on Strings, Trees and Sequences: Computer Science and Computational Biology*, Cambridge Univ. Press, Cambridge, UK, 1997.
[65] Gusfield D., Bansal V., "A fundamental decomposition theory for phylogenetic networks and incompatible characters", in: *Lecture Notes in Comput. Sci.*, vol. 3500, Springer-Verlag, Berlin, 2005, pp. 217–232.

[66] Gusfield D., "Optimal, efficient reconstruction of root-unknown phylogenetic networks with constrained and structured recombination", *J. Comput. Syst. Sci.* **70** (3) (May 2005) 381–398.
[67] Gusfield D., Eddhu S., Langley C., "Optimal, efficient reconstruction of phylogenetic networks with constrained recombination", *J. Bioinform. Comput. Biol.* **2** (1) (2004) 173–213.
[68] Gusfield D., Eddhu S., Langley C., "The fine structure of galls in phylogenetic networks", *Inform. J. Comput.* **16** (4) (2004) 459–469.
[69] Gusfield D., "On the full-decomposition optimality conjecture for hylogenetic networks", Tech. Report CSE-2005, UC Davis, January 2005.
[70] Hallett M., Lagergren J., "Efficient algorithms for lateral gene transfer", in: *Proc. of RECOMB'01*, 2001, pp. 149–156.
[71] Hallett M., Lagergren J., Tofigh A., "Simultaneous identification of duplications and lateral transfer", in: *Prof. of RECOMB'04*, 2004, pp. 164–173.
[72] Hannenhalli S., Pevzner P.A., "Transforming cabbage into turnip polynomial algorithm for sorting signed permutations by reversals", in: *Proceedings of the 27th Annual ACM–SIAM Symposium on the Theory of Computing*, 1995, pp. 178–189.
[73] Hannenhalli S., Pevzner P.A., "Transforming men into mice: polynomial algorithm for genomic distance problem", in: *Proceedings of the 36th IEEE Symposium on Foundations of Computer Science*, 1995, pp. 581–592.
[74] Hannenhalli S., Pevzner P.A., "Transforming cabbage into turnip: polynomial algorithm for sorting signed permutations by reversals", *J. ACM* **46** (1999) 1–27.
[75] Hein J., "Reconstructing the history of sequences subject to gene conversion and recombination", *Math. Biosci.* **98** (1990) 185–200.
[76] Hein J., "A heuristic method to reconstruct the history of sequences subject to recombination", *J. Mol. Evol.* **20** (1993) 402–411.
[77] Heber S., Stoye J., "Finding all common intervals of $k$ permutations", in: *Proceedings of CPM 2001*, in: *Lecture Notes in Comput. Sci.*, vol. 2089, Springer-Verlag, Berlin, 2001, pp. 207–218.
[78] Hoberman R., Sankoff D., Durand D., "The statistical analysis of spatially clustered genes under the maximum gap criterion", *J. Comput. Biol.* **12** (2005) 1083–1102.
[79] Huang J., Mullapudi N., Sicheritz-Ponten T., Kissinger J.C., "A first glimpse into the pattern and scale of gene transfer in Apicomplexa", *Internat. J. Parasitol.* **34** (3) (2004) 265–274.
[80] Hurst L.D., Pal C., Lercher M.J., "The evolutionary dynamics of eukaryotic gene order", *Nat. Rev. Genet.* **5** (4) (2004) 299–310.
[81] Huson D., "SplitsTree—a program for analyzing and visualizing evolutionary data", *Bioinformatics* **14** (1998) 68–73.
[82] Huson D.H., Klopper T., Lockhart P.J., et al., "Reconstruction of reticulate networks from gene trees", in: *Lecture Notes in Comput. Sci.*, vol. 3500, Springer-Verlag, Berlin, 2005, pp. 233–249.
[83] Huynh T.N.D., Jansson J., Nguyen N.B., et al., "Constructing a smallest refining galled phylogenetic network", in: *Lecture Notes in Comput. Sci.*, vol. 3500, Springer-Verlag, Berlin, 2005, pp. 265–280.

[84] Jaitly D., Kearney P., Lin G., Ma B., "Methods for reconstructing the history of tandem repeats and their application to the human genome", *J. Comput. Syst. Sci.* **65** (3) (2002) 494–507.

[85] Kaplan H., Shamir R., Tarjan R.E., "Faster and simpler algorithm for sorting signed permutations by reversals", in: *Proceedings of the 8th Annual ACM–SIAM Symposium on Discrete Algorithms*, 1997, pp. 344–351.

[86] Karlin S., Burge C., "Dinucleotide relative abundance extremes: a genomic signature", *Trends Genet.* **11** (7) (1995) 283–290.

[87] Kececioglu J.D., Sankoff D., "Efficient bounds for oriented chromosome inversion distance", in: *Proceedings of the 5th Annual Symposium on Combinatorial Pattern Matching, CPM '94*, Springer-Verlag, Berlin, 1994, pp. 307–325.

[88] Kececioglu J., Ravi R., "Of mice and men: algorithms for evolutionary distance between genomes with translocations", in: *Proceedings of Sixth ACM–SIAM Symposium on Discrete Algorithms*, 1995, pp. 604–613.

[89] Kececioglu J., Sankoff D., "Exact and approximation algorithms for sorting by reversals, with application to genome rearrangement", *Algorithmica* **13** (1–2) (1995) 180–210.

[90] Kleinjan D.J., van Heyningen V., "Position effect in human genetic disease", *Human Mol. Genet.* **7** (10) (1998) 1611–1618.

[91] Ko M.S., Threat T.A., Wang X., et al., "Genome-wide mapping of unselected transcripts from extraembryonic tissue of 7.5-day mouse embryos reveals enrichment in the t-complex and under-representation on the X chromosome", *Human Mol. Genet.* **7** (1998) 1967–1978.

[92] Kruglyak S., Tang H., "Regulation of adjacent yeast genes", *Trends Genet.* **16** (3) (2000) 109–111.

[93] Kunin V., Goldovsky L., Darzentas N., et al., "The net of life: Reconstructing the microbial phylogenetic network", *Genome Res.* **15** (7) (2005) 954–959.

[94] Lander E.S., Linton L.M., Birren B., Nusbaum C., Zody M.C., Baldwin J., Devon K., Dewar K., Doyle M., FitzHugh W., et al., "Initial sequencing and analysis of the human genome", *Nature* **409** (6822) (2001 February 15) 860–921.

[95] Lawrence J.G., Ochman H., "Reconciling the many faces of lateral gene transfer", *Trends Microbiol.* **10** (1) (2002) 1–4.

[96] Lercher M.J., Blumenthal T., Hurst L.D., "Coexpression of neighboring genes in Caenorhabditis elegans is mostly due to operons and duplicate genes", *Genome Res.* **13** (2) (2003) 238–243.

[97] Lercher M.J., Urrutia A.O., Hurst L.D., "Clustering of housekeeping genes provides a unified model of gene order in the human genome", *Nat. Genet.* **31** (2) (2002) 180–183.

[98] Lercher M.J., Urrutia A.O., Pavlicek A., Hurst L.D., "A unification of mosaic structures in the human genome", *Human Mol. Genet.* **12** (19) (2003) 2411–2415.

[99] Levine M., Tjian R., "Transcription regulation and animal diversity", *Nature* **424** (6945) (2003 July 10) 147–151.

[100] Li Q., Lee B.T., Zhang L.X., "Genome-scale analysis of positional clustering of mouse testis-specific genes", *BMC Genomics* **6** (1) (2005) 7.

[101] Lin Y.C., Lu C.L., Chang H.Y., Tang C.Y., "An efficient algorithm for sorting by block-interchanges and its application to the evolution of vibrio species", *J. Comput. Biol.* **12** (2005) 102–112.
[102] Lu C.L., Wang T.C., Lin Y.C., Tang C.Y., "ROBIN: a tool for genome rearrangement of block-interchanges", *Bioinformatics* **21** (11) (2005) 2780–2782.
[103] Ma B., Li M., Zhang L.X., "From gene trees to species trees", *SIAM J. Comput.* **30** (2000) 729–752.
[104] MacLeod D., Charlebois R.L., Doolittle F., Bapteste E., "Deduction of probable events of lateral gene transfer through comparison of phylogenetic trees by recursive consolidation and rearrangement", *BMC Evol. Biol.* **5** (1) (2005) 27.
[105] Maddison W.P., "Gene trees in species trees", *Systemat. Biol.* **46** (3) (1997) 523–536.
[106] Mathe C., Sagot M.-F., Schiex T., Rouze P., "Current methods of gene prediction, their strengths and weaknesses", *Nucleic Acids Res.* **30** (19) (2002) 4103–4117.
[107] Megy K., Audic S., Claverie J.M., "Positional clustering of differentially expressed genes on human chromosomes 20, 21 and 22", *Genome Biol.* **4** (2) (2003) P1.
[108] Miller W., Makova K.D., Nekrutenko A., Hardison R.C., "Comparative genomics", *Annu. Rev. Genom. Human Genet.* **5** (2004) 15–56.
[109] Mirkin B., Muchnik I., Smith T.F., "A biologically consistent model for comparing molecular phylogenies", *J. Comput. Biol.* **2** (4) (1995) 493–507.
[110] Mirkin B.G., Fenner T.I., Galperin M.Y., Koonin E.V., "Algorithms for computing parsimonious evolutionary scenarios for genome evolution, the last universal common ancestor and dominance of horizontal gene transfer in the evolution of prokaryotes", *BMC Evol. Biol.* **3** (2003) 2.
[111] Moret B.M.E., Nakhleh L., Warnow T., et al., "Phylogenetic networks: Modeling, reconstructibility, and accuracy", *IEEE/ACM Trans. Comput. Biol. Bioinform.* **1** (1) (2004) 13–23.
[112] Moret B.M.E., Wyman S., Bader D.A., Warnow T., Yan M., "A new implementation and detailed study of breakpoint analysis", in: *6th Pacific Symposium on Biocomputing, PSB 2001*, 2001, pp. 583–594.
[113] Siepel A.C., Moret B.M.E., "Finding an optimal inversion median: experimental results", in: *WABI 2001, Algorithms in Bioinformatics, 1st International Workshop*, in: *Lecture Notes in Comput. Sci.*, vol. 2149, Springer-Verlag, Berlin, 2001, pp. 189–203.
[114] Sturtevant A.H., "Genetic studies on *Drosophila simulans* II. Sex-linked group of genes", *Genetics* **6** (1921) 43–64.
[115] Morrison D.A., "Networks in phylogenetic analysis: new tools for population biology", *Internat. J. Parasitol.* **35** (5) (2005) 567–582.
[116] Murphy W.J., Larkin D.M., Everts-van der Wind A., et al., "Dynamics of mammalian chromosome evolution inferred from multispecies comparative maps", *Science* **309** (5734) (2005) 613–617.
[117] Nakhleh L., Jin G., Zhao F., et al., "Reconstructing phylogenetic networks using maximum parsimony", in: *Proc. the 2005 IEEE Computational Systems Bioinformatics Conference*, 2005, pp. 93–102.
[118] Nakhleh L., Warnow T., Linder C.R., et al., "Reconstructing reticulate evolution in species—theory and practice", *J. Comput. Biol.* **12** (6) (2005) 796–811.

[119] Nelson K.E., Clayton R.A., Gill S.R., et al., "Evidence for lateral gene transfer between Archaea and bacteria from genome sequence of Thermotoga maritima", *Nature* **399** (1999) 323–329.
[120] Nordborg M., Tavaré S., "Linkage disequilibrium: what history has to tell us", *Trends Genet.* **18** (2002) 83–90.
[121] Nguyen C.T., Nguyen N.B., Sung W.-K., Zhang L.X., "Reconstructing recombination network from sequence data: The small parsimony problem", Manuscript, 2005.
[122] Nguyen C.T., "The complexity and algorithms for the exemplar problem with gene family", Honors Thesis, School of Computing, National University of Singapore, 2005.
[123] Nguyen C.T., Tay Y.C., Zhang L.X., "Divide-and-conquer approach for the exemplar breakpoint distance", *Bioinformatics* **21** (10) (2005) 2171–2176.
[124] O'Brien S.J., Menotti-Raymond M., Murphy W.J., et al., "The promise of comparative genomics in mammals", *Science* **286** (5439) (1999 October 15) 458–462, 479–481.
[125] Ohno S., *Evolution by Gene Duplication*, Springer-Verlag, Berlin, 1970.
[126] Oliver B., Misteli T., "A non-random walk through the genome", *Genome Biol.* **6** (4) (2005) 214.
[127] Ozery-Flato M., Shamir R., "Two notes on genome rearrangement", *J. Bioinform. Comput. Biol.* **1** (1) (2003) 71–94.
[128] Page R.D., "Maps between trees and cladistic analysis of historical associations among genes, organisms, and areas", *Syst. Biol.* **43** (1994) 58–77.
[129] Page R.D., Charleston M., "From gene to organismal phylogeny: reconciled trees and the gene tree/species tree problem", *Mol. Phys. Evol.* **7** (1997) 231–240.
[130] Page R.D., "GeneTree: comparing gene and species phylogenies using reconciled trees", *Bioinformatics* **14** (9) (1998) 819–820.
[131] Page R.D., "Extracting species trees from complex gene trees: reconciled trees and vertebrate phylogeny", *Mol. Phylogenet. Evol.* **14** (1) (2000) 89–106.
[132] Page R.D., Cotton J.A., "Vertebrate phylogenomics: reconciled trees and gene duplications", in: *Proc. of Pacific Symp. Biocomput.*, 2002, pp. 536–547.
[133] Pevzner P.A., *Computational Molecular Biology: An Algorithmic Approach*, The MIT Press, Cambridge, MA, 2000 (Chapter 10).
[134] Posada D., Crandall K.A., "Intraspecific gene genealogies: trees grafting into networks", *Trends Ecol. Evol.* **16** (1) (2001) 37–45.
[135] Reymond A., Marigo V., Yaylaoglu M.B., et al., "Human chromosome 21 gene expression atlas in the mouse", *Nature* **420** (6915) (2002) 582–586.
[136] Roy P.J., Stuart J.M., Lund J., Kim S.K., "Chromosomal clustering of muscle-expressed genes in Caenorhabditis elegans", *Nature* **418** (2002) 975–979.
[137] Sankoff D., "Edit distances for genome comparisons based on non-local operations", in: *Proc. of the 3rd Annual Symp. on Combin. Pattern Matching, CPM '92*, Springer-Verlag, Berlin, 1992, pp. 121–135.
[138] Sankoff D., Sundaram G., Kececioglu J., "Steiner points in the space of genome rearrangements", *Internat. J. Foundations Comput. Sci.* **7** (1996) 1–9.
[139] Sankoff D., Blanchette M., "The median problem for breakpoints in comparative genomics", in: *Computing and Combinatorics, Proceedings of COCOON '97*, 1997, pp. 251–263.

[140] Sankoff D., "Genome rearrangement with gene families", *Bioinformatics* **15** (1999) 909–917.

[141] Sankoff D., Zhang C.F., Lenert A., "Reversals of fortune", Manuscript, 2005.

[142] Semple C., Steel M., "Unicyclic networks: compatibility and enumeration", *IEEE/ACM Trans. Comput. Biol. Bioinform.* **3** (2006) 84–91.

[143] Setubal J., Meidanis J., *Introduction to Computational Molecular Biology*, PWS Publishing Company, 1997 (Chapter 7).

[144] Smith G.P., "Evolution of repeated DNA sequences by unequal crossover", *Science* **191** (1976) 58–535.

[145] Smith D.R., Doucette-Stamm L.A., Deloughery C., et al., "Complete genome sequence of Methanobacterium thermoautotrophicum deltaH: functional analysis and comparative genomics", *J. Bacteriol.* **179** (22) (1997) 7135–7155.

[146] Snyder M., Gerstein M., "Genomics. Defining genes in the genomics era", *Science* **300** (5617) (2003 April 11) 258–260.

[147] Song Y.S., Hein J., "Constructing minimal ancestral recombination graphs", *J. Comput. Biol.* **12** (2) (2005) 147–169.

[148] Spellman P.T., Rubin G.M., "Evidence for large domains of similarly expressed genes in the Drosophila genome", *J. Biol.* **1** (2002) 5.

[149] Stege U., "Gene trees and species trees: The gene-duplication problem is fixed-parameter tractable", in: *Proc. of the 6th Internat. Workshop on Algorithms and Data Structures, WADS '99, August 1999*, in: *Lecture Notes in Comput. Sci.*, vol. 1663, Springer-Verlag, Berlin, 1999.

[150] Sturtevant A.H., Novitski E., "The homologies of chromosome elements in the genus drosophila", *Genetics* **26** (1941) 517–541.

[151] Swenson K.M., Pattengale N.D., Moret B.M.E., "A framework for orthology assignment from gene rearrangement data", in: *Proceedings of RECOMB 2005 Workshop on Comparative Genomics*, in: *Lecture Notes in Bioinform.*, vol. 3678, Springer-Verlag, Berlin, 2005, pp. 153–166.

[152] Tang M., Waterman M., Yooseph S., "Zinc finger gene clusters and tandem gene duplication", *J. Comput. Biol.* **9** (2) (2002) 429–446.

[153] Templeton A., Crandall K., Sing C., "A cladistic analysis of phenotypic association with haplotype inferred from restriction endonuclease mapping and DNA sequence data. III. Cladogram estimation", *Genetics* **132** (1992) 619–633.

[154] Tesler G., "Efficient algorithms for multichromosomal genome rearrangements", *J. Comput. Syst. Sci.* **65** (3) (2002) 587–609.

[155] Tesler G., "GRIMM: genome rearrangements web server", *Bioinformatics* **18** (3) (2002) 492–493.

[156] Uno T., Yagiura M., "Fast algorithms to enumerate all common intervals of two permutations", *Algorithmica* **26** (2) (2000) 290–309.

[157] Versteeg R., van Schaik B.D., van Batenburg M.F., et al., "The human transcriptome map reveals extremes in gene density, intron length, GC content, and repeat pattern for domains of highly and weakly expressed genes", *Genome Res.* **13** (9) (2003) 1998–2004.

[158] Walter M.E.T., Dias Z., Meidanis J., "A new approach for approximating the transposition distance", in: *Proceedings SPIRE*, 2000, pp. 199–208.
[159] Waterston R.H., Lindblad-Toh K., Birney E., et al., "Initial sequencing and comparative analysis of the mouse genome", *Nature* **420** (6915) (2002 December 5) 520–562.
[160] Williams E.J., Bowles D.J., "Coexpression of neighboring genes in the genome of Arabidopsis thaliana", *Genome Res.* **14** (6) (2004) 1060–1067.
[161] Wang L.S., Zhang K.Z., Zhang L.X., "Perfect phylogenetic networks with recombination", *J. Comput. Biol.* **8** (1) (2001) 69–78.
[162] Watterson G.A., Ewens W.J., Hall T.E., Morgan A., "The chromosome inversion problem", *J. Theoret. Biol.* **99** (1982) 1–7.
[163] Yang J., Zhang L.X., "On counting tandem duplication trees", *Mol. Biol. Evol.* **21** (6) (2004) 1160–1163.
[164] Yang Y.S., Song H.D., Shi W.J., et al., "Chromosome localization analysis of genes strongly expressed in human visceral adipose tissue", *Endocrine* **18** (1) (2002) 57–66.
[165] Yancopoulos S., Attie O., Friedberg R., "Efficient sorting of genomic permutations by translocation, inversion and block interchange", *Bioinformatics* **21** (16) (2005) 3340–3346.
[166] Zhang L.X., "On a Mirkin–Muchnik–Smith conjecture for comparing molecular phylogenies", *J. Comput. Biol.* **4** (1997) 177–188.
[167] Zhang L.X., Ma B., Wang L., Xu Y., "Greedy method for inferring tandem duplication history", *Bioinformatics* **19** (2003) 1497–1504.
[168] Zheng C., Lenert A., Sankoff D., "Reversal distance for partially ordered genomes", *Bioinformatics* **21** (Suppl. 1) (2005) i502–i508.
[169] Zheng C., Sankoff D., "Genome rearrangements with partially ordered chromosomes", in: *Proceeding of COCOON 2005*, in: *Lecture Notes in Comput. Sci.*, vol. 3595, Springer-Verlag, Berlin, 2005, pp. 52–62.
[170] Zmasek C.M., Eddy S.R., "A simple algorithm to infer gene duplication and speciation events on a gene tree", *Bioinformatics* **17** (9) (2001) 821–828.
[171] Zhaxybayeva O., Gogarten J.P., "An improved probability mapping approach to assess genome mosaicism", *BMC Genomics* **4** (1) (2003) 37.

# Translocation Distance: Algorithms and Complexity

LUSHENG WANG

*Department of Computer Science*
*City University of Hong Kong*
*Hong Kong*
*cswangl@cityu.edu.hk*

**Abstract**

With the development of fast sequencing techniques, large-scale DNA molecules are investigated with respect to the relative order of genes in them. Contrary to the traditional alignment approach, genome rearrangements are based on comparison of gene orders and the evolution of gene families. Genome rearrangement has become an important area in computational biology and bioinformatics. There are three basic operations, *reversal*, *translocation*, and *transposition*. Here we study the translocation operations. Multi-chromosomal genomes frequently evolve by *translocation* events that exchange genetic material between two chromosomes. We will discuss both signed and unsigned cases.



ADVANCES IN COMPUTERS, VOL. 68


ISSN: 0065-2458/DOI: 10.1016/S0065-2458(06)68003-0

# 1. Introduction

Genome rearrangement was first studied by Dobzhansky and Sturtevant [8], sixty years ago, who published a milestone paper with an evolutionary tree presenting a rearrangement scenario with 17 reversals for the species Drosophila pseudoobscura and Miranda. Many subsequent studies show that genome rearrangement is a common mode of molecular evolution in plants, mammals, viral, and bacteria [1,11, 13–16,18,24–26].

In the late 1980s, Palmer et al. compared the mitochondrial genomes of *Brassica oleracea* (cabbage) and *Brassica campestris* (turnip) and found that they are very closely related (many genes are 99–99.9% identical) [23]. Another example [22] shows that the only major difference between the two bacteria *Escherichia coli* and *Salmonella typhimurium* is the order of genes in their chromosomes.

Genome rearrangement is based on comparison of gene orders and the evolution of gene families. Genome rearrangement has become an important area in computational biology and bioinformatics. Although the rearrangement process is very complicated, there are three basic operations, *reversal*, *translocation* and *transposition*. Fusions and fissions are also common in mammalian evolution.

In this chapter, we study the *translocation* operations. Multi-chromosomal genomes frequently evolve by translocation events that exchange genetic material between two chromosomes.

A *chromosome* $X = x_1, x_2, \ldots, x_p$ is a sequence of genes, where each gene $x_i$ is represented by an integer. A gene $x_i$ has a direction. When the direction of every gene is known, we use a signed integer to indicate the direction. When the directions of genes are unknown, we use unsigned integers to represent the genes. Throughout this chapter, each $x_i$ in a *signed chromosome* is a signed integer, and each $x_i$ in an *unsigned chromosome* is an unsigned integer. A *signed genome* is a set of signed chromosomes and an *unsigned* genome is a set of unsigned chromosomes.

## 1.1 The Signed Translocation

For two signed chromosomes $X = x_1, x_2, \ldots, x_m$ and $Y = y_1, y_2, \ldots, y_n$ in a genome, a prefix–prefix translocation $\rho_{pp}(X, Y, i, j)$ generates two new chromosomes: $x_1, \ldots, x_{i-1}, y_j, \ldots, y_n$ and $y_1, \ldots, y_{j-1}, x_i, \ldots, x_m$. A prefix–suffix translocation $\rho_{ps}(X, Y, i, j)$ generates two new chromosomes: $x_1, \ldots, x_{i-1}, -y_{j-1}, \ldots, -y_1$ and $-x_m, \ldots, -x_i, y_j, \ldots, y_n$.

Note that the choices of *prefix–prefix* and *prefix–suffix* translocations imply that one can change the direction of a chromosome without increasing the translocation distance. A chromosome $X$ is *identical* to chromosome $Y$ if either $X = Y$ or

$X = -Y$. Genome $A$ is *identical* to genome $B$ if and only if the sets of chromosomes for $A$ and $B$ are the same.

The *translocation distance* between two signed genomes $A$ and $B$, denoted as $d_s(A, B)$, is the minimum number of translocations required to transform $A$ into $B$. Given two genomes, the *signed translocation problem* is to find the minimum number of translocations as well as the sequence of translocation operations to transform one signed genome into the other.

Let $A$ and $B$ are two genomes. The genes at the ends of a chromosome are called head/tail genes. $A$ can be transformed into $B$ by translocations if and only if:

(1) The two genomes contain the same set of genes;
(2) The two genomes contain the same number (must be at least 2) of chromosomes;
(3) The two genomes have the same set of head/tail genes;
(4) For any gene $g$ that is a head/tail gene in $A$, (a) if $g$'s sign in $A$ is different from that in $B$, then $g$ must be a head in one genome and a tail in the other; (b) if $g$ has the same sign in both $A$ and $B$, then $g$ must be either a head in both genomes or a tail in both genomes.

(See [9].)

## 1.2 The Unsigned Translocation

For two unsigned chromosomes $X = x_1, x_2, \ldots, x_m$ and $Y = y_1, y_2, \ldots, y_n$ in a genome, a *translocation* swaps the segments in the chromosomes and generates two new chromosomes. A prefix–prefix translocation $\rho_{pp}(X, Y, i, j)$ generates two new chromosomes: $x_1, \ldots, x_{i-1}, y_j, \ldots, y_n$ and $y_1, \ldots, y_{j-1}, x_i, \ldots, x_m$. A prefix–suffix translocation $\rho_{ps}(X, Y, i, j)$ generates two new chromosomes: $x_1, \ldots, x_{i-1}$, $y_{j-1}, \ldots, y_1$ and $x_m, \ldots, x_i, y_j, \ldots, y_n$.

The *translocation distance* between two unsigned genomes $A$ and $B$, denoted as $d(A, B)$, is the minimum number of translocations required to transform $A$ into $B$. Given two genomes, the *unsigned translocation problem* is to find the minimum number of translocations as well as the sequence of translocation operations to transform one signed genome into the other.

For an unsigned chromosome, the genes at the ends of a chromosome are called *end* genes. Given two unsigned genomes, $A$ and $B$, $A$ can be transformed into $B$ by translocations if and only if the sets of end genes for $A$ and $B$ are identical.

In this chapter, we will review the history on the development of the algorithms for signed and unsigned translocation distance problems and present the best known exact and approximation algorithms for signed case and unsigned case, respectively.

## 2. The Signed Translocation Distance Problem

The signed translocation problem was first studied in [18]. Hannenhalli gave the first polynomial time algorithm to solve the problem [12]. The running time is $O(n^3)$, where $n$ is the total number of genes in the genome. An $O(n^2 \log n)$ algorithm was given in [29]. A linear-time algorithm that computes the minimum number of translocation operations was given in [20]. However, that algorithm cannot give the optimal sequence of translocation operations. Here we present an $O(n^2)$ algorithm originally in [27] that can compute the optimum sequence of translocation operations.

It seems that it is common to have linear-time algorithms to compute the distance values for various kinds of rearrangement operations. However, it takes more time to give an optimal sequence of operations. For example, for the signed reversal distance, a linear-time algorithm that computes the reversal distance value was given in [2]. However, the best known algorithms to give an optimal sequence of reversal operations still take $O(n^2)$ time [3,11,17]. Reference [10] dealt with minimum number of reversals, translocations, fissions and fusions. The value can be computed in linear-time. However, it takes $O(n^2)$ time to give the sequence of the four operations in [10]. The translocation distance is different from the distance studied in [10]. The algorithm makes use of some new and non-trivial properties and structures.

### 2.1 The Breakpoint Graph and the Distance Formula

For a genome $A$, we will construct a graph $G_A$. For each chromosome $X = x_1, x_2, \ldots, x_p$ in genome $A$, we have $2p$ vertices in $G_A$, two vertices $x_i^h$, $x_i^t$ for each gene $x_i$ in $X$. The $2p$ vertices are arranged in a linear order from left to right as

$$l(x_1)r(x_1)l(x_2)r(x_2)\ldots l(x_p)r(x_p), \tag{1}$$

where if $x_i$ is a positive integer, then $l(x_i) = x_i^t$ and $r(x_i) = x_i^h$; and if $x_i$ is a negative integer, then $l(x_i) = x_i^h$ and $r(x_i) = x_i^t$. For each $i \in \{1, 2, \ldots, p-1\}$, there is a black edge $(r(x_i), l(x_{i+1}))$ in $G_A$. Vertices $u$ and $v$ are *neighbors* in $G_A$ if there is a black edge connecting $u$ and $v$ in $G_A$.

Given two genomes $A$ and $B$, we can construct the *breakpoint graph* $G_{AB}$ from $G_A$ by adding a *grey* edge to every pair of vertices $u$ and $v$, where $u$ and $v$ are neighbors in $G_B$. The graph $G_{AB}$ contains two kinds of edges, *black* edge and *grey* edge. Each vertex in $G_{AB}$ (except the first and the last in a chromosome) is incident to two edges, one black and one grey. Thus, each vertex is in a unique cycle in $G_{AB}$. From the construction, each black edge in the cycle is followed by a grey edge and vice visa. A cycle is *long* if it contains at least two black edges. Otherwise, the cycle is *short*. If $A = B$, then all cycles in $G_{AB}$ are short. $d(A, B)$ is closely related to the number of cycles in $G_{AB}$.

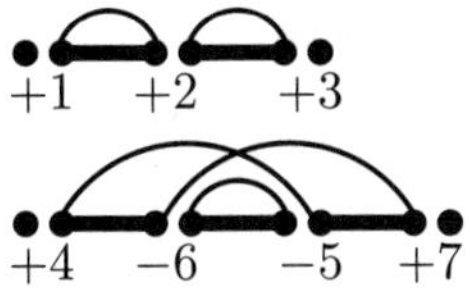


FIG. 1. The breakpoint graph for signed genome.

**Example 1.** Let the two genomes be $A = \{(1, 2, 3), (4, -6, -5, 7)\}$ and $B = \{(1, 2, 3), (4, 5, 6, 7)\}$. Both $A$ and $B$ contain two chromosomes. The breakpoint graph is shown in Fig. 1.

Let $X = x_1, x_2, \ldots, x_p$ be a chromosome in $A$. A *sub-permutation* is an interval $x_i, x_{i+1}, \ldots, x_{i+l}$ in $X$ containing at least three genes such that there is another interval of the same length $y_k, y_{k+1}, \ldots, y_{k+l}$ in a chromosome $Y$ of $B$ satisfying $\{|x_i|, |x_{i+1}|, \ldots, |x_{i+l}|\} = \{|y_k|, |y_{k+1}|, \ldots, |y_{k+l}|\}$, $y_k = x_i$, $y_{k+l} = x_{i+l}$, and $x_{i+1}, \ldots, x_{i+l-1} \neq y_{k+1}, \ldots, y_{k+l-1}$. $x_i$ and $x_{i+l}$ are called the *ending* genes of the sub-permutation.

Let $I = x_i, x_{i+1}, \ldots, x_j$ be an interval for chromosome $X$ in $A$. $V(I) = \{x_i^t, x_i^h, x_{i+1}^t, x_{i+1}^h, \ldots, x_j^t, x_j^h\}$ be the set of vertices in $G_{AB}$. The leftmost vertex and the rightmost vertex in $V(I)$ are referred to as $\mathit{LEFT}(I) = l(x_i)$ and $\mathit{RIGHT}(I) = r(x_j)$. Define $\mathit{IN}(I) = V(I) - \{\mathit{LEFT}(I), \mathit{RIGHT}(I)\}$. An edge $(u, v)$ is *inside* the interval $I$ if both $u$ and $v$ are in $\mathit{IN}(I)$. A sub-permutation $I$ can be viewed as a sub-graph $G_{AB}(I)$ of $G_{AB}$ containing the vertex set $\mathit{IN}(I)$ such that

(a) there is no edge $(u, v)$ such that $u \in \mathit{IN}(I)$ and $v \notin \mathit{IN}(I)$;
(b) the sub-graph corresponding to $I$ has at least one long cycle.

A *minimal sub-permutation* (*minSP* for short) is a sub-permutation such that any other interval in the minimal sub-permutation is not a sub-permutation.

Let $u$ and $v$ be two vertices in (1). $u$ is on the left of $v$ in $X$. A *segment* $[u, v]$ on chromosome $X$ contains all the vertices in (1) starting at $u$ and ending at $v$. A segment $[u, v]$ is *inside* a segment $[x, y]$ if both $u$ and $v$ are in $[x, y]$.

$s_{AB}$ denotes the number of minimal sub-permutations in $G_{AB}$ and $c_{AB}$ denotes the number of cycles in $G_{AB}$. The translocation distance is closely related to $s_{AB}$ and $c_{AB}$. It was shown that

$$d(A, B) \geqslant n - m - c_{AB},$$

where $n$ is the number of genes in the genomes and $m$ is the number of chromosomes in the genomes [12]. Given two *minSP*s in two *different* chromosomes in $A$, one can use one translocation to destroy the two *minSP*s and the resulting breakpoint graph has one more cycle. Thus, roughly speaking, $s_{AB}$ extra translocations are required to destroy all *minSP*s and keep the same number of cycles. However, if there are odd number of *minSP*s, we need one more extra translocation. $o_{AB}$ is defined as

$$o_{AB} = \begin{cases} 1: & \text{if the number of } \mathit{minSP}\text{s is odd,} \\ 0: & \text{otherwise.} \end{cases} \tag{2}$$

Another case that need extra translocations is that in $G_{AB}$ if (1) there are even number of *minSP*s in $G_{AB}$, and (2) all the *minSP*s are contained in a single sub-permutation (and thus all the *minSP*s are on a single chromosome of $A$). Such a single sub-permutation is called an *even isolation*. Note that, there is at most one even isolation. Define

$$i_{AB} = \begin{cases} 1: & \text{if there is an even isolation,} \\ 0: & \text{otherwise.} \end{cases} \tag{3}$$

The following theorem gives the value of the translocation distance and is the key to design polynomial time algorithm solving the problem [12].

**Theorem 1.** [12] *Let $n$ be the number of genes in the genomes and $m$ the number of chromosomes in the genomes. The translocation distance between two signed genomes $A$ and $B$ is*

$$d(A, B) = n - m - c_{AB} + s_{AB} + o_{AB} + 2 \cdot i_{AB}. \tag{4}$$

## 2.2 The General Framework of Polynomial Time Algorithms

Consider two black edges $(u, v)$ and $(f, g)$ in a long cycle in $G_{AB}$, where $(u, v)$ is in chromosome $X$ in $A$ and $(f, g)$ is in chromosome $Y$ in $A$. Consider a translocation $\rho$ acting on $X$ and $Y$ cutting the two black edge $(u, v)$ and $(f, g)$. $\rho$ is a *proper* translocation if the cycle containing $(u, v)$ and $(f, g)$ in $G_{AB}$ becomes two cycles in the new breakpoint graph. Otherwise, $\rho$ is *improper*. Sometimes, the two black edges that a translocation cuts might be in different cycles in $G_{AB}$. In that case, a translocation merges the two cycles into one. A *bad* translocation merges two cycles into one. (See Fig. 2.)

The formula (4) gives the value of the translocation distance between two genomes. We want to find translocations such that after applying such a translocation, the translocation distance is reduced by one.

A proper translocation is *valid* if it does not create any new *minSP*. It is proved in [12] that if there is a proper translocation for $G_{AB}$, there must be a valid proper translocation. As pointed out by Bergeron et al. in [6], a valid proper translocation

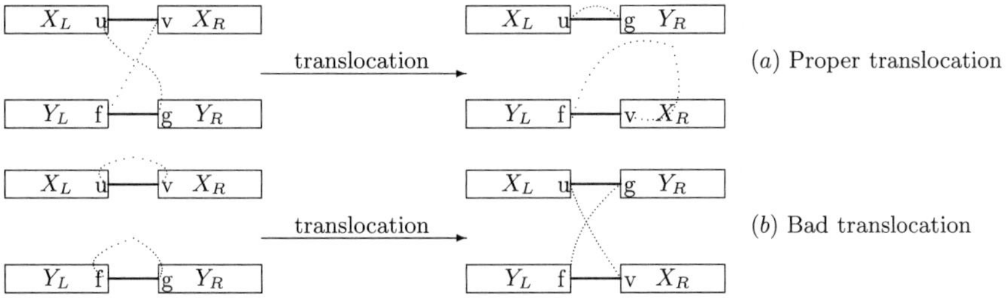


FIG. 2. Proper and bad translocations.

---

**while** the two genomes are not identical **do** choose a correct translocation as follows:

Case 1. There is an even isolation: destroy a *minSP*.
Case 2. If $O_{AB} = 0$, $L = 1$ and there is no even isolation: choose a valid proper translocation such that $L = 2$.
Case 3. $O_{AB} = 1$: Choose a valid proper translocation if possible. Otherwise, choose a correct bad translocation.
Case 4. $O_{AB} = 0$ and $L \geqslant 2$: Choose a correct bad translocation.

---

ALGORITHM 1. The general framework of a polynomial time algorithm.

may create an even isolation. Thus, when applying a valid proper translocation, one has to make sure no even isolation is introduced. A *correct* translocation reduces the distance by one. The general strategy for a polynomial time algorithm is (1) to choose a correct proper translocation to reduce the number of cycles by one; and (2) to choose a correct bad translocation to destroy two *minSP*s and at the same time to create one more cycle. (On average, each *minSP* needs one translocation in this case.) There are some special cases to consider. (i) If there are odd number of *minSP*s, we have to use one more bad translocation to destroy it. (ii) An even isolation costs two extra translocations.

Let $L$ be the number of chromosomes in the genome that contain *minSP*s. The algorithm to find an optimal sequence of correct translocations is given in Algorithm 1.

In Case 2, there must be more than one *SP* in the chromosome. Thus, there exists a grey edge with one end in the middle of the two *SP*s and the other end on another chromosome. Such a grey edge corresponds to a proper translocation (see Section 2.3). Using the method in [27] (see Section 2.3), we can find a valid proper translocation that re-distributes the *minSP*s in the chromosome to the two newly created chromosomes. Thus, $L$ becomes 2.

In Case 3, we do not have to worry about creating an even isolation when using a valid proper translocation. Thus, we always choose a valid proper translocation if possible.

In Case 4, there always exists a translocation that destroys two *minSP*s such that $L \geqslant 2$ or $L = 0$. We can cut the *minSP* $I$ in a chromosome such that there are *minSP*s on both left and right of $I$. If there is no such a chromosome, then either both chromosomes we cut have one *minSP* or both chromosomes we cut have two *minSP*s. In the first case, we have $L$ is even and $L$ is reduced by 2 and in the second case, we can have $L \geqslant 2$.

Suppose there are $n$ genes in the genomes. $d(A, B)$ is at most $O(n)$. The method in [12] can find a bad valid translocation in $O(n)$ time when no proper valid translocation is available. It takes $O(n)$ time to update the value of $L$. All the *minSP*s can be found in $O(n^2)$ time. Thus, the running time depends on the time to find a valid proper translocation.

### 2.2.1 Ideas for the Old Algorithms

The algorithm in [12] simply checks each grey edge in the newly created *minSP* to see if the grey edge leads to a proper valid translocation. For each grey edge, the checking process takes $O(n)$ time. Thus, in the worst case, it takes $O(n^2)$ time to find a proper valid translocation. Since $d(A, B)$ is at most $O(n)$, the total time required is $O(n^3)$.

For the best known algorithm in [29], it takes $O(n \log n)$ time to find a valid proper translocation from the newly created *minSP*. The idea is as follows:

(1) Carefully choose a grey edge in the newly created *minSP* and test if such a grey edge leads to a proper valid translocation.
(2) If such a grey edge does not lead to a proper valid translocation, then the size of the segment containing the proper valid grey edge (originally being a *minSP*) is reduced by half.
(3) Go to Step 1 to work on the new segment whose size is reduced by half.

Step 1 takes $O(n)$. In the worst case, it takes $O(\log n)$ iterations to find a proper valid translocation. Thus, the total time to find a proper valid translocation is $O(n \log n)$. Since $d(A, B)$ is at most $O(n)$, the total time required is $O(n^2 \log n)$.

## 2.3 The $O(n^2)$ Algorithm

In this section, we present the algorithm in [27] that makes use of some new and non-trivial properties and structures. It search the proper valid grey edge from the ends of the newly created *minSP*. It takes $O(n)$ time in total to find a proper valid grey edge.

Since $d(A, B)$ is at most $O(n)$, the total time required is $O(n^2)$.

Now we focus on how to find a valid proper translocation in $O(n)$ time.

A grey edge is *proper* if its two ends are in different chromosomes. For a proper grey edge $(u, v)$, there are two translocations (prefix–prefix and suffix–prefix) to cut the two black edges adjacent to the grey edge. One of the two translocations breaks a long cycle into two and thus is a proper translocation and the other is improper. From now on, we use a proper grey edge $(u, v)$ to refer to its proper translocation, denoted as $\rho(u, v)$. We use the two terms interchangeably.

Note that some proper translocation may not cut two black edges adjacent to a proper grey edge. However, whenever there is a proper translocation $\rho$, there must be a proper grey edge in the long cycle that $\rho$ breaks. In our algorithm, we always focus on the proper translocations indicated by proper grey edges.

If a proper grey edge (translocation) does not produce a new *minSP*, then it is valid. Otherwise, it is not valid. The following lemma shows that in this case, we can find a valid proper grey edge inside the new *minSP*.

**Lemma 1.** [29] *If a proper translocation for $G_{AB}$ produces a new minSP, say, $P$, then there must be a proper grey edge inside $P$ that is valid for $G_{AB}$.*

### 2.3.1 Finding the New *minSP*

Let $min = \{P_1, P_2, \ldots, P_k\}$ be the set of all *minSP*s for $G_{AB}$. *min* can be computed in $O(n^2)$ time [27]. Let $X_1Y_1$ be a new chromosome produced by a proper grey edge in $G_{AB}$, where $X_1$ is from chromosome $X$ in genome $A$ and $Y_1$ is from chromosome $Y$ in $A$. The black edge $(RIGHT(X_1), LEFT(Y_1))$ connecting the two parts $X_1$ and $Y_1$ is called the *connecting edge* in $X_1Y_1$. Obviously, a new *minSP* must contain the connecting edge.

We can find whether a new *minSP* is produced in $X_1Y_1$ in $O(n)$ time. The idea of our algorithm is to search the new chromosome $X_1Y_1$ starting from the two ends of the connecting edge to left and right, respectively. Let $l$ and $r$ be the vertices in $X_1$ and $Y_1$ that we are going to check. $L$ denotes the leftmost vertex in $X_1$ that a new *minSP* could reach and $R$ denotes the rightmost vertex in $Y_1$ that a new *minSP* could reach. $left(u)/right(u)$ denotes the vertex that is on the left/right of vertex $u$ in the breakpoint graph $G_{AB}$. (See Algorithm 2.)

In Step 5, we have to test if an old *minSP* is in $[L, R]$. This can be done in $O(n)$ time by looking at all the old *minSP*s in *min* produced by Algorithm 2.

A new sub-permutation $I$ in $X_1Y_1$ containing the connecting edge is a *nested* sub-permutation if $I$ does not contain any sub-permutation $P' \subset I$ such that $P' \subseteq X_1$ or $P' \subseteq Y_1$.

1. **Initialize** $L = l$ to indicate the rightmost vertex on $X_1$ in a long cycle. **Initialize** $R = r$ to indicate the leftmost vertex in $Y_1$ in a long cycle. (**if** there is no long cycle crossing the connecting edge, **then** return "no new *minSP* is found".)
2. **Let** $(l, u)$ and $(r, v)$ be the grey edges incident to $l$ and $r$, respectively.
   $(a)$ **if** $v \in V(X_1)$ and $v$ is on the left of $L$ **then** set $L = v$.
   $(b)$ **if** $v \in V(Y_1)$ and $v$ is on the right of $R$ **then** set $R = v$
   $(c)$ **if** $u \in V(X_1)$ and $u$ is on the left of $L$ **then** set $L = u$.
   $(d)$ **if** $u \in V(Y_1)$ and $u$ is on the right of $R$ **then** set $R = u$
   $(e)$ **if** $u$ or $v$ is not in $V(X_1Y_1)$ **then** return "no new *minSP* is found".
3. **If** $l \neq L$ **then** $l = left(l)$. **If** $r \neq R$ **then** $r = right(r)$.
4. **If** $l \neq L$ or $r \neq R$ goto Step 2.
5. **If** $[L, R]$ does not contain any *minSP* in *min* **then** return $[L, R]$
   **else return** "no new *minSP* is found".

ALGORITHM 2. Testing whether a new *minSP* exists in O($n$) time.

**Theorem 2.** *Algorithm 2 correctly tests whether $X_1Y_1$ contains a new minSP and if yes, outputs the new minSP. Algorithm 2 runs in* O($n$) *time.*

### 2.3.2 Partition of the New *minSP*

Let $X$ and $Y$ be two chromosomes of $A$. Let $e$ be a proper grey edge and $b$ and $c$ the two black edges adjacent to $e$ in $G_{AB}$. Suppose the proper translocation cutting $b$ and $c$ produces two new chromosomes $X_LX_MY_MY_R$ and $Y_LX_R$ such that $P = X_MY_M$ is a new *minSP*, where $X_M$ is from $X$ and $Y_M$ is from $Y$. See Fig. 3. We use $l(b)$ and $r(b)$ to represent the left and the right ends of edge $b$. Thus, we have $RIGHT(X_M) = l(b)$ and $LEFT(Y_M) = r(c)$.

From Lemma 1, to find a valid grey edge, we only have to consider the grey edges inside $X_MY_M$. This grey edge cannot be $(RIGHT(X_M), LEFT(Y_M))$, since if such a grey edge $(RIGHT(X_M), LEFT(Y_M))$ exists, then $(RIGHT(X_M), LEFT(Y_M)) = (l(b), r(c))$. (See Fig. 3.) Is the original grey edge used to do the translocation operation, and this translocation operation leads to the new *minSP* and is not valid.

**Lemma 2.** *Let $\rho$ be a proper translocation acting on chromosomes $X$ and $Y$ that produces the two new chromosomes $X_LX_MY_MY_R$ and $Y_LX_R$ such that $P = X_MY_M$ is a new minSP. Let $(u, v)$ be a grey edge inside $X_MY_M$. $\rho(u, v)$ acting on $X$ and $Y$ produces two new chromosomes $X' = X_1X_VY_VY_1$ and $Y' = X_2X_UY_UY_2$ such that $V(X_VY_V) \neq \emptyset$, $V(X_UY_U) \neq \emptyset$, $X_V$ and $X_U$ form $X_M$, and $Y_V$ and $Y_U$ form $Y_M$. If $X'$ or $Y'$ contains a new minSP, say, $P'$, then $P'$ must be inside $X_VY_V$ or $X_UY_U$.*

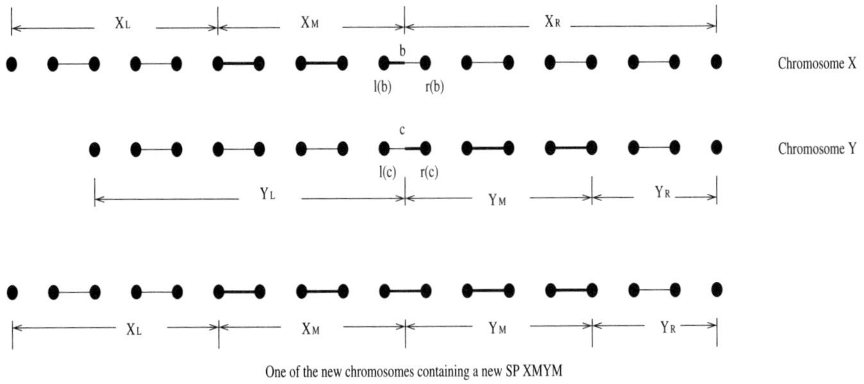


FIG. 3. A proper grey edge (translocation) acting on $X$ and $Y$ generates a new *minSP* in the resulting chromosomes. The bold parts represent segments in the new *minSP*.

---

*findEdge*$(X_M Y_M)$
We can start from the right end $l(b)$ of $X_M$, go to the left in $X_M$ and find the first vertex $v_R$ in $V(X_M)$ satisfying
(1) $v_R$ is connected to vertex $u_R \in V(Y_M)$ via a grey edge $(u_R, v_R)$ in $G_{AB}$.
(2) $(v_R, u_R) \neq (l(b), r(c))$, where $RIGHT(X_M) = l(b)$ and $LEFT(Y_M) = r(c)$.

---

ALGORITHM 3. Finding a grey edge in $X_M Y_M$ such that at least one of the new chromosomes does not contain any *minSP*.

Lemma 1 does not tell us how to find such a valid grey edge. We can use *findEdge*$(X_M Y_M)$ (Algorithm 3) to find a proper grey edge that can produce at most one new *minSP* though it may not be valid. (A grey edge may produce two new *minSP*s in some cases. This moves towards our goal by one step.)

**Lemma 3.** *Let $X_M Y_M$ be the new minSP. The grey edge $(u_R, v_R)$ is found in findEdge$(X_M Y_M)$. $(u_R, u)$ and $(v_R, v)$ denote the two black edges adjacent to the grey edge $(u_R, v_R)$ in $G_{AB}$. $X_N = v_1, v_2, \ldots, v_k$, where $v_k = l(b)$ if $X_N$ is not empty, is the segment of vertices (not including $v_R$) in $X_M$ checked in findEdge$(X_M Y_M)$ before vertex $v_R$ is found in $X_M$. At most one of the two new chromosomes produced by translocation $\rho(u_R, v_R)$ contains a new minSP. In particular, if $X_N$ is not empty, then the new chromosome $X'$ containing the segment $X_N$ does not contain any new minSP.*

**Corollary 1.** *Lemma 3 still holds if the input $X_M Y_M$ of findEdge() is a nested subpermutation, but not a minSP.*

Let $X' = X_1 X_V Y_V Y_1$ be the new chromosome produced by translocation $\rho(u_R, v_R)$ that does not contain any new *minSP*, where $X_1 \cap X_M = \emptyset$, $Y_1 \cap Y_M = \emptyset$, $X_V \subseteq X_M$ and $Y_V \subseteq Y_M$. Let $Y'$ be the other new chromosome produced by $\rho(u_R, v_R)$. According to Lemma 3, $Y'$ may contain a new *minSP*, say, $P$. Lemma 1 says that a valid proper translocation can be found in $P$. In the next subsection, we design a method to repeatedly reduce the size of the new *minSP* and eventually find the valid proper grey edge.

### 2.3.3 Finding the Valid Proper Grey Edge in the New *minSP*

Let $(u_R, v_R)$ be selected in *findEdge*$(X_M Y_M)$. One of the two new chromosomes $X' = X_1 X_V Y_V Y_1$ does not contain any new *minSP*. The other chromosome $Y' = X_2 X_U Y_U Y_2$ (call it *crucial* chromosome) that may contain a new *minSP*. Note that the two segments $X_U$ and $X_V$ form $X_M$ and $Y_U$ and $Y_V$ form $Y_M$ (the order may not be fixed). From Lemmas 2 and 3, the new *minSP* $P$ in $Y'$ must be inside the segment $X_U Y_U$. Next, we try to reduce the range in $X_U Y_U$ that the new *minSP* could be. Since $X_U \subseteq X_M$, $Y_U \subseteq Y_M$ and $X_M Y_M$ is a *minSP* at the very beginning, for any grey edge with one end in $X_U Y_U$, the other end must be in $V(X_M Y_M) = V(X_U) \cup V(X_V) \cup V(Y_U) \cup V(Y_V)$. Thus, it is enough to consider the vertices in $V(X_U) \cup V(X_V) \cup V(Y_U) \cup V(Y_V)$.

A vertex is *ignorable* if it is in $V(X_U Y_U)$, but not in the new *minSP* in $Y'$. We need the following lemma to prune segment $X_U Y_U$.

**Lemma 4.** *If there is a grey edge $(u_1, v_1)$ such that $u_1 \in V(X_V Y_V)$ and $v_1 \in V(X_U Y_U)$, then $v_1$ is ignorable.*

By the definition of *minSP*, the following lemma holds.

**Lemma 5.** *If $u \in V(X_U)$ is ignorable, then any vertex $v$ on the left of $u$ in $X_U$ is ignorable. If $u \in V(Y_U)$ is ignorable, then any $v$ on the right of $u$ in $Y_U$ is ignorable.*

**Lemma 6.** *Let $(u, v)$ be a grey edge inside $X_U Y_U$. If $u$ is ignorable then $v$ is ignorable.*

We can reduce the range of $X_U Y_U$ based on Lemmas 4–6. Let $l$ and $r$ be the rightmost vertex in $X_U$ and the leftmost vertex in $Y_U$ such that there are grey edges $(v_1, l)$ and $(v_2, r)$ with $v_1 \in V(X_V Y_V)$ and $v_2 \in V(X_V Y_V)$. Let $L$ and $R$ be the

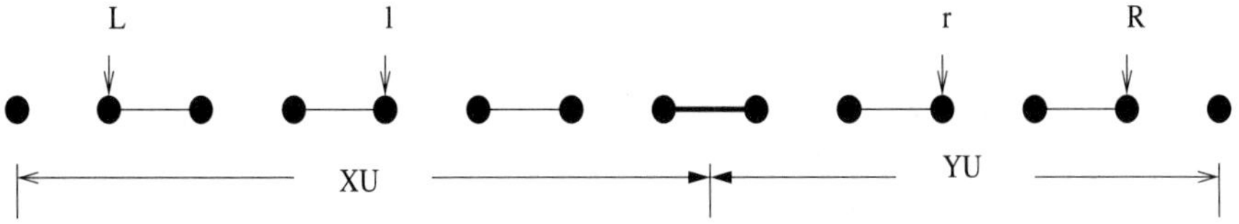


FIG. 4. Illustration of the four pointers in Algorithm 4.

---

*prune*$(X_U, Y_U, X_V, Y_V)$

1. Set $l = right(LEFT(X_U))$ and $r = left(RIGHT(Y_U))$.
2. Search every vertex $v \in V(X_V Y_V)$ and find the rightmost vertex $l$ in $X_U$ and the leftmost vertex $r$ in $Y_U$ such that there are grey edges $(v_1, l)$ and $(v_2, r)$ with $v_1 \in V(X_V Y_V)$ and $v_2 \in V(X_V Y_V)$.
3. Let $L = right(LEFT(X_U))$ and $R = left(RIGHT(Y_U))$.
4. Consider the grey edges $(L, u)$ and $(R, v)$. **if** $u \in V(X_U)$ $(v \in V(Y_U))$ and $u$ $(v)$ is on the right of $l$ (left of $r$), **then** $l = u$ $(r = v)$. **if** $u \in V(Y_U)$ $(v \in V(Y_U))$ and $u$ $(v)$ is on the left of $r$, **then** $r = u$ $(l = v)$.
5. **if** $(l \neq L)$ **then** $L = right(L)$. **if** $(r \neq R)$ **then** $R = left(R)$. **if** $(l \neq L$ or $r \neq R)$ **then** goto Step 4.
6. $l = right(l)$ and $r = left(r)$.
7. Move $r$ to the left until no short cycle is on the left of $r$ in $Y_U$. Move $l$ to the right until no short cycle is on the right of $l$ in $X_U$.
8. output: $[l, r]$.

---

ALGORITHM 4. Reducing the range of the *minSP* in the crucial chromosome.

vertices in $X_U$ and $Y_U$ that we are going to check (based on Lemma 6). Initially, we set $L = right(LEFT(X_U))$ and $R = left(RIGHT(Y_U))$. Figure 4 illustrates the four pointers used in the algorithm.

We can use Algorithm 4 to prune the segment $X_U Y_U$ in $Y'$. We claim that there always exists a grey edge $(u, v)$ with $u \in V(X_U Y_U)$ and $v \in V(X_V Y_V)$.

**Theorem 3.** *If algorithm prune*$(X_U, Y_U, X_V, Y_V)$ *returns* $l$ *and* $r$ *as the two ends of the connecting edge in* $X_2 X_U Y_U Y_2$, *then* $\rho(u_R, v_R)$ *is valid. If* $l$ *or* $r$ *is not the end of the connecting edge,* $\rho(u_R, v_R)$ *is not valid. In this case,* $\rho(u_R, v_R)$ *produces a new minSP contained in the interval* $[l, r]$. *Moreover,* $[l, r]$ *itself is a nested subpermutation in this case.*

Now, we can use *findEdge*() and *prune*() alternately to find a valid grey edge. (See Algorithm 5.)

---

*findValid*$(G_{AB})$
**Output** $(u_R, v_R)$.
1. Arbitrarily select a proper grey edge $(u, v)$ in $G_{AB}$ and apply the translocation.
2. Use Algorithm 3 to test if any of the two new chromosomes contains a new *minSP*. **if** no new *minSP* is found **then** return $(u, v)$ and stop.
3. Let $X_M Y_M$ be the new *minSP* found in Step 2.
4. Call *findEdge*$(X_M Y_M)$ to get $(u_R, v_R)$, and determine $X_U, Y_U, X_V, Y_V$.
5. Call *prune*$(X_U, Y_U, X_V, Y_V)$ to get $[l, r]$. **if** $l = RIGHT(X_U)$ and $r = LEFT(Y_U)$ **then** return $(u_R, v_R)$ and stop.
6. Update $X_M = [l, x]$ and $Y_M = [y, r]$, where $x$ and $y$ are the two ends of the connecting edge and goto Step 4.

---

ALGORITHM 5. Finding a valid proper grey edge (translocation) in O($n$) time.

**Theorem 4.** *Algorithm 5 finds a valid proper grey edge (translocation) in* O($n$) *time.*

**Theorem 5.** *There exists an* O($n^2$) *algorithm for the signed translocation problem.*

## 3. The Unsigned Translocation Distance Problem

In this section, we discuss the complexity for unsigned case and present a ratio-1.75 approximation algorithm. The translocation distance computation for unsigned genomes was first studied by Kececioglu et al. [19]. The problem was prove to be NP-hard by Zhu and Wang in [28].

### 3.1 Breakpoint Graph for Unsigned Genomes

Given two unsigned genomes $A$ and $B$, the *breakpoint* graph $B_{AB}$ is constructed as follows: (1) the vertex set is the set of genes in $A$ in the linear order as in the chromosomes; (2) set a *black* edge between any two vertices that are neighbors in $A$ and set a *grey* edge between any two vertices that are neighbors in $B$. A *nodal* vertex is the vertex for an end gene in a chromosome. Every *nodal* vertex in $B_{AB}$ is incident to one black edge and one grey edge. Any non-nodal vertex is incident to two black and two grey edges.

Unlike the signed breakpoint graphs, the unsigned breakpoint graphs do not admit unique cycle decomposition. For each non-nodal vertex, there are two ways to pair the two black and two grey edges incident to the vertex. Once the choice for the paring of the two black and two grey edges is fixed, we have a decomposition of $B_{AB}$ into alternate-color cycles. Any alternate-color cycle decomposition gives a direction of every gene in genomes $A$ and $B$.

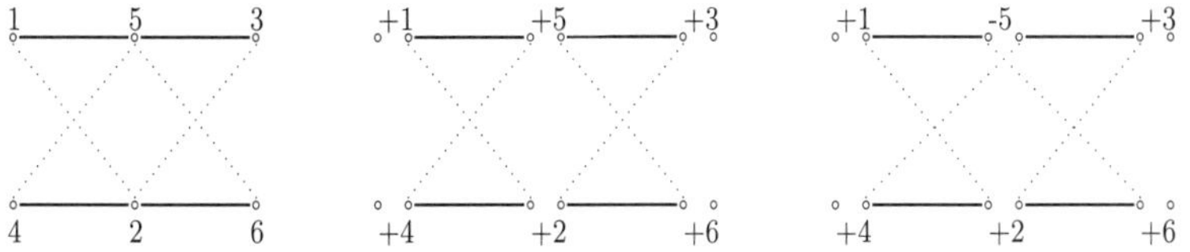


(a) Unsigned breakpoint graph $B_{AB}$. (b) Signed breakpoint graph $G_{\vec{A}_1\vec{B}}$. (c) Signed breakpoint graph $G_{\vec{A}_2\vec{B}}$.

FIG. 5. The signed and unsigned breakpoint graphs for genomes $A$ and $B$.

For example, let $A = \{1, 5, 3; 4, 2, 6\}$ and $B = \{1, 2, 3; 4, 5, 6\}$, both containing two chromosomes separated by a semicolon. The unsigned breakpoint graph $B_{AB}$ is presented in Fig. 5(a). Assign every gene in $B$ a positive direction to get $\vec{B}$=$\{+1, +2, +3; +4, +5, +6\}$. If $\vec{A}_1 = \{+1, +5, +3; +4, +2, +6\}$, the corresponding signed breakpoint graph $G_{\vec{A}_1\vec{B}}$ is as Fig. 5(b) and $d(\vec{A}_1, \vec{B})$=2. If $\vec{A}_2 = \{+1, -5, +3; +4, +2, +6\}$, the corresponding graph $G_{\vec{A}_2\vec{B}}$ is as Fig. 5(c). In this case, $d(\vec{A}_2, \vec{B}) = 3$.

Let $\rho$ be a translocation that transforms genome $A$ into $A_1$. There exists a translocation $\rho_1$ transforming $A_1$ into $A$. Translocation $\rho_1$ is called the *counter translocation* of $\rho$ and $\rho_1$ is denoted as $\bar{\rho}$. Let *spin*$(A)$ be the set of all signed genomes obtained from $A$ by assigning a direction to each gene in $A$. The following theorem gives the relationship between the unsigned and the signed translocation distances.

**Theorem 6.** *Let $A$ and $B$ be two unsigned genomes. $\vec{B}$ is the signed genome obtained from $B$ by setting the direction of every gene as positive. Then,* $d(A, B) = \min_{\vec{A}\in \text{spin}(A)} d(\vec{A}, \vec{B})$.

## 3.2 The NP-Hardness

The reduction is from the maximum alternate-color cycle decomposition problem, which was proved to be NP-hard by Caprara in [7].

> **The maximum alternate-color cycle decomposition problem**
> **Instance:** Unsigned chromosomes $X$ and $Y$, $B_{XY}$ as the breakpoint graph with respect to $X$ and $Y$.
> **Question:** Find an alternate-color cycle decomposition of $B_{XY}$ such that the number of cycles is maximized.

Given two unsigned genomes $A$ and $B$. Consider the cycle decomposition of $B_{AB}$. If vertex $x$ is split into $x^t$ and $x^h$ by a cycle decomposition of $B_{AB}$, each of $x^t$ and $x^h$ must be uniquely in one alternate-color cycle. Vertex $x$ is *used* by cycle $C$ if $x^t$

or $x^h$ is in $C$. Every cycle uses a vertex at most twice in a cycle decomposition of $B_{AB}$. A grey edge is referred to as *inside* $X$ if its two ends are both in $X$. A grey edge *spans* $X$ and $Y$ if one of its end is in $X$ and the other is in $Y$.

The reduction is from the Max-Acd problem. Let $X$ and $Y$ be the two unsigned chromosomes. Without loss of generality, let $X = g_1, g_2, \ldots, g_{n-1}, g_n$ and $Y = 1, 2, \ldots, n$, where $\{g_1, g_2, \ldots, g_n\} = \{1, 2, \ldots, n\}$, $g_1 = 1$, $g_n = n$. We construct two genomes $A$=$\{X_1, X_2\}$ and $B$=$\{Y_1, Y_2\}$ from $X$ and $Y$.

There are $4n - 3 + (n - 2)d$ genes in both genomes $A$ and $B$, where genes in $\{1, 2, \ldots, n\}$ have been used in $X$ and $Y$. The positive integer $d$ is used to control the shape of the long cycles in the decomposition of $B_{AB}$. Chromosome $X_1$ of genome $A$ is constructed by inserting $n - 1$ new genes into the midst of adjacent pairs of genes in chromosome $X$.

$$X_1 = 1, t_{1,1}, g_2, t_{1,2}, \ldots, g_{n-1}, t_{1,n-1}, n, \tag{5}$$

where $t_{1,k} = 3n - 2 + k$, $1 \leqslant k \leqslant n - 1$.

$X_2$ contains two types of new genes, denoted as $t_{2,l}$ and $s_i$ respectively.

$$\begin{aligned} X_2 = {} & t_{2,1}, t_{2,2}, s_1, s_2, \ldots, s_d, \\ & t_{2,3}, t_{2,4}, s_{d+1}, \ldots, s_{2d}, \\ & \ldots, \\ & t_{2,2(n-2)-1}, t_{2,2(n-2)}, s_{(n-3)d+1}, \ldots, s_{(n-2)d}, \\ & t_{2,2(n-1)-1}, t_{2,2(n-1)}, \end{aligned} \tag{6}$$

where $t_{2,l} = n + l$, $1 \leqslant l \leqslant 2(n - 1)$, $s_i = 4n - 3 + i$, and $1 \leqslant i \leqslant (n - 2)d$.

Now construct genome $B = \{Y_1, Y_2\}$. Let $t_{1,k}$, $t_{2,l}$, and $s_i$ be the same integers as used in $A$. Chromosome $Y_1$ is identical to $Y$, $Y_1 = 1, 2, \ldots, n - 1, n$. $Y_2$ is constructed from $X_2$ by inserting $t_{1,k}$ into the midst of $t_{2,2k-1}$ and $t_{2,2k}$ in $X_2$.

$$\begin{aligned} Y_2 = {} & t_{2,1}, t_{1,1}, t_{2,2}, s_1, s_2, \ldots, s_d, \\ & t_{2,3}, t_{1,2}, t_{2,4}, s_{d+1}, \ldots, s_{2d}, \\ & \ldots, \\ & t_{2,2(n-2)-1}, t_{1,n-2}, t_{2,2(n-2)}, s_{(n-3)d+1}, \ldots, s_{(n-2)d}, \\ & t_{2,2(n-1)-1}, t_{1,n-1}, t_{2,2(n-1)}. \end{aligned} \tag{7}$$

**Example.** Suppose $X = 1, 4, 3, 5, 2, 6$ and $Y = 1, 2, 3, 4, 5, 6$. Then the breakpoint graph $G_{XY}$ is shown in Fig. 6(a). For simplicity, set $d = 1$. The two genomes are constructed as $A = \{X_1 = 1, 17, 4, 18, 3, 19, 5, 20, 2, 21, 6;\ X_2 = 7, 8, 22, 9, 10, 23, 11, 12, 24, 13, 14, 25, 15, 16\}$, and $B = \{Y_1 = 1, 2, 3, 4, 5, 6;$

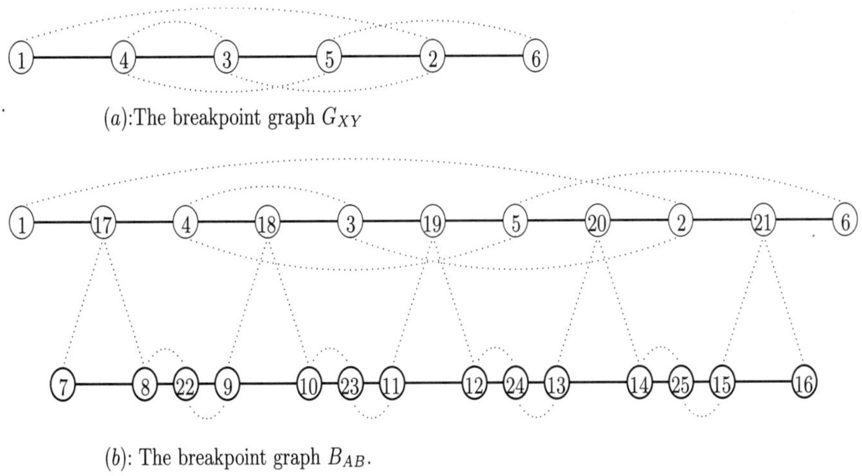

FIG. 6. The breakpoint graphs with respect to chromosomes $X$ and $Y$ and genomes $A$ and $B$.

$Y_2 = 7, 17, 8, 22, 9, 18, 10, 23, 11, 19, 12, 24, 13, 20, 14, 25, 15, 21, 16\}$. The corresponding breakpoint graph $B_{AB}$ is shown in Fig. 6(b).

We can show that there is a decomposition of $G_{XY}$ into $J$ alternate-color cycles if and only if there exist at most $3n - 3 - J$ translocations to transform $A$ into $B$.

**Theorem 7.** *The unsigned translocation distance problem is NP-hard.*

## 3.3 Inapproximability

Now, we study the hardness of approximating the unsigned translocation distance. Consider the breakpoint graph decomposition (BGD) problem [4]. The instance of BGD is the same as Max-Acd, but the objective of BGD is to minimize $cost(\mathcal{C}) = b - |\mathcal{C}|$, where $b$ is the number of black edges of the breakpoint graph and $\mathcal{C}$ is the set of alternate-color cycles. In [4], Berman and Karpinski proved

**Lemma 7.** *For any $\varepsilon > 0$, it is NP-hard to decide if an instance of BGD with $2240p$ breakpoints has the minimum cost of alternate-color cycle decomposition below $(1236 + \varepsilon)p$ or above $(1237 - \varepsilon)p$.*

Now we use the reduction of Theorem 7 to show that approximating the unsigned translocation distance within a factor 1.00017 is difficult.

**Theorem 8.** *For any $\varepsilon > 0$, it is NP-hard to decide if an instance of the unsigned translocation distance problem can be approximated within factor $\frac{5717}{5716} - \varepsilon$, i.e., $1.00017 - \varepsilon$.*

## 3.4 The 1.75 Approximation Algorithm

In this subsection, we present the 1.75 approximation algorithm originated in [5]. The main idea is based on the observation that if we can give a good approximation of the cycle decomposition of the unsigned case, we can get a good approximation solution for the unsigned translocation distance. For the 1.75 approximation algorithm, they give a cycle decomposition that contains the maximum number of 1-cycles and a sufficient number of 2-cycles.

### *3.4.1 Why the Ratio Could Be Better Than 2?*

Now, we give an intuitive explanation that if we keep the maximum number of 1-cycles and maximum number of 2-cycles in assigning signs to genes, then the best performance ratio we can expect is 1.5.

Suppose that we ignore the effect of $s_{AB}$ and $i_{AB}$ in formula (4). That is, we assume that $s_{AB} = 0$ and $i_{AB} = 0$ in the optimal cycle decomposition. Then $d(A, B) = n - N - c$. Let $c_i^*$ be the number of $i$-cycles in the optimal cycle decomposition. Then

$$d(A, B) = n - N - c = n - N - c_1^* - c_2^* - \sum_{i \geqslant 3} c_i^*. \tag{8}$$

$n - N$ is the number of black edges in the breakpoint graph. We further assume that $c_1^* = 0$, $c_2^* = 0$ and all black edges are in 3-cycles in the optimal cycle decomposition. In this case, $d(A, B) = n - N - \frac{n-N}{3} = \frac{2}{3}(n - N)$. If in the approximation solution, we do not care about $i$-cycles for $i \geqslant 3$, the distance for the approximation solution could be $n - N$. Thus, the ratio becomes $\frac{3}{2}$. In our approximation algorithm, we cannot get the maximum number of 2-cycles, but we get a large number of 2-cycles. Besides, we have to design sophisticated ways to deal with the other two parameters $s$ and $f$ in the analysis.

### *3.4.2 The Cycle Decomposition Algorithm*

We use $B_{AB}$ to denote the breakpoint graph for the unsigned genomes $A$ and $B$. A cycle decomposition of $B_{AB}$ can be computed in the following three steps.

*Step* 1: *Decomposition of* 1*-cycles.* If two vertices are joined by a black edge and a grey edge in $B_{AB}$, then assign proper signs to the two vertices to obtain the 1-cycle containing the black edge and the grey edge. Thus, if two genes are neighbors in both genomes, the corresponding 1-cycle is kept in the cycle decomposition.

*Step* 2: *Decomposition of* 2-*cycles.* From $B_{AB}$, we define a new graph, called *match graph*, $F_{AB}$ as follows: (1) For every black edge in $B_{AB}$ with at least one end not assigned a sign in Step 1, we create a vertex of $F_{AB}$. (2) For every two vertices of $F_{AB}$ (representing two black edges in $B_{AB}$), we create an edge connecting them in $F_{AB}$ if the two black edges in $B_{AB}$ can form a 2-cycle. $F_{AB}$ can be constructed in $O(n^2)$ time where $n$ is the number of genes.

Let $M$ denote a maximum match of $F_{AB}$. $|M|$ is the size of the match. A maximum match of any graph can be found in $O(|V||E|^{1/2})$ time, where $|V|$ is the number of vertices and $|E|$ is the number of edges [21]. Since $F_{AB}$ contains at most $n$ vertices and $O(n)$ edges, $M$ can be found in $O(n^{3/2})$ time. Every edge in $M$ represents a 2-cycle of $B_{AB}$. By the construction, two 2-cycles in $M$ cannot share any black edge of $B_{AB}$. However, they may share a grey edge in $B_{AB}$. In that case, the two 2-cycles cannot be kept in the cycle decomposition simultaneously. A 2-cycle in $M$ is *isolated* if it does not share any grey edge with any other 2-cycles in $M$. Otherwise, the 2-cycle is *related.* Since a 2-cycle has two grey edges, it is related to at most two 2-cycles.

A *related component* $U$ consists of related cycles $C_1, C_2, \ldots, C_k$, where $C_i$ is related to $C_{i-1}$ $(2 \leqslant i \leqslant k)$, and every 2-cycle in $U$ is not related to any 2-cycle not in $U$. A related component involves at most two chromosomes, and can be one of the four types shown in Fig. 7.

In our cycle decomposition, we keep all the isolated 2-cycles and alternatively select 2-cycles from every related component. Assume that a maximum match $M$ of $F_{AB}$ contains $z$ isolated 2-cycles. In our cycle decomposition approach, we can keep at least $\lceil \frac{|M|-z}{2} \rceil + z$, i.e., $\lceil \frac{|M|+z}{2} \rceil$ 2-cycles in Step 2.

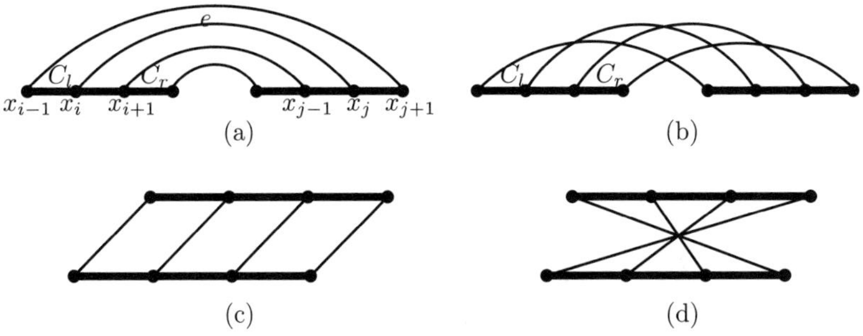


FIG. 7. The four cases of related components including three 2-cycles.

*Step* 3: *Decomposition of other long cycles*. After the decomposition of 2-cycles, the other long cycles can be arbitrarily selected from the remaining graph.

The long cycles created in Step 2 are called *selected* cycles and the cycles created in Step 3 are called *arbitrary* cycles.

Our approximation algorithm for unsigned translocation problem is as follows:

**Approximation algorithm**

Input: $B_{AB}$

**1**. Compute the cycle decomposition of $B_{AB}$ as described before.
**2**. Solve the signed case using the standard algorithm.

Let $n$ be the number of genes in the given genomes. $B_{AB}$ and $F_{AB}$ can be constructed in $O(n^2)$ time. A maximum match of $F_{AB}$ can be found in $O(n^{3/2})$ time. The algorithm in [27] requires $O(n^2)$ time to compute an optimal sequence of translocations for signed case. Thus, the total time required for our approximation algorithm is $O(n^2)$.

**Theorem 9.** *The performance of the approximation algorithm is* 1.75 *and its running time is* $O(n^2)$.

## ACKNOWLEDGEMENT

The work is fully supported by a grant from the Research Grants Council of the Hong Kong Special Administrative Region, China [Project No. CityU 1070/02E].

## REFERENCES

[1] Bafna V., Pevzner P., "Sorting by reversals: Genome rearrangements in plant organelles and evolutionary history of x chromosome", *Mol. Biol. Evol.* **12** (1995) 239–246.
[2] Bader D.A., Moret B.M.E., Yan M., "A linear-time algorithm for computing inversion distance between signed permutation", *J. Comput. Biol.* **8** (2001) 483–491.
[3] Bader D.A., Moret B.M.E., Yan M., "A linear-time algorithm for computing inversion distance between signed permutations with an experimental study", in: *Proceedings of the 7th International Workshop on Algorithms and Data Structures*, August 2001, pp. 365–376.
[4] Berman P., Karpinski M., "On some tighter inapproximability results", ECCC report No. 65, University of Trier, 1998.
[5] Cui Y., Wang L., Zhu D., "A 1.75-approximation algorithm for unsigned translocation distance", in: *ISAAC 2005*, in press.
[6] Bergeron A., Mixtacki J., Stoye J., "On sorting by translocation", in: *RECOMB'05*, 2005, pp. 615–629.

[7] Caprara A., "Sorting by reversals is difficult", in: *Proceedings of the 1st Annual International Conference on Research Computational Molecular Biology*, 1999, pp. 84–93.
[8] Dobzhansky T., Sturtevant A.H., "Inversions in the chromosomes of *drosophila pseudoobscura*", *Genetics* **23** (1938) 28–64.
[9] Feng W., Wang L., Zhu D., "CTRD: a fast applet for computing signed translocation distance between genomes", *Bioinformatics* **20** (17) (2004) 3256–3257.
[10] Tesler G., "Efficient algorithms for multichromosomal genome rearrangements", *J. Comput. Syst. Sci.* **65** (2002) 587–609.
[11] Hannenhalli S., Pevzner P., "Transforming cabbage into turnip: Polynomial algorithm for sorting signed permutations by reversals", *J. ACM* **46** (1) (1999) 1–27.
[12] Hannenhalli S., "Polynomial time algorithm for computing translocation distance between genomes", *Discrete Appl. Math.* **71** (May 1996) 137–151.
[13] Hannenhalli S., Chappey C., Koonin E.V., Pevzner P., "Genome sequence comparison and scenarios for gene rearrangements: A test case", *Genomics* **30** (1995) 299–311.
[14] Hannenhalli S., Pevzner P., "Towards a computational theory of genome rearrangement", in: *Lecture Notes in Comput. Sci.*, vol. 1000, Springer-Verlag, Berlin, 1995, pp. 184–202.
[15] Hannenhalli S., Pevzner P., "To cut or not to cut (applications of comparative physical maps in molecular evolution)", in: *Proceedings of the 7th Annual ACM–SIAM Symposium on Discrete Algorithms*, January 1996, pp. 304–313.
[16] Hannenhalli S., Pevzner P., "Transforming men into mice: Polynomial algorithm for genomic distance problem", in: *Proceedings of the 36 Annual IEEE Symposium on Foundations of Computer Science*, 1995, pp. 581–592.
[17] Kaplan H., Shamir R., Tarjan R.E., "Faster simpler algorithm for sorting signed permutations by reversals", *SIAM J. Comput.* **29** (3) (2000) 880–892.
[18] Kececioglu J., Ravi R., "Of mice and men: Algorithms for evolutionary distances between genomes with translocation", in: *Proceedings of the 6th Annual ACM–SIAM Symposium on Discrete Algorithms*, January 1995, pp. 604–613.
[19] Kececioglu J., Sankoff D., "Exact and approximation algorithms for the inversion distance between two permutations", in: *Proceedings of the 4th Annual Symposium on Combinatorial Pattern Matching*, in: *Lecture Notes in Comput. Sci.*, vol. 684, Springer-Verlag, Berlin, 1993, pp. 87–105.
[20] Li G., Qi X., Wang X., Zhu B., "A linear time algorithm for computing translocation distance between signed genomes", in: *Proceedings of CPM'2004*, in: *Lecture Notes in Comput. Sci.*, vol. 3109, Springer-Verlag, Berlin, 2004.
[21] Lovász L., Plummer M.D., *Matching Theory*, *Annals of Discrete Mathematics*, vol. 29, North-Holland, Amsterdam, 1986.
[22] O'Brien S.J., *Genetics Maps: Locus Maps of Complex Genomes*, sixth ed., Cold Spring Harbor Laboratory Press, Cold Spring Harbor, 1993.
[23] Palmer J.D., Herbon L.A., "Plant mitochondrial DNA evolves rapidly in structure, but slowly in sequence", *J. Mol. Evol.* **28** (1988) 87–97.
[24] Sankoff D., Nadeau J.H., "Comparative genomics: Empirical and analytical approaches to gene order dynamics, map alignment and the evolution of gene families", in: *Series in Computational Biology*, vol. 1, Kluwer Academic Press, Dordrecht, NL, 2000, pp. 225–241.

[25] Sankoff D., "Edit distance for genome comparison based on non-local operations", in: *Proceedings of the 3rd Annual Symposium on Combinatorial Pattern Matching*, 1992, pp. 121–135.

[26] Sankoff D., El-Mabrouk N., "Genome rearrangement", in: T. Jiang, Y. Xu, Q. Zhang (Eds.), *Current Topics in Computational Molecular Biology*, The MIT Press, Cambridge, MA, 1992, pp. 132–155.

[27] Wang L., Zhu D., Liu X., Ma S., "An $O(n^2)$ algorithm for signed translocation", *J. Comput. Syst. Sci.* **70** (2005) 284–299.

[28] Zhu D., Wang L., "On the complexity of unsigned translocation distance", *Theoret. Comput. Sci.*, submitted for publication.

[29] Zhu D.M., Ma S.H., "An improved polynomial time algorithm for translocation sorting problems", *J. Comput.* **25** (2) (2002) 189–196 (in Chinese).

# Computational Grand Challenges in Assembling the Tree of Life: Problems and Solutions

DAVID A. BADER

*College of Computing*
*Georgia Institute of Technology*
*Atlanta, GA 30332*
*USA*

USMAN ROSHAN

*Computer Science Department*
*New Jersey Institute of Technology*
*Newark, NJ 07102*
*USA*

ALEXANDROS STAMATAKIS

*Swiss Federal Institute of Technology*
*School of Computer & Communication Sciences*
*Station 14*
*CH-1015 Lausanne*
*Switzerland*

**Abstract**

The computation of ever larger as well as more accurate phylogenetic (evolutionary) trees with the ultimate goal to compute the tree of life represents one of the grand challenges in High Performance Computing (HPC) Bioinformatics. Unfortunately, the size of trees which can be computed in reasonable time based on elaborate evolutionary models is limited by the severe computational cost inherent to these methods. There exist two orthogonal research directions to overcome this challenging computational burden: First, the development of novel, faster, and more accurate heuristic algorithms and second, the application of high performance computing techniques. The goal of this chapter is to

ADVANCES IN COMPUTERS, VOL. 68
ISSN: 0065-2458/DOI: 10.1016/S0065-2458(06)68004-2

provide a comprehensive introduction to the field of computational evolutionary biology to an audience with computing background, interested in participating in research and/or commercial applications of this field. Moreover, we will cover leading-edge technical and algorithmic developments in the field and discuss open problems and potential solutions.



# 1. Phylogenetic Tree Reconstruction

In this section, we provide an example of Branch and Bound (B&B) applied to reconstructing an evolutionary history (phylogenetic tree). Specifically, we focus on the shared-memory parallelization of the maximum parsimony (MP) problem using B&B based on work by Bader and Yan [1–4].

## 1.1 Biological Significance and Background

All biological disciplines agree that species share a common history. The genealogical history of life is called phylogeny or an evolutionary tree. Reconstructing phylogenies is a fundamental problem in biological, medical, and pharmaceutical research and one of the key tools in understanding evolution. Problems related to phylogeny reconstruction are widely studied. Most have been proven or are believed to be NP-hard problems that can take years to solve on realistic datasets [5,6]. Many biologists throughout the world compute phylogenies involving weeks or years of computation without necessarily finding global optima. Certainly more such computational analyses will be needed for larger datasets. The enormous computational demands in terms of time and storage for solving phylogenetic problems can only be met through high-performance computing (in this example, large-scale B&B techniques).

A phylogeny (phylogenetic tree) is usually a rooted or unrooted bifurcating tree with leaves labeled with species, or more precisely with taxonomic units (called *taxa*) that distinguish species [7]. Locating the root of the evolutionary tree is scientifically difficult so a reconstruction method only recovers the topology of the unrooted tree. Reconstruction of a phylogenetic tree is a statistical inference of a true phylogenetic tree, which is unknown. There are many methods to reconstruct phylogenetic trees from molecular data [8]. Common methods are classified into two major groups: criteria-based and direct methods. Criteria-based approaches assign a score to each phylogenetic tree according to some criteria (e.g., parsimony, likelihood). Sometimes computing the score requires auxiliary computation (e.g. computing hypothetical ancestors for a leaf-labeled tree topology). These methods then search the space of trees (by enumeration or adaptation) using the evaluation method to select the best one. Direct methods build the search for the tree into the algorithm, thus returning a unique final topology automatically.

We represent species with binary sequences corresponding to morphological (e.g. observable) data. Each bit corresponds to a feature, call a *character*. If a species has a given feature, the corresponding bit is one; otherwise, it is zero. Species can also be described by molecular sequence (nucleotide, DNA, amino acid, protein). Regardless of the type of sequence data, one can use the same parsimony phylogeny reconstruction methods. The evolution of sequences is studied under a simplifying assumption that each site evolves independently.

The Maximum Parsimony (MP) objective selects the tree with the smallest total evolutionary change. The *edit distance* between two species as the minimum number of evolutionary events through which one species evolves into the other. Given a tree in which each node is labeled by a species, the *cost* of this tree (tree length) is the sum of the costs of its edges. The cost of an edge is the edit distance between the species at the edge endpoints. The *length* of a tree $T$ with all leaves labeled by taxa is the minimum cost over all possible labelings of the internal nodes.

Distance-based direct methods [9–11] require a distance matrix $D$ where element $d_{ij}$ is an estimated evolutionary distance between species $i$ and species $j$. The distance-based Neighbor-Joining (NJ) method quickly computes an approximation to the shortest tree. This can generate a good early incumbent for B&B. The neighbor-joining (NJ) algorithm by Saitou and Nei [12], adjusted by Studier and Keppler [13], runs in $O(n^3)$ time, where $n$ is the number of species (leaves). Experimental work shows that the trees it constructs are reasonably close to "true" evolution of synthetic examples, as long as the rate of evolution is neither too low nor too high. The NJ algorithm begins with each species in its own subtree. Using the distance matrix, NJ repeatedly picks two subtrees and merge them. Implicitly the two trees become children of a new node that contains an artificial taxon that mimics the distances to the subtrees. The algorithm uses this new taxon as a representative for the new tree. Thus in each iteration, the number of subtrees decrements by one till there are only two left. This creates a binary topology. A distance matrix is *additive* if there exists a tree for which the inter-species tree distances match the matrix distances exactly. NJ can recover the tree for additive matrices, but in practice distance matrices are rarely additive. Experimental results show that on reasonable-length sequences parsimony-based methods are almost always more accurate (on synthetic data with known evolution) than neighbor-joining and some other competitors, even under adverse conditions [14]. In practice MP works well, and its results are often hard to beat.

In this section we focus on reconstructing phylogeny using maximum parsimony (minimum evolution). A brute-force approach for maximum parsimony examines all possible tree topologies to return one that shows the smallest amount of total evolutionary change. The number of unrooted binary trees on $n$ leaves (representing the species or taxa) is $(2n - 5)!! = (2n - 5) \cdot (2n - 7) \cdots 3$. For instance, this means that there are about 13 billion different trees for an input of $n = 13$ species. Hence it is very time-consuming to examine all trees to obtain the optimal tree. Most researchers focus on heuristic algorithms that examine a much smaller set of most promising topologies and choose the best one examined. One advantage of B&B is that it provides instance-specific lower bounds, showing how close a solution is to optimal [15].

The phylogeny reconstruction problem with maximum parsimony (MP) is defined as follows. The input is a set of $c$ characters and a set of taxa represented as length-$c$ sequences of values (one for each character). For example, the input could come from an aligned set of DNA sequences (corresponding elements matched in order, with gaps). The output is an unrooted binary tree with the given taxa at leaves and assignments to the length-$c$ internal sequences such the resulting tree has minimum total cost (evolutionary change). The characters need not be binary, but each usually has a bounded number of states. Parsimony criteria (restrictions on the changes between adjacent nodes) are often classified into Fitch, Wagner, Dollo, and Generalized (Sankoff) Parsimony [7]. In this example, we use the simplest criteria, Fitch parsimony [16], which imposes no constraints on permissible character state changes. The optimization techniques we discuss are similar across all of these types of parsimony.

Given a topology with leaf labels, we can compute the optimal internal labels for that topology in linear time per character. Consider a single character. In a leaf-to-root sweep, we compute for each internal node $v$ a set of labels optimal for the subtree rooted at $v$ (called the Farris Interval). Specifically, this is the intersection of its children's sets (connect children though $v$) or, if this intersection is empty, the union of its children's sets (agree with one child). At the root, we choose an optimal label and pass it down. Children agree with their parent if possible. Because we assume each site evolves independently, we can set all characters simultaneously. Thus for $m$ character and $n$ sequences, this takes $O(nm)$ time. Since most computers can perform efficient bitwise logical operations, we use the binary encoding of a state in order to implement intersection and union efficiently using bitwise AND and bitwise OR. Even so, this operation dominates the parsimony B&B computation.

The following sections outline the parallel B&B strategy for MP that is used in the GRAPPA (Genome Rearrangement Analysis through Parsimony and other Phylogenetic Algorithms) toolkit [2]. Note that the maximum parsimony problem is actually a minimization problem.

## 1.2 Strategy

We now define the *branch*, *bound*, and *candidate* functions for phylogeny reconstruction B&B. Each node in the B&B tree is associated with either a partial tree or a complete tree. A tree containing all $n$ taxa is a *complete tree*. A tree on the first $k$ ($k < n$) taxa is a *partial tree*. A complete tree is a candidate solution. Tree $T$ is *consistent* with tree $T'$ iff $T$ can be reduced into $T'$; i.e., $T'$ can be obtained from $T$ by removing all the taxa in $T$ that are not in $T'$. The subproblem for a node with partial tree $T$ is to find the most parsimonious complete tree consistent with $T$.

We partition the frontier into *levels*, such that level $k$, for $3 \leqslant k \leqslant n$, represents the candidates (i.e., partial trees when $k < n$) containing the first $k$ taxa from the input. The root node that contains the first three taxa (hence, indexed by level 3) since there is only one possible tree topology with three leaves. The branch function finds the immediate successors of a node associated with a partial tree $T_k$ at level $k$ by inserting the $(k + 1)$st taxon at any of the $2k - 3$ possible places. A new node (with this taxon attached) can join in the middle of any of the $2k - 4$ edges not adjacent to the root or anywhere on the path through the root. For example, in Fig. 1, the root on three taxa is labeled (A), its three children at level four are labeled (B), (C), and (D), and a few trees at level five (labeled (1) through (5)) are shown. The search space explored by this approach depends on the addition order of taxa, which also influences the efficiency of the B&B algorithm. This issue is important, but not further addressed in this chapter.

We use depth-first search (DFS) as our primary B&B search strategy, and a heuristic best-first search (BeFS) to break ties between nodes at the same depth.

Next we discuss the bound function for maximum parsimony. A node $v$ associated with tree $T_k$ represents the subproblem to find the most parsimonious tree in the

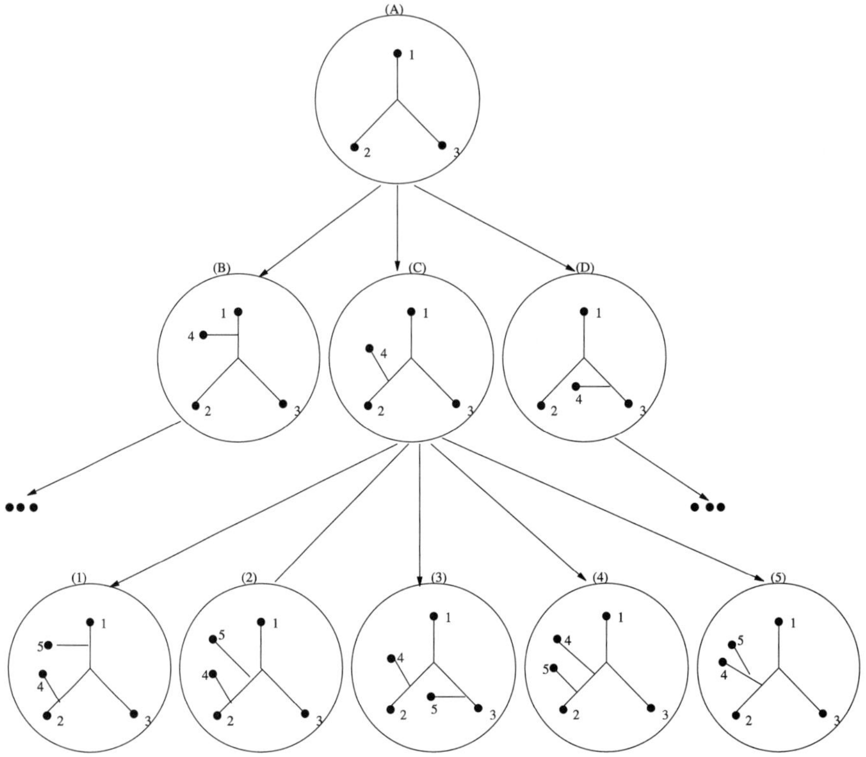


FIG. 1. Maximum Parsimony B&B search space.

search space that is consistent with $T_k$. Assume $T_k$ is a tree with leaves labeled by $S_1, \ldots, S_k$. Our goal is to find a tight lower bound of the subproblem. However, one must balance the quality of the lower bound against the time required to compute it in order to gain the best performance of the overall B&B algorithm.

Hendy and Penny [15] describe two practical B&B algorithms for phylogeny reconstruction from sequence data that use the cost of the associated partial tree as the lower bound of this subproblem. This traditional approach is straightforward, and obviously, it satisfies the necessary properties of the bound function. However, it is not tight and does not prune the search space efficiently. Purdom et al. [17] use single-character discrepancies of the partial tree as the bound function. For each character one computes a difference set, the set of character states that do not occur among the taxa in the partial tree and hence only occur among the remaining taxa. The single-character discrepancy is the sum over all characters of the number of the elements in these difference sets. The lower bound is therefore the sum of the single-character discrepancy plus the cost of the partial tree. This method usually produces much better bounds than Hendy and Penny's method, and experiments show that it usually fathoms more of the search space [17]. Another advantage of Purdom's approach is that given an addition order of taxa, there is only one single-character discrepancy calculation per level. The time needed to compute the bound function is negligible.

Next we discuss the candidate function and incumbent $x_I$. In phylogeny reconstruction, it is expensive to compute a meaningful feasible solution for each partial tree, so instead we compute the upper bound of the input using a direct method such as neighbor-joining [12,13] before starting the B&B search. We call this value the global upper bound, $f(x_I)$, the incumbent's objective function. In our implementation, the first incumbent is the best returned by any of several heuristic methods.

The greedy algorithm [18], an alternative incumbent heuristic, proceeds as follows. Begin with a three-taxa core tree and iteratively add one taxon at a time. For an iteration with an $k$-leaf tree, try each of the $n - k$ remaining taxon in each of the $2k - 2$ possible places. Select the lowest-cost $(k + 1)$-leaf tree so formed.

Any program, regardless of the algorithms, requires implementation on a suitable data structure. As mentioned previously, we use DFS as the primary search strategy and BeFS as the secondary search strategy. For phylogeny reconstruction with $n$ taxa, the depth of the subproblems ranges from 3 to $n$. So we use an array to keep the open subproblems sorted by DFS depth. The array element at location $i$ contains a priority queue (PQ) of the subproblems with depth $i$, and each item of the PQ contains an external pointer to stored subproblem information.

The priority queues (PQs) support best-first-search tie breaking and allow efficient deletion of all dominated subproblems whenever we find a new incumbent. There are many ways to organize a PQ (see [19] for an overview). In the phylogeny reconstruction problem, most of the time is spent evaluating the tree length of a partial tree. The choice of PQ data structures does not make a significant difference. So for simplicity, we use a D-heap for our priority queues. A heap is a tree where each node has higher priority than any of its children. In a D-heap, the tree is embedded in an array. The first location holds the root of the tree, and locations $2i$ and $2i + 1$ are the children of location $i$.

## 1.3 Parallel Framework

Our parallel maximum parsimony B&B algorithm uses shared-memory. The processors can concurrently evaluate open nodes, frequently with linear speedup.

Second, a shared-memory platform makes available a large, shared memory that can hold shared data structures, such as the arrays of priority queues representing the frontier. For example, one of the largest SMP systems to date, the IBM pSeries

690, uses 32 Power4+ 1.9 GHz microprocessors and one terabyte of global memory in its largest configuration. Thus, the data structures representing the search space and incumbent can be shared (concurrently accessed by the processors) with little overhead, and the sheer amount of main memory allows for a tremendous number of active frontier nodes to be saved for later exploration, rather than sequential approaches that often store only a small number of frontier nodes due to space limitations and throw away other nodes that do not seem promising at the time (but may contain the optimal tree). As described in Section 1.2, for each level of the search tree (illustrated in Fig. 1), we use a priority queue represented by binary heaps to maintain the active nodes in a heuristic order. The processors concurrently access these heaps. To ensure each subproblem is processed by exactly one processor and to ensure that the heaps are always in a consistent state, at most one processor can access any part of a heap at once. Each heap $H_i$ (at level $i$) is protected by a lock $Lock_i$. Each processor locks the entire heap $H_i$ whenever it makes an operation on $H_i$.

In the sequential B&B algorithm, we use DFS strictly so $H_i$ is used only if the heaps at higher level (higher on the tree, lower level number) are all empty. In the parallel version, to allow multiple processors shared access to the search space, a processor uses $H_i$ if all the heaps at higher levels are empty or locked by other processors.

The shared-memory B&B framework has a simple termination detection. A processor can terminate its execution when it detects that all the heaps are unlocked and empty: there are no more active nodes except for those being decomposed by other processors. This is correct, but it could be inefficient, since still-active processors could produce more parallel work for the prematurely-halted processors. If the machine supports it, instead of terminating, a processor can declare itself idle (e.g. by setting a unique bit) and go to sleep. An active processor can then wake it up if there's sufficient new work in the system. The last active processor terminate all sleeping processors and then terminates itself.

## 1.4 Impact of Parallelization

There are a variety of software packages to reconstruct sequence-based phylogeny. The most popular phylogeny software suites that contain parsimony methods are PAUP* by Swofford [20], PHYLIP by Felsenstein [21], and TNT and NONA by Goloboff [22,23]. We have developed a freely-available shared-memory code for computing MP, that is part of our software suite, GRAPPA (Genome Rearrangement Analysis through Parsimony and other Phylogenetic Algorithms) [2]. GRAPPA was designed to re-implement, extend, and especially speed up the breakpoint analysis (BPAnalysis) method of Sankoff and Blanchette [24]. Breakpoint analysis is another form of parsimony-based phylogeny where species are represented by ordered sets of genes and distances is measured relative to differences in orderings. It is also solved by branch and bound. One feature of our MP software is that it does not constrain the character states of the input and can use real molecular data and also characters reduced from gene-order data such as Maximum Parsimony on Binary Encodings (MPBE) [25].

The University of New Mexico operates *Los Lobos*, the NSF/Alliance 512-processor Linux supercluster. This platform is a cluster of 256 IBM Netfinity 4500R nodes, each with dual 733 MHz Intel Xeon Pentium processors and 1 GB RAM, interconnected by Myrinet switches. We ran *GRAPPA* on *Los Lobos* and obtained a 512-fold speed-up (linear speedup with respect to the number of processors): a complete breakpoint analysis (with the more demanding inversion distance used in lieu of breakpoint distance) for the 13 genomes in the Campanulaceae data set ran in less than 1.5 hours in an October 2000 run, for a *million-fold* speedup over the original implementation [26,1]. Our latest version features significantly improved bounds and new distance correction methods and, on the same dataset, exhibits a speedup factor of *over one billion*. In each of these cases a factor of 512 speed up came from parallelization. The remaining speed up came from algorithmic improvements and improved implementation.

## 2. Boosting Phylogenetic Reconstruction Methods Using Recursive-Iterative-DCM3

Reconstructing the Tree of Life, i.e., the evolutionary tree of all species on Earth, poses a highly challenging computational problem. Various software packages such as TNT [27–29], PAUP* [30], and RAxML [31] contain sophisticated search procedures for solving MP (Maximum Parsimony) and ML (Maximum Likelihood) on very large datasets. (Section 3 of this chapter describes aspects of the RAxML method in more detail.) The family of Disk Covering Methods (DCMs) [32–35] was introduced to *boost* the performance of a given base method without making changes to the method itself, i.e. use the same search procedures in the base method, except deploy them in a divide and conquer context. DCMs decompose the input set of species (i.e. alignment) into smaller subproblems, compute subtrees on each subproblem using a given *base method*, merge the subtrees to yield a tree on the full dataset, and refine the resulting supertree to make it binary if necessary. Figure 2 shows the four steps of the DCM2 method which was developed for boosting MP and ML heuristics. Figure 3 illustrates the operation of the Strict Consensus Merger supertree method (SCM) which is used for merging the subtrees computed by the base method. SCM is a fast consensus based method that has shown to be more accurate and faster than the Matrix Representation using Parsimony (MRP) method

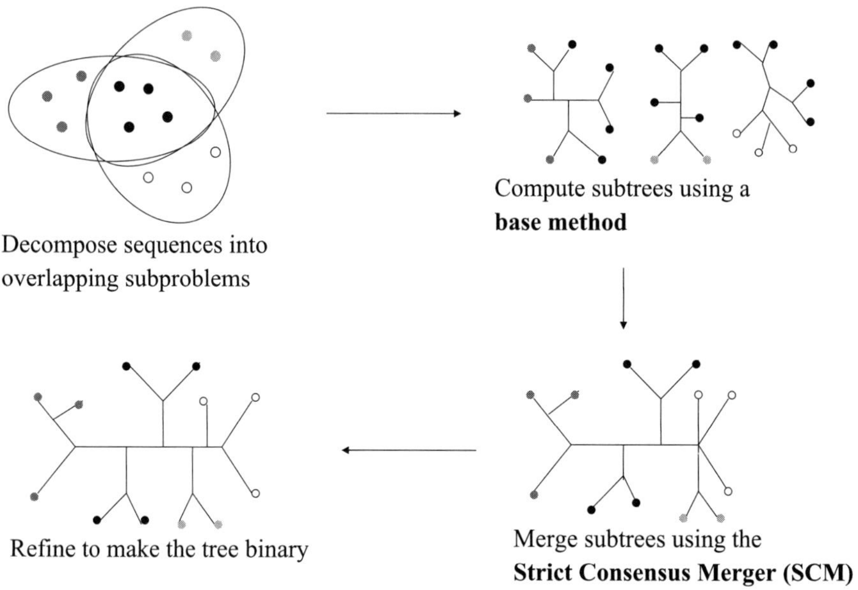
Decompose sequences into overlapping subproblems
Compute subtrees using a **base method**
Merge subtrees using the **Strict Consensus Merger (SCM)**
Refine to make the tree binary

FIG. 2. The DCM2 method was designed for boosting MP and ML heuristics. Steps 2, 3, and 4 are common to most DCMs developed to date.

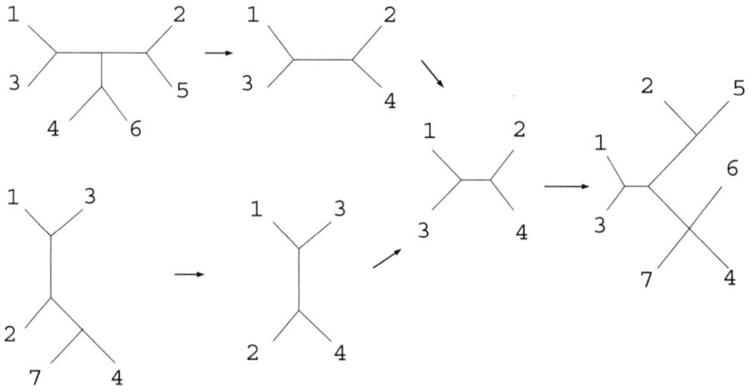

FIG. 3. The Strict Consensus Merger is a consensus-based supertree method that is fast and accurate enough on DCM decompositions. As the figure shows, two subtrees are merged by first computing the set of common taxa and restricting both the input trees to this set. The strict consensus tree, i.e. set of common bipartitions, is computed on the restricted subtrees, and the remaining bipartitions on the two input trees are then attached to the consensus.

for supertree reconstruction on DCM subproblems [36]. DCMs have previously been shown to significantly improve upon NJ, the most widely used distance-based method for phylogeny reconstruction. See [37–40] for various studies showing DCM improvements over NJ.

Rec-I-DCM3 is the latest in the family of Disk Covering Methods (DCMs) and was designed to improve the performance of MP and ML heuristics. Rec-I-DCM3 is an iterative technique which uses the DCM3 decomposition [34] for escaping local minima. Previously it was shown that Rec-I-DCM3 improves upon heuristics for solving MP [34,35]. In this study we show that Rec-I-DCM3 combined with RAxML-III finds highly optimal ML trees, particularly on large datasets. Within the current Section we will refer to RAxML-III as RAxML (as opposed to Section 3 where RAxML refers to RAxML-VI).

We first discuss an essential component of Rec-I-DCM3 which is the DCM3 decomposition. We then describe Rec-I-DCM3 in detail and examine its performance in conjunction with RAxML as the base method.

## 2.1 DCM3 Decomposition

DCM3 is the latest decomposition technique in the family of DCMs. DCM3 was designed as improvement over the previous DCM2 decomposition. As shown previously DCM2 is too slow on large datasets and more importantly, does not always produces subsets that are small enough to give a substantial speedup [35]. The DCM3 decomposition is similar in many ways to the DCM2 technique; the main difference between the two techniques is that DCM2's decomposition is based upon a distance matrix computed on the dataset, while DCM3's decomposition is obtained on the basis of a "guide tree" for the dataset.

We assume we have a tree $T$ on our set $S$ of taxa, and an edge weighting $w$ of $T$ (i.e., $w : E(T) \to \Re^+$). Based upon this edge-weighted tree, we obtain a decomposition of the leaf set using the following steps. Before describing the decomposition we define the short subtree of an edge.

*Short subtrees of edges.* Let $A$, $B$, $C$, and $D$ be the four subtrees around $e$ and let $a, b, c$, and $d$ be the set of leaves closest to $e$ in each of the four subtrees $A$, $B$, $C$, and $D$ respectively (where the distance between nodes $u$ and $v$ is measured as $\sum_{e \in P_{uv}} w(e)$). The set of nodes in $a \cup b \cup c \cup d$ is the "short subtree" around the edge $e$. We will say that $i$ and $j$ are in a short subtree of $T$ if there is some edge so that $i$ and $j$ are in the short subtree around $e$. The graph formed by taking the union of all the cliques on short subtrees is the *short subtree graph* and is shown to be triangulated [35].

DCM3 decomposition

- **Input**
  - Set $S = \{s_1, \ldots, s_n\}$ of $n$ aligned biomolecular sequences.
  - An edge-weighted phylogenetic *guide tree* $T$ leaf-labeled by $S$.
- **Output** $A_i, \ldots, A_k$ with $\bigcup_i A_i = S$, and set $X \subset S$ such that $A_i \cap A_j = X$ for all $i, j$.
- **Algorithm**
  - Compute the *short subtree graph* $G = (V, E)$ where $V = S$ and $E = \{(i, j)\colon i, j \in \text{short subtree of } T\}$.
  - Find a clique separator $X$ in $G$ which minimizes $\max_i |A_i \cup X|$ where $A_1, \ldots, A_k$ are the connected components of $G$ after removing $X$.

FIG. 4. Algorithmic description of the DCM3 decomposition.

We begin the decomposition by first constructing the *short subtree graph*, which is the union of cliques formed on "short subtrees" around each edge. Since the short subtree graph $G$ is triangulated, we can find maximal clique separators in polynomial time (these are just cliques in the graph, as proven in [41]), and hence we can find (also in polynomial time) a clique separator $X$ that minimizes $\max_i |X \cup C_i|$, where $G - X$ is the union of $k$ components $C_1, C_2, \ldots, C_k$. This is the same decomposition technique used in the DCM2 decomposition, but there the graph is constructed differently, and so the decomposition is different. Figure 4 describes the full DCM3 decomposition algorithm and Fig. 5 shows a toy example of the DCM3 decomposition on a eight taxon phylogeny. We now analyze the running time to compute the DCM3 decomposition.

**Theorem 1.** *Computing a DCM3 decomposition takes* $O(n^3)$ *time in the worst case, where n is the number of sequences in the input.*

**Proof.** In the worst case, the input tree can be ultrametric which causes each short subtree to be of size $O(n)$. Thus, for each internal edge ($O(n)$ time) we create a clique for each short subtree ($O(n^2)$ worst case time); the total time taken is $O(n^3)$. The optimal separator and the associated connected components are found by computing a depth-first search ($O(n^2)$ worst case time) for each of the $O(n)$ clique separators; total time taken is $O(n^3)$. Thus, the worst case time is $O(n^3)$. □

Although finding the optimal separator takes $O(n^3)$ time, in practice it takes much longer than computing the short subtree. Rather than explicitly seeking a clique separator $X$ in $G$ which minimizes the size of the largest subproblem, we apply a simple

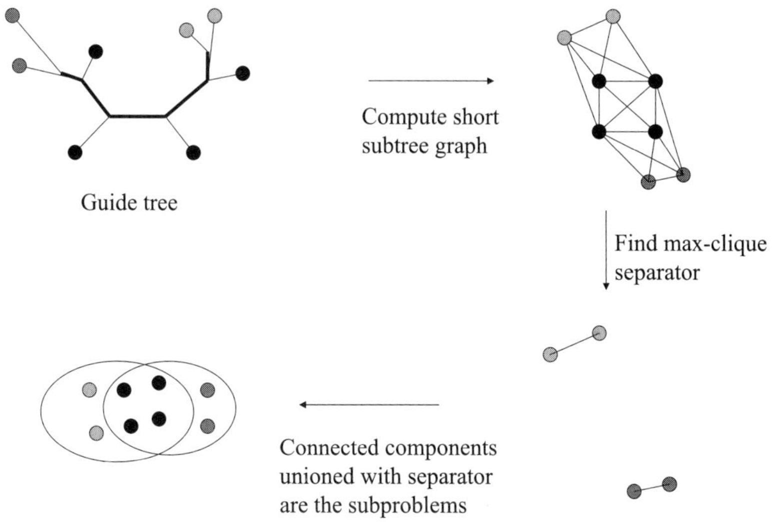


FIG. 5. DCM3 decomposition shown on an eight taxon phylogeny.

heuristic to get a decomposition, which in practice turns out to be a good decomposition. We explain this heuristic below.

*Approximate centroid-edge decomposition.* It has been observed on several real datasets that the optimal separator is usually the one associated with the short subtree of the centroid edge [35], i.e., the edge such that when removed produces subtrees of equal size (in number of leaves). This observation allows us to bypass the computation time associated with dealing with short subtrees. We can compute an *approximated centroid edge* decomposition by finding the centroid edge $e$ and setting the separator to be the closest leaves in each of the subtrees around $e$. The remaining leaves in each of the subtrees around $e$ (unioned with the separator) would then form the DCM3 subproblems (see Fig. 6). This takes linear time if we use a depth-first search. In the rest of this chapter we will use the approximate centroid edge decomposition when we refer to a DCM3 decomposition.

## 2.2 Recursive-Iterative-DCM3 (Rec-I-DCM3)

Recursive-Iterative-DCM3 is the state of the art in DCMs for solving NP-hard optimization problems for phylogeny reconstruction. It is an iterative procedures which applies an existing base method to both DCM3 subsets and the complete dataset. Rec-I-DCM3 can also be viewed as an iterated local search technique [42] which

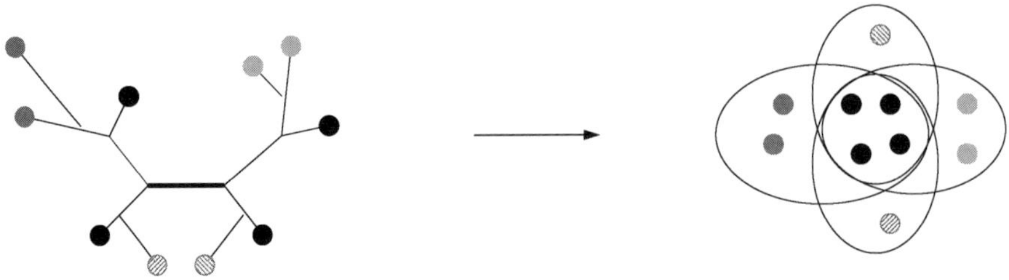

FIG. 6. The faster approximate DCM3 centroid decomposition can be done in O($n$) time. Both, finding the centroid edge and computing the subsets, can be done in O($n$) using a depth first search ($n$ is the number of leaves).

---

Recursive-Iterative-DCM3

- **Input**
  - Input alignment $S$, #iterations $n$, base heuristic $b$, global search method $g$, starting tree $T$, maximum subproblem size $m$.
- **Output** Phylogenetic tree leaf-labeled by $S$.
- **Algorithm** For each iteration do
  - Set $T' = \text{Recursive-DCM3}(S, m, b, T)$.
  - Apply the global search method $g$ starting from $T'$ until we reach a local optimum. This step can be skipped; however, it usually leads to more optimal trees even with a superficial search.
  - Let $T''$ be the resulting local optimum from the previous step. Set $T = T''$.

---

FIG. 7. Algorithm for Recursive-Iterative-DCM3.

uses a DCM3 decomposition to escape local minima. Figure 7 provides a full description of the Rec-I-DCM3 algorithm.

The Recursive-DCM3 routine performs the work of dividing the dataset into smaller subsets, solving the subproblems (using the base method), and then merging the subtrees into the full tree. Recursive-DCM3 is a simple modification of the original DCM3. It is obtained by recursively applying the DCM3 decomposition to DCM3 subsets in order to yield smaller subproblems. The sizes of individual subproblems vary significantly and the inference time per subproblem is not known a priori and difficult to estimate. This can affect performance if the subproblems are solved in parallel [43]. The global search method further improves the accuracy of the Recursive-DCM3 tree and can also find optimal global configurations that were not found by Recursive-DCM3, which only operates on smaller—local—subsets.

However, previous studies [34,35] and results presented in this one show that even a superficial search can yield good results.

## 2.3 Performance of Rec-I-DCM3 for Solving ML

Rec-I-DCM3 has previously shown to boost TNT (currently the fastest software package for solving MP) with the default settings of TNT. In this chapter we set out to determine if Rec-I-DCM3 can improve upon the standard hill-climbing algorithms of RAxML (as implemented in RAxML-III). We study the performance of RAxML and Rec-I-DCM3(RAxML) on several real datasets described below.

### 2.3.1 Real Datasets

We collected 20 real datasets of different sizes, sequence lengths, and evolutionary rates from various researchers. All the alignments were prepared by the authors of the datasets. It is important to use a reliable alignment when computing phylogenies. Therefore, we minimize the use of machine alignments, i.e., those created solely by a computer program with no human intervention. Below we list the size of each alignment along with its sequence length and source.

1. 101 RNA, 1,858 bp [44], obtained from Alexandros Stamatakis.
2. 150 RNA, 1,269 bp [44], obtained from Alexandros Stamatakis.
3. 150 ssu rRNA, 3,188 bp [45], obtained from Alexandros Stamatakis.
4. 193 ssu rRNA [46], obtained from Alexandros Stamatakis.
5. 200 ssu rRNA, 3,270 bp [45], obtained from Alexandros Stamatakis.
6. 218 ssu rRNA, 4,182 bp [47], obtained from Alexandros Stamatakis.
7. 250 ssu rRNA [45], obtained from Alexandros Stamatakis.
8. 439 Eukaryotic rDNA, 2,461 bp [48], obtained from Pablo Goloboff.
9. 476 Metazoan DNA, 1,008 bp, created by Doug Ernisse but unpublished, obtained from Pablo Goloboff with omitted taxon names.
10. 500 rbcL DNA, 1,398 bp [49].
11. 567 three-gene (rbcL, atpB, and 18s) DNA, 2,153 bp [50].
12. 854 rbcL DNA, 937 bp, created by H. Ochoterena but unpublished, obtained from Pablo Goloboff with omitted taxon names.
13. 921 Avian Cytochrome *b* DNA, 713 bp [51].
14. 1,000 ssu rRNA, 5,547 bp [45], obtained from Alexandros Stamatakis.
15. 1,663 ssu rRNA, 1,577 bp [45], obtained from Alexandros Stamatakis.
16. 2,025 ssu rRNA, 1,517 bp [45], obtained from Alexandros Stamatakis.
17. 2,415 mammalian DNA, created by Olaf Bininda-Emonds but unpublished, obtained from Alexandros Stamatakis.

18. 6,722 three-domain (Eukarayote, Archea, and Fungi) rRNA, 1,122 bp, created and obtained by Robin Gutell.
19. 7,769 three-domain (Eukaryote, Archea, and Fungi) + two organelle (mitochondria and chloroplast) rRNA, 851 bp, created and obtained by Robin Gutell.
20. 8,780 ssu rRNA, 1,217 bp [45], obtained from Alexandros Stamatakis.

### 2.3.2 Parameters for RAxML and Rec-I-DCM3

*2.3.2.1 RAxML.* We use default settings of RAxML on each dataset. By default RAxML performs a standard hill-climbing search for ML trees but begins with an estimate of the MP tree (constructed using heuristics implemented in Phylip [52]). We use the HKY85 model [53] throughout the study whenever we run RAxML (even as the base and global methods for Rec-I-DCM3). For more details on RAxML we refer the reader to Section 3 of this chapter where RAxML is thoroughly described.

*2.3.2.2 Rec-I-DCM3.* We use RAxML with its default settings for the base method. However, when applying RAxML on a DCM3 subproblem, we use the guide-tree restricted to the subproblem taxa as the starting tree for the search (as opposed to the default randomized greedy MP tree). This way the RAxML search on the subset can take advantage of the structure stored in the guide-tree through previous Rec-I-DCM3 iterations. We use the *fast* RAxML search for the global search phase of Rec-I-DCM3. This terminates much quicker than the standard (and more through) hill-climbing search (which is also the default one). We can expect better performance in terms of ML scores if the standard RAxML search was used as the Rec-I-DCM3 global search; however, that would increase the overall running time. The initial guide-tree for Rec-I-DCM3 is the same starting tree used by RAxML and the Rec-I-DCM3 search was performed for the same amount of time as the unboosted RAxML. The maximum subproblem size of Rec-I-DCM3 was selected as follows:

- 50% for datasets below 1,000 sequences;
- 25% for datasets between 1,000 and 5,000 sequences (including 1,000);
- 12.5% for datasets above 5,000 sequences (including 5,000).

These subproblem sizes may not yield optimal results for Rec-I-DCM3(RAxML). We selected these based upon performance of Rec-I-DCM3(TNT) [34,35] for boosting MP heuristics.

### 2.3.3 Experimental Design

On each dataset we ran 5 trials of RAxML since each run starts from a randomized greedy MP tree (see [35] and Section 3 for a description of this heuristic). We ran

5 trials of Rec-I-DCM3(RAxML) and report the average best score found by each-method on each dataset. We also report the difference in likelihood scores both in absolute numbers and percentages.

### 2.3.4 Results

Table I summarizes the results on all the real datasets. The − log likelihood improvement is the average RAxML score subtracted from the Rec-I-DCM3(RAxML) score. This is also shown as a percentage by dividing the improvement by the RAxML average score.

Rec-I-DCM3(RAxML) improves RAxML on 15 of the 20 datasets studied here. On datasets below and including 500 taxa Rec-I-DCM3(RAxML) improves upon

TABLE I

THE DIFFERENCE BETWEEN THE REC-I-DCM3(RAXML) AND RAXML − log LIKELIHOOD SCORE AND ALSO PRESENTATION OF IT AS A PERCENTAGE OF THE RAXML − log LIKELIHOOD SCORE

| Dataset size | Improvement as % | − LH Improvement | Max p-distance |
|---|---|---|---|
| 101 | −0.004 | −2.7 | 0.45 |
| 150 (SC) | 0.007 | 3.2 | 0.43 |
| 150 (ARB) | 0 | 0.3 | 0.54 |
| 193 | 0.06 | 38.6 | 0.78 |
| 200 | −0.006 | −6.5 | 0.54 |
| 218 | 0.014 | 21 | 0.42 |
| 250 | 0.014 | 19 | 0.55 |
| 439 | 0 | 0.1 | 0.65 |
| 476 | −0.004 | −4 | 0.89 |
| 500 | 0.011 | 11 | 0.18 |
| 567 | 0.006 | 13.9 | 0.33 |
| 854 | 0.03 | 42 | 0.32 |
| 921 | 0.06 | 109.6 | 0.39 |
| 1,000 | 0.031 | 123 | 0.55 |
| 1,663 | −0.004 | −11.7 | 0.48 |
| 2,025 | −0.002 | −6 | 0.56 |
| 2,415 | 0.004 | 23 | 0.48 |
| 6,722 | 1.251 | 6,877 | 1 |
| 7,769 | 2.338 | 13,290 | 1 |
| 8,780 | 0.03 | 270 | 0.55 |

The negative percentages show where RAxML performed better than Rec-I-DCM(RAxML). These percentages are small (at least −0.006%) and show that Rec-I-DCM3(RAxML) performs almost as well as the unboosted RAxML when it fails to provide a better score. We also list the maximum p-distance of each dataset to indicate its divergence. On most of the divergent datasets Rec-I-DCM3(RAxML) improves over RAxML by a larger percentage as opposed to the more conserved ones.

RAxML in 7 out of 10 datasets. The maximum improvement is 0.06% which is on the most divergent dataset of 193 taxa. On datasets above 500 taxa Rec-I-DCM3(RAxML) improves RAxML in 8 out of 10 datasets with the improvement generally more pronounced. On 6 datasets the improvement is above 0.02% and above 1% on the 6,722 and 7,769 taxon datasets—these two datasets are also highly divergent (as indicated by their maximum pairwise p-distances) and can be considered as very challenging to solve. Interestingly, Rec-I-DCM3(RAxML) does not improve RAxML on the 1,663 and 2,025 taxon datasets despite their large sizes and moderate maximum p-distances. As indicated by the small percentage values (see Table I) Rec-I-DCM3(RAxML) is almost as good as RAxML on these datasets. It is possible there are certain characteristics of these datasets that make them unsuitable for boosting or for divide-and-conquer methods. We intend to explore this in more detail in subsequent studies.

Figures 8 through 11 show the performance of Rec-I-DCM3(RAxML) and RAxML as a function of time on all the datasets. Each data point in the curve is the average of five runs. Variances are omitted from the figures for the purpose of visual clarity and are in general small. The first time point shown on each graph is the time when the Rec-I-DCM3(RAxML) outputs its first tree, i.e., the tree at the end of the first iteration. This tree is always much better in score than the initial guide-tree. Of the 15 datasets where Rec-I-DCM3(RAxML) has a better score than RAxML at the end of the searches, Rec-I-DCM3(RAxML) improves RAxML at every time point on 11 of them. On the remaining 4 RAxML is doing better initially; however, at the end of the search Rec-I-DCM3(RAxML) comes out with a better score.

### *2.3.5 Conclusions*

Our results indicate that Rec-I-DCM3 can improve RAxML on a wide sample of DNA and RNA datasets. The improvement is larger and more frequent on large datasets as opposed to smaller ones. This is consistent with Rec-I-DCM3 results for boosting MP heuristics [35].

The results presented here are using the algorithms of RAxML-III. It remains to be see how the performance of Rec-I-DCM3(RAxML) will be affected if different (and better) ML hill-climbing algorithms are used (such as those implemented in RAxML-VI). We recommend the user to experiment with different subset sizes (such as one-half, one-quarter, and one-eighth the full dataset size) and both, a standard (and thorough) hill-climbing as well as a superficial one for the global search phase of Rec-I-DCM3. Preliminary results (not shown here) show similar improvements of RAxML-VI using Rec-I-DCM3(RAxML-VI) on some of the datasets used in this study.

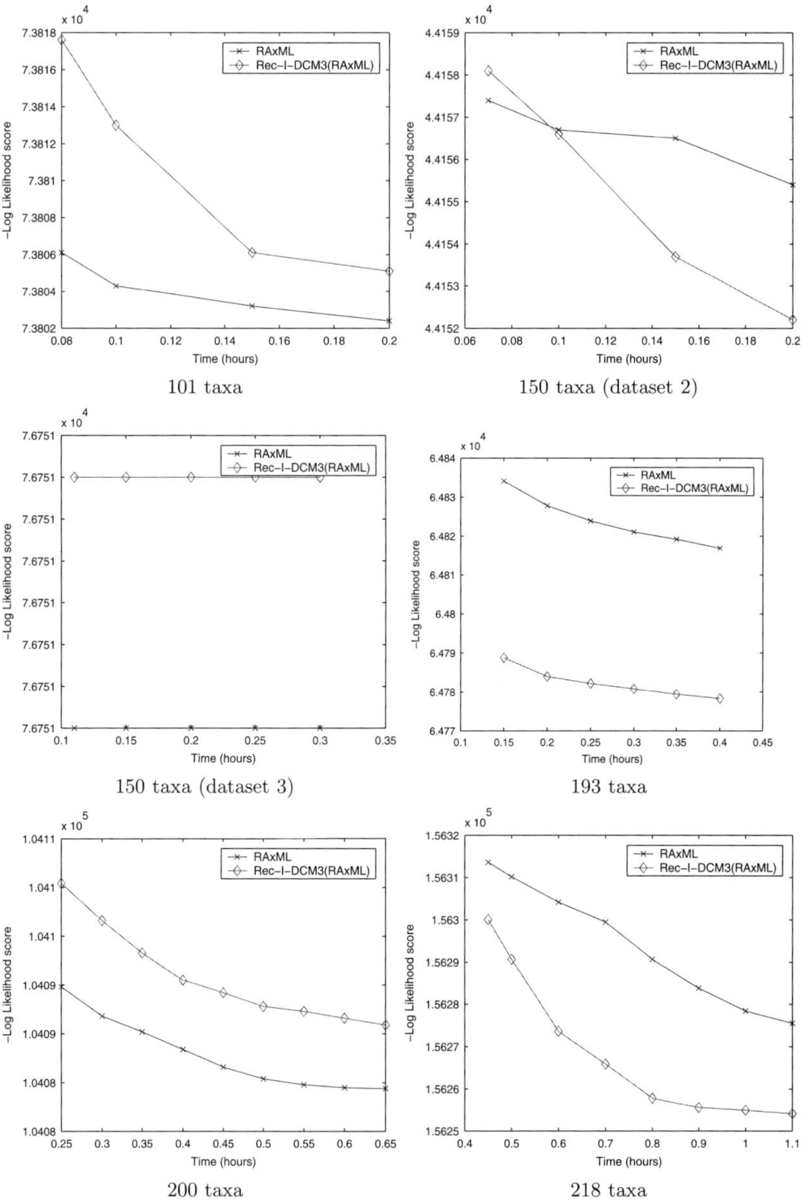


FIG. 8. Rec-I-DCM3(RAxML) improves RAxML on the 150 (dataset 2), 193, and 218 taxon datasets shown here.

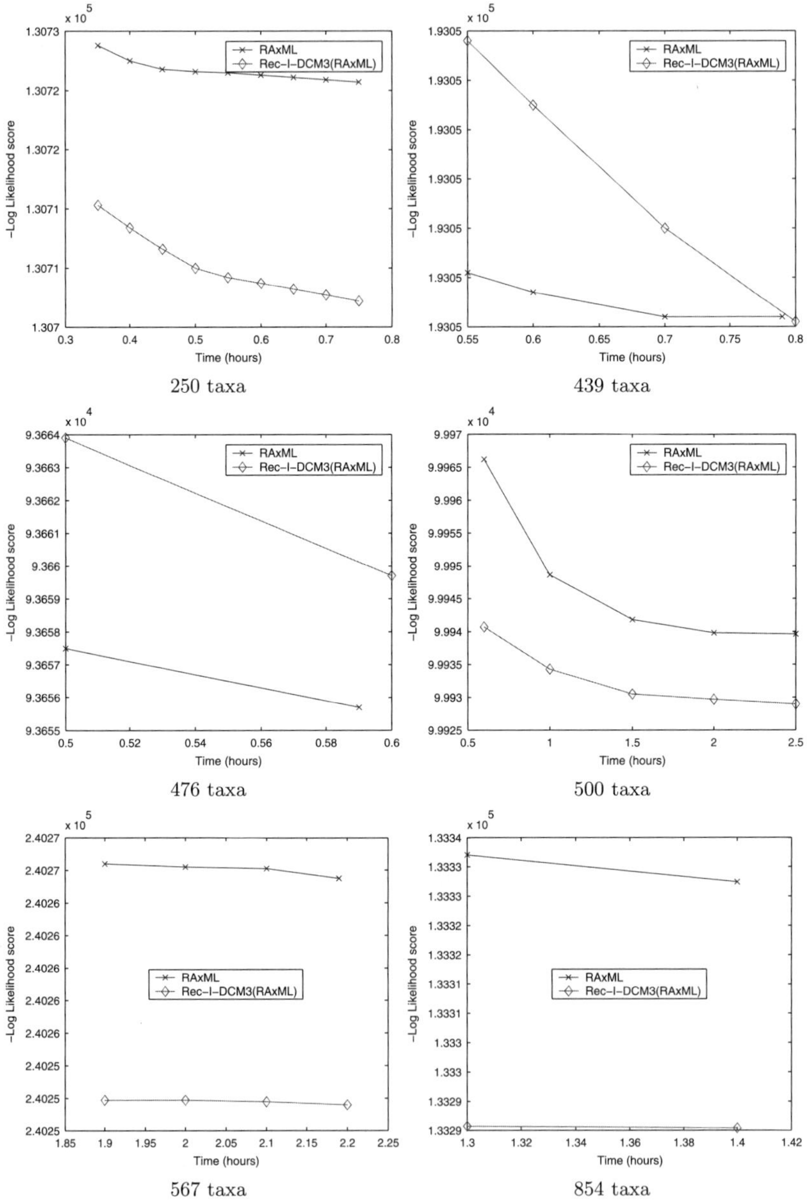


FIG. 9. As the dataset sizes get larger Rec-I-DCM3(RAxML) improves RAxML on more datasets. Here we see improvements on the 250, 500, 567, and 854 taxon datasets.

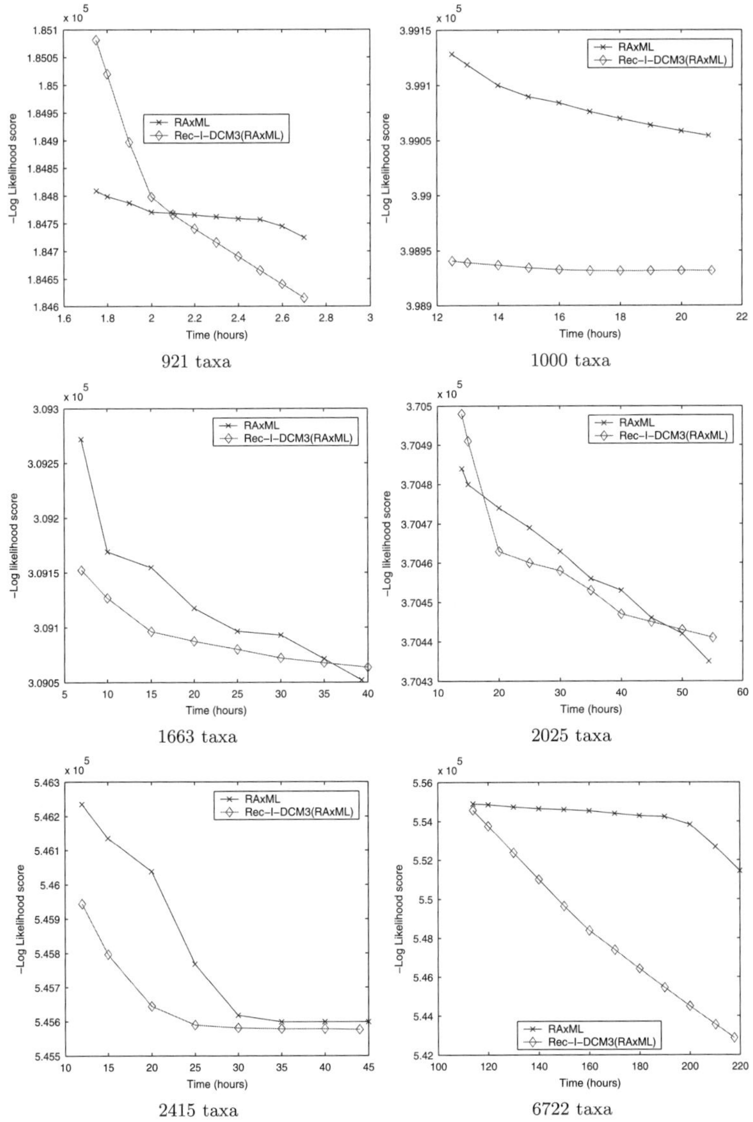


FIG. 10. Rec-I-DCM3(RAxML) improves RAxML on all the datasets shown here except for the 1,663 and 2,025 taxon ones. There we see that Rec-I-DCM3(RAxML) improves RAxML in the earlier part of the search but not towards the very end. It is possible these datasets possess certain properties which make it hard for booster methods like Rec-I-DCM3. On the 6,722 taxon dataset we see a very large improvement of with Rec-I-DCM3(RAxML) (of over 1%—see Table I).

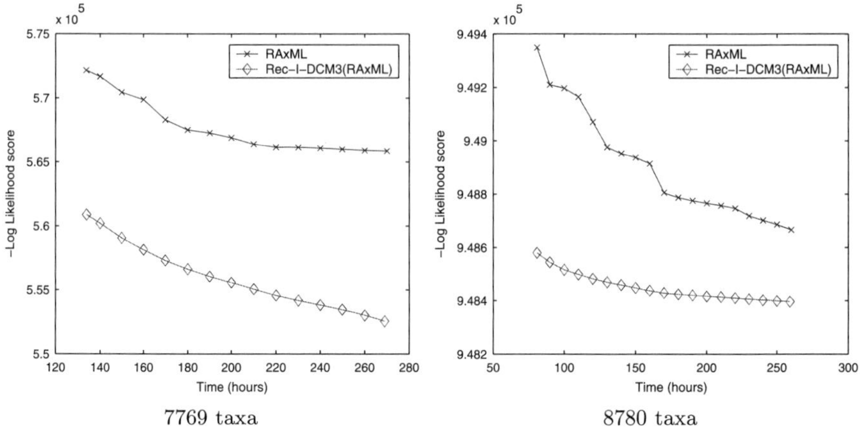


FIG. 11. Rec-I-DCM3(RAxML) improves RAxML on the two largest datasets. On the 7,769 taxon dataset the improvement in score is 2.34% which is the largest over all the datasets examined here.

## 3. New Technical Challenges for ML-Based Phylogeny Reconstruction

The current Section intends to cover the relatively *new* phenomenon of technical problems which arise for the inference of large phylogenies—containing more than 1,000 organisms—with the popular Maximum Likelihood (ML) method [54].

The tremendous accumulation of sequence data over recent years coupled with the significant progress in search (optimization) algorithms for ML and the increasing use of parallel computers allow for inference of huge phylogenies within less than 24 hours. Therefore, large-scale phylogenetic analyses with ML are becoming more common recently [55].

The computation of *the* ML tree has recently been demonstrated to be NP-complete [56]. The problem of finding the optimal ML tree is particularly difficult due to the immense amount of alternative tree topologies which have to be evaluated *and* the high computational cost—in terms of floating point operations—of each tree evaluation per se. To date, the main focus of researchers has been on improving the search algorithms (RAxML [57], PHYML [58], GAML [59], IQPNNI [46], MetaPIGA [60], Treefinder [61]) and on accelerating the likelihood function via algorithmic means by detecting and re-using previously computed values [62,63].

Due to the algorithmic progress which has been achieved there exists a noticeable number of programs which are now able to infer a sufficiently accurate 1,000-taxon tree within less than 24 hours on a single PC processor.

However, due to the increasing size of the data and the complexity of the more elaborate models of nucleotide substitution, a new category of technical problems arises. Those problems mainly concern cache efficiency, memory shortage, memory organization, efficient implementation of the likelihood function (including manual loop unrolling and re-ordering of instructions), as well as the use of efficient data-structures.

The main focus of this section is to describe those problems and to present some recent technical solutions. Initially, Section 3.1 briefly summarizes the fundamental mathematics of ML in order to provide a basic understanding of the compute-intensive likelihood function. The following Section 3.2 covers some of the most recent and most efficient state-of-the-art ML phylogeny programs and shows that performance of most programs is currently *limited by memory efficiency and consumption*. In Section 3.3 the data-structures, memory organization, and implementation details of RAxML are described. RAxML has inherited an excellent technical implementation from fastDNAml which has unfortunately never been properly documented. Finally, Section 3.4 covers applications of HPC techniques and architectures to ML-based phylogenetic inference.

## 3.1 Introduction to Maximum Likelihood

This section does not provide a detailed introduction to ML for phylogenetic trees. The goal is to offer a notion of the complexity and amount of arithmetic operations required to compute the ML score for one *single* tree topology. The seminal paper by Felsenstein [54] which introduces the application of ML to phylogenetic trees and the comprehensive and readable chapter by Swofford et al. [64] provide detailed descriptions of the mathematical as well as computational background.

To calculate the likelihood of a *given* tree topology with *fixed* branch lengths a probabilistic model of nucleotide substitution $P_{ij}(t)$ is required which allows for computing the probability $P$ that a nucleotide $i$ mutates to another nucleotide $j$ within time $t$ (branch length). The model for DNA data must therefore provide substitution transitions:

```
A|C|G|T -> A|C|G|T
```

In order to significantly reduce the mathematical complexity of the overall method the model of nucleotide substitution must be time-reversible [54], i.e. the evolutionary process has to be identic if followed forward or backward in time. Essentially, this means that the maximum number of possible transition types in the General Time Reversible model of nucleotide substitution (GTR [65,66]) is reduced to 6 due to required symmetries. The less general time-reversible models of nucleotide substitution such as the Jukes–Cantor (JC69 [67]) or Hasegawa–Kishino–Yano (HKY85 [68]) model can be derived from GTR by further restriction of possible transition types. It is important to note, that there exists a trade-off between speed and quality among substitution models. The simple JC69 model which only has one single transition type requires significantly less floating point operations to compute $P_{ij}(t)$ than GTR which is the most complex and accurate one.

Thus, model selection has a significant impact on inference times, and therefore—whenever possible—the simpler model should be used for large datasets, e.g. HKY85 instead of GTR. The applicability of a less complex model to a *specific* alignment can be determined by application of likelihood ratio tests. Thus, if the likelihood obtained for a fixed tree topology with HKY85 is not significantly worse than the GTR-based likelihood value, HKY85 should be used. Programs such as Modeltest [69] can be applied to determine the appropriate model of evolution for a specific dataset.

Another very important and rarely discussed modeling issue concerns the way rate heterogeneity among sites (alignment columns) is accommodated in nucleotide substitution models (see discussion on page 152). There exist two competing models which differ significantly in terms of amount of floating point operations and memory consumption.

Given the model of nucleotide substitution and a tree topology with branch lengths where the data (the individual sequences of the multiple alignment) is located at the tips, one can proceed with the computation of the likelihood score for that tree. In order to compute the likelihood a *virtual root* (*vr*) has to be placed into an *arbitrary* branch of the tree in order to calculate/update the individual entries of each *likelihood vector* (also often called partial likelihood) with length *m* (alignment length) in the tree bottom-up, i.e. starting at the tips and moving towards *vr*. If the model of nucleotide substitution is time-reversible the likelihood of the tree is identic irrespectively of where *vr* is placed. After having updated all likelihood vectors the vectors to the right and left of *vr* can be used to compute the overall likelihood of the tree.

Note that, the number *n* (where *n* is the number of taxa) and length of likelihood vectors *m* (where *m* is the number of distinct patterns/columns in the alignment) dominate the memory consumption of typical ML implementations which is thus $O(n * m)$. Section 3.3 describes how the likelihood vector structures can efficiently be implemented to consume only $\Theta(n * m)$ memory.

The process of rooting the tree at $vr$ and updating the likelihood vectors is outlined in Fig. 12 for a 4-taxon tree.

To understand how the individual likelihood vectors are updated consider a subtree rooted at node `p` with immediate descendants `r` and `q` and likelihood vectors `l_p`, and `l_q`, `l_r` respectively. When the likelihood vectors `l_q` and `l_r` have

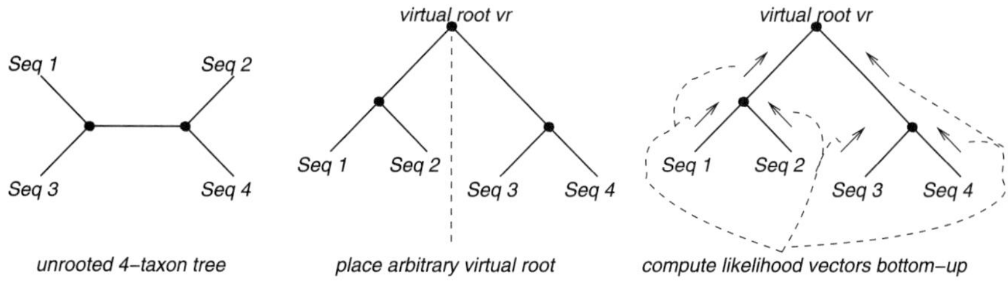


FIG. 12. Computation of the likelihood vectors of 4-taxon tree.

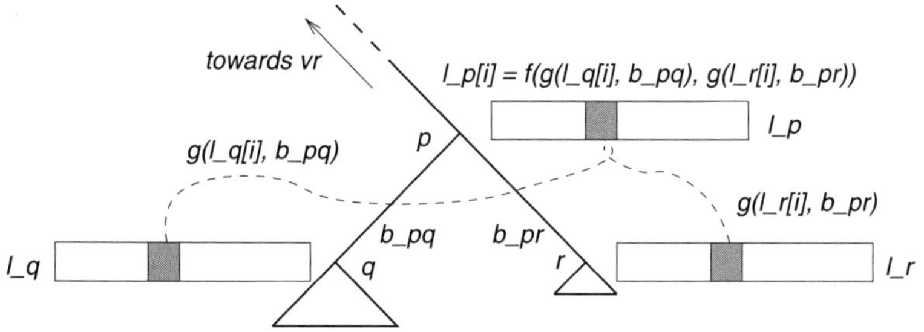


FIG. 13. Updating the likelihood vector of node $p$ at position $i$.

been computed the entries of `l_p` can be calculated—in an extremely simplified manner—as outlined by the pseudo-code below and in Fig. 13:

```
for(i = 0; i < m; i++)
  l_p[i] = f(g(l_q[i], b_pq), g(l_r[i], b_pr));
```

where `f()` is a simple function, i.e. requires just a few FLOPs, to combine the values of `g(l_q[i], b_pq)` and `g(l_r[i], b_pr)`. The `g()` function however is more complex and computationally intensive since it calculates $P_{ij}(t)$. The parameter $t$ corresponds to the branch lengths `b_pq` and `b_pr` respectively. Note, that the `for`-loop can easily be parallelized on a fine-grained level since entries `l_p[i]` and `l_p[i + 1]` can be computed independently (see Section 3.4).

Up to this point it has been described how to compute the likelihood of a tree given some arbitrary branch lengths. In order to obtain the *maximum* likelihood value for a given tree topology the length of *all* branches in the tree has to be optimized. Since the likelihood of the tree is not altered by distinct rootings of the tree the virtual root can be subsequently placed into all branches of the tree. Each branch can then be individually optimized to improve the likelihood value of the entire tree. In general—depending on the implementation—this process is continued until no further branch length alteration yields an improved likelihood score. Branch length optimization can be regarded as maximization of a one-parameter function $lh(t)$ where $lh$ is the phylogenetic likelihood function and $t$ the branch length.

Some of the most commonly used optimization methods are the Newton–Raphson method in fastDNAml [70] or Brent's rule in PHYML [58].

Typically, the two basic operations: computation of the likelihood value and optimization of the branch lengths, require $\approx 90\%$ of the complete execution time of every ML program. For example $92.72\%$ of total execution time for a typical dataset with 150 sequences in PHYML and $92.89\%$ for the same dataset in RAxML-VI. Thus, an acceleration of these functions at a technical level by optimization of the source code and the memory access behavior, or at an algorithmic level by re-use of previously computed values is very important.

A technically extremely efficient implementation of the likelihood function has been coded in fastDNAml. The Subtree Equality Vector (SEV) method [63] represents an algorithmic optimization of the likelihood function which exploits alignment pattern equalities to avoid a substantial amount of re-computations of the expensive `g()` function. An analogous approach to accelerate the likelihood function has been proposed in [62].

As already mentioned another important issue within the HPC context is the mathematical accommodation of rate variation (also called rate heterogeneity) among sites in nucleotide substitution methods, since sites (alignment columns) usually do not evolve at the same speed. It has been demonstrated, e.g. in [71], that ML inference under the assumption of rate homogeneity can lead to erroneous results if rates vary among sites.

Rate heterogeneity among sites can easily be accommodated by incorporating an additional per-site (per-alignment-column) rate vector `r[]` of length $m$ into function `g()`.

The pseudocode for updating the likelihood vectors with per-site rates is indicated below:

```
for(i = 0; i < m; i++)
  l_p[i] = f(g(l_q[i], b_pq, r[i]),
             g(l_r[i], b_pr, r[i]));
```

Often, such an assignment of individual rates to sites corresponds to some functional classification of sites and can be performed based on an a priori analysis of the data. G. Olsen has developed a program called DNArates [72] which performs an ML estimate of the individual per site substitution rates for a given input tree. A similar technique is used in RAxML and the model is called e.g. GTR + CAT to distinguish it from GTR + $\Gamma$ (see below), when the GTR model of nucleotide substitution is used. However, the use of individual per-site rates might lead to over-fitting the data. This effect can be alleviated by using rate categories instead of individual per-site rates, e.g. for an alignment with a length of 1,000 base pairs only $c = 25$ or $c = 50$ distinct rate categories are used. To this end an integer vector `category[]` of length $m$ is used which assigns an individual rate category `cat` to each alignment column, where $1 \leqslant$ `cat` $\leqslant c$. The vector `rate[]` of length $c$ contains the rates. This model will henceforth be called CAT model of rate heterogeneity. The abstract structure of a typical `for`-loop to compute the likelihood under CAT is outlined below:

```
for(i = 0; i < m; i++)
  {
     cat = category[i];
     r = rate[cat];
     l_p[i] = f(g(l_q[i], b_pq, r), g(l_r[i],
                 b_pr, r));
  }
```

However, little has been published on how to optimize per-site evolutionary rates and how to reasonably categorize per-site evolutionary rates. A notable exception, dealing with per-site rate optimization, is a relatively recent paper by Meyer et al. [73]. The current version of RAxML is one of the few ML programs which implements the CAT model.

A computationally more intensive and thus less desirable form of dealing with heterogeneous rates, due to the fact that significantly more memory *and* floating point operations are required (typically factor 4), consists in using either discrete or continuous stochastic models for the rate distribution at each site. In this case every site has a certain probability of evolving at any rate contained in a given probability distribution. Thus, for a discretized distribution with a number $\rho$ of discrete rates, $\rho$ distinct likelihood vector entries have to be computed *per* site `i`. In the continuous case likelihoods must be integrated over the entire probability distribution.

The most commonly used distributions are the continuous [74] and discrete [71] $\Gamma$ distributions. Typically, a discrete $\Gamma$ distribution with $\rho = 4$ points/rates is used since this represents an acceptable trade-off between inference time, memory consumption, and accuracy. Given the *four* individual rates from the discrete $\Gamma$ distribution `r_0,...,r_3` *now four* individual likelihood entries `l_p[i].g_0,...,l_p[i].g_3` *per* site `i` have to be updated as indicated below:

```
for(i = 0; i < m; i++)
  {
     l_p[i].g_0 = f(g(l_q[i], b_pq, r_0),
                    g(l_r[i], b_pr, r_0));
```

```
        l_p[i].g_1 = f(g(l_q[i], b_pq, r_1),
                       g(l_r[i], b_pr, r_1));
        l_p[i].g_2 = f(g(l_q[i], b_pq, r_2),
                       g(l_r[i], b_pr, r_2));
        l_p[i].g_3 = f(g(l_q[i], b_pq, r_3),
                       g(l_r[i], b_pr, r_3));
    }
```

Usually, Biologists have to account for rate heterogeneity in their analyses due to the properties of real world data and in order to obtain *publishable* results.

From an HPC point of view it is evident that the CAT model should be preferred over the $\Gamma$ model due to the significantly lower memory consumption and amount of floating point operations which result in faster inference times. However, little is known about the correlation between the CAT and the $\Gamma$ model, despite the fact that they are intended to model the same phenomenon. A recent experimental study [75] with RAxML on 19 real-world DNA data alignments comprising 73 up to 1,663 taxa indicate that CAT is on average over 5 times faster than $\Gamma$ and—surprisingly enough—also yields trees with even slightly better final $\Gamma$ likelihood values (factor 1.000014 for 50 rate categories, and factor 1.000037 for 25 rate categories). Similar experimental results have been obtained by Derrick Zwickl on different datasets. Citing from [76], p. 62: "*In practice, performing inferences using the* GTR + CAT *model in RAxML has proven to be an excellent method for obtaining topologies that score well under the* GTR + $\Gamma$ *model.*"

The large speedup of CAT over $\Gamma$ which exceeds factor 4 is due to increased cache efficiency, since CAT only uses *approximately one quarter* of the memory and the floating point operations required for $\Gamma$. In fact, the utilization of $\Gamma$ lead to an average increase of L2 cache misses by factor 7.46 and factor 7.41 for the L3 cache respectively. Thus, given the computational advantages of CAT over $\Gamma$, more effort needs to be invested into the design of a more solid mathematical framework for CAT. The current implementation and categorization algorithm in RAxML has been derived from empirical observations [75]. In addition, final likelihood values obtained under the CAT approximation are numerically instable at present such that the likelihood of final trees needs to be re-computed under $\Gamma$ in order to compare alternative trees based on their likelihood values. The recently released RAxML manual (diwww.epfl.ch/~stamatak (software frame)) describes this in more detail.

In order to underline the efficiency of the GTR+CAT approximation over GTR+$\Gamma$ Fig. 14 depicts the GTR + $\Gamma$ Log Likelihood development over time (seconds) on the same starting tree. This alignment of 8,864 Bacteria is currently analyzed with RAxML in cooperation with the Pace Lab at the University of Colorado at Boulder.

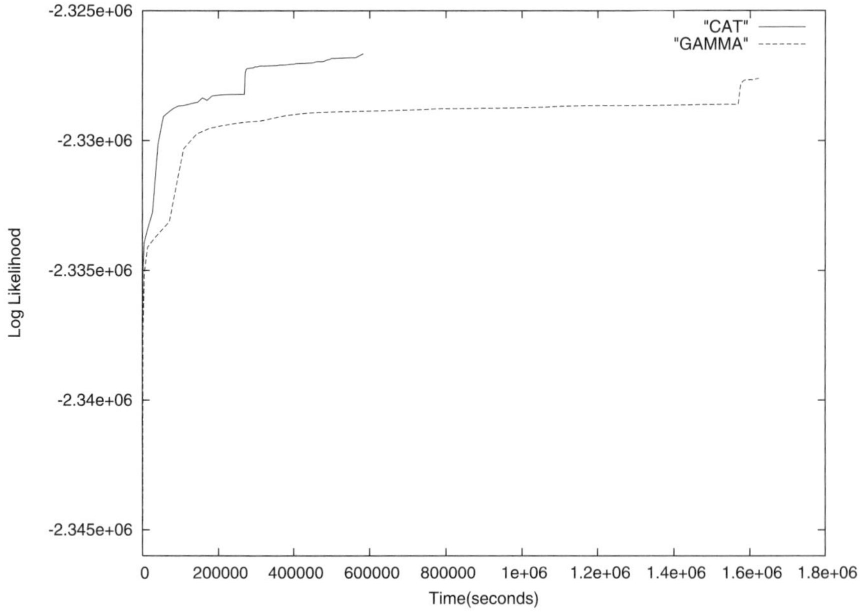


FIG. 14. RAxML Gamma log likelihood development over time for inferences under GTR+CAT and GTR + Γ on an alignment of 8,864 bacteria.

## 3.2 State-of-the-Art Programs

The current Section lists and discusses some of the most popular and widely used sequential and parallel ML programs for phylogenetic inference.

### *3.2.1 Hill-Climbing Algorithms*

In 2003 Guidon and Gascuel published an interesting paper about their very fast program PHYML [58]. The respective performance analysis includes larger simulated datasets of 100 sequences and two well-studied real data sets containing 218 and 500 sequences. Their experiments show that PHYML is extremely fast on real and simulated data.

However, the current hill-climbing and simulated annealing algorithms of RAxML clearly outperform PHYML on real world data, both in terms of execution time and final tree quality [57]. The requirement to improve accuracy on real data [57] and to replace NNI moves (Nearest Neighbor Interchange) by more exhaustive SPR moves (Subtree Pruning Re-grafting, also called subtree rearrangements) has been recognized by the authors of PHYML. In fact, a very promising refinement/extension of the *lazy subtree rearrangement* technique from RAxML [57] has very recently been integrated into PHYML [77].

Irrespective of these differences between RAxML and PHYML, the results in [58] show that well-established sequential programs like PAUP* [30], TREE-PUZZLE [78], and fastDNAml [70] are prohibitively slow on datasets containing more than 200 sequences, at least in sequential execution mode.

More recently, Vinh et al. [46] published a program called IQPNNI which yields better trees than PHYML on real world data but is significantly slower. In comparison to RAxML, IQPNNI is both slower and less accurate [79].

### 3.2.2 Simulated Annealing Approaches

The first application of simulated annealing techniques to ML tree searches was proposed by Salter et al. [80] (the technique has previously been applied to MP phylogenetic tree searches by D. Barker [81]). However, the respective program SSA has not become very popular due to the limited availability of nucleotide substitution models and the focus on the molecular clock model of evolution. Moreover, the program is relatively hard to use and comparatively slow in respect to recent hill-climbing implementations. Despite the fact that Salter et al. where the first to apply simulated annealing to ML-based phylogenetic tree searches there do not exist any published biological results using SSA. However, the recent implementation of a simulated annealing search algorithm in RAxML [79] yielded promising results.

### 3.2.3 Parallel Phylogeny Programs

Despite the fact that parallel implementations of ML programs are technically very solid in terms of performance and parallelization techniques, they significantly lag behind algorithmic development. This means, that programs are parallelized that mostly do not represent the state-of-the-art algorithms any more. Therefore, they are likely to be out-competed by the most recent sequential algorithms in terms of final tree quality and—more importantly—accumulated CPU time.

For example, the largest tree computed with parallel fastDNAml [82] which is based on the fastDNAml algorithm from 1994 contained 150 taxa. Note, that there also exists a distributed implementation of this code [83].

The same argument holds for a technically very interesting JAVA-based distributed ML program: DPRml [84]. Despite the recent implementation of state-of-the-art search algorithms in DPRml, significant performance penalties are caused by using JAVA both in terms of memory efficiency and speed of numerical calculations. Those language-dependent limitations will become more intense when trees comprising over 417 taxa (currently largest tree with DPRml, Thomas Keane, personal communication) are computed with DPRml.

The technically challenging parallel implementation of TrExML [85,86] (original sequential algorithm published in the year 2000) has been used to compute a tree containing 56 taxa. However, TrExML is probably not suited for computation of very large trees since the main feature of the algorithm consists in a more exhaustive exploitation of search space for medium-sized alignments. Due to this exhaustive search strategy the execution time increases more steeply with the number of taxa than in other programs.

The largest tree computed with the parallel version of TREE-PUZZLE [87] contained 257 taxa due to limitations caused by the data structures used (Heiko Schmidt, personal communication). However, TREE-PUZZLE provides mainly advantages concerning quality-assessment for medium-sized trees. IQPNNI has also recently been parallelized with MPI and shows good speedup values [88].

M.J. Brauer et al. [59] have implemented a parallel genetic tree-search algorithm (parallel GAML) which has been used to compute trees of up to approximately 3,000 taxa with the main limitation for the computation of larger trees being memory consumption (Derrick Zwickl, personal communication). However, the new tree search mechanism implemented in the successor of GAML, which is now called GARLI [76] (Genetic Algorithm for Rapid Likelihood Inference, available at http://www.zo.utexas.edu/faculty/antisense/Garli.html) is equally powerful as the RAxML algorithm (especially on datasets $\leqslant$1,000 taxa) but requires higher inference times [76]. However, GARLI is one of the few state-of-the-art programs, that incorporates an outstanding technical implementation and optimization of the likelihood functions.

There also exists a parallel version of Rec-I-DCM3 [34] for ML which is based on RAxML (see Section 2.2 of this chapter). The current implementation faces some scalability limitations due to load imbalance caused by significant differences in the subproblem sizes. In addition, the parallelization of RAxML for global tree optimizations also faces some intrinsic difficulties (see [89] and page 167 in Section 3.4.3).

Finally, there exist the previous parallel and distributed implementations of the RAxML hill-climbing algorithm [90,91].

### 3.2.4 Conclusion

The above overview of recent algorithmic and technical developments, and the maximum tree sizes calculated so far, underlines the initial statement that a part of the computational problems in phylogenetics tends to become technical. This view is shared in the recent paper by Hordijk and Gascuel on the new search technique implemented in PHYML [77]. In order to enable large-scale inference of huge trees a greater part of research efforts should focus on the technical implementation of the likelihood functions, the allocation and use of likelihood vectors, cache efficiency, as well as exploitation of hardware such as Symmetrical Multi-Processing (SMPs), Graphics Processing Units (GPUs), and Multi-Core Processors. Thus, the rest of the current section will mainly focus on these rarely documented and discussed technical issues and indicate some potential directions of future research.

## 3.3 Technical Details: Memory Organization and Data Structures

As already mentioned, the implementation of the likelihood functions in fastDNAml represents perhaps *the* most efficient implementation currently available, both in terms of memory organization and loop optimization. The current version of RAxML has been derived from the fastDNAml source code and extended this efficient implementation.

The current Section reviews some of the—so far undocumented—technical implementation details which will be useful for future ML implementations.

### *3.3.1 Memory Organization and Efficiency*

As outlined in Section 3.1 the amount of memory space required is dominated by the length and number of likelihood vectors. Thus, the memory requirements are of order $O(n * m)$ where $n$ is the number of sequences and $m$ the alignment length. An unrooted phylogenetic tree for an alignment of dimensions $n * m$ has $n$ tips or leaves and $n-2$ inner nodes, such that $2n-2$ vectors of length $m$ would be required to compute the likelihood bottom-up at a given virtual root $vr$. Note that, the computation of the vectors at the tips of the tree (leaf-vectors) is *significantly less expensive* than the computation of inner vectors. In addition, the values of the leaf-vectors are topology-independent, i.e. it suffices to compute them *once* during the initialization of the program. Unlike most other ML implementations however, in fastDNAml a distinct approach has been chosen: The program trades memory for additional computations, i.e. only 3 (!) likelihood vectors are used to store tip-values. This means that tip likelihood vectors will have to be continuously re-computed on-demand during the entire inference process. On the other hand the memory consumption is reduced to $(n + 1) * m$ in contrast to $(2n - 2) * m$. This represents a memory footprint reduction by almost factor 2. This leads to improved cache-efficiency and the capability to handle larger alignments. Experiments with RAxML using the alternative implementation with $n$ precomputed leaf-vectors on a 1,000-taxon alignment have demonstrated that the re-computation of leaf-vector values is in fact more efficient, even with respect to execution times. Due to the growing chasm between CPU and RAM performance and the constantly growing alignment sizes, the above method should be used. The importance and impact of cache efficiency is also underlined by the significant superlinear speedups achieved by the OpenMP implementation of RAxML (see [92] and Fig. 19).

The idea of trading memory for computation with respect to tip vectors has been further developed in the current release of RAxML-VI for High Performance Computing (RAxML-VI-HPC v2.0). This new version does not use or compute any leaf-vectors at all. Instead it uses one global leaf-likelihood vector `globalLeafVector[]` of length 15 which contains the pre-computed likelihood vectors for all 15 possible nucleotide sequence states. Note that, the number of 15 states comes from some intermediate states which are allowed, e.g. apart from `A,C,G,T,-` the letter `R` stands for `A or G` and `Y` for `C or T` etc. When a tip with a nucleotide sequence `sequence[i]` where `i=1,...,m` and alignment length `m` is encountered, the respective leaf-likelihood vector at position `i` of the alignment is obtained by referencing `globalLeafVector[]` via the sequence entry `sequence[i]`, i.e. `likelivector = globalTip[sequence[i]]`. Note that `sequence[]` is a simple array of type `char` which contains the sequences of the alignment. The introduction of this optimization yielded performance improvements of approximately 5–10%. Finally, note that GARLI uses a similar, though more sophisticated implementation of leaf-likelihood vector computations (Derrick Zwickl, personal communication).

With respect to the internal likelihood vectors there also exist two different approaches. In programs such as PHYML or IQPNNI not one but *three* likelihood vectors are allocated to each internal node, i.e. one vector for each direction of the unrooted tree. Thus, PHYML also maintains an unrooted view of the tree with respect to the likelihood vector organization.

If the likelihood needs to be calculated at an arbitrary branch of the tree the required likelihood vectors to the left and right of the virtual root will be immediately available. On the other hand, a very large amount of those vectors will have to be re-computed after a change of the tree topology or branch lengths (see Fig. 15 for an example).

In RAxML and fastDNAml only one inner likelihood vector per internal node, is allocated. This vector is relocated to the one of the three outgoing branches `noderec *next` (see data structure below) of the inner node which points towards the current virtual root. If the likelihood vector `xarray *x` is already located at the correct branch it must not be recomputed. The infrastructure to move likelihood vectors is implemented by a cyclic list of 3 data structures of type `node` (one per outgoing branch `struct noderec *back`) to the likelihood vector data structure. At all times, two of those pointers point to `NULL` whereas one points to the actual address of the likelihood vector (see Fig. 16).

```
typedef struct noderec {
  double z; /* branch length value */
```

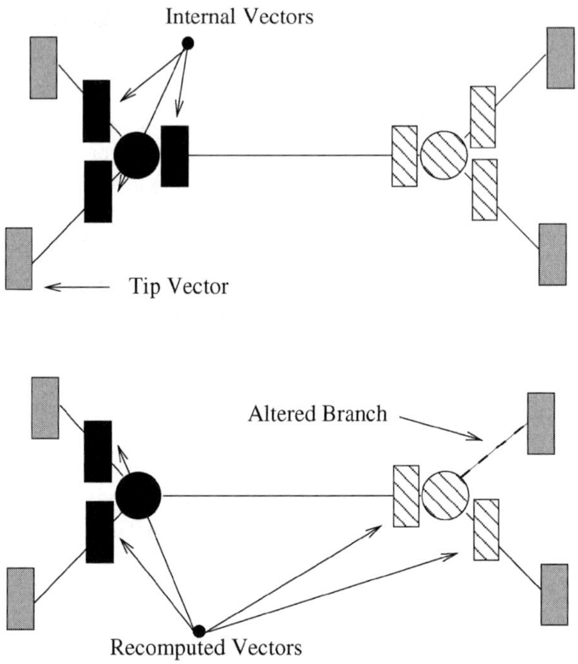


FIG. 15. Likelihood vector update in PHYML.

```
  struct noderec *next;
  /* pointer to next structure in cyclic list*/
  struct noderec *back;
  /* pointer to neighboring node*/
  xarray *x; /* pointer to likelihood vector*/
} node;
```

With respect to the position of the likelihood vectors in the cyclic list of `struct noderec` a tree using this scheme is always rooted. In addition, at each movement of the virtual root, in order to e.g. optimize a branch, a certain amount of vectors must be recomputed. The same holds for changes in tree topology. However, as for the tip vectors, there is a trade-off between additional computations and reduced memory consumption for inner likelihood vectors as well. Moreover, the order by which topological changes are applied to improve the likelihood, can be arranged intelligently, such that only few likelihood vectors need to be updated after each topological change. Currently, there exists no comparative study between those two approaches to memory organization and likelihood calculation. Nonetheless, it

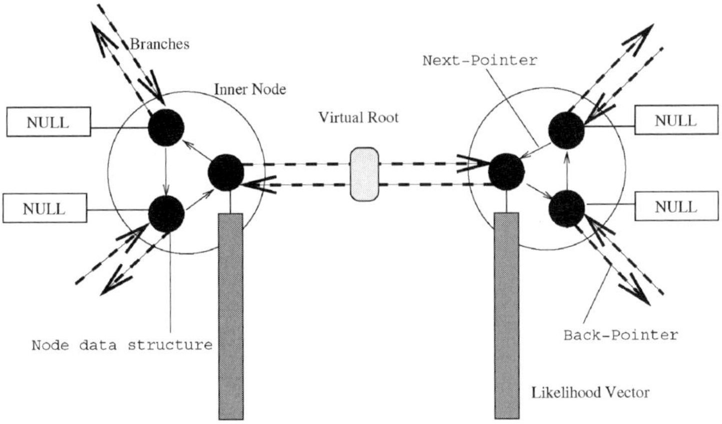


FIG. 16. Likelihood vector organization in RAxML.

would be very useful to compare memory consumption, cache efficiency, and amount of floating point operations for these alternatives under the *same* search algorithm.

It appears however, that the latter approach is more adequate for inference of extremely large trees with ML. Experiments with an alignment of approximately 25,000 protobacteria show that RAxML already requires 1.5 GB of main memory using the GTR + CAT approximation. A very long multi-gene alignment of 2,182 mammalian sequences with a length of more than 50,000 base pairs already required 2.5 GB under GTR + CAT and 9 GB under GTR + $\Gamma$. To the best of the authors knowledge this alignment represents the largest data matrix which has been analyzed under ML to date. Given that the alternative memory organization requires at least 3 times more memory it is less adequate for inference of huge trees.

One might argue, that the application of a divide-and-conquer approach can solve memory problems since it will only have to handle significantly smaller subtrees and sub-alignments. Due to the algorithmic complexity of the problem however, every divide-and-conquer approach to date also performs *global* optimizations on the complete tree.

The extent of the memory consumption problem becomes even more evident when one considers, that the length $m$ of the 25,000 protobacteria alignment is only 1,463 base pairs, i.e. it is relatively short with respect to the large number of sequences. Typically, for a *publishable* biological analysis of such large datasets a significantly greater alignment length would be required [40]. In the final analysis it can be stated that memory organization and consumption are issues of increasing importance in the quest to reconstruct the tree of life which should contain at least 100,000 or 1,000,000 organisms based on the rather more conservative estimates.

The increasing concern about memory consumption is also reflected by the recent changes introduced in the new release of MrBayes [93] (version 3.1.1). Despite the fact that MrBayes performs Bayesian inference of phylogenetic trees the underlying technical problems are the same since the likelihood value of alternative tree topologies needs to be computed and thus likelihood computations consume a very large part of execution time. Therefore, to reduce memory consumption of MrBayes, double-precision arithmetics have been replaced by single-precision operations.

### *3.3.2 Loop Optimization and Model Implementation*

Another aspect of increasing importance in HPC ML program design consists in highly optimized implementations of the likelihood functions. They consume over 90% of total execution time in typical ML implementations, e.g. 92.72% in PHYML and 92.89% in RAxML for a typical dataset of 150 sequences.

Despite the obvious advantages of a generic programming style as used e.g. in PHYML or IQPNNI, each model of sequence evolution such as HKY85 or GTR should be implemented in separate functions. Depending on the selected model RAxML uses function pointers to highly optimized individual functions for each model. This allows for better exploitation of symmetries and simplifications on a per-model basis. As already mentioned the compute-intensive part of the computations is performed by 4–5 `for`-loops (depending on the implementation) over the length of the alignment $m$. For example the manual optimization and complete unrolling of inner loops for the recently implemented protein substitution models in RAxML yielded more than 50% of performance improvement. This increase in performance could not be achieved by the use of highly sophisticated Intel or PGI compilers alone. In addition, instructions within the for-loops have been re-ordered to better suit pipeline architectures.

Another important technical issue concerns the optimization technique used for branch lengths, which consumes 42.63% of total execution time in RAxML and 58.74% in PHYML. Despite the additional cost required to compute the first and second derivative of the likelihood function, the Newton–Raphson method (RAxML, fastDNAml) should be preferred over Brent's method (PHYML) since Newton–Raphson converges *significantly* faster. Due to this observation Brent has recently been replaced by Newton–Raphson in the new version of IQPNNI [88] (version 3.0). In addition, the latest version of IQPNNI also incorporates the BFGS method [94] for multi-dimensional optimization of model parameters (Bui Quang Minh, personal communication). BFGS is very efficient for parameter-rich models such as $\mathrm{GTR} + \Gamma$ or complex protein models, in comparison to the more common approach of optimizing parameters one-by-one. By deploying BFGS the parameter optimization process for the 6 rate parameters of the GTR model in IQPNNI could be accelerated by factor 3–4 in comparison to Brent (Bui Quang Minh, personal communication). Those

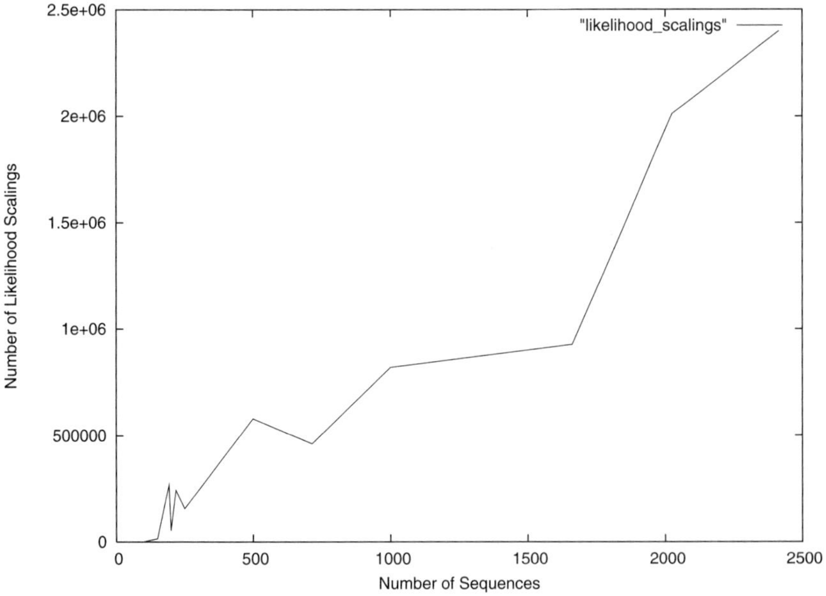


FIG. 17. Number of likelihood scalings.

mathematical improvements lead to a total performance improvement of factor 1.2 up to 1.8 in IQPNNI over the previous version of the program.

A useful discussion of numerical problems and solutions for the inference of large trees can be found in [95]. Another important numerical design decision which concerns the memory-time trade-off is the choice between single (e.g. MrBayes), double (e.g. RAxML, PHYML), and long double (IQPNNI) precision arithmetics for calculating the likelihood. This choice is important since it has an effect on the number of times *very small* likelihood values have to be scaled (scaling events) in order to avoid numerical underflow. Typically, the larger the tree, the more *scaling events* are anticipated. This trend is outlined in Fig. 17 where the $x$-axis indicates the number of sequences in the dataset and the $y$-axis the number of scaling events in RAxML for the evaluation and parameter-optimization of one single tree topology. When single precision is used those computationally relatively expensive operations have to be performed more frequently. On the other hand double and long double require more memory space. Thus, the choice of double precision appears to represent a reasonable trade-off. A porting of RAxML from `double` to `float` for the purposes of the GPGPU implementation [96] (see Section 3.4) did not yield better results in terms of execution times.

## 3.4 Parallelization Techniques

Typically, in ML programs there exist three distinct sources of parallelism which are depicted in Fig. 18:

1. *Fine-grained loop-level parallelism* at the `for`-loops of the likelihood function which can be efficiently exploited with OpenMP on 2-way or 4-way SMPs.
2. *Coarse-grained parallelism* at the level of tree alterations and evaluations which can be exploited using MPI and a master–worker scheme.
3. *Job-level parallelism* where multiple phylogenetic analyses on the same dataset with distinct starting trees or multiple bootstrap analyses are performed simultaneously on a cluster.

### 3.4.1 Job-Level Parallelism

Since implementing job-level parallelism does not represent a very challenging task this issue is omitted. It should be stated however, that this is probably the best way to exploit a parallel computer for real-world biological analyses (including multiple bootstrapping) of large datasets in most practical cases. In order to conduct a biologically "publishable" study, multiple inferences with distinct starting trees and a relatively large number of bootstrap runs should be executed. The typical RAxML

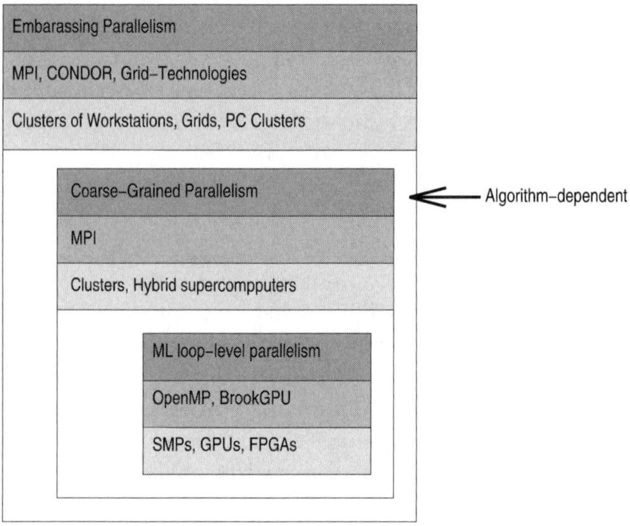


FIG. 18. The three nested sources of parallelism in ML programs.

execution times under elaborate models of nucleotide substitution for trees of 1,000–2,000 taxa range from 12 to 24 hours on an Opteron CPU. Note that, the dedicated High Performance Computing Version of RAxML-VI (released March 2006) only requires about 40–60 hours in sequential execution mode on 7,000–8,000 taxon alignments under the reasonably accurate and fast GTR + CAT approximation. In order to provide a useful tool for Biologists this version has also been parallelized with MPI to enable parallel multiple inferences on the original alignment as well as parallel multiple non-parametric bootstraps.

### 3.4.2 Shared-Memory Parallelism

The exploitation of fine-grained loop-level parallelism is straightforward, since ML programs spend most of their time in the `for`-loops for calculating the likelihood (see Section 3.1). In addition, those loops do not exhibit any dependencies between iteration `i` → `i + 1` such that they can easily be parallelized with OpenMP. As indicated in the pseudo-code below, it suffices to insert a simple OpenMP directive:

```
#pragma omp parallel for private(...)
for(i = 0; i < m; i++)
  l_p[i] = f(g(l_q[i], b_pq), g(l_r[i], b_pr));
```

There are several advantages to this approach: The implementation is easy, such that little programming effort (approximately one week) is required to parallelize an ML program with OpenMP. The memory space of the likelihood vectors is equally distributed among processors, such that higher cache efficiency is achieved than in the sequential case, due to the smaller memory footprint. This has partially lead to *significantly* superlinear speedups with the OpenMP version of RAxML [92] on large/long alignments. Figure 19 indicates the speedup values of the OpenMP version of RAxML on a simulated alignment of 300 organisms with a length of $m = 5{,}000$ base pairs for the Xeon, Itanium, and Opteron architectures.

Moreover, modern supercomputer architectures can be exploited in a more efficient manner by a hybrid MPI/OpenMP approach. Finally, it is a very general concept that can easily be applied to other ML phylogeny programs. An unpublished OpenMP parallelization of PHYML by M. Ott and A. Stamatakis yielded comparable—though not superlinear—results. GARLI (Derrick Zwickl, personal communication) and IQPNNI [97] are also currently being parallelized with OpenMP. However, the scalability of this approach is usually limited to 2-way or 4-way SMPs and relatively long alignments due to the granularity of this source of parallelism. However, this type of parallelism represents a good solution for analyses of long multi-gene alignments which are becoming more popular recently. Figure 20 indicates the parallel performance improvement on 1 versus 8 CPUs on one node of

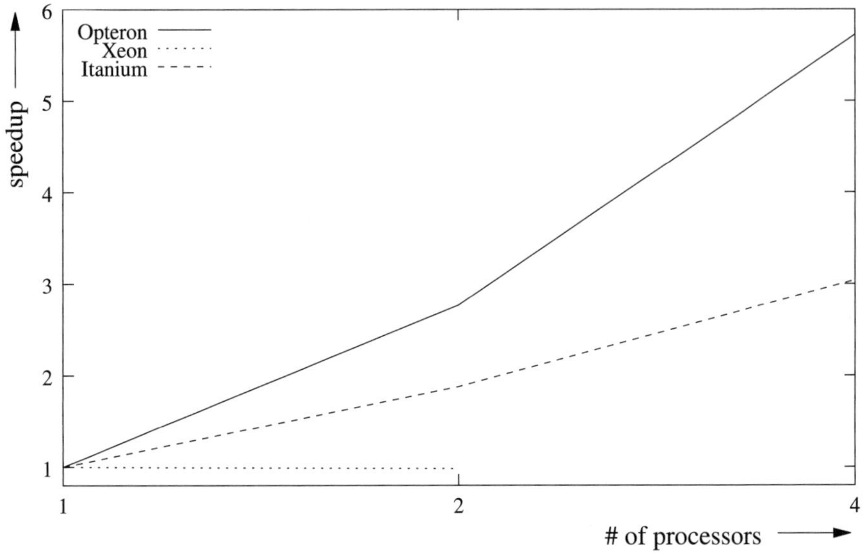


FIG. 19. Speedup of the OpenMP version of RAxML on Xeon, Itanium, and Opteron architectures for a relatively long alignment of 5,000 nucleotides.

the CIPRES project (www.phylo.org) cluster located at the San Diego Supercomputing Center for the previously mentioned multi-gene alignment of mammals during the first three iterations of the search algorithm (speedup: 6.74).

Apart from SMPs another interesting hardware platform to exploit loop-level parallelism are GPUs (Graphics Processing Units). Recently, General Purpose computations on GPUs (GPGPU) are becoming more popular due to the availability of improved programming interfaces such a the BrookGPU [98] compiler and runtime implementation. Since GPUs are essentially vector processors the intrinsic fine-grained parallelism of ML programs can be exploited in a very similar way as on SMPs. RAxML has recently been parallelized on a GPU [96] and achieves a highly improved price/performance and power-consumption/performance ratio than on CPUs. Note that, in [96] only one of the main `for`-loops of the program which accounts for approximately 50% of overall execution time has been ported to the GPU. Despite the incomplete porting and the fact that a mid-class GPU (NVIDIA FX 5700LE, price: \$75, power consumption: 24 W) and high-end CPU (Pentium 4 3.2 GHz, price: \$200, power consumption: $\geqslant$130 W) have been used, an overall speedup of 1.2 on the GPU has been measured. However, there still exists a relatively large number of technical problems, such as unavailability of double precision arithmetics (RAxML had to be ported to `float`) and insufficient memory capacity for

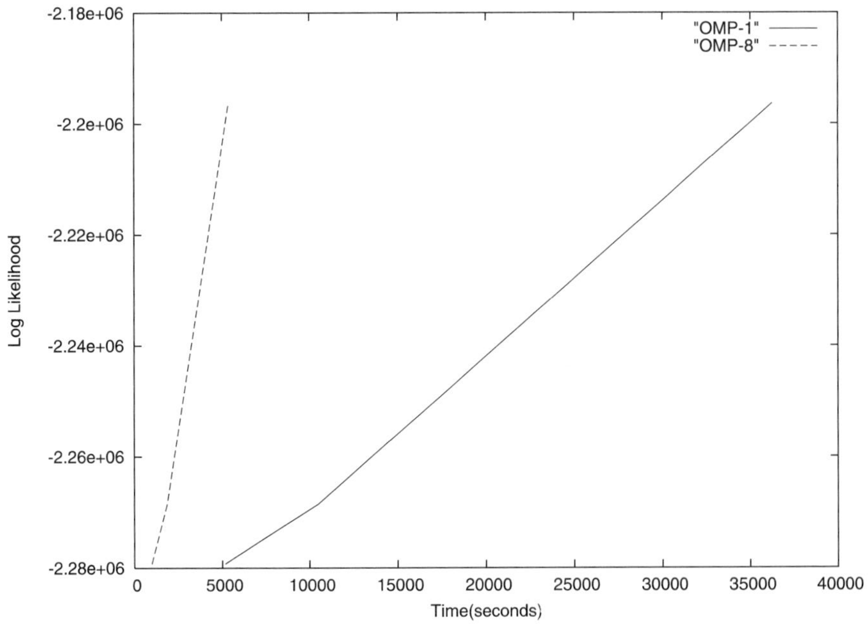


FIG. 20. Run time improvement for the first three iterations of the search algorithm of the OpenMP version of RAxML-VI-HPC on 1 and 8 CPUs on a 51,089 bp long multi-gene alignment of 2,182 mammals.

very large trees (usually up to 512 MB). A natural extension of this work consists in the usage of clusters of GPUs.

### *3.4.3 Coarse-Grained Parallelism*

The coarse-grained parallelization of ML phylogeny programs is less straightforward: The parallel efficiency which can be attained depends strongly on the structure of the individual search algorithms. In addition the rate at which improved topologies are encountered has a major impact on parallel efficiency since the tree structure must be continuously updated at all processes. This can result in significant communication overheads.

For example RAxML frequently detects improved topologies during the initial optimization phase of the tree. One iteration of the search algorithm consists in applying a sequence of $2n$ distinct LSR moves (Lazy Subtree Rearrangements, see [57] for details) to the currently best topology $t_{\text{best}}$. If the likelihood of $t_{\text{best}}$ is improved by the $i$th LSR, $i = 1, \ldots, 2n$, the changed topology is kept, i.e. $t_{\text{best}} := t_i$. Thus, one

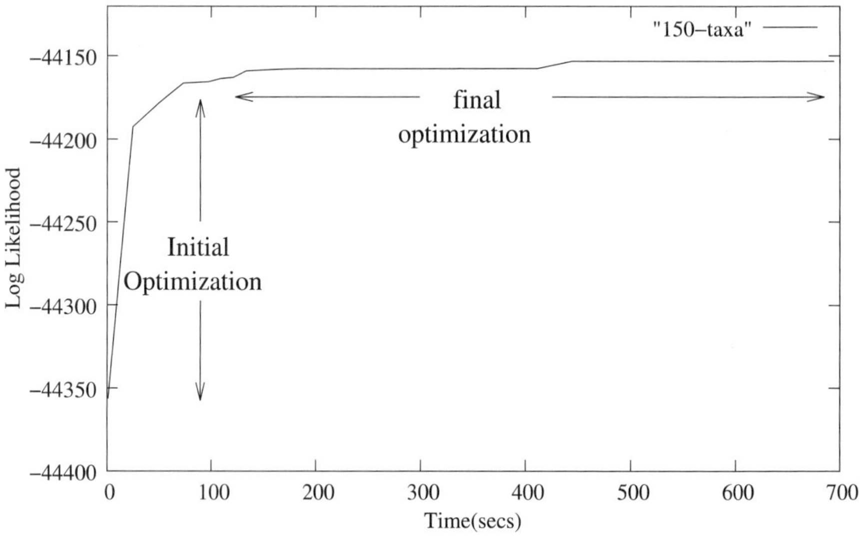


FIG. 21. Typical asymptotic likelihood improvement over time for RAxML on a 150-taxon alignment.

iteration of the sequential algorithm (one iteration of LSRs) generates a sequence of $k \leqslant n$ distinct topologies with improved likelihood values $t_{i_1} \rightarrow t_{i_2} \rightarrow \cdots \rightarrow t_{i_k}$. The likelihood optimization process typically exhibits an asymptotic convergence behavior over time with a steep increase of the likelihood values during the initial optimization phase and a shallow improvement during the final optimization phase (see Fig. 21).

Due to the small execution time of a single LSR even on huge trees, the algorithm can only be parallelized by independently assigning one or more LSR jobs at a time to each worker processes in a master-worker scheme. The main problem consists in breaking up the sequential dependency $t_{i_1} \rightarrow t_{i_2} \rightarrow \cdots \rightarrow t_{i_k}$ of improvements. Since this is very difficult a reasonable approach is to introduce a certain amount of non-determinism. This means that workers will receive topology updates for their local copy of $t_{\text{best}}$ detected by other workers with some delay and in a different order. If during the initial optimization phase of RAxML $k$ is relatively large with respect to $n$, e.g. $k \approx n$ this has a negative impact on the parallel efficiency since a large number of update messages has to be communicated and is delayed. For example, on an alignment with 7,769 organisms every second LSR move yielded a topology with an improved likelihood value during the first iteration of the search algorithm. Thus, the mechanism of exchanging topological alterations between workers represents a potential performance bottleneck. The standard string representation of trees (with parentheses, taxon-names and branch lengths) as used in parallel fastDNAml [82] and an older parallel version of RAxML [91] is becoming inefficient. This is due to the feasibility to compute significantly larger trees caused by recent algorithmic advances. In addition, the starting trees for these large analyses which are usually computed using Neighbor Joining or "quick & dirty" Maximum Parsimony heuristics are worse (in terms of relative difference between the likelihood score of the starting tree and the final tree topology) than on smaller trees. As a consequence improved topologies are detected more frequently during the initial optimization phase with a negative impact on speedup values. Thus, topological changes should be communicated by specifying the actual change only, e.g. remove subtree number $i$ from branch $x$ and insert it into branch $y$. This can still lead to inconsistencies among the local copies of $t_{\text{best}}$ at individual workers but appears to be the only feasible solution for parallelizing the initial optimization phase.

Nonetheless, the final optimization phase which is significantly longer with respect to the total run time of the program is less problematic to parallelize since improved topologies are encountered less frequently. It is important to note, that the above problems mainly concern the parallelization of RAxML but will generally become more prominent as tree sizes grow.

A recent parallelization of IQPNNI [88] with near-optimal relative speedup values demonstrates that these problems are algorithm-dependent. However, as most other programs IQPNNI is currently constrained to tree sizes of approximately 2,000 taxa due to memory shortage. The comments about novel solutions which have to be deployed for communicating and updating topologies still hold.

An issue which will surely become important for future HPC ML program development is the distribution of memory among processes: Currently, most implementations hold the entire tree data structure in memory locally at each worker. Given the constant increase of computable tree sizes, and the relatively low main memory per node (1 GB) of current MPP architectures, such as the IBM BlueGene, it will become difficult to hold the complete tree in memory for trees comprising more than 20,000–100,000 taxa.

## 3.5 Conclusion

Due to the significant progress, which has been achieved by the introduction of novel search algorithms for ML-based phylogenetic inference, analyses of huge phylogenies comprising several hundreds or even thousands of taxa have now become feasible. However, the performance of ML phylogeny programs is increasingly limited by rarely documented and published technical implementation issues. Thus, an at least partial paradigm shift towards technical issues is required in order to advance the field and to enable inference of larger trees with the ultimate, though still distant, goal to compute the tree-of-life.

As an example for the necessity of a paradigm shift one can consider the recent improvements to RAxML: The significant (unpublished) speedups for sequential RAxML-VI over sequential RAxML-V, of 1.66 on 1,000 taxa over 30 on 4,000 taxa up to 67 on 25,000 taxa, have been attained by very simple technical optimizations of the code.[1] The potential for these optimizations has only been realized by the author who has been working on the RAxML-code for almost 4 years after the respective paradigm shift.

To this end, the current Section covered some of those rarely documented but increasingly important technical issues and summarizes how MPP, SMP, hybrid supercomputer, and GPU architectures can be used to infer huge trees.

## Acknowledgements

Bader's research discussed in this chapter has been supported in part by NSF Grants CAREER CCF-0611589, ACI-00-93039, CCF-0611589, DBI-0420513, ITR ACI-00-81404, ITR EIA-01-21377, Biocomplexity DEB-01-20709, and ITR EF/BIO 03-31654; and DARPA Contract NBCH30390004.

## References

[1] Bader D., Moret B.M.E., Vawter L., "Industrial applications of high-performance computing for phylogeny reconstruction", in: Siegel H. (Ed.), *Proc. SPIE Commercial Applications for High-Performance Computing, Denver, CO*, vol. 4528, SPIE, Bellingham, WA, 2001, pp. 159–168.

[2] Moret B.M.E., Wyman S., Bader D., Warnow T., Yan M., "A new implementation and detailed study of breakpoint analysis", in: *Proc. 6th Pacific Symp. Biocomputing, PSB 2001, Hawaii*, 2001, pp. 583–594.

[3] Yan M., "High performance algorithms for phylogeny reconstruction with maximum parsimony", PhD thesis, Electrical and Computer Engineering Department, University of New Mexico, Albuquerque, NM, 2004.

[4] Yan M., Bader D.A., "Fast character optimization in parsimony phylogeny reconstruction", Technical report, Electrical and Computer Engineering Department, The University of New Mexico, Albuquerque, NM, 2003.

[5] Caprara A., "Formulations and hardness of multiple sorting by reversals", in: *3rd Annu. Internat. Conf. Computational Molecular Biology, RECOMB99, Lyon, France*, ACM, New York, 1999.

[1] Performance results and datasets used for RAxML-VI are available on-line at diwww.epfl.ch/~stamatak (material frame).

[6] Pe'er I., Shamir R., "The median problems for breakpoints are NP-complete", Technical Report 71, Electronic Colloquium on Computational Complexity, 1998.
[7] Swofford D., Olsen G., Waddell P., Hillis D., "Phylogenetic inference", in: Hillis A., Moritz C., Mable B. (Eds.), *Molecular Systematics*, Sinauer Associates, Sunderland, MA, 1996, pp. 407–514.
[8] Nei M., Kumar S., *Molecular Evolution and Phylogenetics*, Oxford Univ. Press, Oxford, UK, 2000.
[9] Faith D., "Distance method and the approximation of most-parsimonious trees", *Systematic Zoology* **34** (1985) 312–325.
[10] Farris J., "Estimating phylogenetic trees from distance matrices", *Amer. Naturalist* **106** (1972) 645–668.
[11] Li W.H., "Simple method for constructing phylogenetic trees from distance matrices", *Proc. Natl. Acad. Sci. USA* **78** (1981) 1085–1089.
[12] Saitou N., Nei M., "The neighbor-joining method: A new method for reconstruction of phylogenetic trees", *Mol. Biol. Evol.* **4** (1987) 406–425.
[13] Studier J., Keppler K., "A note on the neighbor-joining method of Saitou and Nei", *Mol. Biol. Evol.* **5** (1988) 729–731.
[14] Rice K., Warnow T., "Parsimony is hard to beat", in: *Computing and Combinatorics*, 1997, pp. 124–133.
[15] Hendy M., Penny D., "Branch and bound algorithms to determine minimal evolutionary trees", *Math. Biosci.* **59** (1982) 277–290.
[16] Fitch W., "Toward defining the course of evolution: Minimal change for a specific tree topology", *Systematic Zoology* **20** (1971) 406–416.
[17] Purdom Jr., Bradford P., Tamura K., Kumar S., "Single column discrepancy and dynamic max-mini optimization for quickly finding the most parsimonious evolutionary trees", *Bioinformatics* **2** (16) (2000) 140–151.
[18] Eck R., Dayhoff M., *Atlas of Protein Sequence and Structure*, National Biomedical Research Foundation, Silver Spring, MD, 1966.
[19] Benaïchouche M., Cung V., Dowaji S., Cun B., Mautor T., Roucairol C., "Building a parallel branch and bound library", in: Ferreira A., Pardalos P. (Eds.), *Solving Combinatorial Optimization Problem in Parallel: Methods and Techniques*, Springer-Verlag, Berlin, 1996, pp. 201–231.
[20] Swofford D., Begle D., *PAUP: Phylogenetic Analysis Using Parsimony*, Sinauer Associates, Sunderland, MA, 1993.
[21] Felsenstein J., "PHYLIP—phylogeny inference package (version 3.2)", *Cladistics* **5** (1989) 164–166.
[22] Goloboff P., "Analyzing large data sets in reasonable times: Solutions for composite optima", *Cladistics* **15** (1999) 415–428.
[23] Nixon K., "The parsimony ratchet, a new method for rapid parsimony analysis", *Cladistics* **15** (1999) 407–414.
[24] Sankoff D., Blanchette M., "Multiple genome rearrangement and breakpoint phylogeny", *J. Comput. Biol.* **5** (1998) 555–570.

[25] Cosner M., Jansen R., Moret B.M.E., Raubeson L., Wang L.S., Warnow T., Wyman S., "An empirical comparison of phylogenetic methods on chloroplast gene order data in Campanulaceae", in: Sankoff D., Nadeau J. (Eds.), *Comparative Genomics: Empirical and Analytical Approaches to Gene Order Dynamics, Map Alignment, and the Evolution of Gene Families*, Kluwer Academic, Dordrecht, Netherlands, 2000, pp. 99–121.

[26] Bader D., Moret B.M.E., "GRAPPA runs in record time", *HPCwire* **9** (47) (2000).

[27] Giribet G., "A review of TNT: Tree analysis using new technology", *Syst. Biol.* **54** (1) (2005) 176–178.

[28] Meier R., Ali F., "The newest kid on the parsimony block: TNT (tree analysis using new technology", *Syst. Entomol.* **30** (2005) 179–182.

[29] Goloboff P., "Analyzing large data sets in reasonable times: solution for composite optima", *Cladistics* **15** (1999) 415–428.

[30] Swofford D.L., *PAUP*: Phylogenetic Analysis Using Parsimony (and Other Methods), Version 4.0*, Sinauer Associates, Underland, MA, 1996.

[31] Stamatakis A., Ludwig T., Meier H., "RAxML-III: A fast program for maximum likelihood-based inference of large phylogenetic trees", *Bioinformatics* **21** (4) (2005) 456–463.

[32] Huson D., Nettles S., Warnow T., "Disk-covering, a fast-converging method for phylogenetic tree reconstruction", *J. Comput. Biol.* **6** (1999) 369–386.

[33] Huson D., Vawter L., Warnow T., "Solving large scale phylogenetic problems using DCM2", in: *Proc. 7th Internat. Conf. on Intelligent Systems for Molecular Biology, ISMB'99*, AAAI Press, Menlo Park, CA, 1999, pp. 118–129.

[34] Roshan U., Moret B.M.E., Warnow T., Williams T.L., "Rec-I-DCM3: a fast algorithmic technique for reconstructing large phylogenetic trees", in: *Proc. of CSB04, Stanford, CA*, 2004.

[35] Roshan U., "Algorithmic techniques for improving the speed and accuracy of phylogenetic methods", PhD thesis, The University of Texas at Austin, 2004.

[36] Roshan U., Moret B.M.E., Williams T.L., Warnow T., "Performance of supertree methods on various dataset decompositions", in: Bininda-Emonds O.R.P. (Ed.), *Phylogenetic Supertrees: Combining Information to Reveal the Tree of Life*, in: Dress A. (Ed.), *Computational Biology*, vol. 3, Kluwer Academic, Dordrecht/Norwell, MA, 2004, pp. 301–328.

[37] Nakhleh L., Roshan U., St. John K., Sun J., Warnow T., "Designing fast converging phylogenetic methods", in: *Proc. 9th Internat. Conf. on Intelligent Systems for Molecular Biology, ISMB'01*, in: *Bioinformatics*, vol. 17, Oxford Univ. Press, Oxford, UK, 2001, pp. S190–S198.

[38] Nakhleh L., Moret B.M.E., Roshan U., John K.S., Warnow T., "The accuracy of fast phylogenetic methods for large datasets", in: *Proc. 7th Pacific Symp. Biocomputing, PSB'2002*, World Scientific Publ., Singapore, 2002, pp. 211–222.

[39] Nakhleh L., Roshan U., St. John K., Sun J., Warnow T., "The performance of phylogenetic methods on trees of bounded diameter", in: *Proc. of WABI'01*, in: *Lecture Notes in Comput. Sci.*, vol. 2149, Springer-Verlag, Berlin, 2001, pp. 214–226.

[40] Moret B.M.E., Roshan U., Warnow T., "Sequence length requirements for phylogenetic methods", in: *Proc. of WABI'02*, 2002, pp. 343–356.

[41] Golumbic M., *Algorithmic Graph Theory and Perfect Graphs*, Academic Press, San Diego, CA, 1980.

[42] Hoos H.H., Stutzle T., *Stochastic Local Search: Foundations and Applications*, Morgan Kaufmann, San Francisco, CA, 2004.

[43] Du Z., Stamatakis A., Lin F., Roshan U., Nakhleh L., "Parallel divide-and-conquer phylogeny reconstruction by maximum likelihood", in: *2005 International Conference on High Performance Computing and Communications*, pp. 776–785.

[44] Stewart C., Hart D., Berry D., Olsen G., Wernert E., Fischer W., "Parallel implementation and performance of fastDNAml—a program for maximum likelihood phylogenetic inference", in: *Proceedings of the 14th IEEE/ACM Supercomputing Conference, SC2001*, 2001.

[45] Ludwig W., Strunk O., Westram R., Richter L., Meier H., Yadhukumar, Buchner A., Lai T., Steppi S., Jobb G., Fvrster W., Brettske I., Gerber S., Ginhart A.W., Gross O., Grumann S., Hermann S., Jost R., Kvnig A., Liss T., Lubmann R., May M., Nonhoff B., Reichel B., Strehlow R., Stamatakis A., Stuckman N., Vilbig A., Lenke M., Ludwig T., Bode A., Schleifer K.H., "ARB: a software environment for sequence data", *Nucl. Acids Res.* **32** (4) (2004) 1363–1371.

[46] Vinh L., Haeseler A., "IQPNNI: Moving fast through tree space and stopping in time", *Mol. Biol. Evol.* **21** (2004) 1565–1571.

[47] Maidak B.L., Cole J.R., Lilburn T.G., Parker C.T. Jr, Saxman P.R., Farris R.J., Garrity G.M., Olsen G.J., Schmidt T.M., Tiedje J.M., "The RDP-II (Ribosomal Database Project)", *Nucl. Acids Res.* **29** (1) (2001) 173–174.

[48] Lipscomb D., Farris J., Kallersjo M., Tehler A., "Support, ribosomal sequences and the phylogeny of the eukaryotes", *Cladistics* **14** (1998) 303–338.

[49] Rice K., Donoghue M., Olmstead R., "Analyzing large datasets: *rbcL* 500 revisited", *Syst. Biol.* **46** (3) (1997) 554–563.

[50] Soltis D.E., Soltis P.S., Chase M.W., Mort M.E., Albach D.C., Zanis M., Savolainen V., Hahn W.H., Hoot S.B., Fay M.F., Axtell M., Swensen S.M., Prince L.M., Kress W.J., Nixon K.C., Farris J.S., "Angiosperm phylogeny inferred from 18s rDNA, *rbcL*, and *atpB* sequences", *Botanical J. Linnean Soc.* **133** (2000) 381–461.

[51] Johnson K.P., "Taxon sampling and the phylogenetic position of Passeriformes: Evidence from 916 avian cytochrome b sequences", *Syst. Biol.* **50** (1) (2001) 128–136.

[52] Felsenstein J., "PHYLIP (phylogeny inference package) version 3.6". Distributed by the author, Department of Genome Sciences, University of Washington, Seattle, 2004.

[53] Swofford D.L., Olsen G.J., "Phylogeny reconstruction", in: Hillis D., Moritz C., Marble B.K. (Eds.), *Molecular Systematics*, second ed., Sinauer Associates, Sunderland, MA, 1996, pp. 407–514.

[54] Felsenstein J., "Evolutionary trees from DNA sequences: A maximum likelihood approach", *J. Mol. Evol.* **17** (1981) 368–376.

[55] Ley R., Backhed F., Turnbaugh P., Lozupone C., Knight R., Gordon J., "Obesity alters gut microbial ecology", *Proc. Natl. Acad. Sci. USA* **102** (31) (2005) 11070–11075.

[56] Chor B., Tuller T., "Maximum likelihood of evolutionary trees is hard", in: *Proc. of RECOMB05*, 2005.

[57] Stamatakis A., Ludwig T., Meier H., "RAxML-III: A fast program for maximum likelihood-based inference of large phylogenetic trees", *Bioinformatics* **21** (4) (2005) 456–463.

[58] Guindon S., Gascuel O., "A simple, fast, and accurate algorithm to estimate large phylogenies by maximum likelihood", *Syst. Biol.* **52** (5) (2003) 696–704.

[59] Brauer M., Holder M., Dries L., Zwickl D., Lewis P., Hillis D., "Genetic algorithms and parallel processing in maximum-likelihood phylogeny inference", *Mol. Biol. Evol.* **19** (2002) 1717–1726.

[60] Lemmon A., Milinkovitch M., "The metapopulation genetic algorithm: An efficient solution for the problem of large phylogeny estimation", *Proc. Natl. Acad. Sci.* **99** (2001) 10516–10521.

[61] Jobb G., Haeseler A., Strimmer K., "TREEFINDER: A powerful graphical analysis environment for molecular phylogenetics", *BMC Evol. Biol.* **4** (2004).

[62] Kosakovsky-Pond S., Muse S., "Column sorting: Rapid calculation of the phylogenetic likelihood function", *Syst. Biol.* **53** (5) (2004) 685–692.

[63] Stamatakis A., Ludwig T., Meier H., Wolf M. "Accelerating parallel maximum likelihood-based phylogenetic tree calculations using subtree equality vectors", in: *Proc. of 15th IEEE/ACM Supercomputing Conference, SC2002*, 2002.

[64] Swofford D., Olsen G., "Phylogeny reconstruction", in: Hillis D., Moritz C. (Eds.), *Molecular Systematics*, Sinauer Associates, Sunderland, MA, 1990, pp. 411–501.

[65] Lanave C., Preparata G., Saccone C., Serio G., "A new method for calculating evolutionary substitution rates", *J. Mol. Evol.* **20** (1984) 86–93.

[66] Rodriguez F., Oliver J., Marin A., Medina J., "The general stochastic model of nucleotide substitution", *J. Theor. Biol.* **142** (1990) 485–501.

[67] Jukes T., Cantor C. III, *Evolution of Protein Molecules*, Academic Press, New York, 1969, pp. 21–132.

[68] Hasegawa M., Kishino H., Yano T., "Dating of the human-ape splitting by a molecular clock of mitochondrial DNA", *J. Mol. Evol.* **22** (1985) 160–174.

[69] Posada D., Crandall K., "Modeltest: testing the model of DNA substitution", *Bioinformatics* **14** (9) (1998) 817–818.

[70] Olsen G., Matsuda H., Hagstrom R., Overbeek R., "fastDNAml: A tool for construction of phylogenetic trees of DNA sequences using maximum likelihood", *Comput. Appl. Biosci.* **20** (1994) 41–48.

[71] Yang Z., "Among-site rate variation and its impact on phylogenetic analyses", *Trends Ecol. Evol.* **11** (1996) 367–372.

[72] Olsen G., Pracht S., Overbeek R., "DNArates distribution", http://geta.life.uiuc.edu/~gary/programs/DNArates.html, unpublished, 1998.

[73] Meyer S., v. Haeseler A., "Identifying site-specific substitution rates", *Mol. Biol. Evol.* **20** (2003) 182–189.

[74] Yang Z., "Maximum likelihood phylogenetic estimation from DNA sequences with variable rates over sites", *J. Mol. Evol.* **39** (1994) 306–314.

[75] Stamatakis A., "Phylogenetic models of rate heterogeneity: A high performance computing perspective", in: *Proc. of IPDPS2006, Rhodos, Greece*, 2006.

[76] Zwickl D., "Genetic algorithm approaches for the phylogenetic analysis of large biological sequence datasets under the maximum likelihood criterion", PhD thesis, University of Texas at Austin, 2006.
[77] Hordijk W., Gascuel O., "Improving the efficiency of SPR moves in phylogenetic tree search methods based on maximum likelihood", *Bioinformatics* (2005).
[78] Strimmer K., Haeseler A., "Quartet puzzling: A maximum-likelihood method for reconstructing tree topologies", *Mol. Biol. Evol.* **13** (1996) 964–969.
[79] Stamatakis A. "An efficient program for phylogenetic inference using simulated annealing", in: *Proc. of IPDPS2005, Denver, CO*, 2005.
[80] Salter L., Pearl D., "A stochastic search strategy for estimation of maximum likelihood phylogenetic trees", *Syst. Biol.* **50** (1) (2001) 7–17.
[81] Barker D., "LVB: Parsimony and simulated annealing in the search for phylogenetic trees", *Bioinformatics* **20** (2004) 274–275.
[82] Stewart C., Hart D., Berry D., Olsen G., Wernert E., Fischer W., "Parallel implementation and performance of fastDNAml—a program for maximum likelihood phylogenetic inference", in: *Proc. of SC2001*, 2001.
[83] Hart D., Grover D., Liggett M., Repasky R., Shields C., Simms S., Sweeny A., Wang P., "Distributed parallel computing using Windows desktop system", in: *Proc. of CLADE*, 2003.
[84] Keane T., Naughton T., Travers S., McInerney J., McCormack G., "DPRml: Distributed phylogeny reconstruction by maximum likelihood", *Bioinformatics* **21** (7) (2005) 969–974.
[85] Wolf M., Easteal S., Kahn M., McKay B., Jermiin L., "TrExML: A maximum likelihood program for extensive tree-space exploration", *Bioinformatics* **16** (4) (2000) 383–394.
[86] Zhou B., Till M., Zomaya A., Jermiin L., "Parallel implementation of maximum likelihood methods for phylogenetic analysis", in: *Proc. of IPDPS2004*, 2004.
[87] Schmidt H., Strimmer K., Vingron M., Haeseler A., "Tree-puzzle: maximum likelihood phylogenetic analysis using quartets and parallel computing", *Bioinformatics* **18** (2002) 502–504.
[88] Minh B., Vinh L., Haeseler A., Schmidt H., "pIQPNNI—parallel reconstruction of large maximum likelihood phylogenies", *Bioinformatics* (2005).
[89] Du Z., Stamatakis A., Lin F., Roshan U., Nakhleh L., "Parallel divide-and-conquer phylogeny reconstruction by maximum likelihood", in: *Proc. of HPCC-05*, 2005, pp. 776–785.
[90] Stamatakis A., Lindermeier M., Ott M., Ludwig T., Meier H., "DRAxML@home: A distributed program for computation of large phylogenetic trees", *Future Generation Comput. Syst.* **51** (5) (2005) 725–730.
[91] Stamatakis A., Ludwig T., Meier H., "Parallel inference of a 10.000-taxon phylogeny with maximum likelihood", in: *Proc. of Euro-Par2004*, 2004, pp. 997–1004.
[92] Stamatakis A., Ott M., Ludwig T., "RAxML-OMP: An efficient program for phylogenetic inference on SMPs", in: *Proc. of PaCT05*, 2005, pp. 288–302.
[93] Huelsenbeck J., Ronquist F., "MrBayes: Bayesian inference of phylogenetic trees", *Bioinformatics* **17** (2001) 754–755.

[94] Press W., Teukolsky S., Vetterling W., Flannery B., *Numerical Recipes in C: The Art of Scientific Computing*, Cambridge Univ. Press, New York, 1992.
[95] Yang Z., "Maximum likelihood estimation on large phylogenies and analysis of adaptive evolution in human influenza virus A", *J. Mol. Evol.* **51** (2000) 423–432.
[96] Charalambous M., Trancoso P., Stamatakis A., "Initial experiences porting a bioinformatics application to a graphics processor", in: *Proceedings of the 10th Panhellenic Conference on Informatics, PCI 2005*, 2005, pp. 415–425.
[97] Minh B., Schmidt H., Haeseler A., "Large maximum likelihood trees", Technical report, John von Neumann Institute for Computing, Jülich, Germany, 2006.
[98] Buck I., Foley T., Horn D., Sugerman J., Hanrahan P., Houston M., Fatahalian K., "BrookGPU website", http://graphics.stanford.edu/projects/brookgpu/index.html, 2005.

# Local Structure Comparison of Proteins

JUN HUAN, JAN PRINS, AND WEI WANG

*Department of Computer Science*
*University of North Carolina at Chapel Hill*
*USA*
*huan@cs.unc.edu*
*prins@cs.unc.edu*
*weiwang@cs.unc.edu*

**Abstract**

Protein local structure comparison aims to recognize structural similarities between parts of proteins. It is an active topic in bioinformatics research, integrating computer science concepts in computational geometry and graph theory with empirical observations and physical principles from biochemistry. It has important biological applications, including protein function prediction. In this chapter, we provide an introduction to the protein local structure comparison problem including challenges and applications. Current approaches to the problem are reviewed. Particular consideration is given to the discovery of local structure common to a group of related proteins. We present a new algorithm for this problem that uses a graph-based representation of protein structure and finds recurring subgraphs among a group of protein graphs.





ADVANCES IN COMPUTERS, VOL. 68
ISSN: 0065-2458/DOI: 10.1016/S0065-2458(06)68005-4

## 1. Introduction

A protein is a chain of amino-acid molecules. In conditions found within a living organism, the chain of amino acids folds into a relatively stable three-dimensional arrangement known as the *native structure*. The native structure of a protein is a key determinant of its function [21,62,68,76]. Exactly how protein function is determined by protein structure is the central question in structural biology, and computational methods to compare the structures of proteins are a vital part of research in this area.

Starting from the 3D coordinates of the atoms in a protein (as obtained by a number of experimental techniques described later), *global structure comparison* can determine the similarity of two complete protein structures. Global structure comparison is widely used to classify proteins into groups according to their global similarity [35].

However, a protein's global structure does not always determine its function. There are well known examples of proteins with similar global structure but different functions. Conversely, there are also examples of proteins with similar function but quite different global structure. For this reason there has been increased interest in *local structure comparison* to identify structural similarity between parts of proteins [23].

This chapter provides an introduction to the protein structure comparison problem, focusing on recent research on local structure comparison. Work in this area combines computational geometry and graph theory from computer science with empirical observations and physical principles from biochemistry. The protein structure comparison problem has important applications in classification and function prediction of proteins, and is also of use in protein folding research and rational drug design [49].

The chapter is organized as follows. In the remainder of this section we describe the factors driving the need for protein structure comparison and present the structure comparison problem, and our area of focus. Section 2 outlines the necessary biological background, including a high-level introduction to protein sequence, structure, and function. Readers with limited knowledge of proteins and protein structure may wish to read this section before proceeding further. In Section 3 we present a taxonomy of current algorithms for the problem of protein local structure comparison. In Section 4, we give an introduction to graph representations of protein structure, and describe how discovering common local structure may be viewed as a data mining problem to identify frequent subgraphs among a collection of graphs. In Section 5, we introduce an efficient subgraph mining algorithm. Results obtained using graph-based local structure comparison on various key problems in protein structure are presented in Section 6. Finally we conclude in Section 7 with some thoughts on future directions for work in this area. This chapter also includes an extensive bibliography on protein structure comparison.

## 1.1 Motivation

This section describes the factors that underscore the need for automated protein structure comparison methods.

### *1.1.1 Rapidly Growing Catalogs of Protein Structure Data*

Recognizing the importance of structural information, the Protein Structure Initiative (PSI, http://www.nigms.nih.gov/psi/) and other recent efforts have targeted the accurate determination of all protein structures specified by genes found in sequenced genomes [13,94]. The result has been a rapid increase in the number of known 3D protein structures. The Protein Data Bank (PDB) [6], a public on-line protein structure repository, contained more than 30,000 entries at the end of year 2005. The number of structures is growing exponentially; more than 5000 structures were deposited to the PDB in 2005, about the same as the total number of protein structures added in the first four decades of protein structure determination [52].

Along with individual protein structures, the structure of certain complexes of interacting proteins are known as well. While the structures of relatively few complexes have been completely determined, there is rapidly growing information about which proteins interact. Among the proteins in yeast alone, over 14,000 binary interactions have been discovered [83]. The IntAct database records 50,559 binary interactions involving 30,497 proteins [32] from many species. Experts believe that many more interactions remain to be identified. For example, among the proteins in yeast it is estimated that there are about 30,000 binary interactions [100].

Additional types of data whose relation to protein structure is of interest are being accumulated as well, such as the cellular localization of proteins, the involvement of proteins in signaling, regulatory, and metabolic pathways, and post-translation structural changes in proteins [1,73]. The rapidly growing body of data call for automatic computational tools rather than manual processing.

### *1.1.2 Structure Comparison Aids Experiment Design*

Protein structure comparison is part of a bioinformatics research paradigm that performs comparative analysis of biological data [84]. The overarching goal is to aid rational experiment design and thus to expedite biological discovery. Specifically, through comparison, the paradigm endeavors to transfer experimentally obtained biological knowledge from known proteins to unknown ones, or to discover common structure among a group of related proteins. Below we review some of the applications of structure comparison including structure classification, functional site identification, and structure-based functional annotation. A comprehensive review can be found in [49].

*1.1.2.1 Structure Classification.* Classification of protein structures is vital to providing easy access to the large body of protein structures, for studying the evolution of protein structures, and for facilitating structure prediction. For example, through global structure classification, domain experts have identified many sequences that have low pairwise sequence identity yet have adopted very similar 3D structures. Such information helps significantly in structure prediction [51].

Traditionally, protein structure classification is a time consuming manual task, for example as used to construct the Structure Classification of Protein (SCOP) database [62]. SCOP is maintained using visual examination of protein structures by domain experts. With the development of automated global structure comparison methods such as CATH [68] and DALI [35], structure classification has become more automated.

In DALI and CATH, the units of classification are protein domains. Domains are organized hierarchically based on their similarity at the sequence, structure, and function level. Classification systems such as DALI and CATH utilize three common steps to derive a hierarchical grouping of protein structures. The first step is to select from all known structures a subset of "representative" structures among which (pairwise) sequence similarity is low. The second step is to compare the set of structures to compute an all-by-all similarity matrix. Based on this matrix, the third step is to perform a hierarchical clustering to group similar structures together. How to compute the similarity between a pair of structures and how to perform hierarchical clustering are the two key components in protein classification. For example, in DALI, proteins are classified at 4 levels according to *class*, *fold*, *functional families*, and *sequence family* and in CATH, proteins are classified into 5 levels according to *class*, *architecture*, *topology*, *homology superfamilies*, and *sequence families*. Though different methods may lead to different classifications, careful comparison of classification systems has revealed that existing systems (DALI, CATH, and SCOP) overlap significantly [21].

#### *1.1.2.2 Functional Site Identification.*

A *functional site* is a group of amino acids in a protein that participate in the function of the protein (e.g. catalyzing chemical reactions or binding to other proteins). Identifying functional sites is critical in studying the mechanism of protein function, predicting protein-protein interaction, and recognizing evolutionary connections between proteins when there is no clear clue from sequence or global structure alignment [3,19,60,99]. See [95] for a recent review of known functional sites in protein structures.

Traditionally, functional sites are derived through expensive experimental techniques such as site-directed mutagenesis. This technique creates a modified protein in which one or more amino acids are replaced in specific locations to study the effect on protein function. However, site-directed mutagenesis studies are both labor intensive and time consuming, as there are many potential functional sites. In search of an alternative approach, more than a dozen methods based on the analysis of protein structure have been developed [95]. All are based on the idea that functional sites in proteins with similar function may be composed of a group of specific amino acids in approximately the same geometric arrangement. The methods differ from each other in algorithmic details as described in Section 3. The essence of the approach is to identify local structure that recurs significantly among proteins with similar function.

#### *1.1.2.3 Structure-Based Functional Annotation.*

There is no question that knowing the function of a protein is of paramount importance in biological research. As expressed by George and his coauthors [26], correct function prediction can significantly simplify and decrease the time needed for experimental validation. However incorrect assignments may mislead experimental design and waste resources.

Protein function prediction has been investigated by recognizing the similarity of a protein with unknown function to one that has a known function where similarity can be determined at the sequence level [105], the expression level [18], and at the level of the gene's chromosome location [70].

In *structure based function annotation*, investigators focus on assigning function to protein structures by recognizing structural similarity. Compared to sequence-based function assignment, structure-based methods may have better annotation because of the additional information offered by the structure. Below, we discuss a recent study performed by Torrance and his coauthors [95] as an example of using local structure comparison for function annotation.

Torrance et al. first constructed a database of functional sites in enzymes [95]. Given an enzyme family, the functional sites for each protein in the family were either manually extracted from the literature or from the PSI-Blast alignment [95]. With the database of functional sites, Torrance et al. then used the JESS method [5] to search for occurrences of functional sites in the unknown structure. The most likely function was determined from the types of functional sites identified in the unknown structure. Torrance's method achieves high annotation accuracy as evaluated in several functional families.

In summary, the potential to decrease the time and cost of experimental techniques, the rapidly growing body of protein structure and structure related data, and the large number of applications necessitate the development of automated comparison tools for protein structure analysis. Next, we discuss the challenges associated with structure comparison.

## 1.2 Challenges

We decompose the challenges associated with structure comparison into three categories: (1) the nature of protein structure data and structure representation methods, (2) the tasks in structure comparison, and (3) the computational components of structure comparison methods.

### *1.2.1 The Nature of Protein Structure*

In order to compare protein structures automatically, it is necessary to describe protein structure in a rigorous mathematical framework. To that end, we adopt the three-level view of protein structures used by Eidhammer and his coauthors in [21], which is a popular view in designing structure comparison algorithms. Another commonly used biological description of protein structure is introduced in Section 2.

Following Eidhammer's view, a protein is described as a set of elements. Common choices for the elements are either atoms or amino acids (or more precisely *amino acid residues*). Other choices are possible, see Section 4.2. Once the elements are fixed, the protein *geometry*, protein *topology*, and element *attributes* are defined. We illustrate definitions for these using amino acid residues as the protein elements.

- *Geometry* is given by the 3D coordinates of the amino acid residues, for example as represented by the coordinates of the $C_\alpha$ atom, or by the mean coordinates of all atoms that comprise the amino acid residue.
- *Attributes* are the physico-chemical attributes or the environmental attributes of the amino acid residues. For example, the hydrophobicity is a physico-chemical attribute of the residue. The solvent accessible surface area of an amino acid residue is an environmental attribute of the residue.
- *Topology* describes physico-chemical interactions between pairs of amino acid residues. A typical example is to identify pairs of amino acid residues that may interact through the van der Waals potential.

#### *1.2.1.1 Structure Representations.*

The choice of mathematical framework for representation of a protein structure varies considerably. We review three common choices below.

- *Point sets.* A protein is represented as a set of points, each point represents the 3D location of an element in the protein structure. In addition, each point may be labeled with the attributes of the represented element, such as the charge, the amino acid identity, the solvent accessible area, etc.
- *Point lists.* A protein is represented by an ordering of elements in a point set that follows their position in the primary sequence.
- *Graphs.* A protein is represented as a labeled graph. A node in the graph represents an element in the protein structure, usually labeled by the attributes of the element. An edge connecting a pair of nodes represents the physico-chemical interactions between the pair of elements and may be labeled with attributes of the interaction.

All the methods are *element-based* methods since they describe a protein structure using elements in the structure. Though not commonly used, there are methods that describe a protein structure without breaking the structure into a set of elements. See [21] for further details.

### *1.2.2 Tasks in Structure Comparison*

To outline the challenges associated with structure comparison, it is convenient to group current structure comparison methods into common tasks, according to the final goal of the comparison. The categorization we use is not unique, further division is possible, and we expect that new tasks will emerge to augment the list in the future. However, our current categorization summarizes well all the methods that we will describe in this chapter and is useful as a starting point for the introduction of structure comparison algorithms.

- *Global structure comparison*
  - Computing the alignment of a group of two or more structures.
  - Computing the overall similarity between two structures.
  - Searching a set of proteins to find those that are similar to a given protein structure.
- *Local structure comparison*
  - Identifying common substructures among a group of proteins.
  - Searching a set of proteins for occurrences of a particular substructure.
  - Searching a database of substructures for the substructures that appear in a particular protein structure.

The tasks within a specific type of structure comparison (global or local) are closely related. For example, the computation of the pair-wise global structure similarity is usually done after aligning the two structures. Tasks in different types of structure comparison can also be related. For example, in computing the global alignment of two structures, one way is to first compute the shared substructures as "seeds" and then to select and connect such set of seeds to produce the global alignment [35].

### 1.2.3 Components of Structure Comparison Tasks

The tasks listed in the previous section can be decomposed into a number of components. These include a basic notion of similarity between structures, or between a structure pattern and a structure. A scoring function measures the quality of the similarity, and a search procedure uses the scoring function to search a space of potential solutions. Finally the results of a task must be displayed in a meaningful fashion. In this section, we elaborate each of these concepts.

#### 1.2.3.1 Defining Pattern or Structure Similarity.

A *structure pattern* is a geometric arrangement of protein elements, for example four specific amino acids placed at the vertices of a tetrahedron of specified dimensions. We list three considerations in defining similarity between structures or between a pattern and a structure.

- *Level of Structure Representation*
  We may choose atoms, amino acid residues, or secondary structure elements (SSE), as the elements for protein structure comparison. The choice of elements are made according to the specific goal of the comparison and the preference of the investigators. The general concern in choosing a detailed representation where elements are atoms or amino acid residues is that the coordinates of such

elements in protein structures are subject to experimental noise and hence any comparison algorithms should have a certain level of robustness to perturbation of the geometry of the structure. In addition, a detailed representation often leads to a more extensive computation than a coarse representation such as SSE. On the other hand, by choosing SSEs as structure elements, we may miss valuable information about a protein structure. Early structure comparison used SSE as elements extensively, mainly for the purpose of efficient computation. Recent research tends to use amino acid residues or atoms because of the detailed representation.

- *Sequence Order in Structure Comparison*
  In sequence-order dependent structure comparison, the primary sequence order of the structure elements must be preserved in a pattern or an alignment. Otherwise, we carry out a sequence-independent structure comparison.
- *Pair-Wise or Multi-Way Structure Comparison*
  In pair-wise comparison, we find the similarity of a pair of structures, or find a pattern in common to two structures. A generalization of pair-wise structure comparison is a multi-way comparison that involves more than two structures.

As a few examples, most structure alignment algorithms, such as DALI [35], compute the pairwise alignment of two structures that preserves the sequence order of structure elements and hence are sequence dependent, pair-wise global structure comparison methods. In contrast to structure alignment, most of the structure pattern discovery methods, such as those based on graphs [39], search for common local structure patterns without enforcing the sequence order and hence are sequence independent, multi-way (or pair-wise) local structure comparison methods.

*1.2.3.2 Scoring Functions.* A scoring function quantifies the fitness of a structure pattern or an alignment to the observed data. Choosing the right scoring function involves a certain level of art. Ideally, the right scoring function should correlate precisely with the desired consequence of the analysis, e.g. the evolutionary connection of a pair of structures in an global alignment. Practically, such ideal scoring functions are very difficult to obtain due to the limited knowledge we have. Therefore, investigators often resort to "generic" scoring functions. For example, the root-mean-squared-deviation (RMSD) [21] is usually used to compute the closeness of two structures with a known 1–1 correspondence of structure elements in the two protein structures. In computing RMSD, we superimpose one structure onto the other such that the sum of the squared distances between corresponding elements is minimized. A closed-form definition of this scoring function can be found in [50, 36].

*1.2.3.3 Search Procedures.* In protein structure comparison with a given scoring function, a search procedure is often utilized to identify the best solution. One of the most widely used search procedures is the subgraph matching algorithm that determines whether a pattern (specified by one graph) matches a structure (specified by another graph) (see Section 5 for further details). Computational efficiency is the major concern for designing a search procedure.

*1.2.3.4 Results Presentation.* Usually the final step of structure comparison is to present the results to end-users. One commonly used presentation method is visualization. An equally popular one is to form a hypothesis for a biological experiment. For example, recognizing the occurrence of a functional sites in a protein offers information about the possible function of the protein. Usually, both presentation methods are used after structure comparison.

## 1.3 Our Focus in Structure Comparison

We focus on protein local structure comparison and present an overview of the frontier of the research, balancing algorithmic developments and biological applications. We single out local structure comparison because it has become popular in recent structure comparison research. The transition from global structure comparison to local structure comparison is well supported by a wide range of experimental evidence.

- *Protein function is usually carried out by a small region of the protein.* It is well known that in a protein there are a few key residues, that if mutated, interfere with the structural stability or the function of the protein. Those important residues usually are in spatial contact in the 3D protein structure and hence form a "cluster" in the protein structure. On the other hand, much of the remaining protein structure, especially surface area, can tolerate mutations [15,81]. For example, in a model protein T4 Lysozyme, it was reported that single amino acid substitutions occurring in a large fraction of a protein structure (80% of studied amino acids) tend not to interrupt the function and the folding of the protein [58].

  Biology has accumulated a long list of sites that have functional or structural significance. Such sites can be divided into the following three categories:
  - catalytic sites of enzymes;
  - the binding sites of ligands;
  - the folding nuclei of proteins.

  Local structure similarity among proteins can implicate structurally conserved amino acid residues that may carry functional or structural significance [14,103, 20,53].

- *Similar global structure may not correlate with similar function.* For example, it is well known that the TIM barrels are a large group of proteins with a remarkably similar fold, yet widely varying catalytic function [63]. A striking result was reported in [65] showing that even combined with sequence conservation, global structure conservation may still not be sufficient to produce functional conservation. In this study, Neidhart et al. first demonstrated an example where two enzymes (mandelate racemase and muconate lactonizing enzyme) catalyze different reactions, yet the structure and sequence identities are sufficiently high that they are very likely to have evolved from a common ancestor. Similar cases have been reviewed in [28].

  It has also been noticed that similar function does not require similar structure. For example, the most versatile enzymes, hydro-lyases and the O-glycosyl glucosidases, are associated with 7 folds [31]. In a systematic study using the structure database SCOP and the functional database Enzyme Commission (EC), George et al. estimated 69% of protein function (at EC sub-subclass level) is indeed carried by proteins in multiple protein superfamilies [27].
- *Local similarity detection can offer evidence for protein evolution.* There are two putative mechanisms to explain similarity between protein structures. One is *convergent evolution*, a process whereby proteins adopt similar structure and function through different evolutionary paths [77]. Convergent evolution has been studied in the serine protease family, porphyrin binding proteins [77], and the ATP/GTP binding proteins [99]. Another one is *divergent evolution*, a process where proteins from the same origin become so diverse that their structure and sequence homology falls below detectable level [57]. Though the exact evolutionary mechanism is still debated, studying local structure similarity can help in understanding how protein structure and function evolve.

Various other interesting topics such as structure database search and structure-based functional inference are beyond the scope of this chapter and have been omitted. Topics in local structure comparison that are not covered in this chapter may be found in related books such as [21].

## 2. Background

Genome sequencing projects are working to determine the complete genome sequence for several organisms. The sequencing projects have produced significant impact on bioinformatics research by stimulating the development of sequence analysis tools such as methods to identify genes in a genome sequence, methods to predict alternative splicing sites for genes, methods that compute the sequence homology among genes, and methods that study the evolutionary relation of genes, to name a few.

Proteins are the products of genes and the building blocks for biological function. Below, we review some basic background on proteins, protein structure, and protein function. See [10] for topics that are not covered here.

## 2.1 Protein Structure

### 2.1.1 *Proteins are Chains of Amino Acids*

Proteins are chains of $\alpha$-amino acid molecules. An *$\alpha$-amino acid* (or simply an amino acid) is a molecule with three chemical groups and a hydrogen atom covalently bonded to the same carbon atom, the $C_\alpha$ atom. These groups are: a carboxyl group (–COOH), an amino group (–NH2), and a side chain with variable size (symbolized as *R*) [10]. The first carbon atom in a side chain (one that is connected to the $C_\alpha$ atom) is the $C_\beta$ atom and the second one is the $C_\gamma$ atom and so forth. Figure 1 illustrates an example of amino acids.

Different amino acids have different side chains. There are a total of 20 amino acids found in naturally occurring proteins. At physiological temperatures in a solvent environment, proteins adopt stable three-dimensional (3D) organizations of amino acid residues that are critical to their function.

### 2.1.2 *Protein Structure is Described in Four Levels*

The levels are as follows:

- *Primary structure* describes the amino acid sequence of a protein.

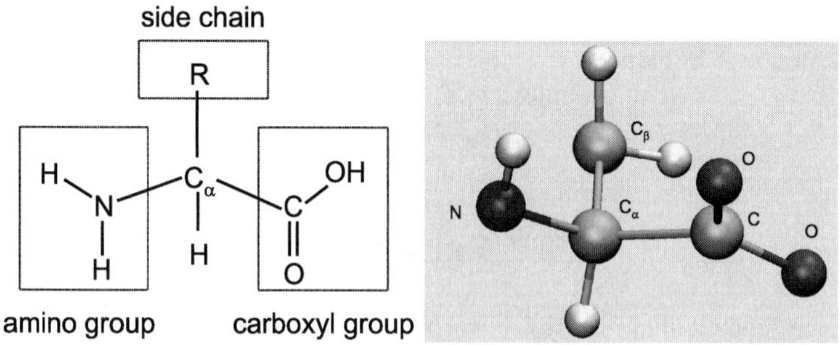


FIG. 1. Left: A schematic illustration of an amino acid. Right: The 3D structure of an amino acid (Alanine) whose side chain contains a single carbon atom. The atom types are shown; unlabeled atoms are hydrogens. The schematic diagram is adopted from [10] and the 3D structure is drawn with the VMD software.

- *Secondary structure* describes the pattern of hydrogen bonding between amino acids along the primary sequence. There are three common types of secondary structures: α-helix, β-sheet, and turn.
- *Tertiary (3D) structure* describes the protein in terms of the coordinates of all of its atoms.
- *Quaternary structure* applies only to proteins that have at least two amino acid chains. Each chain in a multi-chain protein is a *subunit* of the protein and the spatial organization of the subunits of a protein is the quaternary structure of the protein. A single-subunit protein does not have a quaternary structure.

#### 2.1.2.1 Primary Structure.

In a protein, two amino acids are connected by a *peptide bond*, a covalent bond formed between the carboxyl group of one amino acid and the amino group of the other with elimination of a water molecule. After the condensation, an amino acid becomes an *amino acid residue* (or just a *residue*, for short). The $C_\alpha$ atom and the hydrogen atom, the carbonyl group (CO), and the NH group that are covalently linked to the $C_\alpha$ atom are the *main chain atoms*; the rest of the atoms in an amino acid are *side chain atoms*.

In Fig. 2, we show the primary sequence of a protein with three amino acid residues. At one end of the sequence (the left one), the residue contains the full amino group ($-NH_3$) and is the N terminal of the sequence. The residue at the opposite end contains the full carboxyl group (–COOH) and is the C terminal of the sequence. By convention a protein sequence is drawn left to right from its N terminal to its C terminal.

Various protein sequencing techniques can determine the primary sequence of a protein experimentally.

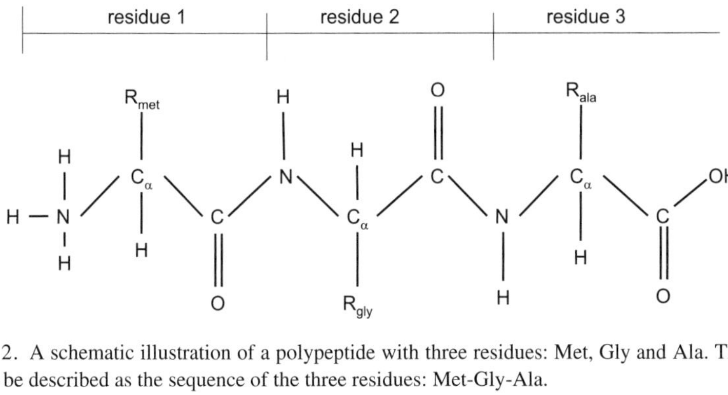


FIG. 2. A schematic illustration of a polypeptide with three residues: Met, Gly and Ala. The peptide can also be described as the sequence of the three residues: Met-Gly-Ala.

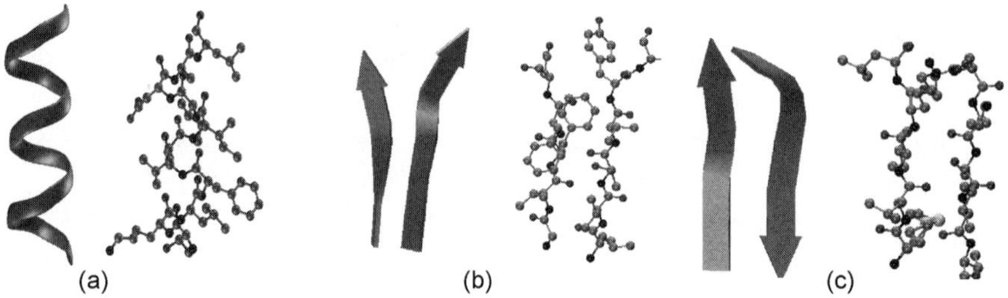


FIG. 3. A schematic illustration of the α-helix and the β-sheet secondary structures. (a) The ribbon representation of the α-helix secondary structure (on the left) and the ball-stick representation showing all atoms and their chemical bonds in the structure (on the right). We also show the same representations for the parallel β-sheet secondary structure (b) and the anti-parallel β-sheet secondary structure (c). The α-helix is taken from protein myoglobin 1MBA at positions 131 to 141 as in [22]. The parallel β-sheet secondary structure is taken from protein 2EBN at positions 126 to 130 and 167 to 172. The anti-parallel β-sheet secondary structure is taken from protein 1HJ9 at positions 86 to 90 and 104 to 108.

*2.1.2.2 Secondary Structure.* A segment of protein sequence may fold into a stable structure called secondary structure. Three types of secondary structure are common in proteins:

- α-helix;
- β-sheet;
- turn.

An α-helix is a stable structure where each residue forms a hydrogen bond with another one that is four residues apart in the primary sequence. We show an example of the α-helix secondary structure in Fig. 3.

A β-sheet is another type of stable structure formed by at least two β-strands that are connected together by hydrogen bonds between the two strands. A *parallel* β-sheet is a sheet where the two β-strands have the same direction while an *anti-parallel* β-sheet is one that does not. We show examples of β-sheets in Fig. 3.

A *turn* is a secondary structure that usually consists of 4–5 amino acids to connect α-helices or β-sheets.

Unlike the protein primary sequence, protein secondary structure is usually obtained after solving the 3D structure of the protein.

*2.1.2.3 Tertiary Structure and Quaternary Structure.* In conditions found within a living organism, a protein folds into its native structure. The tertiary structure refers to the positions of all atoms, generally in the native structure. The process of adopting a 3D structure is the *folding* of the protein. Protein 3D structure is critical for a protein to carry out its function.

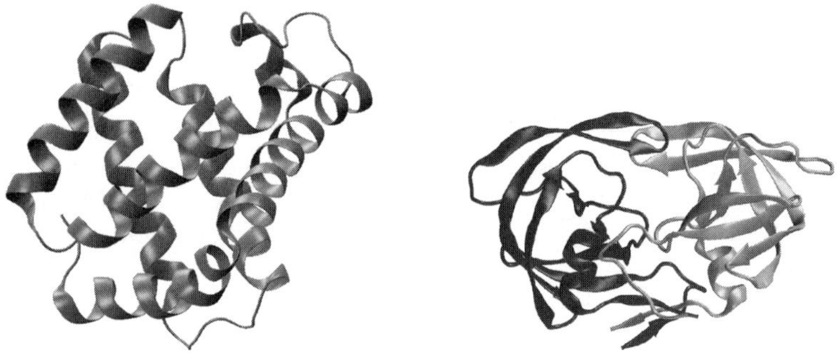

FIG. 4. Left: The schematic representation (cartoon) of the 3D structure of protein myoglobin. Right: The schematic representation (cartoon) of the 3D structure of protein HIV protease. HIV protease has two chains.

In Fig. 4, we show a schematic representation of a 3D protein structure (myoglobin). In the same figure, we also show the quaternary structure of a protein with two chains (HIV protease).

Two types of experimental techniques are used to determine the 3D structure of a protein. In X-ray crystallography, a protein is first crystallized and the structure of the protein is determined by X-ray diffraction. Nuclear Magnetic Resonance spectroscopy (NMR) determines the structure of a protein by measuring the distances among protons and specially labeled carbon and nitrogen atoms [72]. Once the interatom distances are determined, a group of 3D structures (an *ensemble*) is computed in order to best fit the distance constraints.

### 2.1.3 Protein Structures are Grouped Hierarchically

**2.1.3.1 Domains.** A unit of the tertiary structure of a protein is a *domain*, which is the whole amino acid chain or a (consecutive) segment of the chain that can fold into stable tertiary structure independent of the rest of the protein [10]. A domain is often a unit of function i.e. a domain usually carries out a specific function of a protein. Multi-domain proteins are believed to be the product of *gene fusion* i.e. a process where several genes, each which once coded for a separate protein, become a single gene during evolution [72].

**2.1.3.2 Structure Classification.** The *protein structure space* is the set of all possible protein structures. Protein structure space is often described by a hierarchical structure called *protein structure classification*, at the bottom of which are individual structures (domains). Structures are grouped hierarchically based on their secondary structure components and their closeness at the sequence, functional, and evolutionary level [72].

Here we describe a structure hierarchy, the SCOP database (Structure Classification of Proteins) [62]. SCOP is maintained manually by domain experts and considered one of the gold standards for protein structure classification. For other classification systems see [68].

In SCOP, the unit of the classification is the domain (e.g. multi-domain proteins are broken into individual domains that are grouped separately). At the top level (most abstract level), protein in SCOP are assigned to a "class" based on the secondary structure components. The four major classes in SCOP are:

- $\alpha$ domain class: ones that are composed almost entirely of $\alpha$-helices;
- $\beta$ domain class: ones that are composed almost entirely of $\beta$-sheets;
- $\alpha/\beta$ domain class: ones that are composed of alpha helices and parallel beta sheets;
- $\alpha + \beta$ domain class: ones that are composed of alpha helices and antiparallel beta sheets.

These four classes cover around 85% of folds in SCOP. Another three infrequently occurring classes in SCOP are: multi-domain class, membrane and cell surface domain class, and small protein domain class.

Proteins within each SCOP class are classified hierarchically at three additional levels: fold, superfamily, and family. In Fig. 5, we show a visualization developed by the Berkeley Structural Genomics Center, in which globally similar structures are grouped together and globally dissimilar structures are located far away from each other. This figure shows segregation between four elongated regions corresponding to the four SCOP protein classes: $\alpha$, $\beta$, $\alpha/\beta$, and $\alpha+\beta$. Further details about protein structure classification can be found in [62].

## 2.2 Protein Function

Proteins are the molecular machinery that perform the function of living organisms. Protein function can be described by the role(s) that the protein plays in an organism. Usually, protein function description is made at the molecular level, e.g. the role a protein plays in a chemical reaction. Protein function can also be described at a physiological level concerning the whole organism, e.g. the impact of a protein on the functioning of an organism. We describe protein function at 3 different levels according to [69]:

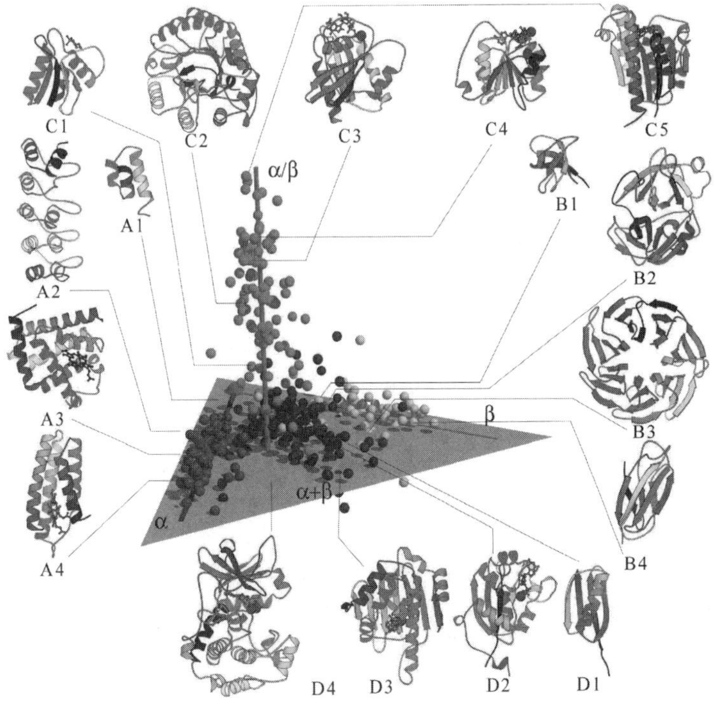


FIG. 5. The top level structural classification of proteins based on their secondary structure components. Source: http://www.nigms.nih.gov/psi/image_gallery/structures.html. Used with permission.

- *Molecular function*: A protein's molecular function is its catalytic activity, its binding activity, its conformational changes, or its activity as a building block in a cell [72].
- *Cellular function*: A protein's cellular function is the role that the protein performs as part of a biological pathway in a cell.
- *Phenotypic function*: A protein's phenotypic function determines the physiological and behavioral properties of an organism.

We need to keep in mind that protein function is context-sensitive with respect to many factors other than its sequence and structure. These factors include (but are not limited to) the cellular environment in which a protein is located, the post-translation modification(s) of the protein, and the presence or absence of certain ligand(s). Though often not mentioned explicitly, these factors are important for protein function.

In this chapter, we concentrate on the molecular function of a protein. We do so since (1) it is generally believed that native structure may most directly be related to the molecular function [26], (2) determining the molecular function is the first step in the determination of the cellular and phenotypic function of a protein.

## 3. A Taxonomy of Local Structure Comparison Algorithms

The goal of local structure comparison is to recognize structure patterns in proteins where the patterns may be known a priori or not. When patterns are known, the recognition problem is a *pattern matching* problem in which we determine whether a pattern appears in a protein. When patterns are unknown, the recognition problem is a *pattern discovery* problem in which we find structure patterns that appear in all or many of the protein structures in a group.

As discussed in Section 1, a structure pattern is a geometric arrangement of elements, usually at the amino acid residue level. Some other terminology also used for structure patterns includes *structure templates* [95], and *structure motifs* [21]. A typical pattern matching algorithm contains the following components:

- a definition of structure patterns;
- a scoring function that determines the fitness of a pattern to a structure;
- a search procedure that recognizes patterns in a protein or a group of proteins, based on pattern definition and the scoring function.

The scoring function is also called a *matching condition* [21]. An *instance* of a structure pattern $S$ in a protein $P$ is a group of amino acid residues in $P$ that *matches* with $S$ under a certain matching condition.

Before we proceed to details of individual algorithms, Fig. 6 presents a taxonomy of protein local structure comparison algorithms, together with sample algorithms in each category. Our categorization is not unique but it serves two purposes: (1) it offers an overview of the algorithms that are discussed in this chapter and (2) it simplifies the presentation since we find that algorithms in the same category often involve the same set of design issues.

At the top level of our taxonomy, we distinguish between pattern matching and pattern discovery algorithms. Our discussion of pattern discovery is further divided into two parts based on whether the primary sequence order of amino acid residues is significant in the pattern or not. The first group is termed *sequence-dependent* pattern discovery and the second is *sequence-independent* pattern discovery. For the more

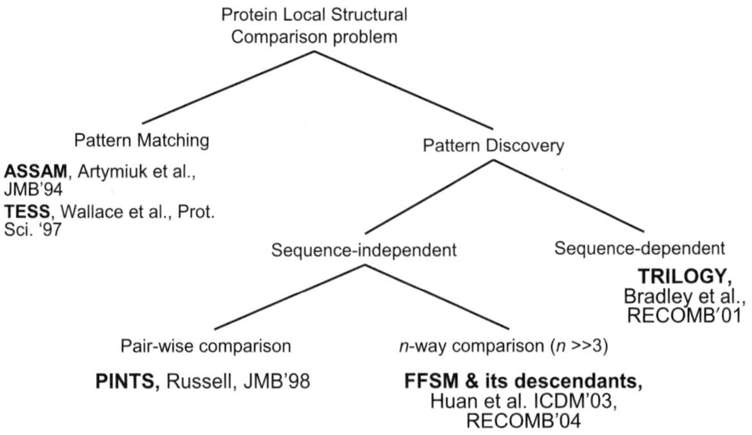


FIG. 6. A taxonomy of local structure comparison algorithms.

challenging sequence-independent pattern discovery, we subdivide the algorithms into two groups: one that detects patterns that are shared by two protein structures and one that detects patterns that occur frequently among an arbitrary group of protein structures. The following sections survey algorithms in each category of the taxonomy.

## 3.1 Pattern Matching

There are three types of subproblems in pattern matching [21]:

- *occurrence* pattern matching determines whether a pattern occurs in a protein structure,
- *complete* pattern matching finds all occurrences of a pattern in a protein structure,
- *probabilistic* pattern matching calculates the probability that a pattern appears in a protein structure.

The solution of the complete pattern matching problem can be used to answer the occurrence pattern matching problem, but sometimes the latter can be computed directly more efficiently. In the following discussion, we present two algorithms for the complete pattern matching problem: one based on subgraph isomorphism and the other one based on geometric hashing. For probabilistic pattern matching, see [2].

### 3.1.1 ASSAM

The algorithm ASSAM is one of the most successful pattern matching algorithms in local structure comparison of proteins [3]. ASSAM recognizes a predefined pattern in a protein structure by transforming both the pattern and the structure to graphs and using subgraph matching to determine a possible matching(s). Below, we discuss the details of the ASSAM in graph construction and subgraph matching.

#### 3.1.1.1 Pattern Definition.

ASSAM uses a graph to represent a structure pattern where

- A node in the ASSAM graph represents an amino acid residue and is labeled by the identity of the residue.
- Two nodes are connected by an edge labeled by the distance vector (to be defined) between the two residues.

In ASSAM, an amino acid residue is represented as a two-element tuple $(p_1, p_2)$ where $p_1$ and $p_2$ are two points in a 3D space. These two points are selected to specify the spatial location and the side chain orientation of the residue and are called the "pseudo atoms" in ASSAM.[1] One of the two pseudo atoms in a residue $R$ is designated as the "start" atom, denoted by $S(R)$, and the other is the "end" atom, denoted by $E(R)$.

The *distance vector* $V_{R,R'}$ between two amino acid residues $R$ and $R'$ is a sequence of four distances

$$V_{R,R'} = d\big(S(R), S(R')\big), d\big(S(R), E(R')\big), d\big(E(R), S(R')\big), d\big(E(R), E(R')\big)$$

where $d(x, y)$ is the Euclidian distance of two points $x$ and $y$. The distance vector is used as an edge label in the graph.

ASSAM represents structure patterns in the same way that it represents full protein structures.

#### 3.1.1.2 Graph Matching.

Distance vector $V_{R_1,R_2}$ matches distance vector $V_{R'_1,R'_2}$ if:

$$\begin{aligned}
&\big|d\big(S(R_1), S(R_2)\big) - d\big(S(R'_1), S(R'_2)\big)\big| \leqslant d_{ss},\\
&\big|d\big(S(R_1), E(R_2)\big) - d\big(S(R'_1), E(R'_2)\big)\big| \leqslant d_{se},\\
&\big|d\big(E(R_1), S(R_2)\big) - d\big(E(R'_1), S(R'_2)\big)\big| \leqslant d_{es},\\
&\big|d\big(E(R_1), E(R_2)\big) - d\big(E(R'_1), E(R'_2)\big)\big| \leqslant d_{ee}
\end{aligned}$$

[1] They are pseudo atoms since they may be located at positions that do not correspond to a real atom.

where $d_{ss}$, $d_{se}$, $d_{es}$, $d_{ee}$ are bounds on the allowed variation in distances. These inequalities help make the matching robust in the presence of experimental errors in the determination of element coordinates.

A structure pattern $U$ *matches* a protein structure $V$, if there exists a 1–1 mapping between vertices in $U$ and a subset of vertices in $V$ that preserves node labels and for which the edge labels in the pattern match the corresponding edge labels in $V$.

ASSAM adapts Ullman's backtracking algorithm for subgraph isomorphism [97] to solve the pattern matching problem. We discuss the details of Ullman's algorithm in Section 4.3.

### 3.1.2 TESS

In TESS both protein structures and structure patterns are represented as point sets, and the elements of the set are individual atoms. TESS determines whether a pattern matches a structure using geometric hashing [101]. Specifically, the matching is done in two steps. In the *preprocessing* step, TESS builds hash tables to encode the geometry of the protein structure and the structure pattern. In the *pattern matching* step, TESS compares the contents of the hash tables and decides whether the pattern structure matches the protein structure.

With minor modifications, TESS can be extended to compare a structure pattern with a group of structures. See [71] for other pattern matching algorithms that also use geometric hashing.

*3.1.2.1 Pattern Definition.* TESS represents a structure pattern as a set of atoms $P = \{a_1, \ldots, a_n\}$ where $n$ is the size of $P$. Each atom is represented by a two-element tuple $a_i = (p_i, id_i)$ where $p_i$ is a point in a 3D space and $id_i$ is the identity of the atom.

*3.1.2.2 Preprocessing in TESS.* To build a hash table encoding the geometry of a protein structure, TESS selects three atoms with their coordinates from each amino acid residue and builds a 3D Cartesian coordinate system for each selection. A 3D Cartesian coordinate system is also called a *reference frame* in TESS. For each reference frame, the associated amino acid residue is its *base* and the three selected atoms are the *reference atoms* of the frame. Predefined reference atoms exist for all 20 amino acid types [101].

Given three reference atoms $p_1$, $p_2$, $p_3$ where each atom is treated as a point, TESS builds a reference frame $Oxyz$ in the following way:

- the origin of the $Oxyz$ system is the midpoint of the vector $\overrightarrow{p_1 p_2}$,
- the vector $\overrightarrow{p_1 p_2}$ defines the positive direction of the $x$-axis,

- point $p_3$ lies in the $xy$ plane and has positive $y$ coordinate,
- the positive direction of $z$-axis follows the right-hand rule.

Given a reference frame for an amino acid, TESS recomputes the coordinates of all atoms in the protein relative to this reference frame. The transformed coordinates of an atom are discretized into an *index* that is mapped to a value using a hash table. The associated value of an index is a two-element tuple $(r, a)$ where $r$ is the identifier of the base of the reference frame and $a$ is the identifier of the corresponding atom.

TESS builds a reference frame for each amino acid residue in a protein structure and enters every atom in the protein structure into the hash table relative to this reference frame. For a protein with a total of $R$ residues and $N$ atoms, there are a total of $R \times N$ entries in the TESS hash table since each reference frame produces a total of $N$ entries and there are a total of $R$ frames.

A structure pattern in TESS is treated like a protein structure; TESS performs the same preprocessing step for a structure pattern as for a protein.

*3.1.2.3 Pattern Matching.* For a pair of reference frames, one from a protein structure and the other one from a structure pattern, TESS determines whether there is a *hit* between the protein structure and the structure pattern. A hit occurs when each atom in the structure pattern has at least one corresponding atom in the protein structure. TESS outputs all pairs of reference frames where a hit occurs.

TESS has been successfully applied to recognize several structure patterns, including the Ser-His-Asp triad, the active center of nitrogenase, and the active center of ribonucleases, in order to predict the function of several proteins [101].

## 3.2 Sequence-Dependent Pattern Discovery

Discovering common structure patterns from a group of proteins is more challenging than matching a known pattern with a structure. Here we introduce two algorithms: TRILOGY [9] and SPratt [48,47] that take advantage of sequence order (and separation) information of amino acid residues in a protein structure to speed up pattern discovery. Patterns identified by these methods are *sequence-dependent* structure patterns.[2]

### *3.2.1 TRILOGY*

TRILOGY identifies sequence-dependent structure patterns in a group of protein structures [9]. There are two phases in TRILOGY: initial pattern discovery and pat-

[2] Amino acid residues in sequence-dependent patterns are in sequence order but not necessarily consecutive in the sequence.

tern growth. Before we discuss the two phases in details, we present the pattern definition and matching condition used in TRILOGY.

#### 3.2.1.1 Pattern Definition.

In TRILOGY, a three-residue pattern (a triplet) $P$ is a sequence of amino acid residues and their primary sequence separations such that

$$P = R_1 d_1 R_2 d_2 R_3$$

where $R_i$ $(i \in [1, 3])$ is a list of three amino acid residues sorted according to primary sequence order in a protein and $d_i$ $(i \in [1, 2])$ is the number of residues located between $R_i$ and $R_{i+1}$ along the primary sequence (the *sequence separation*).

Each residue $R$ in TRILOGY is abstracted by a three-element tuple $(p, v, id)$ where $p$ is a point representing the $C_\alpha$ atom in $R$, $v$ is the vector of $C_\alpha C_\beta$ atoms, and $id$ is the identity of the residue.

#### 3.2.1.2 Pattern Matching.

A triplet $P = R_1 d_1 R_2 d_2 R_3$ matches a protein structure if there exists a triplet $P' = R'_1 d'_1 R'_2 d'_2 R'_3$ in the structure such that

- (1) the corresponding amino acid residues ($R_i$ and $R'_i$, $i \in [1, 3]$) have similar amino acid types,
- (2) the maximal difference between the corresponding sequence separations $|d_i - d'_i|$, $i \in [1, 2]$, is no more than a specified upper-bound (e.g. 5),
- (3) the geometry of two triplets matches. This suggests that:
  - the difference between the related $C_\alpha$–$C_\alpha$ distances is within 1.5 Å,
  - the angle difference between two pairs of matching $C_\alpha$–$C_\beta$ vectors is always within 60°.

If a protein satisfies condition (1) and (2) but not necessarily (3) it is a *sequence match* of the triplet $P$. If a protein satisfies condition (3) but not necessarily (1) or (2) it is a *geometric match* of the triplet $P$. By definition, a protein matches a triplet $P$ if there is a sequence match *and* a geometric match to $P$.

The pattern definition and matching condition for larger patterns with $d$ amino acids are defined similarly to the above, but use $2d - 1$ element tuples instead of triples.

#### 3.2.1.3 Triplet Discovery.

TRILOGY takes as inputs a group of protein structures and produces a sequence alignment of the structures using information provided in the HSSP database [78].

After sequence alignment, all possible triplets are discovered. For each triplet, TRILOGY collects two pieces of information: the total number of sequence matches and the number of structure matches, and assigns a score to the triplet according to a hypergeometric distribution. Only highly scored triplets are used to generate longer patterns.

#### 3.2.1.4 Pattern Growth.

If a highly scored triplet shares two residues with another triplet, the two patterns are "glued" together to generate a larger pattern with four amino acid residues in the format of $R_i d_i R_4$ where $\{R_i\}$, $i \in [1, 4]$, and $d_i$, $i \in [1, 3]$, are defined similarly to ones in triplets. Longer patterns in TRILOGY are generated similarly.

### 3.2.2 SPratt

Like TRILOGY, the SPratt algorithm also uses the primary sequence order information to detect common structure patterns in a group of protein structures [48,47]. Unlike TRILOGY, SPratt discards the requirement that the sequence separation between two residues should be conserved. In the following discussion, we present the details of the SPratt algorithm.

#### 3.2.2.1 Pattern Definition.

In SPratt, a pattern $P$ is a list of amino acid residues

$$P = p_1, \ldots, p_n$$

where $n$ is the length of $P$. Each residue in SPratt is abstracted as a two-element tuple $(p, id)$ where $p$ is a point representing the $C_\alpha$ atom in $R$ and $id$ is the identity of the residue. Additional information such as the secondary structure information and the solvent accessible area may be included to describe a residue.

#### 3.2.2.2 Pattern Matching.

A pattern $P$ of length $n$ matches with a protein structure $Q$ if we can find a sequence of amino acid residues $S = s_1, \ldots, s_n$ sorted according to the primary sequence order in $Q$ such that

- the residue identity of $s_i$ matches with the residue identify of $p_i$, $i \in [1, n]$.
- the root-mean-squared-deviation (RMSD) value of the corresponding locations in $P$ and $S$ is below some threshold.

#### 3.2.2.3 Pattern Discovery.

Pattern discovery in SPratt is done in three steps. First, SPratt picks an amino acid residue and selects all neighboring residues within a cutoff distance. It converts the set of neighboring amino acid residues into two strings, called *neighbor strings*: one that includes all residues that precede the target residue in the sequence and the second that includes all residues that follow.

Both strings are sorted according to the primary sequence order. For each amino acid residue and each protein structure in a data set, SPratt computes the neighbor strings and puts all the strings together. Encoding neighboring residues in this way, the neighbor strings reflect the primary sequence order but not the separation between any residues.

Second, the Pratt string matching algorithm [46] is used to identify all sequence motifs that occur in a significant part of the data set.

Third, for each sequence motif, the geometric conservation of the motifs (measured by the pairwise RMSD distance between all the instances of the sequence motif) is evaluated. SPratt selects only those with significant geometric conservation.

## 3.3 Sequence-Independent Pattern Discovery

### 3.3.1 Discovering Sequence-Independent Structure Patterns in a Pair of Structures

In the previous section, we discussed algorithms that identify sequence-dependent structure patterns. In this section, we discuss algorithms that identify structure patterns without the constraint of sequence order, or *sequence-independent* structure patterns.

We divide sequence-independent structure pattern discovery algorithms into two groups according to whether they work on a pair of structures or on an arbitrary collection of structures. In this section, we review pairwise sequence-independent pattern discovery methods and in the next section we show how pairwise comparison can be extended to multiway comparison of protein structures. Pairwise sequence-independent pattern discovery methods include:

- Geometric hashing methods that represent protein structures as point sets and use geometric matching to find structure patterns [67,23].
- Graph matching methods that model protein structures as labeled graphs and perform subgraph matching to detect conserved patterns [30,61,92,89,104].

### 3.3.2 Geometric Hashing

This class of methods model a protein structure as point sets and use the geometric hashing technique to obtain common point subset from two structures. There is no fundamental difference in applying geometric hashing for pairwise structure pattern identification and that of pattern matching as exemplified by the TESS algorithm in Section 3.1.2. Below, we present the pattern definition used in geometric hashing. Rather than repeating the discussion of preprocessing and geometric matching that are common to almost all geometric hashing based methods, we present an analysis of computational complexity. We also show how different techniques may reduce the asymptotic complexity of the computation.

#### *3.3.2.1 Pattern Definition.*

A structure is represented as a set of amino acid residues $P = \{a_1, \dots, a_n\}$ where $n$ is the size of $P$. Each residue is represented by a two-element tuple $a_i = (p_i, id_i)$ where $p_i$ is a point in a 3D space that represents the spatial location of the residue (e.g. its $C_\alpha$ atom) and $id_i$ is the identity of the residue.

This definition was originally used by Nussinov and Wolfson [67]. The complexity of preprocessing a single protein structure with $n$ residues is bounded by $O(n^4)$. This is because there are a total of $\binom{n}{3}$ triplets in a protein. For each triplet we build one reference frame. For each reference frame, we compute the new coordinates of all $n$ residues in the protein according to the frame. The complexity of this preprocessing step is hence $n \cdot O\binom{n}{3} = O(n^4)$.

At the matching stage, two structures are preprocessed and the results are stored in a single hash table. After preprocessing, we scan the hash table once to report the shared structure patterns. Clearly, the post processing step is bounded by the total number of entries in the hash table which is itself bounded by $O(n^4)$. Therefore the overall computational complexity is $O(n^4)$.

Nussinov and Wolfson present an algorithm to speed up the computation from $O(n^4)$ to $O(n^3)$. In the improved version, rather than using a triplet to build a reference framework, two points are used to build a reference framework. There are a total of $O(n^2)$ point pairs in a data set with $n$ points and hence the overall complexity is reduced to $O(n^3)$.

A more efficient algorithm with complexity $O(n^2)$ has been proposed by Fischer et al. [23]. For a protein structure with $n$ residues, rather than building a total of $O(n^3)$ (or $O(n^2)$, if using residue pairs) reference frames, Fischer's method builds a total of $n$ reference frames. This is done by always picking up three residues that are consecutive in the primary sequence and building one reference frame for each such triplet. There are a total of $O(n)$ such triplets so the overall complexity is $O(n^2)$.

Geometric hashing has been applied to recognize local structure similarity for proteins even if they have globally different structures [23].

### *3.3.3 Graph-Based Methods*

This group of methods utilizes graph theory to model protein structure and uses subgraph isomorphism to detect recurring patterns among a pair of protein structures [91,61,79]. In this group of algorithms, a protein structure is modeled by a graph where each node models an amino acid residue, labeled by the residue identity and an edge connects a pair of residues, labeled by a variety of information related to the geometry of the protein as well as the possible physico-chemical interactions between the pair of residues. Below we review PINTS [77,93] in detail. For related methods, see [24,61,79,107].

### 3.3.3.1 *PINTS.*

PINTS takes as input two protein structures and identifies all structure patterns common to the two structures [91].

*Pattern Definition.* PINTS uses a graph to represent a structure pattern where

- A node in the PINTS graph represents an amino acid residue and is labeled by the identity of the residue.
- Two nodes are connected by an edge labeled by the distance vector (to be defined) between the two residues.

In PINTS, an amino acid residue $R$ is a three-element tuple $(p_1, p_2, p_3)$ that represents the $C_\alpha$ atom, the $C_\beta$ atom, and a functional atom in the residue $R$. One functional atom is defined for each of the 20 amino acid residue types.

A *distance vector* between two residues $R_1$, $R_2$ in PINTS is a three-element tuple $(d_\alpha^{R_1,R_2}, d_\beta^{R_1,R_2}, d_f^{R_1,R_2})$ where $d_\alpha^{R_1,R_2}, d_\beta^{R_1,R_2}, d_f^{R_1,R_2}$ are the (Euclidian) distances between the $C_\alpha$, $C_\beta$, and functional atoms in the side chain of the two residues.

*Graph Matching.* The distance vector $V_{R_1,R_2}$ matches the distance vector $V_{R'_1,R'_2}$ if

$$\left|d_\alpha^{R_1,R_2} - d_\alpha^{R'_1,R'_2}\right| \leqslant d_\alpha,$$
$$\left|d_\beta^{R_1,R_2} - d_\beta^{R'_1,R'_2}\right| \leqslant d_\beta,$$
$$\left|d_f^{R_1,R_2} - d_f^{R'_1,R'_2}\right| \leqslant d_f$$

where $d_\alpha$, $d_\beta$, $d_f$ are predefined tolerances. PINTS uses values 7.5, 6.6, and 6 Å, respectively.

A structure pattern $P$ *matches* a structure $Q$ if there exists 1–1 mapping of residues in $P$ to a set of residues in $Q$ such that corresponding nodes have identical node labels and corresponding edges are labeled by matching distance vectors.

*Pattern Discovery.* PINTS uses a modified Ullman's subgraph isomorphism test to identify all shared subgraphs of two graphs. An overview of the Ullman's subgraph isomorphism algorithm can be found in Section 4.3.

The statistical significance of identified patterns is estimated using a sophisticated model [93], which involves the RMSD between the two instances of the patterns, the number of residues in the pattern, the abundance of those residues, and their connectivity along the sequence.

Many interesting patterns have been identified by the PINTS method including the serine protease active center, the NAD binding motif in NAD binding proteins, and binding pockets of chorismate mutases.

### 3.3.4 Discovering Sequence-Independent Structure Patterns in Multiple Structures

In this section, we present a review of sequence-independent pattern discovery methods that work on a group of two or more structures. These methods are:

- Delaunay tessellation;
- Geometric hashing;
- Frequent subgraph mining.

*3.3.4.1 Delaunay Tessellation.* This class of methods [54,12,96] identifies local structural patterns based on the Delaunay Tessellation technique.

Delaunay tessellation partitions a structure into an aggregate of non-overlapping, irregular tetrahedra that identify the nearest neighbor residue quadruplets for any protein. The decomposition is unique and can be made robust in the presence of uncertainty of the residue positions [4]. Recurring structural patterns can be identified from tetrahedra recurring in multiple structures. Studies have explored the hypothesis that four-residue packing motifs can be defined as structure and sequence specific residue signatures and can be utilized in annotation of structural and functional classes of both protein structures (if available) and genomic sequences [96]. Earlier studies identified residue packing patterns based on the analysis of protein structures in a family represented as a network of residue contacts obtained by Delaunay tessellation [12,42].

*3.3.4.2 Geometric Hashing.* Recently geometric hashing has been applied to perform multiple structure alignment [56] and to identify functional sites in protein structures [87,85]. It has been also applied to atom-level representations of protein structures [85].

The extension of geometric hashing methods to find common structural patterns among multiple structures [87,85] and similarly for an extension based on PINTS [104] suffer from limited scalability since they may have exponential running time in the total number of structures.

*3.3.4.3 Frequent Subgraph Mining.* In frequent subgraph mining, a protein structure is represented by a graph. Given a group of graphs and a matching condition (usually specified as subgraph isomorphism), the goal of frequent subgraph mining is to discover all frequent subgraphs in the collections of graphs [108,40]. We discuss frequent subgraph mining algorithms in detail in the next two sections. These methods have excellent scaling behavior as the number of structures increases.

# 4. Pattern Discovery Using Graph Mining

Graphs have been utilized in many application domains as a rigorous representation of real data. Such data include the topology of communication networks, social networks, citation networks, chemical 2D structures, protein 3D structures, RNA structures, gene phylogeny data, protein-protein interaction data, and signaling, regulatory, and metabolic pathways. For example, the 2D structure of a chemical can be modeled as an undirected labeled graph where each node corresponds to an atom in the chemical, labeled by the atom type, and an edge corresponds to a chemical bond, labeled by the bond type. With graph representations, automated classifiers have been built to identify the toxic chemicals among a mix of toxic and non toxic chemicals [8].

Graphs have also been widely utilized for representing protein structure in protein structure comparison [3]. In the following discussion, we first give a formal definition of labeled graphs (graphs with node and edge labels) and then discuss two methods that use graphs to represent protein structures. A more sophisticated method developed in our recent research, which combines existing graph representations of protein structures, is discussed in Section 6.

## 4.1 Labeled Graphs

### *4.1.1 Labeled Simple Graphs*

We define first labeled simple graphs and then labeled multigraphs and pseudographs.

**Definition 4.1.** A *labeled simple graph* (graph) is a four-element tuple $G = (V, E, \Sigma, \lambda)$ where $V$ is a set of vertices or nodes and $E \subseteq V \times V$ is a set of edges joining two distinct nodes. $\Sigma$ is the set of nodes and edge labels and $\lambda : V \cup E \to \Sigma$ is a function that assigns labels to nodes and edges.

The *size* of a graph $G$, denoted by $|G|$ is the cardinality of its node set. The *degree* of a node $v$ is the number of edges incident with $v$. We use $V[G]$ and $E[G]$ to denote the set of nodes and edges for a graph $G$, respectively. We usually assume node labels and edge labels are disjoint and a total ordering is defined for the label set $\Sigma$.

A *graph database* is a list of labeled graphs where each graph is assigned an integer identifier called *graph id*. A simple graph $G$ is *undirected*, if the binary relation $E[G] \subset V \times V$ is symmetric, otherwise, $G$ is *directed*. Unless stated otherwise, all graphs are undirected in our discussion.

### 4.1.2 Multigraphs and Pseudographs

A *multigraph* is a graph where there may exist at least two edges between the same pair of nodes. A *graph loop* is a degenerate edge which joins a node to itself. A simple graph can have neither loops nor multiple edges, but a *pseudograph* can have both. We define a labeled multigraph and pseudograph in the following way.

**Definition 4.2.** A *labeled multigraph* is a four-element tuple $G = (V, E, \Sigma, \lambda)$ where $\lambda : V \cup E \to 2^{\Sigma}$ is a function that assigns (multiple) labels to nodes and edges. $2^{\Sigma}$ is the powerset of a set $\Sigma$. The interpretations of $V$, $E$, and $\Sigma$ are the same as those of simple graphs. If a labeled multigraph contains graph loops, it is a *labeled pseudograph*.

**Example 1.** In Fig. 7, we show a graph database with three graphs $P$, $Q$, and $S$ with graph id 10, 20, and 30, respectively. The edge $(p_2, p_5)$ in graph $P$ has multiple labels $\{x, y\}$ and hence $P$ is a multigraph. Graphs $Q$ and $S$ are simple graphs. Throughout our discussion, we use capital letters to represent graphs and lower case letters with subscripts to denote nodes in graphs. The order of nodes in a graph is arbitrary.

### 4.1.3 Paths, Cycles, and Trees

We also use the following graph-related terms:

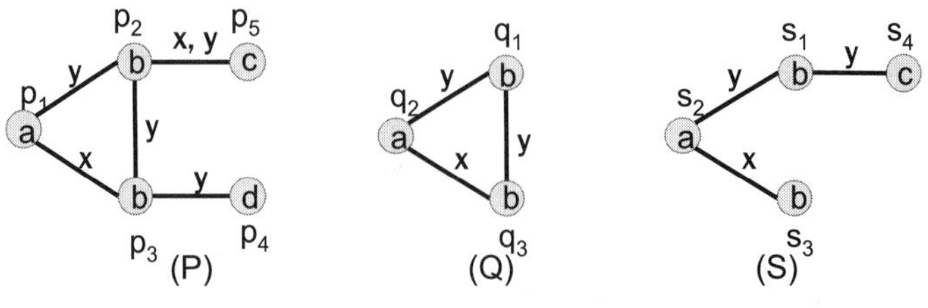


FIG. 7. A database $\mathcal{G}$ of three labeled graphs. The labels of nodes and edges are specified within the nodes and along the edges.

- A *simple path* (path) is an $n$-node undirected graph $L$ where $V[L] = \{l_i\}$, $i \in [1, n]$ and $E[L] = \{(l_i, l_{i+1})\}$, $i \in [1, (n-1)]$. $n > 0$ is the *length* of the path $L$.
- A graph $G$ is *connected* if for each pair of distinct nodes $(u, v)$, there exists a path $L \subseteq G$ such that $l_1 = u$ and $l_n = v$ where $n$ is the length of $L$.
- A *cycle* $O$ is an $n$-node path $L$ with one additional edge connecting $l_1$ and $l_n$. $n$ is the *length* of $O$.
- A *acyclic* graph is a graph with no cycle.
- A *tree* is a connected acyclic graph.

## 4.2 Representing Protein Structures

Graphs have been widely used to represent protein structures. In general at the amino acid residue level, a node in a graph represents an amino acid residue, and an edge represent the binary relation between a pair of residues. Depending on the applications, the binary relation may be distances between pairs of amino acid residues (distance matrix) or the physico-chemical contacts between residues (contact maps). We discuss the details of distance matrices and contact maps in protein structure representation below.

### 4.2.1 Protein Distance Matrix

A matrix $(x_{i,j})$ $(1 \leqslant i, j \leqslant n)$ is the distance matrix for a protein $P$ with $n$ elements, if the entry $x_{i,j}$ is the (Euclidian) distance of the $i$th and $j$th element in protein $P$. For each protein structure, there is exactly one distance matrix but the reserve is not true. Given a distance matrix $X$, there are at most two structures corresponding to the matrix. This is because inter-element distances are the same for a mirror image of a structure. To be efficiently handled by computer algorithms, distances in a distance matrix are discretized.

Using a distance matrix at the residue level, a protein structure is represented by a graph where a node represents an amino acid residue and an edge connecting a pair of amino acid residue is labeled by the discretized distance between the two residues.

### 4.2.2 Protein Contact Maps

A protein contact map is the same as the protein distance matrix representation, except each $x_{i,j}$ is not a distance but rather a Boolean indicating whether the pair of amino acid residues are in "contact" or not. There are many ways to define the "contact" relation. The most common way is a distance based method where a pair of residues are in contact if their distance is below a certain distance threshold and not otherwise [37]. More sophisticated methods such as Delaunay Tessellation and almost-Delaunay are also used to define the contact relation [42].

### 4.3 Subgraph Isomorphism

A fundamental part of recurring subgraph identification is to decide whether a pattern $G$ occurs in a graph $G'$. To make this more precise, we use the follow definition.

**Definition 4.3.** A graph $G$ is *subgraph isomorphic* to another graph $G'$ if there exists a 1–1 mapping $f : V[G] \to V[G']$ such that:

- $\forall u \in V[G], (\lambda(u) \subseteq \lambda'(f(u)))$,
- $\forall u, v \in V, ((u, v) \in E[G] \Rightarrow (f(u), f(v)) \in E[G'])$, and
- $\forall (u, v) \in E[G], (\lambda(u, v) \subseteq \lambda'(f(u), f(v)))$.

$G'$ in the above definition is a *supergraph* of $G$. The bijection $f$ is a *subgraph isomorphism* from $G$ to $G'$ and the node image $f(V[G])$ of $V$ is an *occurrence* of $G$ in $G'$. With a slight abuse of notation, we use the term "subgraph" to refer to a "subgraph isomorphic" relation. Two graphs $G$ and $G'$ are *isomorphic*, denoted by $G = G'$ if they are mutually subgraphs of each other. Non-isomorphic subgraph $G$ of $G'$ is a *proper subgraph* of $G'$, denoted by $G \subset G'$. A *proper supergraph* is defined similarly.

An induced subgraph is one that preserves all edges in the larger graph. In other words, a graph $G$ is *induced subgraph isomorphic* to another graph $G'$ if $G \subseteq G'$ with a bijection $f : V[G] \to V \subseteq V[G']$ such that $E = (V \times V) \cap E[G']$. We call a graph $G$ an *induced subgraph* of $G'$ if $G$ is induced subgraph isomorphic to $G'$.

**Example 2.** In Fig. 8, we show three graphs that are duplicated from Fig. 7 for the readers' convenience. The function $f : q_1 \to p_2, q_2 \to p_1$, and $q_3 \to p_3$ is

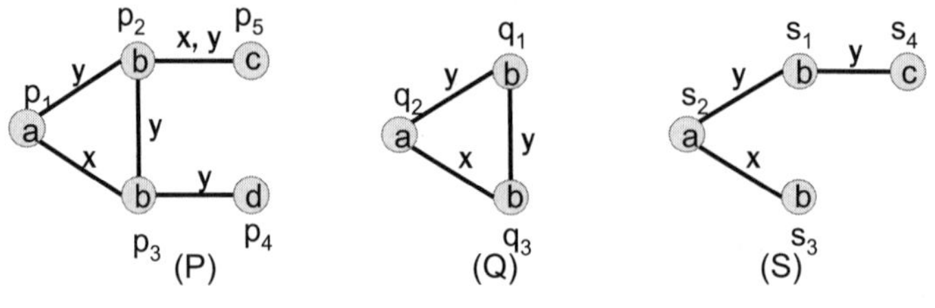


FIG. 8. A database $\mathcal{G}$ of three labeled graphs duplicated from Fig. 7. The label(s) of nodes/edges are specified within the nodes/along the edges.

a subgraph isomorphism from graph $Q$ to $P$ and hence $Q$ occurs in $P$. The set $\{p_1, p_2, p_3\}$ is an occurrence (and the only one) of graph $Q$ in $P$. We notice that $Q$ is also an induced subgraph of $P$ since $Q$ preserves all edges of $P$ in the node image $\{p_1, p_2, p_3\}$. Similarly, $S$ occurs in $P$ but $S$ is not an induced subgraph of $P$.

### *4.3.1 Ullman's Algorithm*

Ullman's algorithm is one of the most widely used algorithms to solve the subgraph isomorphism problem [97]. Though Ullman originally developed the algorithm for unlabeled and undirected graphs, this algorithm is so flexible that it can be used for virtually all types of graphs with little extra effort regardless of whether these graphs are labeled or unlabeled, have multiple edges or not, have graph loops or not, and are directed or undirected. In the following discussion, we present the basic form of Ullman's subgraph isomorphism algorithm for unlabeled and undirected graphs. See [38] if interested in subgraph isomorphism in other types of graphs.

In Ullman's algorithm, the pattern graph and graph to be matched with (the parent graph) are represented by standard adjacency matrices $A(n, n)$ and $B(m, m)$ where $n$ and $m$ are the total numbers of nodes in graph $A$ and $B$ respectively and $a_{i,j}$ equals 1 if the $i$th node and the $j$th node of $A$ are connected and 0 otherwise. Throughout this section, we use $a_{i,j}$ to refer to the entry of a matrix $A$ at the $i$th row and the $j$th column.

Ullman used a specially designed $n \times m$ binary matrix $M$, referred to as the *permutation matrix*, where each row has exactly one 1 and each column has at most a single 1, to encode a 1–1 mapping from nodes of $A$ to those of $B$. To see that $M$ stands for a 1–1 mapping, we interpret an entry $m_{ij} = 1$ in $M$ as a match between the $i$th node in $A$ and the $j$th node in $B$. Since each row of $M$ has exactly one 1, each node in $A$ maps to exactly one node in $B$; since each column of $M$ has at most a single 1, no two nodes in $A$ can match to the same node in $B$. In other words, $M$ encodes a 1–1 mapping from nodes of $A$ to those of $B$.

Using linear algebra, we obtain $C = M(MB)^T$ where $X^T$ is the transpose of matrix $T$. One important theorem about graph matching is that $M$ stands for a subgraph isomorphism from $A$ to $B$, if and only if:

$$\forall(i, j\colon 1 \leqslant i, j \leqslant n,\ a_{ij} = 1 \Rightarrow c_{ij} = 1). \tag{1}$$

To search for all successful matches, Ullman's algorithm enumerates the space of all possible permutation matrices $M$ using a backtrack method. The proof the theorem and the algorithmic details of the backtrack search can be found in [97].

## 4.4 A Road Map of Frequent Subgraph Mining

Because graphs are ubiquitous data types in many application domains including protein structure analysis [40,39], identifying recurring patterns of graphs has attracted much recent research interest. Recurring subgraph patterns provide insights of the underlying relationships of the objects that are modeled by graphs and are the starting point for subsequent analysis such as clustering and classification. Successful applications of recurring subgraph pattern identification include improving storage efficiency of databases [17], efficient indexing [29,86], and web information management [110,75]. With no surprise, algorithms for graph based modeling and analysis are going through a rapid development [39].

Here, we introduce an efficient algorithm for mining graph databases: Fast Frequent Subgraph Mining (FFSM) [40]. With minor modifications, this same algorithm can be used to mine trees, cliques, quasi-cliques from a graph database or tree patterns in a tree database [40]. Before we introduce the details of our algorithm, we define the frequent subgraph mining problem, followed by an introduction to related work.

### 4.4.1 The Frequent Subgraph Mining Problem

Given a set $\Sigma$, the *graph space* $G^*$ is all possible simple connected graphs with labels from $\Sigma$. Given a group of graphs $\mathcal{G} \subseteq G^*$, the *support* of a simple graph $G$, denoted by $s(G)$, is the fraction of $\mathcal{G}$ in which $G$ occurs.

The frequent subgraph mining problem is defined as:

**Definition 4.4.** Given a graph database $\mathcal{G}$ and a parameter $0 < \sigma \leqslant 1$, the *frequent subgraph mining* problem is to identify all simple graphs $G \in G^*$ such that the support of $G$ is at least $\sigma$.

An algorithm that solves the frequent subgraph mining problem is referred to as a *frequent subgraph mining algorithm.* We consider only connected graphs in a graph space since unconnected graphs can be viewed as a group of connected graphs. Once connected frequent subgraphs are identified, unconnected ones can be obtained using frequent item set mining techniques, as observed in [55].

### 4.4.2 Overview of Existing Algorithms

Since frequent subgraph mining is computationally challenging, early research focused on either approximation techniques such as SUBDUE [34] or methods that are only applicable for small databases like Inductive Logic Programming [16].

Recent research in frequent subgraph mining focuses on the efficiency of the algorithms because most of the algorithms solve exactly the same problem and produce the same answer. All scalable algorithms take advantage of the *anti-monotonicity* of frequency, which asserts that any supergraph of an infrequent subgraph pattern remains infrequent. The algorithms contain three components that are discussed in the sequel:

- Searching for initial seeds: preprocessing the input graph database and identifying a set of initial frequent subgraph patterns as "seeds." Graph topology of seeds is usually simple, e.g. frequent single node, single edge, or paths.
- Proposing candidate subgraphs: for each seed, a new set of patterns are proposed that are supergraphs of the seed and are likely to be frequent.
- Validating candidate subgraphs: for each proposed candidate, the support value is computed. Only frequent ones are left as seeds for the next iteration.

Components (2) and (3) may be utilized repeatedly in order to obtain all frequent subgraphs.

Below, we divide existing frequent subgraph mining methods into three groups based on how candidates are proposed:

- Edge based methods: generate new subgraphs by adding one edge to existing frequent subgraphs.
- Path based methods: decompose a graph into a set of paths and enumerate graphs by adding a path at a time.
- Tree based methods: first identify all frequent tree patterns and then discover cyclic graph patterns.

There are other types of graph mining algorithms that focus on mining a smaller subset of frequent subgraphs. For example, maximal frequent subgraph mining [41] identifies only those frequent subgraphs for which none of their supergraphs are frequent. Coherent subgraph mining uses mutual information to select subgraphs that may be infrequent in an overall data set [42]. For a more recent review of different subgraph mining algorithms, see [41].

## 4.4.3 Edge Based Frequent Subgraph Mining

### 4.4.3.1 Level-wise Search: The FSG Algorithm.

FSG (Frequent Subgraph Mining) [55] identifies all frequent patterns by a level-wise search procedure. At the first step, FSG preprocesses the input graph database and identifies all frequent single edge patterns. At a subsequent step, e.g. at step $k$, FSG identifies the set of frequent subgraphs with edge size (i.e. number of edges) $k$. This set is denoted as $C_k$. The task at step $k$ is subdivided into two phases: candidate subgraph processing and candidate subgraph validation, with the details covered below (see Algorithm 1).

$F_1 \leftarrow \{e \mid s(e) \geqslant \sigma\}$ # *all frequent edges*
$k \leftarrow 2$
**while** $F_{k-1} \neq \emptyset$ **do**
    $C_k \leftarrow$ FSG-join$(F_{k-1}, k)$
    $F_k \leftarrow$ FSG-validation$(C_k, \mathcal{G}, \sigma)$
    $k \leftarrow k + 1$
**end while**
$F \leftarrow \bigcup_{i \in [1,k]} F_i$

ALGORITHM 1. FSG$(\mathcal{G}, \sigma)$: Frequent subgraph mining.

*Candidate Subgraph Proposing.* Given a set of frequent graphs with edge size $k-1$ (number of edges), denoted by $F_{k-1}$, FSG constructs candidate frequent subgraphs with edge size $k$ by "joining" two frequent subgraphs with size $k-1$. Two graphs are "joinable" if they have the same edge size $l > 0$ and they share a common subgraph of edge size $l-1$. The "join" between two joinable graphs $G_1, G_2$ with edge size $k-1$ produces a set of graphs that are supergraphs of both graphs with edge size $k$. In other words, in FSG, the join operation is defined as:

$$FSG\_join(G_1, G_2) = \begin{cases} \{G \mid G_1 \subseteq G, G_2 \subseteq G, |E[G]| = k\} \\ \quad \text{if } G_1 \text{ and } G_2 \text{ are joinable,} \\ \emptyset \quad \text{otherwise.} \end{cases}$$

We use $|E[G]|$ to denote the edge size of a graph $G$.

FSG applies the join operation for every pair of joinable graphs in $F_{k-1}$ to produce a list of candidate $k$ edge patterns $C_k$. The join operation is illustrated in Fig. 9 and the pseudo code is presented in Algorithm 2.

*Candidate Subgraph Validation.* FSG determines the true frequent subgraphs with edge size $k$ from the set $C_k$ by computing the support value of each member

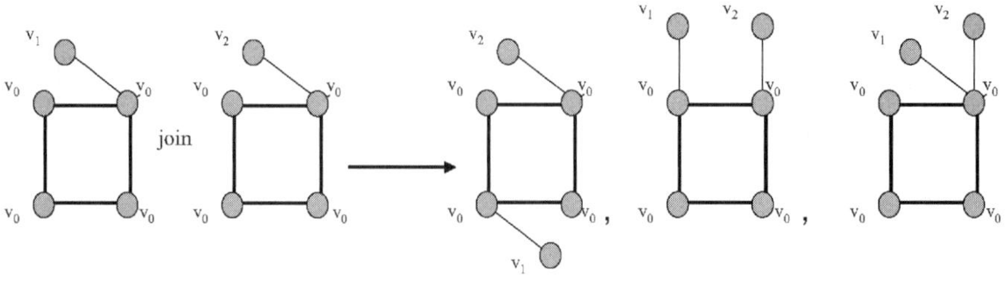


FIG. 9. An example of the join operation in FSG.

```
1: C_k ← ∅
2: for each G_1, G_2 ∈ F_{k-1} do
3:   if there exists e_1 ∈ E[G_1] and e_2 ∈ E[G_2] such that G_1 − e_1 = G_2 − e_2
4:     C_k = {G | G_1 ⊂ G, G_2 ⊂ G, |E(G)| = k} # joinable
5:   end if
6: end for
7: return C_k
```

ALGORITHM 2. FSG-join($F_{k-1}, k$): Join pairs of subgraphs in $F_{k-1}$.

```
1: F_k ← ∅
2: for each G ∈ C_k do
3:   s(G) ← 0
4:   for each G' ∈ 𝒢 do
5:     if G ⊆ G' then s(G) ← s(G) + 1 end # computing support value
6:   end for
7:   if s(G) ⩾ σ then F_k ← F_k ∪ {G} end
8: end for
9: return F_k
```

ALGORITHM 3. FSG-validation($C_k, \mathcal{G}, \sigma$): Validate frequent subgraphs.

in the set $C_k$. To compute the support value of a graph $G$, FSG scans the database of graphs and for each graph $G'$ in the graph database, FSG uses subgraph isomorphism test to determine whether $G$ is a subgraph of $G'$ and updates the support value of $G$ if it is. As the results of the validation phase, the set of frequent subgraph with edge size $k$ is computed. The pseudo code of the FSG-validation is presented in Algorithm 3.

*Putting It All Together.* Algorithms 1–3 present the pseudo code for the FSG algorithm, which identifies all subgraphs $F$ in a graph database $\mathcal{G}$ with support threshold $0 < \sigma \leqslant 1$. We simplified the FSG algorithm to explain its basic structure; see [55] for details of performance improvements in FSG.

#### 4.4.3.2 Depth-First Search: The gSpan Algorithm.

*gSpan* utilizes a depth-first algorithm to search for frequent subgraphs [108]. gSpan, like FSG, also preprocesses a graph database and identifies all frequent single edges at the beginning of the algorithm. gSpan designed a novel extension operation to propose candidate subgraphs. In order to understand the extension operation developed by gSpan, we will introduce the depth-first code representation of a graph, developed in gSpan.

*Depth-First Code of Graphs.* Given a connected graph $G$, a depth-first search $S$ of $G$ produces a chain of nodes in $G$ and we denote the nodes in $V[G]$ as $1, 2, \ldots, n$ where $n$ is the size of the graph $G$. Node $n$ is the *rightmost* node and the path from root to $n$ is named the rightmost path.

Each edge in $G$ is represented by a 5-element tuple $e = (i, j, \lambda(i), \lambda(i, j), \lambda(j))$ where $i, j$ are nodes in $G$ ($i < j$) and $\lambda$ is the labeling function of $G$ that assigns labels to nodes and edges.

We define a total order $\preccurlyeq$ of edges in $G$ such that $e_1 \preccurlyeq e_2$ if $i_1 < i_2$, or ($i_1 = i_2$ and $j_1 \leqslant j_2$).

Given a graph $G$ and a depth-first search $S$, we may sort edges in a graph $G$ according to the total order $\preccurlyeq$ and concatenate such sorted edges together to produce a single sequence of labels. Such a sequence of labels is a depth first code of the graph $G$. There may be many depth first codes for a graph $G$ and the smallest one (using lexicographical order of sequences) is the *canonical DFS form* of $G$, denoted by $DFS(G)$. The depth first tree that produces the canonical form of $G$ is its *canonical DFS tree*.

*Candidate Subgraph Proposing.* In gSpan, a frequent subgraph $G$ is *extended* to a candidate frequent subgraph $G'$ by choosing a node $v$ in the rightmost path of a canonical DFS tree in $G$ and adding an edge $(v, w)$ to $G$ where $w$ is a node in $G$ or not. The restriction that we only introduce an edge into the rightmost path looks strange at the first glance but an important observation of gSpan is that it is guaranteed that we can still enumerate all frequent subgraphs with this extension. See [108] for the detailed proof.

*Candidate Subgraph Validation.* gSpan uses the same procedure used by FSG (a scan of a graph database and use subgraph isomorphism to determine the support value) to select frequent subgraphs from a set of candidates.

Comparing to level-wise search algorithm FSG, gSpan has better memory utilization due to the depth-first search, which leads to an order of magnitude speedup in several benchmarks [109].

*Putting It All Together.* Algorithms 4–6 present the gSpan algorithm.

*Other Edge-Based Depth-First Algorithms.* Instead of enumerating all the subgraph isomorphisms, the method proposed by Borgelt and Berhold [8] also uses an edge-based depth-first scheme to discover all frequent subgraphs. Different from gSpan, the method keeps a list of all subgraph isomorphisms ("embedding") of a frequent subgraph $G$. The intuition is to avoid subgraph isomorphism testing, which generally becomes the performance limiting factor of gSpan when dealing with large and complex graphs (dense graphs with few distinct labels). Another edge-based depth first search method FFSM [40] also keeps embedding and frequent subgraph.

$F_1 \leftarrow \{e \mid s(e) \geqslant \sigma\}$ # *all frequent edges*
$F \leftarrow F_1$
$k \leftarrow 1$
**for each** $G \in F_1$ **do**
    $F \leftarrow F \cup$ gSpan-search$(G, k, \mathcal{G}, \sigma)$
**end for**

ALGORITHM 4. gSpan$(\mathcal{G}, \sigma)$: Frequent subgraph mining.

$k \leftarrow k + 1$
$C_k \leftarrow$ gSpan-extension$(G, k)$
$F_k \leftarrow$ gSpan-validation$(C, \mathcal{G}, \sigma)$
**for each** $G' \in F_k$ **do**
    $F \leftarrow F \cup$ gSpan-search$(G', k, \mathcal{G}, \sigma)$
**end for**
**return** $F$

ALGORITHM 5. gSpan-search$(G, k, \mathcal{G}, \sigma)$.

$C_k \leftarrow \{G' \mid G \subset G', |E[G']| = k, DFS(G) \sqsubseteq DFS(G')\}$
**return** $C_k$

ALGORITHM 6. gSpan-extension$(G, k)$.

FFSM has developed a hybrid candidate proposing algorithm with both a join and an extension operation with improved efficiency. We cover details of FFSM in Section 5.

*4.4.3.3 Path-Based Frequent Subgraph Mining.* Below we introduce the algorithm proposed by Vanetik et al. that discovers all frequent subgraphs using paths as a building block [98]. We name this algorithm PGM (Path-based Graph Mining).

*Path Cover and Path Number of Graphs.* A *path cover* of a graph $G$ is set of edge-disjoint paths that cover edges in $G$ exactly once. A *minimal path cover* of a graph $G$ is a path cover of $G$ with the minimal number of paths. The cardinality of a minimal path cover of a graph $G$, denoted by $p(G)$, is the *path number* of $G$.

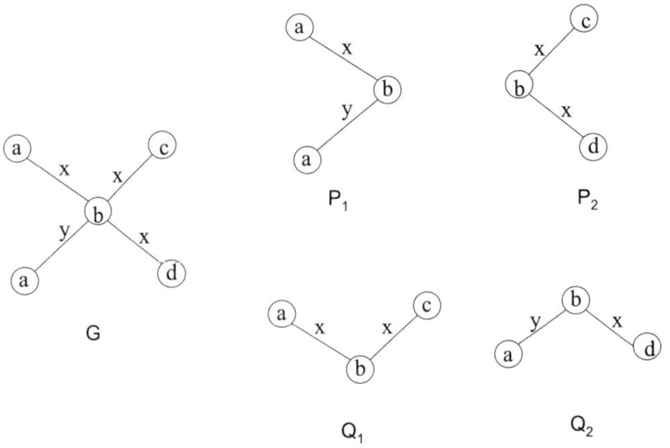


FIG. 10. A graph $G$ and two of its path covers.

The computation of a path number is straightforward. For a connected graph $G = (V, E)$, the path number is $p(G) = |\{v \mid v \in E, d(v) \text{ is odd }\}|/2$ where $d(v)$ is the degree of a node $v$ [98].

In Fig. 10, we show a graph $G$ and two of its path covers $P = \{P_1, P_2\}$ and $Q = \{Q_1, Q_2\}$. Since $G$ has four nodes with odd degree, the path number of $G$ is $p(G) = 4/2 = 2$. Therefore both path cover $P$ and $Q$ are minimal path covers of $G$.

*Representing Graphs by Paths.* In PGM, each graph is represented in a novel way as a set of paths and a relation among the set of paths. More specifically, PGM represents a graph $G$ as a three-element tuple $G = (V, P, \pi)$ where

- $V$ is the set of nodes in $G$,
- $P$ is a path cover of $G$, and
- $\pi : \mathcal{P} \to V$ is a 1–1 mapping of nodes in path cover $P$ to $V$ where $\mathcal{P} = \bigcup_{p \in P} p$ is the set of all nodes in the path cover $P$.

The function $\pi$ is named the *composition relation* in PGM. We can prove that with a node set $V$, a path cover $P$ of a graph $G$, and a composition relation that maps nodes in $P$ to $V$, we can reconstruct the graph $G$ exactly. The proof is given in [98].

*Candidate Subgraph Proposing.* In PGM, each graph is represented as a set of paths $P$, a set of nodes $V$, and the composition relation of $V$ to nodes in $P$. Two $n$-path represented graphs $G_1 = P_{1_1}, P_{1_2}, \ldots, P_{1_n}$ and $G_2 = P_{2_1}, P_{2_2}, \ldots, P_{2_n}$ are "joinable" if they differ from each other by at most one path. In other words, $G_1$ and $G_2$ are joinable if $|G_1 \cap G_2| \geqslant n - 1$.

For two joinable graphs $G_1, G_2$, PGM produces a set of graphs that are supergraphs to both $G_1$ and $G_2$ and selects those that are frequent in a graph database. PGM follows the general approach of Algorithm 1, using this definition of joining.

#### *4.4.3.4 Tree-Based Frequent Subgraph Mining: the GASTON Algorithm.*

We describe the algorithm GASTON [66], which introduced a new frequent subgraph enumeration method by first identifying all frequent trees and then constructing cyclic graphs. The two steps are covered in the following discussions.

*Frequent Tree Identification.* GASTON discovers all frequent trees using a similar strategy to that used by the edge-based depth-first algorithms. First all frequent edges are discovered. Second, single edges are extended to trees with two edges, infrequent trees are pruned, and the same search goes on until no more frequent trees are identified. GASTON uses a novel tree normalization scheme that can be computed incrementally in constant time. Using this tree normalization scheme, GASTON guarantees that each frequent tree is enumerated once and only once efficiently.

*Frequent Cyclic Graph Identification.* For a frequent tree $T$, GASTON constructs a set of frequent graphs that use $T$ as their spanning tree. Let's denote set $C_E$ as the set of unconnected node pairs in a tree $T$, i.e. $C_E = \{(i, j) \mid i < j, (i, j) \notin T\}$ (we require $i < j$ to avoid redundant pairs in an undirected tree). GASTON uses a "close" operation which introduces an edge to an pair of unconnected nodes in a tree or a graph. By applying the close operation repeatedly, GASTON enumerates all frequent cyclic graphs in which $T$ is a spanning tree.

As a final comment for GASTON, as pointed out by Nijssen and Kok, the task of constructing frequent cyclic graphs from a tree $T$ is similar to the frequent item set mining problem [11] if we treat each edge in $C_E$ as an "item." In fact, any algorithms that solves the frequent item set problem can potentially be adapted to solve the problem of constructing frequent cyclic graphs from a tree in GASTON.

## 5. FFSM: Fast Frequent Subgraph Mining

Here, we introduce an efficient algorithm for mining frequent subgraphs in graph databases: Fast Frequent Subgraph Mining (FFSM). With little effort, this same algorithm can be used to mine trees, cliques, quasi-cliques from a graph database or tree patterns in a tree database [40].

### 5.1 New Definitions

#### *5.1.1 Graph Automorphism*

One of the critical problems in graph mining is the graph automorphism problem: given two graphs $P$ and $Q$, determine whether $P$ is isomorphic to $Q$. We solve the graph automorphism problem by graph normalization, i.e. assigning unique ids for graphs. To that end, we introduce the following definitions.

**Definition 5.1.** A *graph normalization function* is a 1–1 mapping $\psi$ from $G^*$ to an arbitrary set $\Gamma$, i.e. $\psi(G) = \psi(G') \Rightarrow G = G'$ where $G^*$ is a graph space (i.e. all possible graphs with vertex and edge labels chosen from a fixed set).

We work on a subclass of normalization procedures that maps a graph to a sequence of labels. The label sequence $\psi(G)$ is the *canonical form* of the graph $G$.

### 5.1.2 Canonical Adjacency Matrix of Graphs

In FFSM, we represent each graph by an adjacency matrix $M$ such that every diagonal entry of $M$ is filled with the label of a node and every off-diagonal entry is filled with the label of the corresponding edge, or zero if there is no edge. In the sequel with no confusion of graphs, we use capital letters to denote matrices and use the corresponding lower case letters with subscripts to denote an individual entry of a matrix. For instance, we use $m_{i,j}$ to denote the entry on the $i$th row and $j$th column of an $n \times n$ matrix $M$, where $0 < j \leqslant i \leqslant n$.

*5.1.2.1 Code.* In general there are many valid adjacency matrix for a single graph. For example, any permutation of the node set corresponds to a (possibly different) adjacency matrix, if we layout the nodes along the diagonal line of the adjacency matrix accordingly. Therefore, there may be up to $n!$ different adjacency matrices for a graph of $n$ nodes. The right part of Fig. 11 shows three adjacency matrices for the labeled graph $P$ shown in the same figure. When we draw a matrix, we assume that the rows are numbered 1 through $n$ from top to bottom, and the columns are numbered 1 through $m$ from left to right for an $n \times m$ matrix $M$. For simplicity, we only show the lower triangular part of an adjacency matrix since the upper half is a mirror image of the lower one. In order to select a unique representation, we define a total order of all adjacency matrices for a graph.

**Definition 5.2.** Given an $n \times n$ adjacency matrix $M$ of a graph $G$ with $n$ nodes, we define the *code* of $M$, denoted by *code*$(M)$, as the sequence $s$ formed by concatenating lower triangular entries of $M$ (including entries on the diagonal) where $s = m_{i,j}$ where $1 \leqslant j \leqslant i \leqslant n$.

For an adjacency matrix $M$, each diagonal entry of $M$ is referred to as a *node entry* and each off-diagonal none-zero entry in the lower triangular part of $M$ is referred to as an *edge entry*. We order edge entries according to their relative positions in the code of the matrix $M$ in such way that the *first* edge entry of $M$ as the leftmost one in $code(M)$ and the *last* edge entry as the rightmost one in $code(M)$.

**Example 3.** In Fig. 11, we show three adjacency matrices for a graph $P$ in the same figure. For adjacency matrix $M_1$, the edge entry set is $\{m_{2,1}, m_{3,1}, m_{3,2}, m_{4,2}, m_{4,3}\}$ where $m_{2,1}, m_{4,3}$, and $m_{4,2}$ are the first, last, second-to-last edge entries of $M$, respectively.

*5.1.2.2 Canonical Form.* We use standard lexicographic order on sequences to define a total order of two arbitrary codes $p$ and $q$. Given a graph $G$, its *canonical form* is the maximal code among all its possible codes. The adjacency matrix $M$ which produces the canonical form is the *canonical adjacency matrix* (CAM) of graph $G'$, denoted by $\mathcal{M}(G)$. For example, after applying the total ordering, we have $code(M_1)$ = "$axbxyb0yyb$" $\geqslant$ $code(M_2)$ = "$axb0ybxyyb$" $\geqslant$ $code(M_3)$ = "$bybyyb0xxa$." Therefore the adjacency matrix $M_1$ shown in Fig. 11 is the CAM of the graph $P$ it represents, and $code(M_1)$ is the canonical form of $P$.

Notice that we use maximal code rather than the minimal code used by [55,45] in the above canonical form definition. This definition provides important properties for subgraph mining, as explained below.

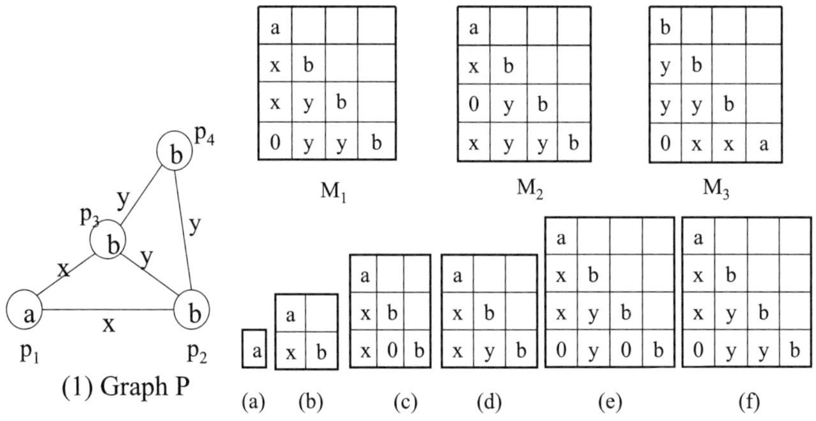


FIG. 11. Left: A labeled graph $P$. Upper right: Three adjacency matrices for the graph $P$. Lower right: Examples of maximal proper submatrices. Matrix (a) is the proper maximal submatrix of matrix (b), which itself is the proper maximal submatrix of (c) and so forth.

## 5.2 Organizing a Graph Space by a Tree

A graph space is the set of all possible graphs that draw labels from a fixed label set. In the following, we introduce a partial order on graphs and show that with the partial order we can define a tree on any graph space.

### *5.2.1 A Partial Order of Graphs*

In order to define a partial order, we first define the maximal proper submatrix of a CAM.

**Definition 5.3.** Given a CAM $M$ with at least two edge entries in the last row, a matrix $N$ is the *maximal proper submatrix* of $M$ if $N$ is obtained by replacing the last edge entry (and the corresponding entry of upper triangular part) of $M$ by the value "0." Similarly, if $M$ has only one edge entry in the last row, $N$ is the *maximal proper submatrix* of $M$ if $N$ is obtained from $M$ by removing the last row (column) of $M$.

Since $M$ represents a connected graph, it is not necessary to consider a case such that there is no edge entry in the last row of $M$. Several examples of the maximal proper submatrices are given at the bottom of Fig. 11. We notice that the empty string is a prefix of any string, and hence an empty matrix is the maximal proper submatrix of any matrix with size 1.

**Definition 5.4.** Given a graph space $G^*$, we define a binary relation $\preccurlyeq$ on graphs in $G^*$ such that $G \preccurlyeq G'$ if one of the following three conditions is true:

- $G = G'$;
- $\mathcal{M}(G)$ is a maximal proper submatrix of $\mathcal{M}(G')$;
- there exists a $G''$ such that $G \preccurlyeq G'' \preccurlyeq G'$.

**Example 4.** In Fig. 12, we have that $A \preccurlyeq B \preccurlyeq C \preccurlyeq D \preccurlyeq E \preccurlyeq F$ because of the maximal proper submatrix relation they have.

**Theorem 1.** $\preccurlyeq$ *is a partial order.*

**Proof.** To prove that $\preccurlyeq$ is a partial order, we need to prove the following three properties:

- reflective: $G \preccurlyeq G$ for all graphs $G$,

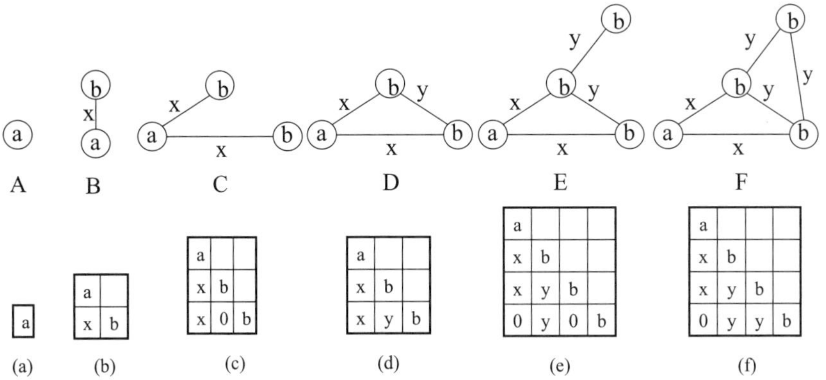


FIG. 12. Examples of the partial order $\preccurlyeq$. Upper: A group of graphs. Lower: The related CAM representations.

- anti-symmetric: $G \preccurlyeq G'$ and $G' \preccurlyeq G$ implies that $G = G'$,
- transitive: $G \preccurlyeq G'$ and $G' \preccurlyeq G''$ imply that $G \preccurlyeq G''$.

All the three properties are the direct results of the definition of the binary relation $\preccurlyeq$ and maximal proper submatrix. □

### 5.2.2 CAM Tree

Given a graph space $G^*$, we define a directed graph $\mathcal{D}$ according to the partial order $\preccurlyeq$.

- Each node in $\mathcal{D}$ is a distinct connected graph in $G^*$, represented by its CAM;
- An ordered edge $(G', G)$ connecting two graphs $G$ and $G'$ if $G$ is the minimal one such that $G' \preccurlyeq G$.

We notice that each graph can have at most one maximal proper submatrix and hence has only one incoming edge. In other words, the directed graph we defined is acyclic. In the following, we show that $\mathcal{D}$ is a tree, which is denoted as the *CAM tree* of the graph space. Before we do that, in Fig. 13 we show the CAM tree of all subgraphs of the graph $P$ from Fig. 11.

The following theorem guarantees that the directed acyclic (DAG) graph $\mathcal{D}$ we constructed is a rooted tree.

**Theorem 2.** *The graph $\mathcal{D}$ we constructed in Section 5.2 is a rooted tree with the empty graph as its root.*

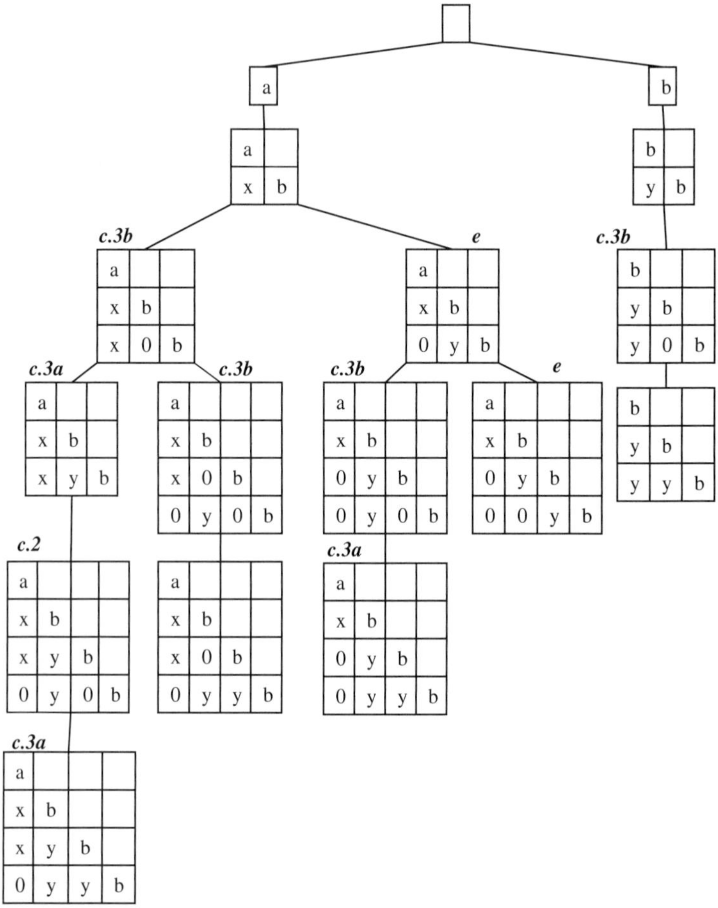


FIG. 13. The CAM Tree of all subgraphs of the graph $P$ in Fig. 11. Every matrix obtained by a join operation is specified by a label starting with **c**. and then the type of the join operation e.g. **c.3a** stands for join case3a. A CAM obtained by an extension operation is labeled with **e**. The join and extension operations are discussed in Sections 5.3 and 5.4, respectively. CAMs (size $\geqslant 3$) without label are explained in Section 5.3 where suboptimal CAMs are discussed. CAMs with up to one edge are obtained by an initial step (discussed in Section 5.4) which involves directly scanning nodes/edges labels in a graph database.

**Proof.** We already have shown that $\mathcal{D}$ is a DAG. To prove that a DAG is a tree, all we need to do is to prove that for any graph $G$, there exists a sequence of graphs $G_1, G_2, \ldots, G_n$ such that $G_1$ is an empty graph, $G_n = G$ and $G_i \preccurlyeq G_{i+1}$ for $1 \leqslant i < n$. This is proved by the following theorem. □

**Theorem 3.** *Given a CAM $M$ of a connected graph $G$ and $M$'s submatrix $N$, $N$ represents a connected subgraph of $G$.*

**Proof.** Since $N$ must represent a subgraph of $G$, it is sufficient to show the subgraph $N$ represents is connected. To prove this, it is sufficient to show that in $N$ there is no row $i$ (with the exception of the first row) that contains no edge entry. We prove this claim by contradiction. We assume that in the matrix $M$, there exists at least one such row $i$ that it does not contain any edge entry. Then we claim that we can find another row $j$ ($j > i$) such that $j$ contains an edge entry connecting the $j$th node and one of the nodes in the first $i - 1$ rows (if not, the graph $M$ corresponds to is not connected). If we perform a swap of row $i$ and $j$ and we claim that the code of the newly obtained adjacency matrix is lexicographically greater than that of $M$. This fact contradicts to the definition of CAM, which asserts the CAM of a graph has the largest code. □

## 5.3 Exploring the CAM Tree

The current methods for enumerating all the subgraphs might be classified into two categories: one is the join operation adopted by FSG and AGM [45,55]. A join operation takes two "joinable" frequent $k$-edge graphs $G_1$ and $G_2$ and produces a $(k + 1)$-edge graph candidate $G$ such that both $G_1$ and $G_2$ are subgraphs of $G$. Two $k$-edge graphs are *joinable* if they share a common $(k - 1)$-edge subgraphs. The join operation is expensive, as shown in [55], in that a single join operation might generate many graph candidates and one candidate might be redundantly proposed by many distinct join operations.

On the other hand, [8,108] use an extension operation to grow a frequent graph. An extension operation produces a $(k + 1)$-edge graph candidate from a frequent $k$-edge graph $G$ by adding one additional edge to $G$ (with or without introducing an additional node). This operation is also costly since for a given graph, there are many nodes in the graph that an additional edge might be attached to.

In order to derive a hybrid method with improved efficiency, we list some of the key challenges to achieve:

- Can we interleave join and extension operation to achieve maximal efficiency?
- Can we design a join operation such that every distinct CAM is generated only once?
- Can we improve a join operation such that only a few graphs can be generated from a single operation (say at most two)?
- Can we design an extension operation such that all the edges might be attached to only a single node rather than many nodes in a graph?

In order to meet these challenges, we have introduced two new operations, FFSM-Join and FFSM-Extension, we have augmented the CAM tree with a set of *sub-optimal canonical adjacency matrices*, and designed an embedding based subgraph enumeration method. Experimental evidence demonstrates our method can achieve an order of magnitude speed up over the current state-of-the-art subgraph mining algorithm gSpan [108]. Further details are discussed in the following sections.

### 5.3.1 FFSM-Join

The purpose of the join operation is "superimposing" two graphs to generate a new candidate graph. Depending on the different characteristics of the graphs, the join operation in our algorithm might produce one or two graph candidates.

Given an adjacency matrix $A$ of a graph $G$, we define $A$ as an "*inner*" matrix if $A$ has at least two edge entries in the last row. Otherwise, $A$ is an "*outer*" matrix. Given two adjacency matrices $A$ $(m \times m)$ and $B$ $(n \times n)$ sharing the same maximal proper submatrix, let $A$'s last edge be $a_{m,f}$ and $B$'s last edge be $b_{n,k}$, and we define $join(A, B)$ by the following three cases:

**join case 1: both A and B are inner matrices**

1: **if** $f \neq k$ **then**

2: $join(A, B) = \{C\}$ where $C$ is a $m \times m$ matrix such that

$$c_{i,j} = \begin{cases} a_{i,j}, & 0 < i, j \leqslant m,\ i \neq n \text{ or } j \neq k, \\ b_{i,j}, & \text{otherwise.} \end{cases}$$

3: **else**

4: $join(A, B) = \emptyset$

5: **end if**

**join case 2: A is an inner matrix and B is an outer matrix** $join(A, B) = \{C\}$ where $C$ is a $n \times n$ matrix and

$$c_{i,j} = \begin{cases} a_{i,j}, & 0 < i, j \leqslant m, \\ b_{i,j}, & \text{otherwise.} \end{cases}$$

**join case 3: both A and B are outer matrices**

1: let matrix $D$ be a $(m+1) \times (m+1)$ matrix where (case 3b)

$$d_{i,j} = \begin{cases} a_{i,j}, & 0 < i, j \leqslant m, \\ b_{m,j}, & i = m+1, 0 < j < m, \\ 0, & i = m+1, j = m, \\ b_{m,m}, & i = m+1, j = m+1. \end{cases}$$

2: **if** $(f \neq k, a_{m,m} = b_{m,m})$ **then**
3: $C$ is $m \times m$ matrix where (case 3a)

$$c_{i,j} = \begin{cases} a_{i,j}, & 0 < i, j \leqslant m, i \neq n \text{ or } j \neq k, \\ b_{i,j}, & \text{otherwise.} \end{cases}$$

4: $join(A, B) = \{C, D\}$
5: **else**
6: $join(A, B) = \{D\}$
7: **end if**

In join case 3, when joining two outer matrices $M_1$ and $M_2$ (both with size $m$), we might obtain a matrix with the same size. We refer this join operation as *case3a*. It is also possible that we obtain a matrix having size $(m + 1)$ and this case is referred as *case3b*.

We notice that the join operation is symmetric with respect to $A$ and $B$ with the only exception of join case 3b. In other words, $join(A, B) = join(B, A)$ for join case 1, 2 and 3a and $join(A, B) \neq join(B, A)$ in join case3b. In order to remove the potential duplications resulting from this symmetry, we require that $code(A) \geqslant code(B)$ in all join cases except join case 3b. Equality is permitted since self-join is a valid operation. If the inequality is not satisfied $(code(A) < code(B))$, a join operation produces an empty set.

Figure 14 shows examples for the join operation for all four cases. At the bottom of Fig. 14, we show a case where a graph might be redundantly proposed by FSG $\binom{6}{2} = 15$ times (joining of any pair of distinct five-edge subgraphs $G_1$, $G_2$ of the graph $G$ will restore $G$ by the join operation proposed by FSG). As shown in the graph, FFSM-Join completely removes the redundancy after "sorting" the subgraphs by their canonical form.

However, the join operation is not "complete" in the sense that it may not enumerate all the subgraphs in the CAM tree. Interested readers might find such examples in the CAM tree we presented in Fig. 13. Clearly we need another operation, which is discussed below.

### 5.3.2 FFSM-Extension

Another enumeration technique in the current subgraph mining algorithms is the extension operation that proposes a $(k + 1)$-edge graph candidate $G$ from a $k$-edge graph $G_1$ by introducing one additional edge. In these algorithms, the newly introduced edge might connect two existing nodes or connect an existing node and a node introduced together with the edge. A simple way to perform the extension operation is to introduce every possible edge to every node in a graph $G$. This method clearly

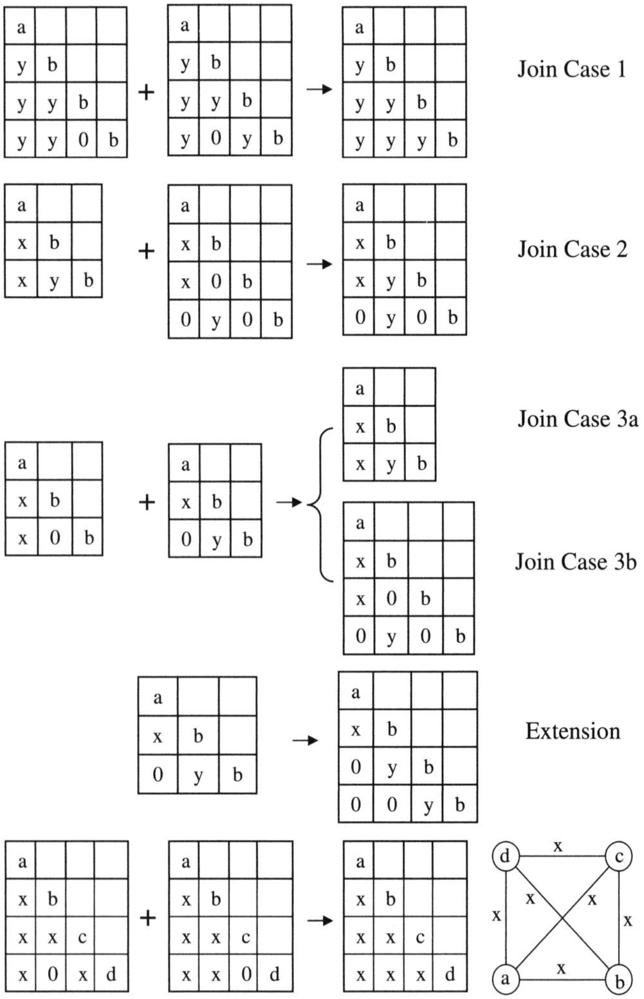


FIG. 14. Examples of the join/extension operation.

has complexity of $O(\Sigma_V \times \Sigma_E \times |G|)$ where $\Sigma_V$, $\Sigma_E$ stand for the set of available vertex and edge labels for a graph $G$, respectively for a single extension. It suffers from the large size of graph candidates as well as the large amount of available node/edge labels.

gSpan [108] developed an efficient way to reduce the total number of nodes that need to be considered. In gSpan, the extension operation is only performed on nodes

**if** ($A$ is an outer adjacency matrix) **then**
  **for** $(n_l, e_l) \in \Sigma_V \times \Sigma_E$ **do**
    $S \leftarrow \emptyset$
    create an $n \times n$ matrix $B = (b_{i,j})$ such that

$$b_{i,j} = \begin{cases} a_{i,j}, & 0 < i,j \leqslant n, \\ 0, & i = n+1,\ 0 < j < n, \\ e_l, & i = n+1,\ j = n, \\ n_l, & i = n+1,\ j = n+1. \end{cases}$$

    $S \leftarrow S \cup \{B\}$
  **end for**
**else**
  $S \leftarrow \Phi$
**end if**

ALGORITHM 7. FFSM-Extension(A).

on the "rightmost path" of a graph. Given a graph $G$ and one of its depth first search trees $T$, the *rightmost path* of $G$ with respect to $T$ is the rightmost path of the tree $T$. gSpan chooses only one depth first search tree $T$ that produces the canonical form of $G$ for extension. Here, we refer to [108] for further details about the extension operation.

In FFSM, we further improve the efficiency of the extension operation by choosing only a single node in a CAM and attaching an newly introduced edge to it together with an additional node. As proved by Theorem 4, this extension operation, combined with the join operation, unambiguously enumerates all the nodes in the CAM tree.

The pseudo code presenting the extension operation is shown in Algorithm 7.

### 5.3.3 Suboptimal CAM Tree

Using the CAM tree of the graph $P$ in Fig. 13, we can verify that the join and extension operations, even combined together, can not enumerate all subgraphs in $P$. We investigated this and found this problem can be solved by introducing the suboptimal canonical adjacency matrices, as defined below.

**Definition 5.5.** Given a graph $G$, a *suboptimal Canonical Adjacency Matrix* (simply, suboptimal CAM) of $G$ is an adjacency matrix $M$ of $G$ such that its maximal proper submatrix $N$ is the CAM of the graph $N$ represents.

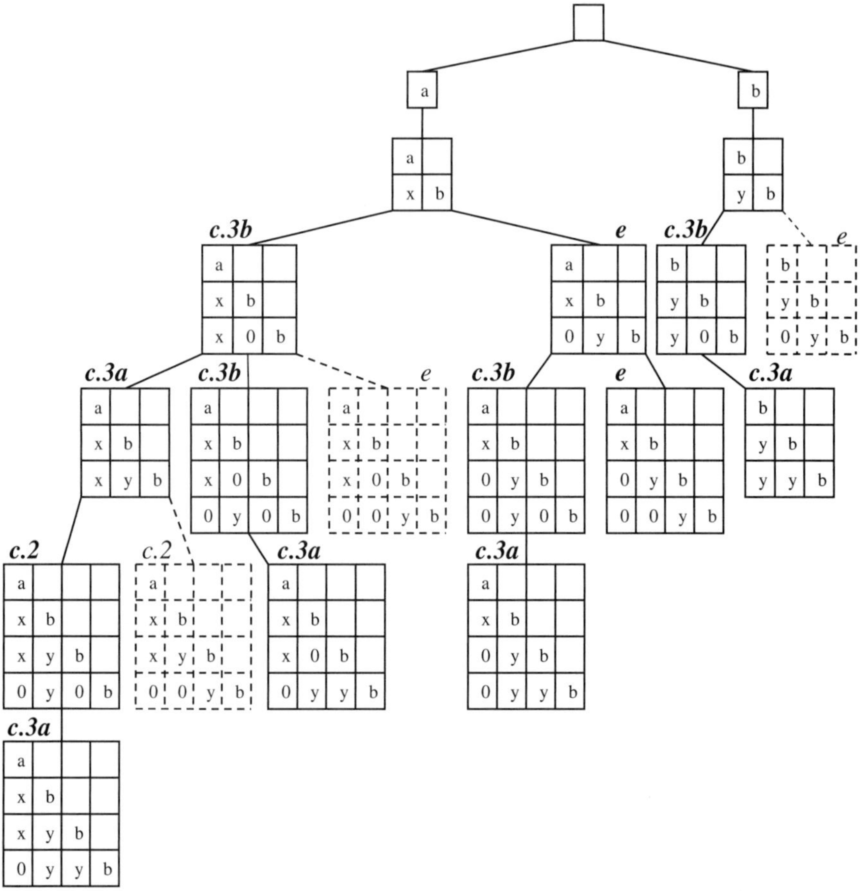


FIG. 15. The suboptimal CAM Tree for the graph $P$ shown in Fig. 11. Matrices with solid boundary are CAMs and those with dashed line boundary are proper suboptimal CAMs. The label on top of an adjacency matrix $M$ indicates the operation by which $M$ might be proposed from its parent. The labeling follows the same conventions used in Fig. 13.

By definition, every CAM is a suboptimal CAM. We denote a *proper suboptimal CAM* as a suboptimal CAM that is not the CAM of the graph it represents. Several suboptimal CAMs (the matrices with dotted boundaries) are shown in Fig. 15. Clearly, all the suboptimal CAMs of a graph $G$ could be organized in a tree in a similar way to the construction of the CAM tree. One such example for the graph $P$ in Fig. 11 is shown in Fig. 15.

With the notion of suboptimal CAM, the suboptimal CAM tree is "complete" in the sense that all vertices in a suboptimal CAM tree can be enumerated using join and extension operations. This is formally stated in the following theorem.

**Theorem 4.** *For a graph G, let $C_{k-1}(C_k)$ be set of the suboptimal CAMs of all the $(k-1)$-vertex ($k$-vertex) subgraphs of G ($k \geqslant 3$). Every member of set $C_k$ can be enumerated unambiguously either by joining two members of set $C_{k-1}$ or by extending a member in $C_{k-1}$.*

**Proof.** Let $A$ be a $m \times m$ suboptimal CAM in set $C_k$. We consider the following five cases according to the edge entries in $A$'s last row and second-to-last row:

- TypeA $M$ has three or more edge entries in the last row;
- TypeB $M$ has exactly two edge entries in the last row;
- TypeC $M$ has exactly one edge entry in the last row and more than one edge entries in the second-to-last row;
- TypeD $M$ has exactly one edge entry $e_{m,n}$ in the last row and one edge entry in the second-to-last row and $n \neq m-1$;
- TypeE $M$ has exactly one edge entry $e_{m,n}$ in the last row and one edge entry in the second-to-last row and $n = m-1$.

As shown in the appendix in [40], a TypeA suboptimal CAM can be produced by two suboptimal CAMs following join case1. Similarly, a TypeB suboptimal CAM corresponds to the join case3a, a TypeC suboptimal CAM corresponds to join case2, a TypeD suboptimal CAM corresponds to join case3b, and a TypeE suboptimal CAM corresponds to the extension operation. □

## 5.4 Mining Frequent Subgraphs

In the above discussions, we introduced a novel data structure (CAM tree) for organizing all connected subgraphs of a single connected undirected graph. This, however, can be easily extended to a set of graphs (connected or not), denoted as a graph database. A single CAM tree can be built for such a graph database. If we have such a tree built in advance (regardless of the required space and computational complexity), any traversal of the tree reveals the set of distinct subgraphs of the graph database. For each such subgraph, its support can be determined by a linear scan of the graph database, frequent ones can be reported subsequently. This method clearly suffers from the huge number of available subgraphs in a graph database and therefore is very unlikely scale to large graph databases.

1: $P \leftarrow \{\mathcal{M}(e) \mid e \text{ is an edge}, s(e) \geqslant \sigma\}$
2: $F \leftarrow$ FFSM-Explore($P, P$)
3: **return** $F$

ALGORITHM 8. FFSM($\mathcal{G}, \sigma$).

1: **for each** $X \in P$ **do**
2:    **if** ($X.isCAM$) **then**
3:      $F \leftarrow F \cup \{X\}, C \leftarrow \emptyset$
4:      **for each** $Y \in P$ **do**
5:        $C \leftarrow C \cup$ FFSM-Join($X, Y$)
6:      **end for**
7:      $C \leftarrow C \cup$ FFSM-Extension($X$)
8:      $C \leftarrow \{G \mid G \in C, G \text{ is frequent}, G \text{ is suboptimal}\}$
9:      $F \leftarrow F \cup$ FFSM-Explore($C, F$)
10:    **end if**
11: **end for**
12: **return** $F$

ALGORITHM 9. FFSM-explore($P, F$).

In the following pseudo code, we present an algorithm which takes advantage of the following simple fact: if a subgraph $G$ is not frequent (support of $G$ is less than a user posted threshold), none of its supergraphs is frequent. This suggest that we can stop building a branch of the tree as soon as we find that the current node does not have sufficient support in a graph database.

In the pseudo code of Algorithms 8 and 9, symbol $\mathcal{M}(G)$ denotes the CAM of the graph $G$. $X.isCAM$ is a Boolean variable indicate whether the matrix $X$ is the CAM of the graph it represents. $s(G)$ is the support value of a graph $G$ (or its CAM $\mathcal{M}(G)$).

## 5.5   Performance Comparison of FFSM

We have evaluated the performance of the FFSM algorithm with various types of graphs. The experimental study was carried out using a single processor of a 2 GHz Pentium PC with 2 GB memory, running RedHat Linux 7.3. The FFSM algorithm was implemented using the C++ programming language and compiled using g++ with O3 optimization. We compared our algorithm to gSpan, which is the state-of-the-art algorithm for graph mining. The gSpan executable, compiled in a similar environment, was provided by X. Yan and J. Han [108].

### 5.5.1 Chemical Compound Data Sets

**5.5.1.1 Data Sets.** We use three chemical compound data sets to evaluate the performance of the FFSM algorithm. The first data set is the PTE data set [90] that can be downloaded from http://web.comlab.ox.ac.uk/oucl/research/areas/machlearn/PTE/. This data set contains 337 chemical compounds each of which is modeled by an undirected graph. There are a total of 66 atom types and four bond types (single, double, triple, aromatic bond) in the data set. The atoms and bonds information are stored in two separate files and we follow exactly the same procedure described in [108] to construct the graph representations of chemical structures.

The next two data sets are derived from the DTP AIDS Antiviral Screen data set from National Cancer Institute. Chemicals in the data set are classified into three classes: confirmed active (CA), confirmed moderately active (CM) and confirmed inactive (CI) according to experimentally determined activities against HIV virus. There are a total of 423, 1083, and 42,115 chemicals in the three classes, respectively. For our own purposes, we formed two data sets consisting of all CA compounds and of all CM compounds and refer to them as DTP CA and DTP CM respectively. The DTP datasets can be downloaded from http://dtp.nci.nih.gov/docs/aids/aids_data.html.

**5.5.1.2 Performance Comparison.** We evaluate the performance of FFSM using various support thresholds. The result is summarized in Figs. 16 and 17. We find that FFSM has a maximal 7 fold speedup over gSpan on the DTP CM data

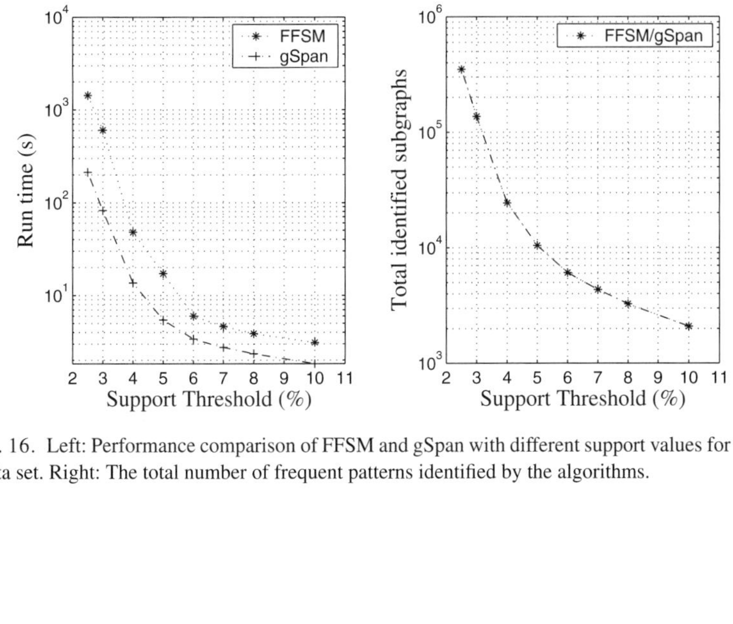


FIG. 16. Left: Performance comparison of FFSM and gSpan with different support values for the DTP CM data set. Right: The total number of frequent patterns identified by the algorithms.

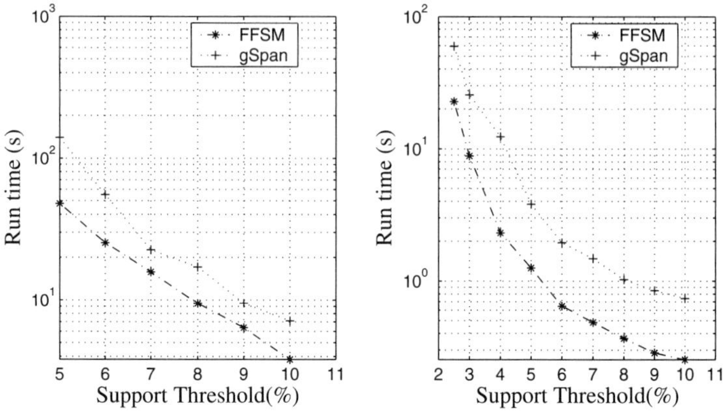


FIG. 17. Performance comparison of FFSM and gSpan with different support values for the DTP CA data set (left) and PTE (right).

set. For DTP CA and PTE data set, FFSM usually has a 2 to 3 fold speedup from gSpan.

### 5.5.2 Synthetic Data Sets

#### 5.5.2.1 Data Sets.

We used a graph generator offered by M. Kuramochi and G. Karypis [55] to generate synthetic graph databases with different characteristics. There are six parameters to control the set of synthetic graphs:

- $|D|$, total graph transactions generated,
- $|T|$, average graph size for the generated graphs, in terms of number of edges,
- $|L|$, the total number of the potentially frequent subgraphs,
- $|I|$, the size of the potentially frequent subgraphs, in terms of number of edges,
- $|V|$, total number of available labels for vertices, and
- $|E|$, total number of available labels for edges.

We use a single string to describe the parameter settings, e.g.

$$\text{“}D10kT20L200I9V4E4\text{”}$$

represents a synthetic graph database which contains a total of $|D| = 10\text{k}$ (10,000) graph transactions. Each graph on average contains $|T| = 20$ edges with up to $|V| = 4$ vertex labels and $|E| = 4$ edge labels. There are total of $|L| = 200$ potential frequent patterns in the database with average size $|I| = 9$.

*5.5.2.2 Performance Comparison.* In Fig. 18, we show how the FFSM algorithm scales with increasing support. The total number of identified frequent subgraphs is also given.

At the left part of Fig. 19, we show performance comparison between FFSM and gSpan with different average graph sizes (left) or different number of node/edge

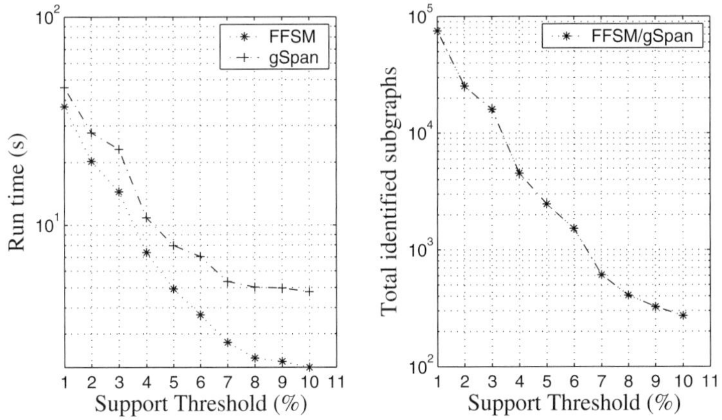


FIG. 18. FFSM and gSpan performance comparison under different support values. Parameters used: D10kT20I9L200E4V4.

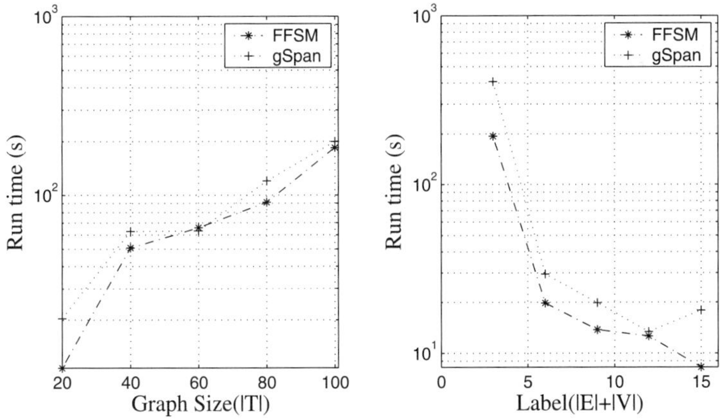


FIG. 19. FFSM and gSpan performance comparison under different graph sizes ($|T|$) ranging from 20 to 100 (left) or different total labels ($|V| + |E|$) ranging from 3 to 18 (right). The ratio of the $|V|$ to $|E|$ is fixed to $2:1$ for any given total number of labels. For example, if there are total 15 labels, we have 10 vertex labels and 5 edge labels. Other parameters setting: D10kI7L200E4V4 (left) and D10kT20I7L200 (right). The support threshold is fixed at 1% in both cases.

labels (right). For almost all circumstances, FFSM is faster than gSpan though the value of the speedup varies from data set to data set.

### 5.5.3 Mining Protein Contact Graphs

**5.5.3.1 Data Sets.** We collect a group of serine proteases from the Structure Classification of Proteins database [62] with SCOP id 50514 (eukaryotic serine proteases). For each protein, we map it to a graph, known as the "contact map" of the protein, in the following way:

- A node represents an amino acid residue in a protein, labeled by the residue identity.
- An edge connects two residues as long as the two residue are in "contact." Edges are not labeled.

In our representation, an amino acid residue is abstracted as two element tuple $(p, id)$ where $p$ is a point representing the $C_\alpha$ atom of the residue and *id* is the identity of the residue. Given a set of points in a 3D space (each point represents a $C_\alpha$ atom in a protein), we compute all possible Delaunay tessellations of the point set (in the format of point pairs), with the condition that each point may move away from its location by up to $\varepsilon > 0$ Å. The result is known as the almost-Delaunay edges for the point set [4]. We define that two residues are in *contact* if they are connected by an almost-Delaunay edges with $\varepsilon = 0.1$ Å and with length up to 8.5 Å. The same data set and the way we represent proteins as graphs are discussed in detail in [39] and the data set is downloadable from http://www.cs.unc.edu/~huan/FFSM.shtml.

**5.5.3.2 Performance Comparison.** The current gSpan is specifically developed for small graphs (with no more than 200 edges in any graphs in a data set).

TABLE I
PERFORMANCE COMPARISON BETWEEN FFSM AND FSG

| $\sigma$ | FFSM(s) | FSG(s) |
|---|---|---|
| 100 | 0.0433 | 0.433 |
| 95 | 0.2 | 1.633 |
| 90 | 0.537 | 3.6 |
| 85 | 2.243 | 14.1 |
| 80 | 11.64 | 61.433 |
| 75 | 104.58 | 700.217 |
| 70 | 1515.15 | 17643.667 |

$\sigma$ support threshold (percentage). Performance of FFSM and FSG are measured in seconds.

We compare FFSM with another graph mining algorithm FSG [55]. FFSM always an order of magnitude faster than FSG. Table I summarizes the results.

So far, we show the performance comparison between different graph mining algorithms. In the next section, we show how graph mining may be applied to protein structures to derive common structure patterns.

# 6. Applications

In this section we describe the use of the FFSM algorithm presented in Section 5 to identify family-specific structural motifs for a number of protein families.

## 6.1 Identifying Structure Motifs

### *6.1.1 Representing Protein Structure As a Labeled Graph*

We model protein structure as a labeled graph where a node represents an amino acid residue, labeled by the amino acid identity, and an edge joins a pair of amino acids, labeled by the Euclidian distance between two $C_\alpha$ atoms. To reduce complexity, we eliminate edges with distances larger than 12.5 Å [23,107]. We partition the one-dimensional distance space into bins in order to tolerate position uncertainty. The width of such bins is referred to as the *distance tolerance* and popular choices are 1 Å [61], 1.5 Å [9], and 2 Å [79]. We use 1.5 Å exclusively in our experimental study.

Given the graph representation, a recurring pattern may be composed of points with no possible physical and chemical interactions among them. This distributed set of points, though geometrically conserved, is hard to assign any biological interpretation to and is usually considered uninteresting by domain experts. To avoid spending computational resources on such patterns, we designate a subset of edges as *contacts* where a contact is an edge joining a pair of points (amino acids) that we believe may interact with each other (as described below). We require that each pattern is a connected component with respect to the contact edges. Similar strategies are used to derive structural patterns with high quality by others [59].

#### *6.1.1.1 Defining Contacts of Amino Acid Residues.*

There are many ways to define whether two amino acids are in contact or not. In our study, two points are in *contact* if they can be connected by a Delaunay edge [88] with point coordinates perturbation up to $\varepsilon \geqslant 0$. Such Delaunay edges (with point coordinate perturbations) are extensions of the commonly used Delaunay edges that are defined on static points [4]. We further restrict the contact edges to have distances no greater than some upper limit ranging from 6.5 to 8.5 Å; this value represents an upper limit on the distance over which there can be significant interaction between amino acid residues.

The graph model presented here is similar to that used by other groups [77,104]. The major difference is that in our representation, geometric constraints such as distances between amino acids are part of the graph representation in order to obtain geometrically conserved patterns rather than using a loosely constrained graph, to reduce the number of spurious patterns.

### *6.1.2 Graph Database Mining*

We apply the FFSM algorithm to find recurring patterns from protein structures. To enforce maximal geometric constraints, we only report fully connected subgraph (i.e. cliques) with all inter-residue distances specified. In graph matching, we require that matching nodes have the same label and matching edges have the same label and type (contact or not). Enforcing these, we guarantee that the structural patterns reported by our system have well defined composition of amino acid identity and three dimensional shape.

### *6.1.3 Statistical Significance of Motifs*

We derived an empirical evaluation of the statistical significance of structural patterns. We randomly sampled proteins from the protein structure space and applied our pattern mining algorithm to search for patterns. The experiments were repeated many times to estimate the probability that we observe at least one pattern using randomly selected proteins. The lower this probability is, the higher confidence we have about the significance of any structural patterns that are found among a group of proteins.

*6.1.3.1 Estimating Significance by Random Sampling.* In our experimental study, we randomly sampled 20 proteins (without replacement) from an non-redundant PDB list [102] and applied our algorithm to search for patterns with support $\geqslant 15$ and with pattern size of at least 4 amino acid residues. These parameters were set up to mimic a typical size and search of a SCOP family. We repeated the experiment 100,000 times, and did not find a single recurring geometric pattern. Limited by the available computational resources, we did not test the system further; however, we are convinced that the chance of observing a random spatial motif in our system is rather small.

*6.1.3.2 Estimating Significance using the Hyper-Geometric Distribution.* We estimate the statistical significance of a structural motif $m$ by computing the $P$-value associated with its occurrences in an existing protein family. To that end, we used the structures in the Culled PDB list [102], as a set of structures $M$ that sample the entire protein structure population (all possible protein structures, crystallized or not).

Our null hypothesis $H_0$ is that the pattern $m$ randomly occurs in the protein structure population. Given an existing protein family $F \subset M$, a set of proteins $S \subseteq M$ where $m$ occurs, the probability of observing a set of at least $k$ proteins in $F$ contain $m$ under the null hypothesis is given by the following hyper-geometric distribution [9]:

$$P\text{-}value = 1 - \sum_{i=0}^{k-1} \frac{\binom{|F|}{i}\binom{|M|-|F|}{|T|-i}}{\binom{|M|}{|T|}} \tag{2}$$

where $|X|$ is the cardinality of a set $X$. For example, if a pattern $m$ occurs in every member of a family $F$ and never outside $F$ (i.e. $F = S$) for a large family $F$, we estimate that this pattern is statistically specifically associated with the family; the statistical significance of the case is measured by a $P$-*value* close to zero.

We adopt the Bonferroni correction for multiple independent hypotheses [82]: $0.001/|C|$, where $|C|$ is the set of categories. The correction is used as the threshold for significance of the $P$-value of an individual test. Since the total number of SCOP families is 2327, a significant $P$-value is $\leqslant 10^{-7}$.

## 6.2 Case Studies

As a proof-of-concept, we applied the method to identify family-specific motifs, i.e. structural patterns that occur frequently in a family and rarely outside it. In Table II, a group of four SCOP families are listed which have more than twenty members. This group of families has been well studied in literature and hence comparison of our results with experimental data is feasible.

### *6.2.1 Eukaryotic Serine Proteases*

The structural patterns identified from the ESP family were documented at the top part of Table II. The data indicated that the patterns we found are highly specific to the ESP family, measured by $P$-*value* $\leqslant 10^{-82}$. We further investigated the spatial distribution of the residues covered by those patterns, by plotting all residues covered by at least one pattern in the structure of a trypsin: 1HJ9, shown in Fig. 20. Interestingly, as illustrated by this figure, we found that all these residues are confined to the vicinity of the catalytic triad of 1HJ9, namely: HIS57-ASP102-SER195, confirming a known fact that the geometry of the catalytic triad and its spatially adjacent residues are rigid, which is probably responsible for functional specificity of the enzyme.

TABLE II
STRUCTURAL PATTERNS IDENTIFIED IN THE EUKARYOTIC SERINE PROTEASE, PAPAIN-LIKE CYSTEINE PROTEASE, AND NUCLEAR BINDING DOMAINS

| Pattern | Composition | $\kappa$ | $\delta$ | $-\log(P)$ | Pattern | Composition | $\kappa$ | $\delta$ | $-\log(P)$ |
|---|---|---|---|---|---|---|---|---|---|
| Eukaryotic Serine Protease (ID: 50514) $N$: 56 $\sigma$: 48/56, $T$: 31.5 | | | | | | | | | |
| 1 | DHAC | 54 | 13 | 100 | 20 | AGGG | 50 | 58 | 85 |
| 2 | ACGG | 52 | 9 | 100 | 21 | ACGAG | 49 | 4 | 100 |
| 3 | DHSC | 52 | 10 | 100 | 22 | SCGA | 49 | 6 | 100 |
| 4 | DHSA | 52 | 10 | 100 | 23 | DACS | 49 | 7 | 100 |
| 5 | DSAC | 52 | 12 | 100 | 24 | DGGS | 49 | 8 | 100 |
| 6 | DGGG | 52 | 23 | 100 | 25 | SACG | 49 | 10 | 98 |
| 7 | DHSAC | 51 | 9 | 100 | 26 | DSGC | 49 | 15 | 98 |
| 8 | SAGC | 51 | 11 | 100 | 27 | DASC | 49 | 20 | 92 |
| 9 | DACG | 51 | 14 | 100 | 28 | SAGG | 49 | 31 | 90 |
| 10 | HSAC | 51 | 14 | 100 | 29 | DGGL | 49 | 53 | 83 |
| 11 | DHAA | 51 | 18 | 100 | 30 | DSAGC | 48 | 9 | 99 |
| 12 | DAAC | 51 | 32 | 99 | 31 | DSSC | 48 | 12 | 97 |
| 13 | DHAAC | 50 | 5 | 100 | 32 | SCSG | 48 | 19 | 93 |
| 14 | DHAC | 50 | 6 | 100 | 33 | AGAG | 48 | 19 | 93 |
| 15 | HACA | 50 | 8 | 100 | 34 | SAGG | 48 | 23 | 88 |
| 16 | ACGA | 50 | 11 | 100 | 35 | DSGS | 48 | 23 | 94 |
| 17 | DSAG | 50 | 16 | 100 | 36 | DAAG | 48 | 27 | 89 |
| 18 | SGGC | 50 | 17 | 100 | 37 | DASG | 48 | 32 | 87 |
| 19 | AGAG | 50 | 27 | 95 | 38 | GGGG | 48 | 71 | 76 |
| Papain-like cysteine protease (ID: 54002) $N$: 24, $\sigma$: 18/24, $T$: 18.4 | | | | | | | | | |
| 1 | HCQS | 18 | 2 | 34 | 4 | WGNS | 18 | 4 | 44 |
| 2 | HCQG | 18 | 3 | 34 | 5 | WGSG | 18 | 5 | 43 |
| 3 | WWGS | 18 | 3 | 44 | | | | | |
| Nuclear receptor ligand-binding domain (ID: 48509) $N$: 23, $\sigma$: 17/23, $T$: 15.3 | | | | | | | | | |
| 1 | FQLL | 20 | 21 | 43 | 3 | DLQF | 17 | 8 | 39 |
| 2 | DLQF | 18 | 7 | 42 | 4 | LQLL | 17 | 40 | 31 |
| FAD/NAD-linked reductase (ID: 51943) $N$ : 20 $\sigma$: 15/20, $T$: 90.0 | | | | | | | | | |
| 1 | AGGG | 17 | 34 | 34 | 2 | AGGA | 17 | 91 | 27 |

$N$: Total number of structures included in the data set. $\sigma$: The support threshold used to obtain recurring structural patterns, $T$: processing time (in unit of seconds). Composition: the sequence of one-letter residue codes for the residue composition of the pattern, $\kappa$: the actual support value of a pattern in the family, $\delta$, the background frequency of the pattern, and $P$: the functional enrichment defined by Eq. (2). The packing patterns were sorted first by their support values in descending order, and then by their background frequencies in ascending order. The two patterns from FAD/NAD-linked reductase show functional enrichment in NAD(P)-binding Rossman fold protein with $-\log(P)$ value 8 and 6, respectively. This is further discussed in Section 6.2.

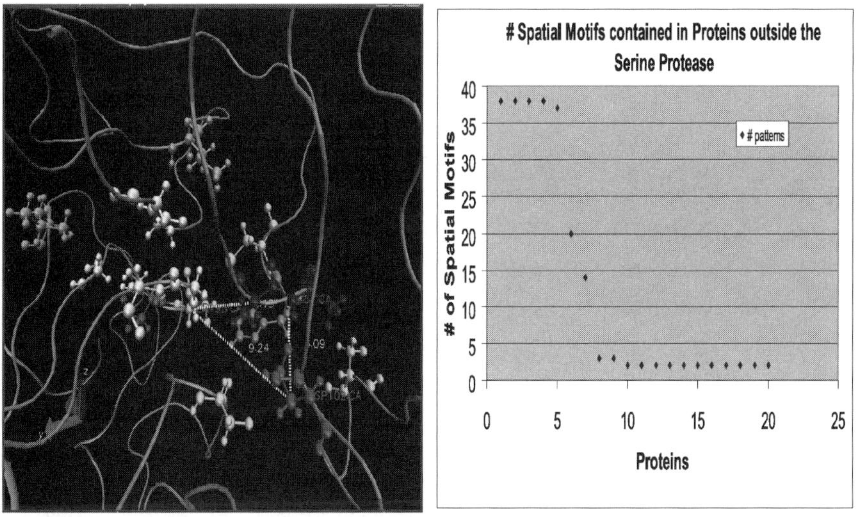


FIG. 20. Left: Spatial distribution of residues found in 38 common structural patterns within protein 1HJ9. The residues of catalytic triad, HIS57-ASP102-SER195, are connected by white dotted lines. Right: Instances of ESP structural patterns occurring in proteins outside the ESP data set. The top 7 proteins, where more than ten structural patterns occur, were found to be eukaryotic serine proteases not annotated in SCOP.

We found that there are five patterns that occur significantly ($P$-*value* $< 10^{-7}$) in another SCOP family: Prokaryotic Serine Protease (details not shown). This is not surprising since prokaryotic and eukaryotic serine proteases are similar at both structural and functional levels and they share the same SCOP superfamily classification. None of the patterns had significant presence outside these two families.

The SCOP classification (v1.65) used in this chapter was released in December 2003. The submissions to PDB since that time offer a good test of our method to see if we would annotate any new submissions as ESPs. We searched all new submissions for occurrences of the 32 structural patterns we had extracted from the ESP family and found seven proteins: 1pq7a, 1os8a, 1op0a, 1p57b, 1s83a, 1ssxa, and 1md8a, that contain quite a few patterns, as shown in Fig. 20. All of these proteins are confirmed to be recently published eukaryotic serine proteases as indicated by the headers in corresponding PDB entries.

Finally, we observed that if we randomly sample two proteins from the ESP family and search for common structural patterns, we obtain an average of 2300 patterns per experiment for one thousand runs. Such patterns are characterized by poor statistical significance and are not specific to known functional sites in the ESP. If we require a structural pattern to appear in at least 24 of a 31 randomly selected ESP proteins and repeat the same experiment, we obtain an average of 65 patterns per experiment with much improved statistical significance. This experiment demonstrates that obtaining structural patterns from a group of proteins helps improve the quality of the result, as observed by [104].

### *6.2.2 Papain-Like Cysteine Protease and Nuclear Binding Domain*

We applied our approach to two additional SCOP families: Papain-Like Cysteine Protease (PCP, ID: 54002) and Nuclear Receptor Ligand-Binding Domain (NB, ID: 48509). The results are documented in the middle part of Table II.

For the PCP family, we have identified five structural patterns which covered the catalytic CYC-HIS dyad and nearby residues ASN and SER which are known to interact with the dyad [14], as shown in Fig. 21. For the NB family, we identified four patterns[3] which map to the cofactor binding sites [103], shown in the same figure. In addition, four members missed by SCOP: 1srv, 1khq, and 1o0e were identified for

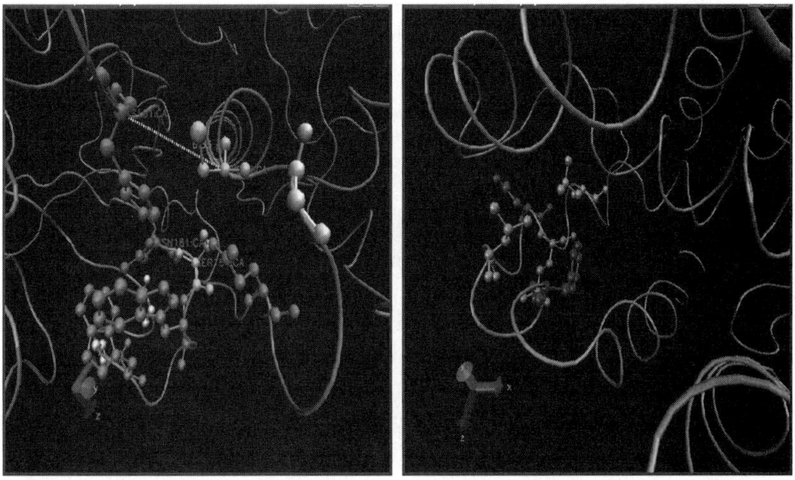

FIG. 21. Left: Residues included in the patterns from PCP family in protein 1CQD. The residues in catalytic dyad CYS27-HIS161 are connected by a white dotted line and two important surrounding residues ASN181 and SER182 are labeled. Right: Residues included in patterns from the NB family in protein 1OVL. The labeled residue GLN 435 has direct interaction with the cofactor of the protein.

[3] Structural patterns 2 and 3 have the same residue composition but they have different residue contact patterns and therefore are regarded as two patterns. They do not map to the same set of residues.

the PCP family and six members 1sj0, 1rkg, 1osh, 1nq7, 1pq9, 1nrl were identified for the NB family.

### 6.2.3 FAD/NAD Binding Proteins

In the SCOP database, there are two superfamilies of NADPH binding proteins, the FAD/NAD(P)-binding domains and the NAD(P)-binding Rossmann-fold domains, which share no sequence or fold similarity. This presents a challenging test case for our system to check whether we are able to find patterns with biological significance across the two groups.

We applied the FFSM to the largest family in the SCOP FAD/NAD(P)-binding domain: FAD/NAD-linked reductases (SCOPID: 51943). With support threshold 15/20, we obtained two recurring structural patterns from the family, and both showed strong statistical significance in the NAD(P)-binding Rossmann-fold superfamily as shown in bottom part of Table II.

In Fig. 22, we show a pattern that is statistically enriched in both families; it has conserved geometry and is interacting with the NADPH molecule in two proteins belonging to the two families. Notice that we do not include any information from NADPH molecule during our search, and we identified this pattern due to its strong structural conservation among proteins in a SCOP superfamily. The two proteins have only 16% sequence similarity and adopt different folds (DALI z-score 4.5). The result suggest that significant common features can be inferred from proteins with no apparent sequence and fold similarity.

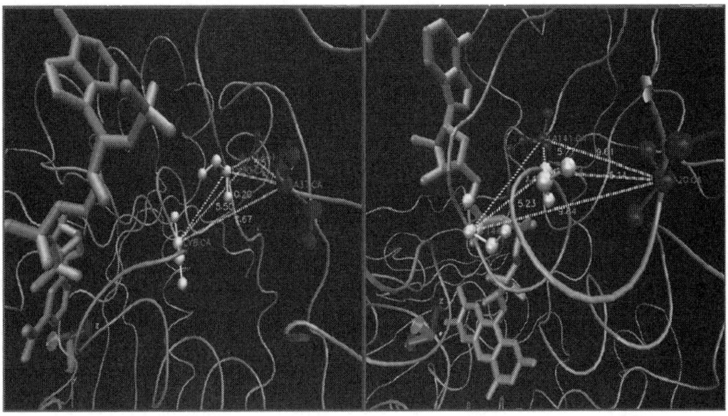

FIG. 22. The pattern appears in two proteins 1LVL (belongs to the FAD/NAD-linked reductase family without Rossman fold) and 1JAY (belongs to the 6-phosphogluconate dehydrogenase-like, N-terminal domain family with Rossman fold) with conserved geometry.

# 7. Conclusions and Future Directions

## 7.1 Conclusions

Structure comparison of proteins is a major bioinformatics research topic with various biological applications including structure classification, function annotation, functional site identification, protein design, and protein engineering.

In studying structure comparison, new computational techniques have been identified and some of these techniques are applicable to domains outside bioinformatics.

In the future, we expect to witness the successes of structure comparison in both algorithmic improvements and new applications. Our optimistic view is based on the following two factors:

- Computers are becoming more powerful.
- The recently started proteomics research efforts will rapidly produce a large volume of structure and structure-related data.

Below, we review plausible future directions that we think are important for structure comparison.

## 7.2 Future Directions

Here we review the possible future direction of structure comparison in two subdirections: (1) identifying applications in the biological/biomedical domain, (2) developing new computational techniques.

### *7.2.1 Future Applications of Structural Comparison*

Three future applications of structure comparison are discussed.

*7.2.1.1 Understanding Dynamic Protein Structures.* There is no question that understanding the dynamics of proteins structures offers great information for biological research. For example, enormous insights can be gained if we can directly observe the process of protein folding using experimental techniques [106].

Currently, the Nuclear Magnetic Resonance spectroscopy (NMR) is the major experimental technique to measures a protein's native structure in a solvent environment. NMR determines the average protein structure by measuring the distances among protons and specially labeled carbon and nitrogen atoms [72]. NMR has been applied to obtain protein structure, protein–protein complexes, and protein-ligand complexes which account for approximately 10% of the overall structures in PDB.

There are also several specialized methods that have been developed to report the dynamic structure of proteins in specialized biological processes such as protein folding and domain movement in multi-domain proteins [106,44].

Protein dynamics brings significant opportunities to the current structure comparison method because of the rich information stored in the trajectory of protein structures. We envision two types of comparisons: *intra-structure comparison*, which analyzes the protein structure motion and detects important features for a single protein, and *inter-structure comparison*, which compares dynamics data for multiple protein structures and identifies common features.

Though techniques to collect structure dynamics data are in their infancy, we believe that such techniques, as well as computational methods for molecular dynamics, will mature rapidly and be successful in helping domain experts gain useful insights into various biological processes.

*7.2.1.2 Predicting Protein–Protein Interaction.* Protein–protein interaction refers to the ability of proteins to form complexes. Protein–protein interaction data is usually formed as an undirected graph whose nodes are proteins and edges connect two protein if the proteins can form a stable/transient complex [1].

Protein–protein interaction data bring new challenges for structure comparison. In order to elucidate common structural motifs involved in protein–protein interaction and finally to predict the interaction computationally, we need to compare multiple protein complexes rather than single structures. We also need to be able to define the boundary of the interaction, based on the structure of the complexes.

*7.2.1.3 Predicting Protein Subcellular Localization.* Knowledge about where a protein may be located in a cell is of paramount importance for biological research and pharmaceutical companies. For example, an outer membrane protein is one that is transported to the outer membrane after its synthesis. Knowing a protein is an outer membrane protein simplifies the drug design process since outer membrane proteins can be accessed easily by drugs [25]. As another example, knowing the localization of a protein offers important information for assembling metabolic pathways [80].

Predicting the subcellular localization is one of the active research topics in bioinformatics research [25,64,80]. Protein subcellular localization has been investigated in two ways. The first approach relies on sequence motifs as descriptors to assign subcellular localization for protein sequences. This approach is based on the observation that continuous stretches of amino acid residues may encode the signal that guides a protein to a specific location. The second approach utilizes the amino acid composition of proteins to predict the possible localization. This technique is motivated by the observation that residue composition of a protein highly correlates with the localization of the proteins [64].

Recently there is evidence showing that protein structure is also important for predicting the related subcellular localization. For example, the β-barrel is known as a signature for outer membrane proteins. This observation has resulted in significant improvement of the prediction accuracy, as reported in [25]. As another example, the FKBP-type peptidyl prolyl cis-trans isomerase (PPIase) is a large group of proteins with 4 possible subcellular localizations. As reported by Himukai et al., the subcellular localization of these proteins is correlated with the conserved structure domain around the active sites of the protein [33]. As shown in this preliminary study, incorporating structure comparison can improve the accuracy of the protein subcellular prediction.

### *7.2.2 New Computational Techniques in Structure Comparison*

Facing the challenges of handling large and complex structure data, we believe new computational techniques will be invented for structure comparison. The possible directions are

(1) developing approximate matching in pattern discovery,
(2) inventing efficient index structures to speed up pattern matching in a structure database,
(3) devising new data visualization techniques for structure comparison,
(4) integrating data from different sources for structure comparison, and
(5) statistical structure comparison.

We conclude this chapter with a brief description of statistical structure comparison.

*7.2.2.1 Comparison Based on Statistical Analysis.* As shown in sequence analysis methods, statistical models such as Hidden Markov Model (HMM) are useful for recognizing sequence similarity that is not easily detectable by straightforward alignment methods. Given the success of statistical tools in sequence comparison, it is natural to consider extending those tools (and possibly to introduce new ones) for structure comparison of proteins.

Here we review a recently developed algorithm 3dHMM [2] whose goal is to build a rigorous description of protein 3D structure family using HMM. In outline, 3dHMM takes a group of aligned 3D structure and a query structure as inputs and computes the best alignment of the query structure to the structure group in the following way:

(1) estimating the 3D Gaussian for each position (the $C_\alpha$ atom in each amino acid residue) of the aligned structures,
(2) estimating the deletion probability for each position using the aligned structures (assuming the alignment is not gap-free),
(3) using a modified Viterbi algorithm [74] to find the best alignment of the query structure to the HMM model, and
(4) using the Forward algorithm [74] to calculate the probability that the query structure was generated from the HMM model.

The 3dHMM method has been applied to several protein families and has achieved better results in terms of identifying structure homology than the traditional RMSD calculation.

There are many other types of statistical analysis tools, such as Markov Random Field [7], Hidden Markov Random Field, and Bayesian Networks [43]. It will be interesting to see their applicability in protein structure comparison.

## REFERENCES

[1] Aebersold R., Mann M., "Mass spectrometry-based proteomics", *Nature* **422** (March 13, 2003) 198–207.
[2] Alexandrov V., Gerstein M., "Using 3d hidden Markov models that explicitly represent spatial coordinates to model and compare protein structures", *BMC Bioinformatics* **9** (5) (2004).
[3] Artymiuk P.J., Poirrette A.R., Grindley H.M., Rice D.W., Willett P., "A graph-theoretic approach to the identification of three-dimensional patterns of amino acid side-chains in protein structures", *J. Mol. Biol.* **243** (1994) 327–344.
[4] Bandyopadhyay D., Snoeyink J., "Almost-Delaunay simplices: Nearest neighbor relations for imprecise points", in: *ACM–SIAM Symposium on Distributed Algorithms*, 2004, pp. 403–412.
[5] Barker J.A., Thornton J.M., "An algorithm for constraint-based structural template matching: Application to 3d templates with statistical analysis", *Bioinformatics* **19** (13) (2003) 1644–1649.
[6] Berman H.M., Westbrook J., Feng Z., Gilliland G., Bhat T.N., Weissig H., Shindyalov I.N., Bourne P.E., "The protein data bank", *Nucl. Acids Res.* **28** (2000) 235–242.
[7] Besag J., "Spatial interaction and the statistical analysis of lattice systems", *J. Royal Statist. Soc. B* **36** (1974) 192–236.
[8] Borgelt C., Berhold M.R., "Mining molecular fragments: Finding relevant substructures of molecules", in: *Proc. International Conference on Data Mining'02*, 2002, pp. 51–58.
[9] Bradley P., Kim P.S., Berger B., "TRILOGY: Discovery of sequence-structure patterns across diverse proteins", *Proc. Natl. Acad. Sci.* **99** (13) (June 2002) 8500–8505.
[10] Branden C., Tooze J., *Introduction to Protein Structure*, Garland Publishing, New York, 1991.

[11] Burdick D., Calimlim M., Gehrke J., "Mafia: A maximal frequent itemset algorithm for transactional databases", in: *ICDE*, 2001.

[12] Cammer S.A., Carter C.W., Tropsha A., "Identification of sequence-specific tertiary packing motifs in protein structures using Delaunay tessellation", *Lecture Notes in Comput. Sci. Engrg.* **24** (2002) 477–494.

[13] Chance M.R., Bresnick A.R., Burley S.K., Jiang J.S., Lima C.D., Sali A., Almo S.C., Bonanno J.B., Buglino J.A., Boulton S., Chen H., Eswar N., He G., Huang R., Ilyin V., McMahan L., Pieper U., Ray S., Vidal M., Wang L.K., "Structural genomics: A pipeline for providing structures for the biologist", *Protein Sci.* **11** (2002) 723–738.

[14] Choi K.H., Laursen R.A., Allen K.N., "The 2.1 angstrom structure of a cysteine protease with proline specificity from ginger rhizome, zingiber officinale", *Biochemistry* **38** (36) (September 7, 1999) 11624–11633.

[15] Cordes M.H., Sauer R.T., "Tolerance of a protein to multiple polar-to-hydrophobic surface substitutions", *Protein Sci.* **8** (2) (1999) 318–325.

[16] Dehaspe L., Toivonen H., King R.D., "Finding frequent substructures in chemical compounds", in: *4th International Conference on Knowledge Discovery and Data Mining*, 1998, pp. 30–36.

[17] Deutsch A., Fernandez M.F., Suciu D., "Storing semistructured data with STORED", in: *SIGMOD*, 1999, pp. 431–442.

[18] D'haeseleer P., Liang S., Somogyi R., "Genetic network inference: From co-expression clustering to reverse engineering", *Bioinformatics* **16** (8) (2000) 707–726.

[19] Dodson G., Wlodawer A., "Catalytic triads and their relatives", *Trends Biochem. Sci.* **23** (9) (September 1998) 347–352.

[20] Dokholyan N.V., Buldyrev S.V., Stanley H.E., Shakhnovich E.I., "Identifying the protein folding nucleus using molecular dynamics", *J. Mol. Biol.* **296** (2000) 1183–1188.

[21] Eidhammer I., Jonassen I., Taylor W.R., *Protein Bioinformatics: An Algorithmic Approach to Sequence and Structure Analysis*, John Wiley & Sons, Ltd, New York, 2004.

[22] Fersht A., *Structure and Mechanism in Protein Science*, W.H. Freeman Co., New York, 1999.

[23] Fischer D., Wolfson H., Lin S.L., Nussinov R., "Three-dimensional, sequence order-independent structural comparison of a serine protease against the crystallographic database reveals active site similarities: Potential implication to evolution and to protein folding", *Protein Sci.* **3** (1994) 769–778.

[24] Gardiner E.J., Artymiuk P.J., Willett P., "Clique-detection algorithms for matching three-dimensional molecular structures", *J. Mol. Graph. Model.* **15** (1997) 245–253.

[25] Gardy J.L., Spencer C., Wang K., Ester M., Tusnady G.E., Simon I., Hua S., deFays K., Lambert C., Nakai K., Brinkman F.S., "Psort-b: Improving protein subcellular localization prediction for gram-negative bacteria", *Nucleic Acids Res.* **31** (13) (2003) 3613–3617.

[26] George R.A., Spriggs R.V., Bartlett G.J., Gutteridge A., MacArthur M.W., Porter C.T., Al-Lazikani B., Thornton J.M., Swindells M.B., "Effective function annotation through residue conservation", *Proc. Natl. Acad. Sci.* **102** (2005) 12299–12304.

[27] George R.A., Spriggs R.V., Thornton J.M., Al-Lazikani B., Swindells M.B., "Scopec: A database of protein catalytic domains Supp", *Bioinformatics* (Suppl. 1) (2004) I130–I136.

[28] Gerlt J.A., Babbitt P.C., "Divergent evolution of enzymatic function: Mechanistically diverse superfamilies and functionally distinct suprafamilies", *Annu. Rev. Biochem.* **70** (2001) 20946.

[29] Goldman R., Widom J., "Dataguides: Enabling query formulation and optimization in semistructured databases", in: *VLDB'97*, 1997.

[30] Grindley H.M., Artymiuk P.J., Rice D.W., Willett P., "Identification of tertiary structure resemblance in proteins using a maximal common subgraph isomorphism algorithm", *J. Mol. Biol.* **229** (1993) 707–721.

[31] Hegyi H., Gerstein M., "The relationship between protein structure and function: A comprehensive survey with application to the yeast genome", *J. Mol. Biol.* **288** (1999) 147–164.

[32] Hermjakob H., Montecchi-Palazzi L., Lewington C., Mudali S., Kerrien S., Orchard S., Vingron M., Roechert B., Roepstorff P., Valencia A., Margalit H., Armstrong J., Bairoch A., Cesareni G., Sherman D., Apweiler R., "Intact—an open source molecular interaction database", *Nucl. Acids Res.* **32** (2004) D452–D455.

[33] Himukai R., Kuzuhara T., Horikoshi M., "Relationship between the subcellular localization and structures of catalytic domains of fkbp-type ppiases", *J. Biochem. (Tokyo)* **126** (5) (1999) 879–888.

[34] Holder L.B., Cook D.J., Djoko S., "Substructures discovery in the subdue system", in: *Proc. AAAI'94 Workshop Knowledge Discovery in Databases*, 1994, pp. 169–180.

[35] Holm L., Sander C., "Mapping the protein universe", *Science* **273** (1996) 595–602.

[36] Horn B.K.P., "Closed-form solution of absolute orientation using unit quaternions", *J. Opt. Soc. Amer. A: Opt. Image Sci. Vision* **4** (4) (1987) 629–642.

[37] Hu J., Shen X., Shao Y., Bystroff C., Zaki M.J., "Mining protein contact maps", in: *2nd BIOKDD Workshop on Data Mining in Bioinformatics*, 2002.

[38] Huan J., Bandyopadhyay D., Wang W., Snoeyink J., Prins J., Tropsha A., "Comparing graph representations of protein structure for mining family-specific residue-based packing motifs", *J. Comput. Biol.* **12** (6) (2005) 657–671.

[39] Huan J., Wang W., Bandyopadhyay D., Snoeyink J., Prins J., Tropsha A., "Mining protein family specific residue packing patterns from protein structure graphs", in: *Proceedings of the 8th Annual International Conference on Research in Computational Molecular Biology, RECOMB*, 2004, pp. 308–315.

[40] Huan J., Wang W., Prins J., "Efficient mining of frequent subgraph in the presence of isomorphism", in: *Proceedings of the 3rd IEEE International Conference on Data Mining, ICDM*, 2003, pp. 549–552.

[41] Huan J., Wang W., Prins J., Yang J., "SPIN: Mining maximal frequent subgraphs from graph databases", in: *Proceedings of the 10th ACM SIGKDD International Conference on Knowledge Discovery and Data Mining*, 2004, pp. 581–586.

[42] Huan J., Wang W., Washington A., Prins J., Shah R., Tropsha A., "Accurate classification of protein structural families based on coherent subgraph analysis", in: *Proceedings of the Pacific Symposium on Biocomputing, PSB*, 2004, pp. 411–422.

[43] Huang C., Darwiche A., "Inference in belief networks: A procedural guide", *Internat. J. Approx. Reasoning* **15** (3) (1996) 225–263.

[44] Hubbell W.L., Cafiso D.S., Altenbach C., "Identifying conformational changes with site-directed spin labeling", *Natl. Struct. Biol.* **7** (9) (2000) 735–739.

[45] Inokuchi A., Washio T., Motoda H., "An apriori-based algorithm for mining frequent substructures from graph data", in: *PKDD'00*, 2000, pp. 13–23.

[46] Jonassen I., "Efficient discovery of conserved patterns using a pattern graph", *Comput. Appl. Biosci.* **13** (5) (1997) 509–522.

[47] Jonassen I., Eidhammer I., Conklin D., Taylor W.R., "Structure motif discovery and mining the PDB", *Bioinformatics* **18** (2002) 362–367.

[48] Jonassen I., Eidhammer I., Taylor W.R., "Discovery of local packing motifs in protein structures", *Proteins* **34** (1999) 206–219.

[49] Jones S., Thornton J.M., "Searching for functional sites in protein structures", *Curr. Opin. Chem. Biol.* **8** (2004) 3–7.

[50] Kabsch W.A., "Discussion of solution for best rotation of two vectors", *Acta Crystallogr. A* **34** (1978) 827–828.

[51] Kelley L.A., MacCallum R.M., Sternberg M.J., "Enhanced genome annotation using structural profiles in the program 3d-pssm", *J. Mol. Biol.* **299** (2) (2000) 499–520.

[52] Kendrew J.C., Bodo G., Dintzis H.M., Parrish R.G., Wyckoff H., Phillips D.C., "A three-dimensional model of the myoglobin molecule obtained by X-ray analysis", *Nature* **181** (1958) 662–666.

[53] Koonin E.V., Wolf Y.I., Karev G.P. (Eds.), *Power Laws, Scale-Free Networks and Genome Biology*, Springer-Verlag, Berlin, 2004.

[54] Krishnamoorthy B., Tropsha A., "Development of a four-body statistical pseudo-potential to discriminate native from non-native protein conformations", *Bioinformatics* **19** (12) (2003) 1540–1548.

[55] Kuramochi M., Karypis G., "Frequent subgraph discovery", in: *Proc. International Conference on Data Mining'01*, 2001, pp. 313–320.

[56] Leibowitz N., Fligelman Z.Y., Nussinov R., Wolfson H.J., "Automated multiple structure alignment and detection of a common substructural motif", *Proteins* **43** (3) (May 2001) 235–245.

[57] Lupasa A.N., Pontingb C.P., Russell R.B., "On the evolution of protein folds: Are similar motifs in different protein folds the result of convergence, insertion, or relics of an ancient peptide world?", *J. Struct. Biol.* **134** (2001) 191–203.

[58] Matthews B.W., "Structural and genetic analysis of the folding and function of t4 lysozyme", *FASEB J.* **10** (1996) 35–41.

[59] Coatney M., Parthasarathy S., "Motifminer: A toolkit for mining common substructures in molecular data", *Knowledge Inform. Syst. J.* (2003).

[60] Meng E.C., Polacco B.J., Babbitt P.C., "Superfamily active site templates", *Proteins* **55** (4) (2004) 962–976.

[61] Milik M., Szalma S., Olszewski K.A., "Common structural cliques: A tool for protein structure and function analysis", *Protein Engrg.* **16** (8) (2003) 543–552.

[62] Murzin A.G., Brenner S.E., Hubbard T., Chothia C., "SCOP: A structural classification of proteins database for the investigation of sequences and structures", *J. Mol. Biol.* **247** (1995) 536–540.

[63] Nagano N., Orengo C.A., Thornton J.M., "One fold with many functions: The evolutionary relationships between TIM barrel families based on their sequences, structures and functions", *J. Mol. Biol.* **321** (2002) 741–765.
[64] Nakashima H., Nishikawa K., "Discrimination of intracellular and extracellular proteins using amino acid composition and residue-pair frequencies", *J. Mol. Biol.* **238** (1) (1994) 54–61.
[65] Neidhart D.J., Kenyon G.L., Gerlt J.A., Petsko G.A., "Mandelate racemase and muconate lactonizing enzyme are mechanistically distinct and structurally homologous", *Nature* **347** (1990) 692–694.
[66] Nijssen S., Kok J.N., "A quickstart in frequent structure mining can make a difference", in: *Proceedings of the 10th ACM SIGKDD International Conference on Knowledge Discovery and Data Mining*, 2004, pp. 647–652.
[67] Nussinov R., Wolfson H.J., "Efficient detection of three-dimensional structural motifs in biological macromolecules by computer vision techniques", *Proc. Natl. Acad. Sci.* **88** (1991) 10495–10499.
[68] Orengo C.A., Michie A.D., Jones S., Jones D.T., Swindells M.B., Thornton J.M., "CATH—a hierarchic classification of protein domain structures", *Structure* **5** (8) (1997) 1093–1108.
[69] Orgengo C., Jones D., Thornton J., *Bioinformatics: Genes, Proteins, and Computers*, BIOS Scientific Publishers Ltd, 2003.
[70] Overbeek R., Fonstein M., D'Souza M., Pusch G.D., Maltsev N., "The use of gene clusters to infer functional coupling", *Proc. Natl. Acad. Sci.* **96** (6) (1999) 2896–2901.
[71] Pennec X., Ayache N., "A geometric algorithm to find small but highly similar 3d substructures in proteins", *Bioinformatics* **14** (6) (1998) 516–522.
[72] Petsko G.A., Ringe D., *Protein Structure and Function*, New Science Press Ltd, Middlesec House, 34–42 Cleveland Street, London W1P 6LB, UK, 2004.
[73] Phizicky E., Bastiaens P.I.H., Zhu H., Snyder M., Fields S., "Protein analysis on a proteomic scale", *Nature* **422** (March 13, 2003) 208–215.
[74] Rabiner L.R., Juang B.H., "An introduction to hidden Markov models", *IEEE ASSP Magazine* (January 1986) 4–15.
[75] Raghavan S., Garcia-Molina H., "Representing web graphs", in: *Proceedings of the IEEE International Conference on Data Engineering*, 2003.
[76] Richardson J.S., "Class-directed structure determination: Foundation for a protein structure initiative", *Adv. Protein Chem.* **34** (1981) 167–339.
[77] Russell R.B., "Detection of protein three-dimensional side-chain patterns: New examples of convergent evolution", *J. Mol. Biol.* **279** (1998) 1211–1227.
[78] Sander C., Schneider R., "Database of homology-derived protein structures and the structural meaning of sequence alignment", *Proteins* **9** (1) (1991) 56–68.
[79] Schmitt S., Kuhn D., Klebe G., "A new method to detect related function among proteins independent of sequence and fold homology", *J. Mol. Biol.* **323** (2) (2002) 387–406.
[80] Schneider G., Fechner U., "Advances in the prediction of protein targeting signals", *Proteomics* **4** (6) (June 2004) 1571–1580.
[81] Schwehm J.M., Kristyanne E.S., Biggers C.C., Stites W.E., "Stability effects of increasing the hydrophobicity of solvent-exposed side chains in staphylococcal nuclease", *Biochemistry* **37** (19) (1998) 6939–6948.

[82] Shaffer J.P., "Multiple hypothesis testing", *Annu. Rev. Psychol.* (1995) 561–584.
[83] Sharan R., Suthram S., Kelley R.M., Kuhn T., McCuine S., Uetz P., Sittler T., Karp R.M., Ideker T., "Conserved patterns of protein interaction in multiple species", *Proc. Natl. Acad. Sci.* **102** (6) (2005) 1974–1979.
[84] Sharan R., Ideker T., Kelley B.P., Shamir R., Karp R.M., "Identification of protein complexes by comparative analysis of yeast and bacterial protein interaction data", in: *ACM RECOMB*, 2004, pp. 282–289.
[85] Shatsky M., Shulman-Peleg A., Nussinov R., Wolfson H.J., "Recognition of binding patterns common to a set of protein structures, in: *RECOMB*, 2005, submitted for publication.
[86] Shearer K., Bunks H., Venkatesh S., "Video indexing and similarity retrieval by largest common subgraph detection using decision trees", *Pattern Recogn.* **34** (5) (2001) 1075–1091.
[87] Shulman-Peleg A., Nussinov R., Wolfson H.J., "Recognition of functional sites in protein structures", *J. Mol. Biol.* **339** (3) (June 2004) 607–633.
[88] Singh R.K., Tropsha A., Vaisman I.I., "Delaunay tessellation of proteins", *J. Comput. Biol.* **3** (1996) 213–222.
[89] Spriggs R.V., Artymiuk P.J., Willett P., "Searching for patterns of amino acids in 3D protein structures", *J. Chem. Inform. Comput. Sci.* **43** (2003) 412–421.
[90] Srinivasan A., King R.D., Muggleton S.H., Sternberg M., "The predictive toxicology evaluation challenge", in: *Proc. of the 15th International Joint Conference on Artificial Intelligence, IJCAI*, 1997, pp. 1–6.
[91] Stark A., Russell R.B., "Annotation in three dimensions. Pints: Patterns in non-homologous tertiary structures", *Nucl. Acids Res.* **31** (13) (2003) 3341–3344.
[92] Stark A., Shkumatov A., Russell R.B., "Finding functional sites in structural genomics proteins", *Structure (Camb)* **12** (2004) 1405–1412.
[93] Stark A., Sunyaev S., Russell R.B., "A model for statistical significance of local similarities in structure", *J. Mol. Biol.* **326** (1998) 1307–1316.
[94] Terwilliger T.C., Waldo G., Peat T.S., Newman J.M., Chu K., Berendzen J., "Class-directed structure determination: Foundation for a protein structure initiative", *Protein Sci.* **7** (1998) 1851–1856.
[95] Torrance J.W., Bartlett G.J., Porter C.T., Thornton J.M., "Using a library of structural templates to recognise catalytic sites and explore their evolution in homologous families", *J. Mol. Biol.* **347** (2005) 565–581.
[96] Tropsha A., Carter C.W., Cammer S., Vaisman I.I., "Simplicial neighborhood analysis of protein packing (SNAPP): A computational geometry approach to studying proteins", *Methods Enzymol.* **374** (2003) 509–544.
[97] Ullman J.D., "An algorithm for subgraph isomorphism", *J. Assoc. Comput. Machinery* **23** (1976) 31–42.
[98] Vanetik N., Gudes E., Shimony E., "Computing frequent graph patterns from semi-structured data", in: *Proc. International Conference on Data Mining'02*, 2002.
[99] Via A., Ferre F., Brannetti B., Valencia A., Helmer-Citterich M., "Three-dimensional view of the surface motif associated with the p-loop structure: cis and trans cases of convergent evolution", *J. Mol. Biol.* **303** (4) (November 2000) 455–465.

[100] von Mering C., Huynen M., Jaeggi D., Schmidt S., Bork P., Snel B., "String: A database of predicted functional associations between proteins", *Nucl. Acids Res.* **31** (2003) 258–261.

[101] Wallace A.C., Borkakoti N., Thornton J.M., "Tess: A geometric hashing algorithm for deriving 3d coordinate templates for searching structural databases. Application to enzyme active sites", *Protein Sci.* **6** (11) (1997) 2308–2323.

[102] Wang G., Dunbrack R.L., "PISCES: A protein sequence culling server", *Bioinformatics* **19** (2003) 1589–1591; http://www.fccc.edu/research/labs/dunbrack/pisces/culledpdb.html.

[103] Wang Z., Benoit G., Liu J., Prasad S., Aarnisalo P., Liu X., Xu H., Walker N.P., Perlmann T., "Structure and function of nurr1 identifies a class of ligand-independent nuclear receptors", *Nature* **423** (3) (2003) 555–560.

[104] Wangikar P.P., Tendulkar A.V., Ramya S., Mali D.N., Sarawagi S., "Functional sites in protein families uncovered via an objective and automated graph theoretic approach", *J. Mol. Biol.* **326** (3) (2003) 955–978.

[105] Weir M., Swindells M., Overington J., "Insights into protein function through large-scale computational analysis of sequence and structure", *Trends Biotechnol.* **19** (Suppl. 10) (2001) s61–s66.

[106] Weiss S., "Measuring conformational dynamics of biomolecules by single molecule fluorescence spectroscopy", *Nature Struct. Biol.* **7** (9) (2000) 724–729.

[107] Weskamp N., Kuhn D., Hullermeier E., Klebe G., "Efficient similarity search in protein structure databases by *k*-clique hashing", *Bioinformatics* **20** (2004) 1522–1526.

[108] Yan X., Han J., "gspan: Graph-based substructure pattern mining", in: *Proc. International Conference on Data Mining'02*, 2002, pp. 721–724.

[109] Yan X., Han J., "Closegraph: Mining closed frequent graph patterns", in: *KDD'03*, 2003.

[110] Zaki M.J., "Efficiently mining frequent trees in a forest", in: *SIGKDD'02*, 2002.

# Peptide Identification via Tandem Mass Spectrometry

XUE WU

*Department of Computer Science*
*University of Maryland, College Park*
*College Park, MD 20742*
*USA*

NATHAN EDWARDS

*Center for Bioinformatics and Computational Biology*
*University of Maryland, College Park*
*College Park, MD 20742*
*USA*

CHAU-WEN TSENG

*Department of Computer Science*
*University of Maryland, College Park*
*College Park, MD 20742*
*USA*
*Center for Bioinformatics and Computational Biology*
*University of Maryland, College Park*
*College Park, MD 20742*
*USA*

**Abstract**

Peptide identification is an important component of the rapidly growing field of proteomics. Tandem mass spectrometry has the potential to provide a high-throughput method for biologists to identify peptides in complex samples. In this chapter, we provide an introduction to how tandem mass spectrometry works and how it may be used for peptide identification. We discuss two techniques for analyzing mass spectra, de novo sequencing and protein sequence database search. Finally, we present an experimental comparison of OMSSA, X!Tandem

ADVANCES IN COMPUTERS, VOL. 68


ISSN: 0065-2458/DOI: 10.1016/S0065-2458(06)68006-6

and Mascot, three popular protein database search algorithms used in peptide identification. We find these search algorithms are of comparable precision and can generally correctly identify peptides for mass spectra of high quality. However, low quality mass spectra present problems for all three algorithms and can lead to many incorrect peptide identifications. Improving algorithms for peptide identification using tandem mass spectrometry should thus be a rewarding area of research.



## 1. Introduction

Most of the properties of living organisms arise from the class of molecules known as proteins. Understanding how proteins function is thus a central goal of biology. Since organisms produce proteins by first transcribing DNA to RNA, then translating RNA to a protein, a great deal of information on proteins can be derived indirectly by analyzing DNA. For instance, gene finding algorithms can analyze genomic DNA to identify protein-coding portions of DNA (genes) to predict what proteins are produced. Biologists can also experimentally detect the presence of transcribed (expressed) DNA (either by sequencing Expressed Sequence Tags (ESTs) or through hybridization with short DNA probe sequences on microarrays) to deduce what proteins are present in a cell.

However, there are several limitations to analyzing proteins indirectly. First, while the presence of transcribed DNA is strong evidence for the presence of the corresponding translated protein, the quantity of protein present is not necessarily correlated with the quantity of transcribed DNA. More importantly, proteins are known to be much more diverse than protein-coding genes in an organism. For instance, the Human Genome Project has identified roughly 22,000 genes in the human genome, even though there are about 400,000 known human proteins. The much larger number of proteins is probably due to alternative splicing and post-translational modifications of proteins.

As a result, scientists have realized simply studying genomic and transcribed DNA is not sufficient for fully understanding the presence and activity of proteins in an organism. This has led to the rise of the field of proteomics, the study of all proteins of an organism [1]. Proteomics strives to provide detailed information about protein structure, interaction, and functions. There are many areas in proteomics, focusing on areas such as protein separation, protein identification, protein quantification, protein structure, protein interactions, and protein function.

Earlier research in the field of proteomics focused on studying proteins using techniques from analytical chemistry. In the 1980s and early 1990s, researchers mainly targeted improving the sensitivity of protein identification techniques based on separating proteins through different types of gel electrophoresis. X-ray crystallography and nuclear magnetic resonance techniques were used to identify the 3D structure of a large number of proteins. Chemical-based techniques were used to identify protein amino acid sequence, but were much slower and less efficient than comparable techniques for sequencing DNA.

More recently, mass spectrometry (MS) has developed into an active research area that has the potential to provide reliable high-throughput methods for identifying and analyzing proteins. Mass spectrometry is a well-established scientific instrumentation technique from analytical chemistry that can be applied to biological samples to identify protein content. Researchers have found that the tandem mass spectrometry technique (MS/MS), when used in conjunction with liquid chromatography (LC), can quickly determine the protein content of biological samples in a wide variety of contexts.

In a high-throughput setting, a complex mixture of unknown proteins can be cut into short amino acid sequences (peptides) using a digestion enzyme such as trypsin; fractionated using liquid chromatography into reduced complexity samples on the basis of some physical or chemical property such as hydrophobicity; and then have tandem mass spectra taken for selected observed peptides in each fraction. The end result of such an experiment is a set of a few hundred to a few thousand tandem mass spectra, each of which represents a peptide of about 6–20 amino acid residues. In many cases amino-acid sequences of 8–10 residues carry sufficient information content to determine the protein from which the peptide is derived. This experimental protocol employing LC-MS/MS can thus potentially identify hundreds of proteins from a complex mixture in several hours of instrument time. In addition, protein mass spectrometry can also be used for analyzing functional protein complexes by identifying not only the members of the complexes, but also the interactions among the members.

Combined with advances in analytical protein chemistry and ever expanding protein databases, mass spectrometry thus has the potential to become the mainstream quantitative technology for systematical protein study. However, because of frequent noise in mass spectra data and high data generation speed, the analysis and interpretation of enormous amounts of protein mass spectra data can be very challenging. Even though computer scientists and statisticians have developed many computer software tools for interpreting the experimental data, high performance algorithms with carefully designed score functions are needed to give precise results that are portable and comparable.

In this chapter, we provide an overview of how mass spectrometry can be used to identify proteins in a high-throughput setting. We describe algorithms used to interpret mass spectra results, and experimentally compare the precision of some popular protein sequence database search algorithms currently used by biologists.

## 2. Tandem Mass Spectrometry

Mass spectrometry is an analytical chemistry technique used to find the chemical composition of a physical sample. This is done by using a mass spectrometer to split the sample into a collection of charged gas particles (ions) with different masses, then measuring their relative abundance by magnetically accelerating the ions and sending them to a detector. Since the acceleration of a particle in a magnetic fields is based on its mass-to-charge ratio ($m/z$), a mass spectrometer can determine the masses of ions very precisely. Because the atomic masses of different chemicals differ, information on the mass of all ions detected can thus be used to identify the chemical composition of a physical sample. The output of a mass spectrometer is a set of detected ion mass-to-charge ratios, typically represented as a mass spectrum, as shown in Fig. 1. In the figure, the $x$-axis represents the mass-to-charge ratio of each ion, and the $y$-axis represents the intensity of each ion (number of particles detected). Intensity is normalized with respect to the peak with the highest intensity.

Proteins are macromolecules composed of sequences of twenty different amino acids, as shown in Fig. 2. Short sequences of amino acids are usually referred to as peptides to distinguish them from full protein sequences. Because each of the twenty amino acids has a different residue with unique chemical structure, all amino acids except two have different atomic masses (as shown in Table I), allowing them to be identified using mass spectrometry. The two exceptions are leucine and isoleucine, which are isomorphic (two molecules with the same chemical composition, but whose atoms are arranged differently) and therefore have the same mass.

As it turns out, proteins are fairly well-suited to identification using mass spectrometry. Proteins and peptides may be ionized using techniques such as electrospray

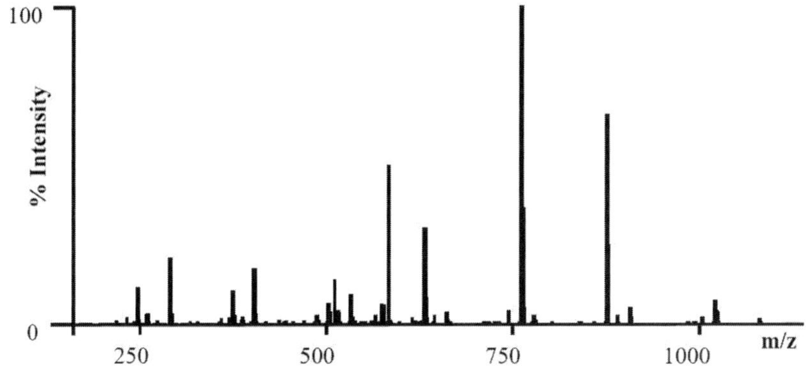


FIG. 1. A mass spectrum consists of a set of ion peaks detected at different mass/charge ($m/z$) ratios.

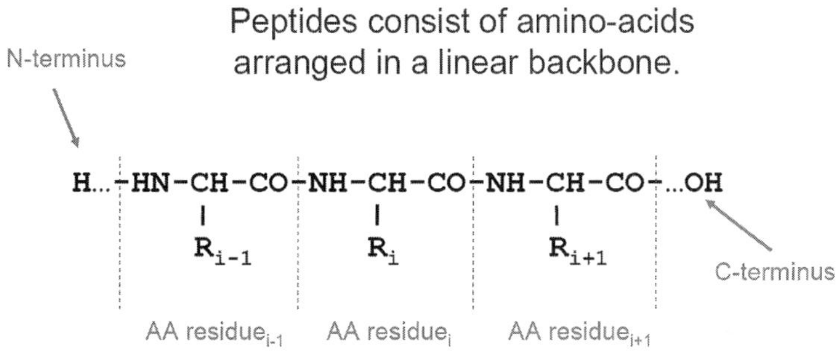


FIG. 2. Proteins/peptides are composed of sequences of amino acids (AA) that share a common backbone, but have different residues.

TABLE I
MASSES FOR ALL 20 AMINO ACID RESIDUES IN DALTONS

| | Amino-acid | Residual MW | | Amino-acid | Residual MW |
|---|---|---|---|---|---|
| A | Alanine | 71.03712 | M | Methionine | 131.04049 |
| C | Cysteine | 103.00919 | N | Asparagine | 114.04293 |
| D | Aspartic acid | 115.02695 | P | Proline | 97.05277 |
| E | Glutamic acid | 129.04260 | Q | Glutamine | 128.05858 |
| F | Phenylalanine | 147.06842 | R | Arginine | 156.10112 |
| G | Glycine | 57.02147 | S | Serine | 87.03203 |
| H | Histidine | 137.05891 | T | Threonine | 101.04768 |
| 1 | Isoleucine | 113.08407 | V | Valine | 99.06842 |
| K | Lysine | 128.09497 | W | Tryptophan | 186.07932 |
| L | Leucine | 113.08407 | Y | Tyrosine | 163.06333 |

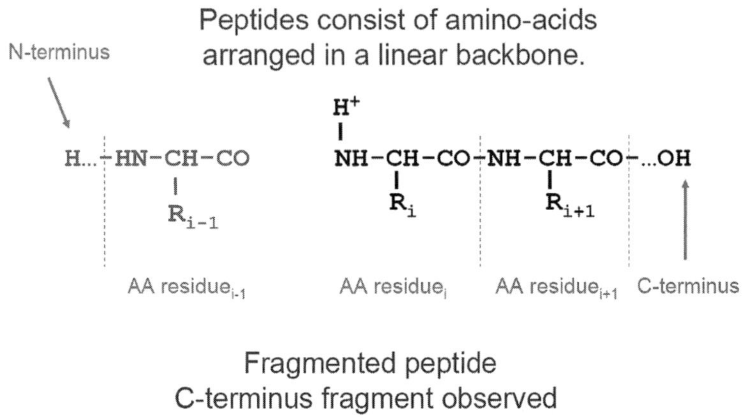


FIG. 3. Peptides become ionized (obtain a charge) when a proton ($H^+$) becomes attached.

ionization or matrix-assisted laser desorption/ionization (MALDI) to attach extra proton(s) to the sequence of amino acids, as shown in Fig. 3. Once ionized, its mass may be measured using a mass spectrometer. Finding the mass of an entire protein is not very useful since the protein mass is too large and many proteins may have the same mass. However, proteins can be split into smaller peptides fragments that are easier to identify.

A common approach for fragmenting proteins is utilizing enzymatic digestion. For instance, the enzyme trypsin will break a protein amino acid sequence at the carboxyl side (or "C-terminus") of the amino acids lysine and arginine, unless the two residues are followed by the amino acid proline (i.e., KR unless followed by P). Because the pattern recognized by trypsin is fairly common, a protein digested by trypsin is usually broken up into a large number of short peptide fragments. Figure 4 illustrates an example of protein digestion, where multiple instances of the original long protein amino acid sequence are digested by an enzyme, producing different unique peptides (each colored differently). Digestions are not necessarily perfect, so there may be missed opportunities for digestion that yield larger peptides.

Once digestion is complete, a mass spectrometer can measure the mass/charge ratios of all the resulting peptides, as shown in Fig. 5. In fact, proteins can be identified directly from the masses of their peptide fragments after digestion. A technique known as peptide mass fingerprinting attempts to identify proteins from all the possible peptides produced from after digestion by a particular enzyme. Different enzymes may be used to obtain sets of fingerprints to better distinguish between proteins.

In practice, biologists seem to prefer using a more precise technique called tandem mass spectrometry (MS/MS) that can improve the precision of protein identification

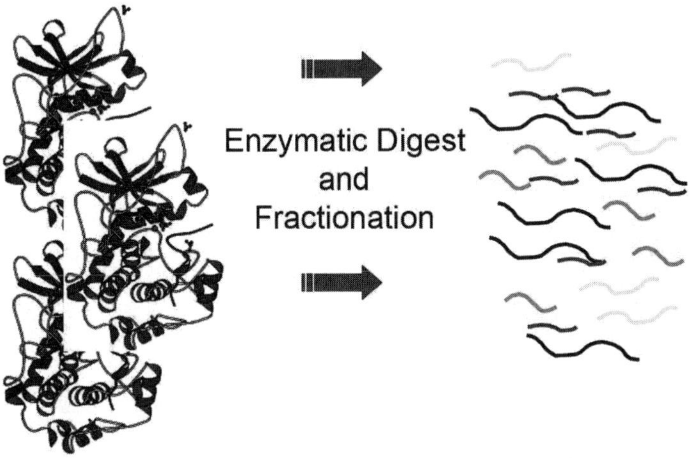


FIG. 4. Enzymes digest proteins by breaking long amino acid sequences into short peptides at specific amino acid positions.

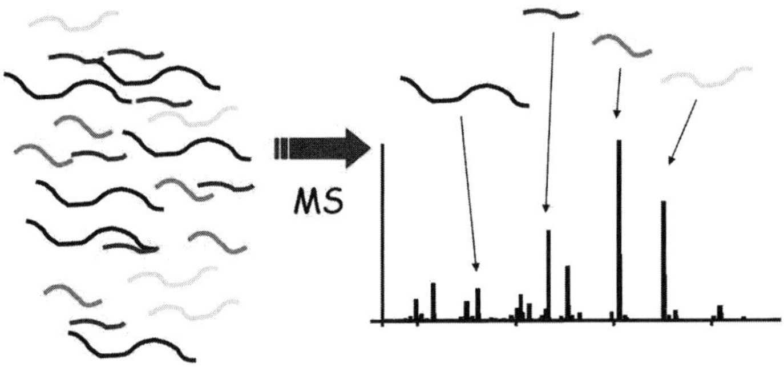


FIG. 5. A mass spectrometer can measure the mass/charge ($m/z$) ratios of ionized peptides from a protein. The set of measured $m/z$ ratios can potentially be used as a peptide mass fingerprint to identify proteins.

by fragmenting digested peptides even further. First, the different peptides resulting from enzymatic digestion are separated as much as possible using techniques such as 1D/2D gel electrophoresis or liquid chromatography (LC), where peptides are separated (according to physical size and/or chemical properties) by forcing them through a gel or capillary tube filled with a combination of water and organic solvents.

Once a single peptide has been separated, it can be fragmented further using techniques such as collision-induced-dissociation (CID), which shoots peptides at high

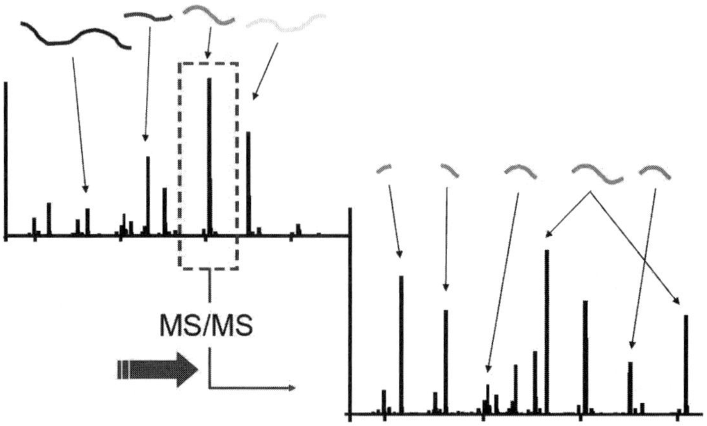


FIG. 6. In tandem mass spectrometry (MS/MS), peptides are fragmented further in order to determine their amino acid sequence.

speed through a cloud of inert gas particles. The resulting ions are now all fragments of the original (precursor/parent) peptide fragment, and greatly simplify the task of identifying its amino acid sequence. An example of tandem mass spectrometry is shown in Fig. 6.

Because the CO–NH bonds connecting amino acids are weak, they tend to break first when a peptide is fragmented. Assuming the original ion carried only a single positive charge ($H^+$ proton), the charge will be on either the peptide fragment containing the N-terminus or the C-terminus of the peptide. If the charge is on the fragment containing the N-terminus, the resulting fragment is labeled as a $b_i$ ion, where $i$ indicates the number of amino acids composing the ion. Otherwise, the charge must be on the fragment containing the C-terminus, and the fragment is labeled a $y_i$ ion. Figure 7 shows an example of what $b$ and $y$ ions can be produced depending on which CO–NH bond is broken for a sequence of amino acids. Other types of ions may be created during fragmentation ($a$ and $x$ ions if the CH–CO bond is broken, $c$ and $z$ ions if the NH–CH bond is broken), but with much lower probability since those bonds are stronger than the CO–NH bond.

To illustrate in greater detail how tandem mass spectrometry works, we use as an example applying LC-MS/MS to the peptide SGFLEEDELK. We assume this peptide is produced from a particular protein after it has been digested by some enzyme. Liquid Chromatography is used to separate copies of this peptide from other peptides. An early instance of this peptide is ionized and its mass-to-charge ratio is measured by the mass spectrometer. Using some predetermined criteria, the tandem mass spectrometer software selects this ion for further fragmentation. This peptide

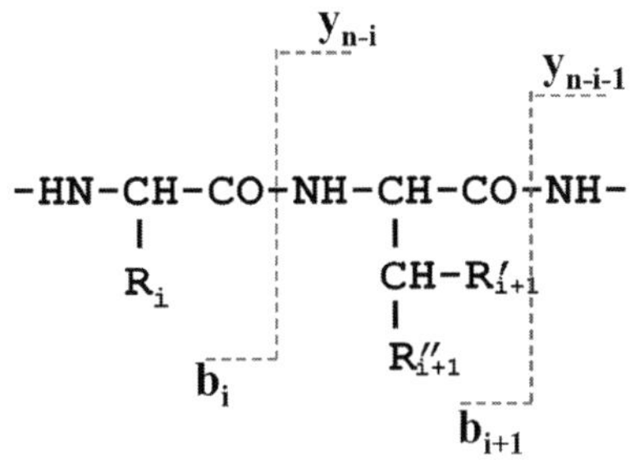


FIG. 7. Different possible *b* and *y* peptide fragment ions are produced depending on which CO–NH bond is broken, and which peptide fragment retains the positive charge ($H^+$).

Peptide: S-G-F-L-E-E-D-E-L-K

| MW | ion | | | ion | MW |
|---|---|---|---|---|---|
| 88 | $b_1$ | S | GFLEEDELK | $y_9$ | 1080 |
| 145 | $b_2$ | SG | FLEEDELK | $y_8$ | 1022 |
| 292 | $b_3$ | SGF | LEEDELK | $y_7$ | 875 |
| 405 | $b_4$ | SGFL | EEDELK | $y_6$ | 762 |
| 534 | $b_5$ | SGFLE | EDELK | $y_5$ | 633 |
| 663 | $b_6$ | SGFLEE | DELK | $y_4$ | 504 |
| 778 | $b_7$ | SGFLEED | ELK | $y_3$ | 389 |
| 907 | $b_8$ | SGFLEEDE | LK | $y_2$ | 260 |
| 1020 | $b_9$ | SGFLEEDEL | K | $y_1$ | 147 |

FIG. 8. All possible *b* and *y* ions produced by peptide SGFLEEDELK and their masses (in Daltons).

ion now becomes a precursor ion. Additional ions of the same mass are fragmented further, and their mass-to-charge ratios are measured and recorded.

Figure 8 displays all the possible *b* and *y* ions produced by fragmenting the peptide SGFLEEDELK, as well as their molecular weights (in Daltons). Additional ions are also possible for many reasons (e.g., precursor ion fragments multiple times, precursor ion does not break at the CO–NH bond, chemical modifications to the precursor ion or its fragments, etc.), but *b* and *y* ions are most frequently observed.

Figure 9 displays an example of a mass spectrum that could result if many possible *b* and *y* ion from the precursor ion was produced and measured. The peaks representing *b* and *y* are ordered from left to right relative to the number of amino acids in each ion, since the mass (and $m/z$ ratio) of a peptide increases with the additional of amino acids to a peptide. Ions containing about half the number of amino acids

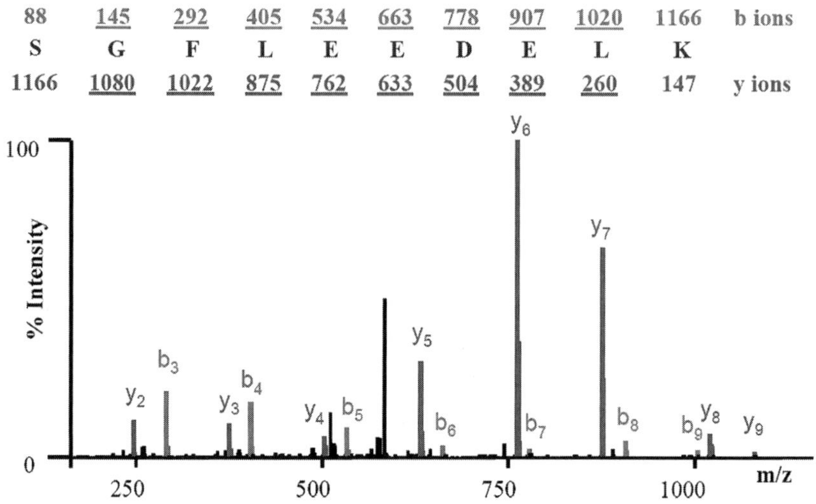


FIG. 9. Position of mass/charge ($m/z$) ratios for many $b$ and $y$ ion peaks produced by peptide SGFLEEDELK.

in the precursor ion are more likely to be observed (i.e., have more intense peaks) in practice.

Note that in Fig. 9 some $b$ and $y$ ions are not observed (with measurable intensity), as those ions were not created with high enough frequency to be observed. In comparison, some fairly large (non-ion) peaks are found. These peaks may be present for a number of reasons. They may have been produced by peptide fragmentation at bonds other than CO–NH. These (non $b$ or $y$ ion) peaks can also represent ionized particles generated from peptides or non-protein substances other than the precursor ion, since liquid chromatography is not completely effective at separating different peptides.

## 3. Algorithms for Peptide Identification

We have just seen how tandem mass spectrometry can each hour automatically capture hundreds of mass spectra representing potential proteins in a biological sample. Trained chemists can examine mass spectra manually to identify proteins, but cannot possibly keep up with rate data is produced by modern tandem mass spectrometers. As a result, biologists are forced to rely on software tools implementing different algorithms for identifying proteins.

There are two main classes of software algorithms for mass spectra based peptide identification. De novo sequencing algorithms attempt to deduce the amino acid sequence from scratch by examining the mass spectrum. In comparison, database search algorithms compare the experimental mass spectrum against theoretical spectra for peptides derived from a protein sequence database. This section provides an overview of techniques used in both approaches.

## 3.1 De Novo Sequencing

We begin with the approach taken by de novo sequence. De novo peptide identification algorithms attempts to determine the peptide sequence using only the peptide fragment information of the tandem mass spectrum, without relying on any knowledge about existing proteins. De novo techniques work by discovering pairs of ions peaks in mass spectra that differ in their mass-to-charge ($m/z$) ratio exactly by the mass of a single amino acid [2–6].

Figure 10 presents an example of a mass spectrum where the mass difference between pairs of peaks matches the mass of an amino acid, specifically E and L. Such peak pairs can provide evidence for a particular amino acid existing at a given position in a peptide. For the mass spectrum in Fig. 10, the two pairs of adjacent peaks marked seem to indicate the precursor peptide contains the peptide fragment EL or LE, depending on whether the peaks are $b$ or $y$ ions.

De novo techniques work very well if the mass spectrum is of high quality, with a large fraction of all $b$ and $y$ ions clearly represented by peaks in the spectrum. In fact, if all $b$ or all $y$ ions are present, the amino acid sequence of the peptide can be derived by simply reading off the sequence of amino acid masses in order by following the sequence "ladder".

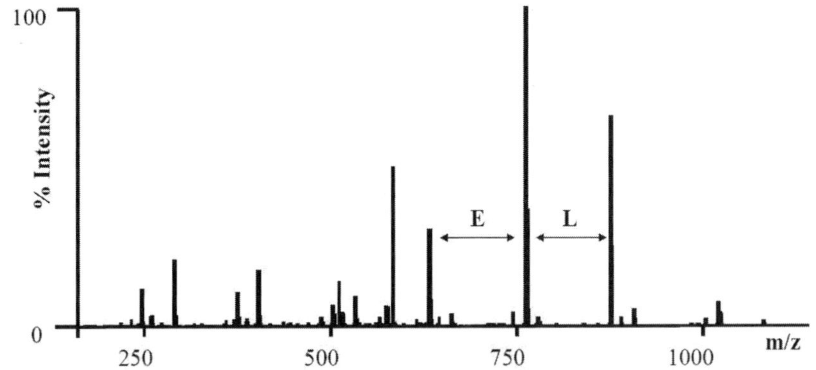


FIG. 10. Discovering pairs of $m/z$ ion peaks that differ exactly by the mass of a single amino acid.

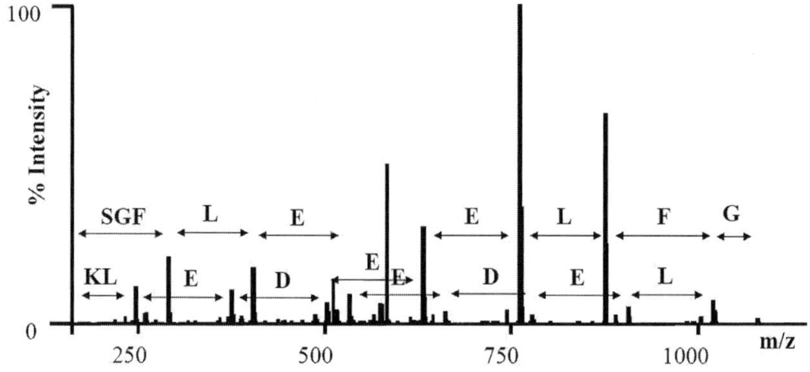


FIG. 11. De novo peptide identification relies on discovery of a sequence of amino acids identified by pairs of ion peaks.

For instance, the mass spectrum shown in Fig. 11 is an example of a very high quality spectrum with almost all *b* and *y* ions present. If the difference in mass between a pair of peaks matches the mass of an amino acid, the gap between the pair of peaks is labeled with the appropriate amino acid. We see that the peptide sequence LEEDEL can be discovered by following the sequence of *b* ions from left to right. In addition, the mass of the first *b* ion peak is equal to the sum of the masses of the amino acids S, G, and F, so we can deduce the first three amino acids in the peptide sequence is some combination of S, G, and F. Following the sequence of *y* ion from right to left, we discover the peptide sequence GFLEEDE. In addition, the mass of the last *y* ion peak is equal to the sum of the masses of the amino acids K and L. Combining the two sequences, we see the only possible peptide capable of generating both sets of *b* and *y* ions is SGFLEEDELK.

De novo techniques have the advantage of working without being limited by the list of protein sequences found in a protein database. De novo techniques can also be used to discover novel peptides and unexpected post-translational modifications (e.g., acylation, methylation, phosphorylation) in a computationally efficient way, since post-translational modifications to proteins are easily represented as additional peptide mass differences to be considered.

However, de novo techniques do not work nearly as well for lower quality mass spectra, where many ion peaks may be missing and non-ion peaks are present. If on a small portion of the ion ladder is present, de novo techniques can only identify short portions of amino acid sequences. De novo interpretations will then produce a long list of possible peptide sequences containing the peptide sequence fragment identified. In practice, the proportion of spectra that can be identified conclusively using a de novo analysis is usually fairly small, because tandem mass spectra often do not contain enough information to form an unambiguous conclusion.

More recently, researchers have found ways to improve de novo analysis algorithms through the use of Hidden Markov Models (HMMs) [7–9]. HMMs were initially introduced in late 1960s and early 1970s for human speech recognition. It includes a class of statistical models used to capture statistical characteristics of time series and linear sequences. HMM is basically a double embedded stochastic process with first order Markov chain as underlying (hidden) stochastic process and state dependent probabilistic function as the observable stochastic process. Because of the nice mathematical properties of HMM, it was introduced into computational biology in late 1980s and used to profile protein sequences [10,11]. Later, HMM was also used to model gene structure and predict protein structure by fold recognition.

The researchers developing NovoHMM proposes a de novo peptide sequencing approach using a generative HMM of mass spectra [12]. The model emulates the whole mass spectra generation process in a probabilistic way that allows for better amino acid prediction. Results show NovoHMM outperforms other de novo sequencing algorithms that use mass spectrum graphs for generating candidate peptides.

## 3.2 Sequence Database Search Algorithms

A different approach for identifying peptides using mass spectra is based on searching protein databases containing protein amino acid sequences. Tools implementing these database search algorithms are commonly known as mass spectra (MS) search engines.

The first step of these algorithm is to computationally digest protein sequences with specific enzymes. In other words, the algorithm predicts which peptides may be produced if the protein is entirely or partially digested by an enzyme. It does so by searching for all the amino acid pattern recognized by the enzyme, and cutting the protein sequence at those points to yield a list of possible peptides. The database search algorithm can then generate a hypothetical mass spectrum for each peptide produced by enzyme digestion, simply by adding the masses of all amino acids for each peptide.

Once the list of hypothetical mass spectra for peptide sequences is generated, the database search algorithm can attempt to identify the peptide by comparing the actual experimental spectrum with hypothetical spectra created for each possible peptide. Using criteria such as a score function based on the number of matched ion peaks, the algorithm can then rank the best matches found and predict possible peptide sequences. For instance, the MS search engine X!Tandem computes a *hyperscore* for each match by summing the intensities of all matched *b* and *y* ions, then multiplying the result by the factorials of the number of matched *b* and *y* ions [13].

Probably the major advantage of database search algorithms is that they do not need to find evidence for all amino acids in a peptide, but just enough to uniquely distinguish a peptide from all other peptides in the database. As a result these algorithms can better identify proteins from low quality spectra (with many missing *b* and *y* ions and non-ion peaks) than de novo techniques.

The database search approach also has several weaknesses. First, to be identified the amino acid sequence of a protein must be present in the sequence database. Novel proteins or alternative splicing isoform proteins not in the database will not be matched by the algorithm, even if the spectrum is very high quality and the peptide can be easily identified using de novo techniques. It is possible to computationally derive additional versions of hypothetical spectra corresponding to mutations, alternative splicing, or post-translational modifications, but the total number of combinations that may need to be considered grows exponentially and quickly becomes computationally infeasible. Second, as protein databases grow larger performance degrades as the number of hypothetical spectra also grows. Finally, it becomes harder for database search algorithms to clearly distinguish the correct peptide mapping as the number of protein sequence candidates increase.

Since the first database search program SEQUEST [14], there have been many algorithms [15–32] designed to identify peptides by searching protein sequence database. The database search algorithms differ in many ways, including heuristics for filtering noise, match score functions, and methods for searching the protein sequence database. We discuss some of the more commonly used MS search engines and point out their main features.

SEQUEST [14] is one of the first algorithms to identify proteins by correlating peptide tandem mass spectrum with amino acid sequence in protein database. It matches the experimental mass spectrum with the theoretical spectrum of a peptide sequence, scoring matches based on a cross-correlation function. Post-processing tools such as PeptideProphet [24] apply statistical analysis of SEQUEST scores to calculate e-values and improve the sensitivity of true peptide identifications.

Mascot [27], developed by Perkins et al., is probably the most widely used protein identification software. It uses an adapted scoring function to score matches between experimental and theoretical spectra. First, experimental MS/MS spectrum are condensed into a small set of masses representing a fingerprint of the spectrum. A probabilistic model is used to compare this mass fingerprint (whose peak values are ignored) against the generated theoretical masses from potential peptides in the protein sequence database. Mascot outputs a probability-based score for each match so the significance of the results can be more easily judged.

OMSSA [22] is a probability-based protein identification method from NCBI. After the filtering steps, it calculates a score based on the statistic significance of a match. The basic assumption used by OMSSA is that the number of product ion matches follows a Poisson distribution. It calculates an e-value based on the number of random matches against N theoretical spectra.

SCOPE [33] uses a comprehensive probabilistic scoring models to more precisely evaluate the probability of a spectrum matching theoretical spectrum from protein sequence databases.

X!Tandem [13] is a multi-step algorithm for quick peptide identification from mass spectra. It filters out sequence candidates in multiple searching steps, while considering more stringent searching criteria in each step. The central assumption used by X!Tandem to improve the performance of filtering is that for each identifiable protein, there is at least one detectable tryptic peptide. It can thus use a quick match algorithm to look for fully digested tryptic peptides, and then look for a more comprehensive list of peptides using heuristics limited to the proteins where at least one match has been found. The score function used by X!Tandem is based on a hypergeometric distribution calculated as the dot product of the intensities of the matching ions, multiplied by the factorials of the number of matched $b$ and $y$ ions. The e-value calculated by X!Tandem is based on just how unlikely a greater hyperscore is to be found, based on statistical analysis of current hyperscores.

InsPecT [34] is a recent MS/MS search algorithm that performs high-throughput identification of peptide mass spectra. Its emphasis is on efficiently identifying post-translational modifications and mutations with high confidence. InsPecT is able to search a broad range of post-translational modifications efficiently by constructing a very good filter for reducing the possible search space.

PepHMM [35] is an algorithm recently proposed that uses HMMs for peptide identification. PepHMM builds a HMM to capture the correlation among matched and unmatched ions to improve the precision of peptide identification. The proposed HMM can be used as a general post-process model for any experimental spectrum to theoretical spectrum matching scheme. Once trained the HMM can be used to reassess spectra comparison results.

Some methods combining both de novo sequencing techniques and database search based peptide identification strategy have been proposed. Mann [26] uses a sequence tag of three or so amino-acids derived directly from the tandem mass spectrum to search a protein sequence database. This approach was not widely adopted due to the lack of an automated technique for sequence tag derivation. ProteinProphet [36] is a tool that combines information from multiple search algorithms in order to better identify proteins.

# 4. Comparing Mass Spectra Search Engines

## 4.1 Previous Comparisons

As more biologists begin using mass spectrometry as a high-throughput method for identifying proteins and peptides, the accuracy of different mass spectrometry search engines has become a topic of high interest. However, there has been only a small number of researchers at work comparing different MS search algorithms.

Elias et al. [37] analyzed two different set of mass spectra data with Mascot and SEQUEST, and suggested Mascot and SEQUEST results greatly overlapped for LTQ spectrum. They also analyzed the difference caused by spectrum machine (LTQ or QToF) and suggest that the two methods are complementary to each other at spectrum level, but basically same at peptide/protein level. Chamrad et al. [38] compared Mascot, MS-Fit, ProFound and SEQUEST for their sensitivity and selectivity as a function of search parameters. Kapp et al. [39] performed a comprehensive comparison of SEQUEST and Mascot and found that Sequest had better performance in terms of sensitivity, while Mascot did better in terms of specificity.

We found that comparisons performed by different groups of researchers differed greatly in terms of goals and search parameters, making their conclusions hard to compare and reconcile. As a result we decided to perform our own comparison of three popular MS search engines. We present our results in this section.

## 4.2 Evaluation Environment

For our comparison we selected three widely used MS search engines: OMSSA 1.0.3, X!Tandem 05-06-01, and Mascot 2.1.0. We generated two sets of mass spectra using two standard protein mix samples provided by Calibrant Biosystems and Children's National Medical Center. The first set of data includes 5494 spectra and are generated from 8 proteins, 20 fmol each. The second set includes 18,675 spectra and are generated from 6 proteins, 0.5 pmol each. The samples are processed by Thermofinigan LTQ ion trap. All tandem mass spectra are searched against Swissprot database release 48.6 with the same search criteria.

## 4.3 Evaluation Results

We first present results from the *8 protein mix* data set. The peptide assignment results are selected based on e-values. Here we chose the most frequently used e-value cutoff of 0.05. In other words, a peptide $p$ is assigned to a mass spectrum only if the peptide identification algorithm selects $p$ as the most likely peptide, and estimates its e-value as 0.05 or better (i.e., 1 in 20 chance a false peptide would score as well).

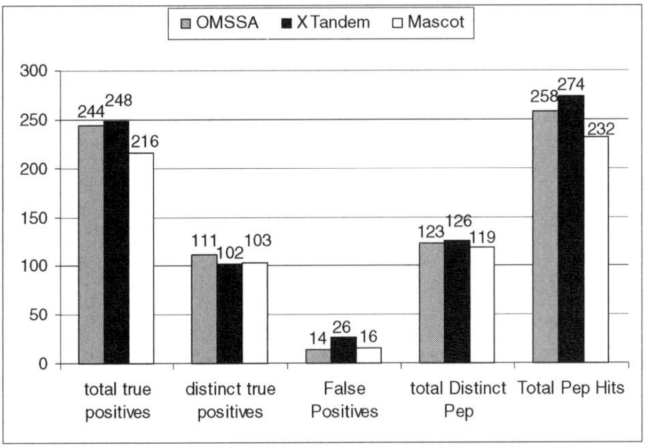


FIG. 12. Summary of number of peptide assignments made by each MS search algorithm (by type).

Using this cutoff value, all three MS search algorithms were able to find peptide assignments for around 5% of mass spectra examined.

Figure 12 compares peptide identification accuracy based on a classification of peptide assignments as total true positives (peptide assigned belongs to actual protein in sample), distinct true positives, false positives (peptide assigned does not belong to actual protein in sample), total peptide hits and distinct peptide hits. Results show three algorithms have similar number of peptide assignments for each category. Using a e-value cutoff of 0.05 yields about 14–26 false peptide assignments out of 232–274 total assignments, around 5–10%, a slightly lower accuracy rate than expected. Even though X!Tandem has more true positive peptide assignments, it also has more false positive peptide assignments. Mascot has the smallest number of total peptide hits, but its distinct true positive peptide number is similar to X!Tandem's. The number of OMSSA assignments is between the results for X!Tandem and Mascot.

To determine which search algorithm is more precise, in Fig. 13 we constructed a Venn Diagram based on distinct true positive peptides, which is important for discovering what proteins the different MS search engine algorithms can actually identify. The Venn Diagram shows the distinct true positive peptide assignments overlap among three algorithms. The Venn diagram shows the assigned distinct true positive peptides have great overlap among three algorithms. 83 out of 121 distinct true positive peptides are detected by all three algorithms. The percentage of true positive peptides detected only by individual algorithm are 4% (5) for OMSSA, 2% (2) for both X!Tandem and Mascot. These peptides only count as 8% of the total number of true positive peptides. These results imply that all three peptide identifi-

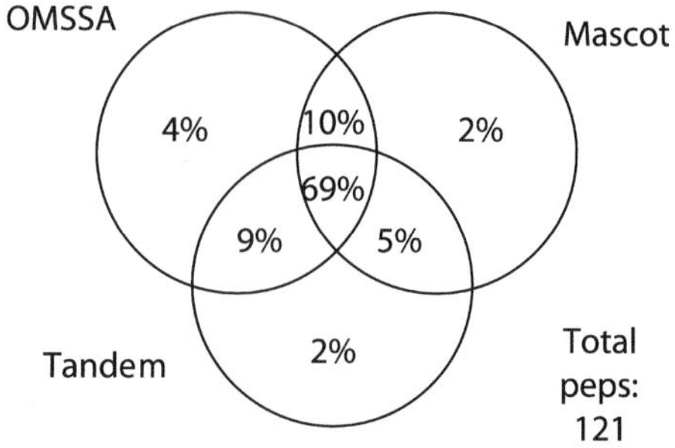


FIG. 13. Venn diagram showing % agreement between different MS search algorithms for true positive (correct) peptide assignments.

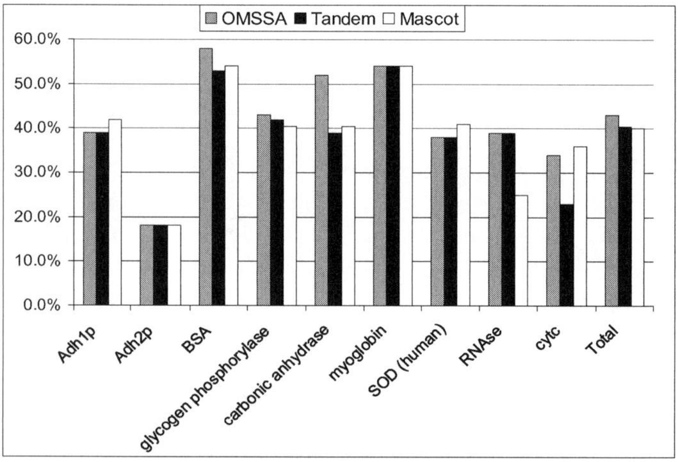


FIG. 14. Protein coverage (percent of protein sequence matched to peptide) for different MS search algorithms.

cation algorithms are roughly comparable in terms of accuracy, no single algorithm is obviously more precise than the other two algorithms.

*Protein coverage* describes the percentage of a protein's amino acid sequence that is identified by peptides identified from mass spectra. It is another important criteria to measure the performance of mass spectra search algorithms. The more true positive proteins it can find and the greater the protein coverage ratio it can achieve, the more precise the algorithm is. Figure 14 shows the protein coverage ratio for 8 standard protein mix by three search algorithms. Again, the protein coverage rates for three algorithms are very close, though OMSSA shows minor improvements over Mascot and X!Tandem.

To further explore the difference between three algorithms, we performed pairwise comparisons of peptide assignments for each spectrum based on the 8 standard protein mix spectra data set, as shown in Fig. 15. For each graph, peptide assignments are plotted according to their scores for the MS search engine represented by each axis, with higher scores indicating greater confidence in the peptide assignment.

High quality mass spectra will tend to be clustered near the top right corner of each graph (high scores from both search algorithms), while low quality mass spectra will tend to be clustered near the bottom left corner of each graph (low scores from both algorithms). When two search engines tend to agree in their peptide predictions, peptides predictions will line up along the diagonal. Predictions for mass spectra far along either axis will be the most interesting, indicating one MS search algorithm was able to identify a peptide with high confidence, while the other algorithm was not able to make any peptide assignment with confidence.

In Fig. 15, the "square" dots stand for spectrum for which both algorithm assigned true positive peptide, the "star" dots stand for spectrum for which both algorithm assigned false positive peptide, the "triangle" dots stand for spectrum for which the first algorithm assigned true positive peptide and the second algorithm assigned false positive peptide, and the "cross" dots stand for spectra for which the first algorithm assigned false positive peptide and the second algorithm assigned true positive peptide.

In OMSSA–Tandem comparison graph, the four kinds of dots are basically distributed along the diagonal, which means both OMSSA and X!Tandem have similar peptide assignments for the spectra. However, in Tandem–Mascot and Mascot–OMSSA comparison graphs, there are peptide assignments off the diagonal. Results thus indicate Mascot missed some true positive peptide assignments compared to OMSSA and X!Tandem.

Since the three database search algorithms use very different heuristics for preprocessing mass spectra, input parameters can have a great influence on peptide identification results. We found Mascot was not examining some peptides, so we changed the precursor ion mass tolerance for Mascot from 2 Daltons to 5 Daltons in order to include the possible missed peptides. The new results are shown in Fig. 16. We see that Mascot results are now more similar to both X!Tandem and OMSSA, with fewer peptide assignments falling along the X!Tandem and OMSSA axes. Mascot therefore appears to be more sensitive with respect to the mass tolerance selected for precursor ions, causing it to lose some high-scoring peptide candidates with smaller mass tolerances.

Examining the graphs in Fig. 16, we see in the Tandem–Mascot graph there are still several triangle dots (true positive for X!Tandem and false positive for Mascot)

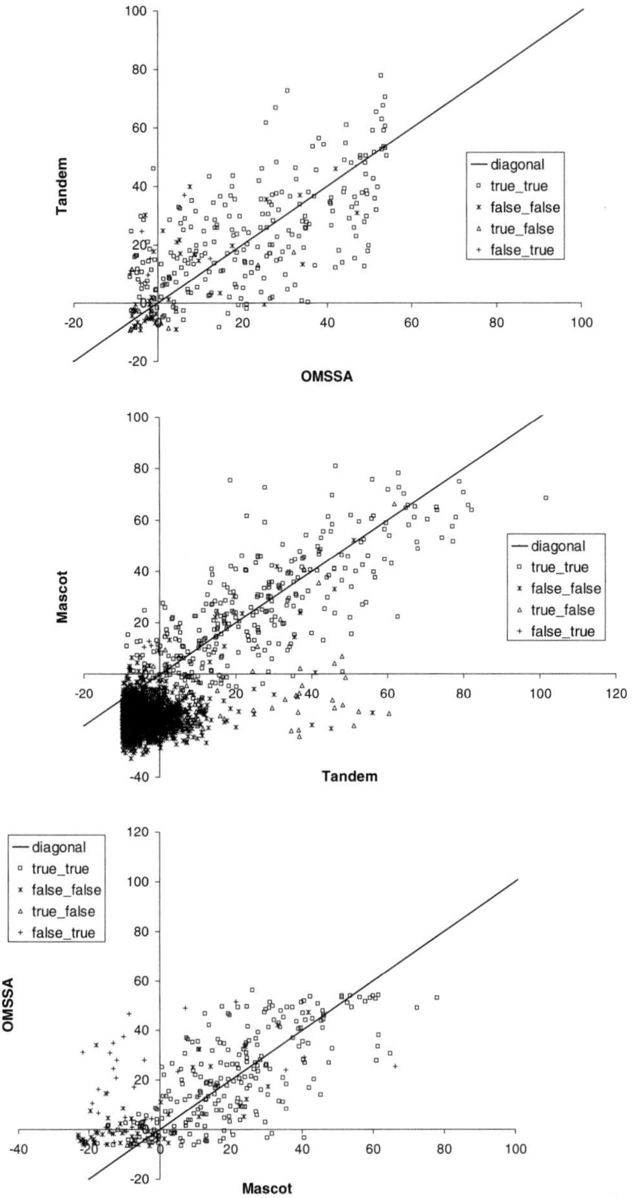


FIG. 15. Spectra peptide assignment comparison (precursor ion mass tolerance = 2 Daltons).

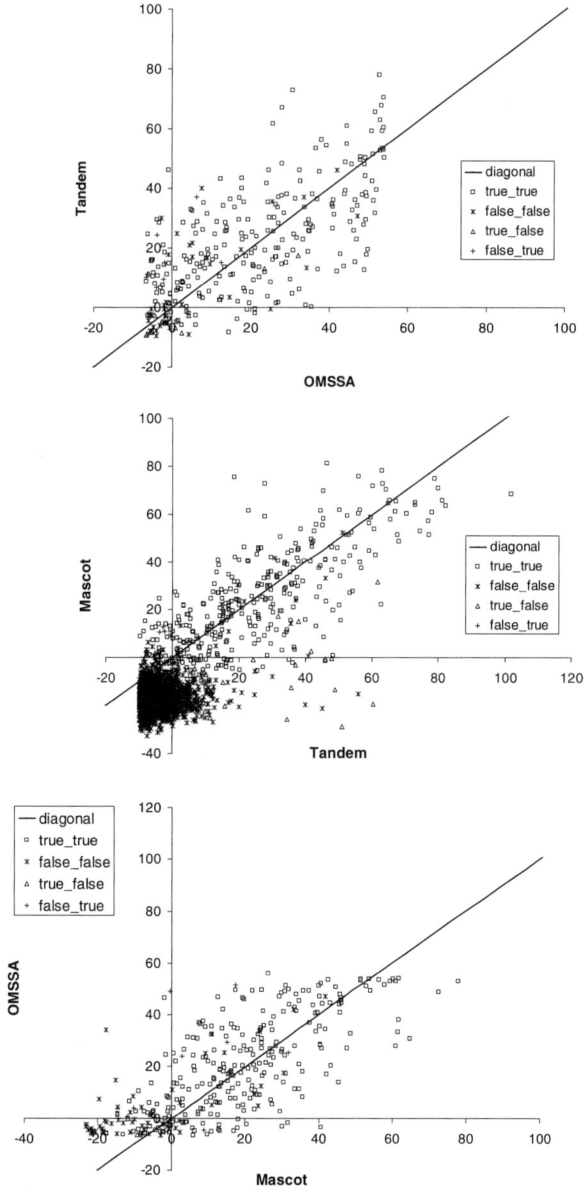


FIG. 16. Spectra peptide assignment comparison (Mascot precursor ion mass tolerance = 5 Daltons, X!Tandem & OMSSA = 2 Daltons).

off the diagonal near the Tandem axis. We manually examined ten of these mass spectra and peptide assignments in an attempt to discover the reason for the discrepancy. For these ten spectra, all X!Tandem scores ($-10\log(\text{e-value})$) are greater than 15 and all Mascot scores ($-10\log(\text{e-value})$) are less than 0. These spectra are the dots in the most outer range of the dots banded along the diagonal.

Among the peptide assignments for these ten spectra, we found three Mascot peptide assignments have only a 1–2 amino acid difference from X!Tandem peptide assignments; two Mascot assignments are equally bad as X!Tandem assignments; one Mascot assignment is better than the X!Tandem assignments, and four Mascot assignments are worse than X!Tandem assignments. Despite much higher X!Tandem confidence scores compared to Mascot for these ten mass spectra, we found X!Tandem was only slightly more accurate than Mascot in making the correct peptide assignment. As a result, it appears the peptide assignments are generally similar for X!Tandem and Mascot.

To further confirm our observations, we collected and analyzed the same set of results for mass spectra generated from a separate 6 standard protein mix. This second set of mass spectra data included more noise, and we found false positive peptide assignment rates to be higher for all three algorithms. However, the general results of the comparison were similar.

## 4.4 Summary of Observations

Considering the result of our experimental comparison of three popular MS search algorithms, we found them to be of mostly similar quality (though Mascot appears to require larger tolerances for precursor ions to avoid missing some legitimate candidate peptides). Using an e-value cutoff of 0.05, each MS search algorithm was able to correctly assign mass spectra to a peptide present in the protein mix sample between 90–95% of the time. What we find to be of interest is that even though all three MS search algorithms are of similar accuracy, they only fully agreed on the correct peptide assignments in around 69% of the cases examined. For 24% of mass spectra only 2 of 3 MS search algorithms made the correct assignment. In 8% of the time, only a single MS search algorithm assigned the mass spectra to the correct peptide.

These results indicate that even though all three MS search algorithms are identifying peptides from mass spectra with similar precision, the algorithms are obviously using different heuristics and scoring functions that can yield different results for the same mass spectrum. Looking at pairwise comparisons of mapping scores, we believe what we are observing is that all three MS search algorithms can generally correctly identify peptides for mass spectra of high quality. For lower quality mass spectra missing $b$ or $y$ ions and containing more noise (non-ion peaks), accurate peptide identification is more difficult because no single peptide stands out as the best match. Slight differences between MS search algorithms can then lead to incorrect peptides being selected. More research is needed to improve MS search algorithms to avoid such errors and improve the precision of peptide identification via tandem mass spectrometry.

## 5. Conclusions

High-throughput peptide identification through tandem mass spectrometry has the potential to expand the field of protein identification in the same way fast automated DNA sequencing has transformed molecular biology. In this chapter, we discussed the equipment and algorithms used in protein identification, as well as experimentally comparing the precision of three popular MS search engines. Our study results demonstrate that despite the different searching scheme, probability model, and varying quality of mass spectra, the three algorithms give fairly similar results for peptide identification. Nonetheless, improvements in mass search engines would improve the precision of peptide identification, allowing biologists to fully take advantage of high-throughput protein identification using tandem mass spectrometry.

ACKNOWLEDGEMENTS

The authors wish to thank Paul Rudnick from Calibrant Biosystems and Kristy Brown and Eric Hoffman from the Children's National Medical Center for providing the experimental mass spectra data used in our analysis.

REFERENCES

[1] Patterson S.D., Aebersold R.H., "Proteomics: the first decade and beyond", *Nature Genetics* **3** (2003) 311–323.

[2] Dancik V., Addona T., Clauser K., Vath J., Pevzner P., "De novo peptide sequencing via tandem mass spectrometry", *J. Comput. Biol.* **6** (1999) 327–342.

[3] Bafna V., Edwards N., "On de novo interpretation of tandem mass spectra for peptide identification", in: *Proceedings of the 7th Annual International Conference on Computational Molecular Biology*, 2003.

[4] Chen T., Kao M.Y., Tepel M., Rush J., Church G.M., "A dynamic programming approach to de novo peptide sequencing via tandem mass spectrometry", *J. Comput. Biol.* **8** (3) (2001) 325–337.

[5] Ma B., Zhang K., Lajoie G., Doherty-Kirby C., Hendrie C., Liang C., Li M., "Peaks: Powerful software for peptide de novo sequencing by tandem mass spectrometry", *Rapid Commun. Mass Spectrom.* **17** (20) (2003) 2337–2342.

[6] Taylor J.A., Johnson R.S., "Sequence database searches via de novo peptide sequencing by tandem mass spectrometry", *Rapid Commun. Mass Spectrom.* **11** (9) (1997) 1067–1075.

[7] Rabiner L.R., "A tutorial on hidden Markov models and selected applications in speech recognition", *Proc. IEEE* **77** (2) (1989) 257–286.

[8] Juang B.H., Rabiner L.R., "The segmental $k$-means algorithm for estimating parameters of hidden Markov models", *IEEE Trans. Acoustics Speech Signal Process.* **38** (1990) 1639–1641.

[9] Juang B.H., Rabiner L.R., "A probabilistic distance measure between HMMs", *IEEE Trans. Acoustics Speech Signal Process.* **64** (2) (1985) 391–408.

[10] Eddy S.R., "Profile hidden Markov models", *Bioinformatics* **14** (9) (1998) 755–763.

[11] Krogh A., Brown M., Mian I.S., Sjolander K., Haussler D., "Hidden Markov models in computational biology: Applications to protein modeling", *J. Mol. Biol.* **235** (5) (1994) 1501–1531.

[12] Fischer B., Roth V., Roos F., Grossmann J., Baginsky S., Widmayer P., Gruissem W., Buhmann J.M., "Novohmm: A hidden Markov model for de novo peptide sequencing", *Anal. Chem.* **77** (2005) 7266–7273.

[13] Craig R., Beavis R., "Tandem: Matching proteins with tandem mass spectra", *Bioinformatics* **20** (2004) 1466–1467.

[14] Yates J.R., Eng J., Clauser K., Burlingame A., "Search of sequence databases with uninterpreted high-energy collision-induced dissociation spectra of peptides", *J. Amer. Soc. Mass Spectrom.* **7** (1996) 1089–1098.

[15] Anderson D.C., Li W., Payan D.G., Noble W.S., "A new algorithm for the evaluation of shotgun peptide sequencing in proteomics: Support vector machine classification of peptide ms/ms spectra and Sequest scores", *J. Proteome Res.* **2** (2) (2003) 137–146.

[16] Colinge J., Masselot A., Giron M., Dessingy T., Magnin J., "Olav: Towards high-throughput tandem mass spectrometry data identification", *Proteomics* **3** (8) (2003) 1454–1463.

[17] Creasy M.D., Cottrell J.S., "Error tolerant searching of uninterpreted tandem mass spectrometry data", *Proteomics* **2** (10) (2002) 1426–1434.

[18] Demine R., Walden P., "Sequit: Software for de novo peptide sequencing by matrix-assisted laser desorption/ionization post-source decay mass spectrometry", *Rapid Commun. Mass Spectrom.* **18** (8) (2004) 907–913.

[19] Elias J.E., Gibbons F.D., King O.D., Roth F.P., Gygi S.P., "Intensity-based protein identification by machine learning from a library of tandem mass spectra", *Nat. Biotechnol.* **22** (2) (2004) 214–219.

[20] Field H.I., Fenyo D., Beavis R.C., "Radars, a bioinformatics solution that automates proteome mass spectral analysis, optimises protein identification, and archives data in a relational database", *Proteomics* **2** (1) (2002) 36–47.

[21] Havilio M., Haddad Y., Smilansky Z., "Intensity-based statistical scorer for tandem mass spectrometry", *Anal. Chem.* **75** (3) (2003) 435–444.

[22] Geer L.Y., Markey S., Kowalak J., Wagner L., Xu M., Maynard D., Yang X., Shi W., Bryant S.H., "Open mass spectrometry search algorithm", *J. Proteome Res.* **3** (2004) 958–964.

[23] Hansen B.T., Jones J.A., Mason D.E., Liebler D.C., "Salsa: A pattern recognition algorithm to detect electrophile-adducted peptides by automated evaluation of cid spectra in lc-ms-ms analyses", *Anal. Chem.* **73** (8) (2001) 1676–1683.

[24] Keller A., Nesvizhskii A.I., Kolker E., Aebersold R., "Empirical statistical model to estimate the accuracy of peptide identifications made by ms/ms and database search", *Anal. Chem.* **74** (20) (2002) 5383–5392.

[25] MacCoss M.J., Wu C.C., Yates J.R., "Probability-based validation of protein identifications using a modified Sequest algorithm", *Anal. Chem.* **72** (21) (2002) 5593–5599.

[26] Mann M., Wilm M., "Error-tolerant identification of peptides in sequence databases by peptide sequence tags", *Anal. Chem.* **66** (1994) 4390–4399.

[27] Perkins D.N., Pappin D., Creasy D., Cottrell J., "Probability-based protein identification by searching sequence databases using mass spectrometry data", *Electrophoresis* **20** (1999) 3551–3567.

[28] Sadygov R.G., Yates J.R., "A hypergeometric probability model for protein identification and validation using tandem mass spectral data and protein sequence databases", *Anal. Chem.* **75** (15) (2003) 3792–3798.

[29] Sadygov R.G., Liu H., Yates J.R., "Statistical models for protein validation using tandem mass spectral data and protein amino acid sequence databases", *Anal. Chem.* **76** (6) (2004) 1664–1671.

[30] Yates J.R., Eng J.K., McCormack A.L., Schieltz D., "Method to correlate tandem mass spectra of modified peptides to amino acid sequences in the protein database", *Anal. Chem.* **67** (8) (1995) 1426–1436.

[31] Zhang N., Aebersold R., Schwikowski B., "Probid: A probabilistic algorithm to identify peptides through sequence database searching using tandem mass spectral data", *Proteomics* **2** (10) (2002) 1406–1412.

[32] Zhang W., Chait B.T., "Profound: An expert system for protein identification using mass spectrometric peptide mapping information", *Anal. Chem.* **72** (11) (2000) 2482–2489.

[33] Bafna V., Edwards N.J., "Scope: A probabilistic model for scoring tandem mass spectra against a peptide database", *Science* **17** (2001) S13–S21.

[34] Tanner S., Shu H., Frank A., Wang L.C., Zandi E., Mumby M., Pevzner P.A., Bafna V., "Inspect: Fast and accurate identification of post-translationally modified peptides from tandem mass spectra", *Anal. Chem.* **77** (2005) 4626–4639.

[35] Wan Y., Yang A., Chen T., "Pephmm: A hidden Markov model based scoring function for tandem mass spectrometry", *Anal. Chem.* **78** (2) (2006) 432–437.

[36] Nesvizhskii A.I., Keller A., Kolker E., Aebersold R., "A statistical model for identifying proteins by tandem mass spectrometry", *Anal. Chem.* **75** (2003) 4646–4658.

[37] Elias J.E., Haas W., Faherty B.K., Gygi S.P., "Comparative evaluation of mass spectrometry platforms used in large-scale proteomics investigations", *Nature Methods* **2** (2005) 667–675.

[38] Chamrad D.C., Körting G., Stühler K., Meyer H.E., Klose J., Blüggel M., "Evaluation of algorithms for protein identification from sequence databases using mass spectrometry data", *Proteomics* **4** (2004) 619–628.

[39] Kapp E.A., Schütz F., Connolly L.M., Chakel J.A., Meza J.E., Miller C.A., Fenyo D., Eng J.K., Adkins J.N., Omenn G.S., Simpson R.J., "An evaluation, comparison, and accurate benchmarking of several publicly available ms/ms search algorithms: Sensitivity and specificity analysis", *Proteomics* **5** (2005) 3475–3490.

# Author Index

Numbers in *italics* indicate the pages on which complete references are given.

## C

**D**

## S

**T**

# Subject Index

**H**

## M



## N

**T**

U



V



W



X



Y



Z

# Contents of Volumes in This Series

**Volume 58**



**Volume 59**



**Volume 60**

**Volume 67**